THE Flower Garden

BY E. R. JANES

—

WITH MANY ILLUSTRATIONS BY
ARTHUR H. HALL

PENGUIN BOOKS

Penguin Books Ltd, Harmondsworth, Middlesex
U.S.A.: Penguin Books Inc., 3300 Clipper Mill Road, Baltimore 11, Md
CANADA: Penguin Books (Canada) Ltd, 178 Norseman Street, Toronto 18, Ontario
AUSTRALIA: Penguin Books Pty Ltd, 762 Whitehorse Road, Mitcham, Victoria
SOUTH AFRICA: Penguin Books (S.A.) Pty Ltd, Gibraltar House, Regent Road, Sea Point, Cape Town

—

First published 1952
Reprinted 1953, 1956

Made and printed in Great Britain
by Wyman & Sons Ltd,
London, Reading, and Fakenham

CONTENTS

Foreword

THERE is no magic or mystery about gardening – it is just common sense. The 'green finger' theory can be discredited, too, for through the ages there have been men with a special aptitude for certain jobs – whether making a violin or milking a cow; but this comes only after close application, and in this gardening is similar to any other job.

The purpose of this book is to show people of average ability the easiest way of beautifying their gardens, and, incidentally, their homes, by the application of common sense. I cannot pretend that they will suddenly become skilled, or that their gardens will quickly produce miracles. Instead, each must develop his or her garden, working on sound basic principles, which includes the avoidance of wasteful action.

Throughout I shall endeavour to provide a sound foundation on which the reader's knowledge can be built, with his interest always increasing as he plies his pleasurable hobby. Perhaps, when he is tired, I shall be unpopular at first, but he will soon discover the joy of slumber after an evening in the garden, and find that – apart from the small amount of pleasant fatigue it brings with it – probably no human hobby gives as much satisfaction as gardening. Unlike many others, it does not make a man weary of it or regretful. Indeed, the cultivation of flowers is one of the sanest of human pleasures, which cannot but ennoble and enrich the mind. Besides, what is more fascinating than to have a hobby in which new discoveries are constantly being made, in which one has never finished learning, and which beautifies our surroundings so lavishly?

It is natural that the newcomer, perhaps accustomed to the fixed routine of other pursuits, may expect rules which, if followed, will give certain definite results, but these I cannot give, for climate, soil, aspect, shelter, and many other connected factors vary widely, so that an exact formula would be useless. When asked for fixed rules, an old professor friend of mine used to say 'Gardening is not an exact science', a truth which a little practice will quickly verify. But I can give certain principles which are sufficient to guide newcomers, and aid those of experience, to beautify their gardens, if they will only study detail and use the priceless gift of observation, possessed by most but developed horticulturally by few.

With sound rules to guide, observation, initiative, and pertinacity will produce a garden of beauty, which will be restful for the hours of leisure. Public gardens, however beautiful, cannot have the same qualities as the garden made by one's own hands; hence this book.

E. R. J.

· 1 ·

Soils and Manures

THE soil we cultivate is composed of rock dissolved by the elements during countless ages. This dissolved rock also contains organic matter composed of the droppings of birds and animals mixed with the decayed deposits of trees, grasses, and other herbage in varying stages of decay. The organic matter, without which the soil would be almost sterile and non-productive, is known as humus.

Soils are roughly classified according to texture, depending largely upon the size of the soil particles. Thus, at one end of the scale we have clay soils composed of very fine particles which cling closely together – known as heavy soils – and at the other, sandy soils composed of coarse particles which fall apart readily – known as light soils. Although known as heavy soil, dry particles of clay weigh much less than dry particles of sand, and this soil is heavy only because the clinging nature of the small particles prevents water from passing through quickly. It is therefore heavier than sand only because of its high water content. Sandy soils, however, because of the coarseness of their particles allow water to pass quickly, and because of lack of moisture and the openness of the material of which they are formed, may be worked at any time and appear to be much lighter to handle. They are therefore known as light soils. Their lightness depends largely upon the size of the particles, and varies according to the rock formation of the district. Between the two extremes there is a great variety of soils, classified roughly into clays, clay loams, sandy loams, heavy sands, etc., the texture of all depending upon the amount of sand in the clay at one end, and the amount of clay in the sand at the other.

These are all the dissolved rock of the neighbourhood. In addition there is another type of soil known as alluvial, generally found in deep valleys, composed of surface soils of various types washed down the slopes through the ages, sometimes containing chalk, sand, loam, and clay in varying mixtures, according to the locality, and in deposits of varying depth, sometimes many feet. Such soil, unless it contains too great a proportion of sand or stones, is generally very fertile. Usually alluvial soils contain a high proportion of organic matter, unless this has been exhausted by bad husbandry.

The most fertile soils are the deep alluvials and the deep loams, but well-worked clays can be very fertile, while even the porous, overdrained, coarse-particled sandy soils can be made fertile by the addition of much humus.

The physical condition of soil is of great importance, because plants, like human beings or animals, require air, water, and suitable food. Many soils unworked for a long period become so closely packed that surplus water cannot pass out, and therefore air cannot enter, a condition which leaves them cold and almost inert. Also, when closely packed, planting and sowing is almost impossible and the roots of plants are condemned to exist, and sometimes to die, in a medium which they cannot penetrate physically and from which they cannot obtain the food they need because the temperature of waterlogged soil is too low in spring for the soil bacteria, upon which supplies of nitrogen depend, to function because of low temperature and lack of air.

This in itself has an important bearing upon the growth of plants, which are all balanced intimately. The root system and top growth of healthy plants always correspond, and when the root system is healthy and able to increase by branching and re-branching in long continued sequence, and consequently to send up larger and larger amounts of food to be manufactured, the top growth increases accordingly. Each plant is therefore as big as its roots, and vice versa.

It is difficult to upset the balance of nature; this is shown by the treatment given to a fruit tree which is growing too strongly and is therefore unfruitful. If the top growth of such a tree is pruned very hard without root pruning it generally grows more strongly than before, until a balance with the roots is effected, but if root only is pruned, without a corresponding reduction of the top, little growth is made for a season or two until the severed roots have regained their grip and thus restored the balance. This natural phenomenon is sometimes utilized to restore wild-growing fruit trees to fertility, as fruit buds form when the foliage grows sparsely, but it is rarely that any root restriction is necessary for the flower garden. One of the first essentials, therefore, is to provide an unrestricted root run under conditions of unlimited root expansion in soil at the right temperature, abundantly supplied with suitable plant-food and a teeming population of soil bacteria to convert the raw material into suitable food for plants.

For these reasons, deep digging is necessary. Digging should always be done in the autumn or early winter months if possible, because during the winter exposure to the elements disintegrates the cloying particles which cling closely together – leading to bad drainage and low temperatures – and leaves them loosely heaped to a depth of several inches in a workable condition, known as a good tilth – a condition when soil and sowing operations in the spring are easy. To achieve this, rain, frost, snow, and wind all play their part. There is an old saying among farmers that a heavy fall of snow is as good as a coating of manure, but this has probably arisen because heavy snow is generally followed by long and sometimes severe frost, and of all the elements frost, especially if followed by harsh winds, is the great reducer of proud soils. On the heavy soils too, and on some of the lighter, frost releases supplies of minerals othersise locked up and unavailable. Soil is in good tilth for sowing or planting when a handful tightly pressed together refuses to 'ball up' or remain compressed.

In addition to minor trace elements, generally present in most soils, plants require three main things – nitrogen, phosphates, and potash. On good deep soils, and in cases where abundant farmyard manure or compost is available, enough nitrogen is supplied by humus – the most important link in cultivation. Humus supplies nitrogen through the medium of soil bacteria, helps to retain moisture during drought, and maintains a good balance between excessive moisture and drought. Indeed, without enough humus it is almost impossible, even in a comparatively wet climate such as ours, to prevent some stony and sandy soils from drying out excessively after a few days' drought. Humus also supplies an almost invisible gelatinous seal which, while affording good drainage, holds the soil particles together and prevents them from being blown away in summer or washed away in winter. The natural process known as erosion has become particularly bad in some districts in the United States, where huge tracts of land have been lost to cultivation because of the lack of humus in districts which a couple of centuries ago were either forest or prairie. In the case of the forests, the natural plant population – in this case trees – feed luxuriously by extracting minerals, i.e. phosphates and potash, from the rocks or subsoil below and from the abundant supplies of humus, sometimes several feet in depth, resulting from the yearly droppings of leaves mixed with the excreta of animals and birds, and occasionally their dead bodies – conditions which can be found in some British woods today.

On the prairies the position was very similar, for the tall-growing prairie grasses and herbage died down annually, to decay and provide the humus, with perhaps an occasional prairie fire to burn all vegetation to the ground and provide abundant potash. The early settlers, after the initial heavy work of clearing the forests, were able to cultivate without additional manure for many years, sometimes generations, until the great layer of humus was exhausted, but much of this original fertile land has had to be abandoned because without the nitrogen and the binding seal provided by humus the soil has become inert, barren and liable to be washed into the nearest gully or river-bed in winter and blown away in dust storms in summer. Even in this country I have seen something similar. I remember seeing two tractors cultivating adjoining pieces of land. One piece had been starved of humus deliberately to induce certain plants to starve quickly and so to produce seeds in the short English summer, while the other was land which for many years had been enriched heavily with humus annually for vegetable production. It was a March day with a heavy wind blowing. On the poor land, devoid of humus, the tractor was hidden in a swirling cloud of dust which obliterated it and its driver from sight. On the rich land there was no dust except that blown over from the poor piece. This teaches us that, for continued fertility, humus is a primary necessity.

Those lucky enough to occupy a new house built on an old, rich meadow generally find themselves working a garden with a high humus content, because generations of decaying grasses and accumulated droppings of cattle have converted the upper layer of soil into a tolerable imitation of the rich, humus-laden prairies, a fact which is seldom appreciated until the customary good growth begins to wane. Rich humus-laden top spit from meadows unploughed for generations, if at all, has always been valued by professional gardeners for the pot culture of plants, for which purpose it is generally cut a few inches deep and stacked in a square-sided heap, grass side downwards. In this state it is generally called potting loam or turf loam.

Undoubtedly the most satisfactory plant-food or manure is

farmyard manure, which, if used in a partially decayed condition, contains everything necessary for the growth of plants. Such manure was used by generations of our forefathers with great success, especially in the great gardens of noblemen, where gardening with plentiful labour and unlimited supplies of manure from the cowsheds was brought to a very high pitch. The head gardeners generally knew little about plant nutrition, but they were painstaking, observant workers who, by very careful methods, obtained astonishingly good results. Farmyard manure – or muck – was all they had, and with this and a dressing of lime every few years they obtained results which would hardly be believed today, except by a handful of first-class, large-scale market growers who too have always believed in the muck which has led to their success. There is ample proof, therefore, that farmyard manure is a complete plant food, containing the three main elements required for plants, with the additional advantage that it is composed of the very bulky humus-forming excreta of cattle, the use of which, by annual dressings of the land, maintains a high humus content. Valuable trace elements are also present in farmyard manure.

But the population of our country then was small, and the animal population relatively large, for in addition to the large herds of cattle on great estates and farms our large cities housed thousands of horses, from which a vast supply of valuable manure was also obtained. Even less than sixty years ago this was sent into the country in innumerable train-loads, while the huge horse-drawn vans of the market growers rumbled heavily through the night to deposit their loads of vegetables in some city and return next morning piled high with manure.

Now our cities are filled with motor cars and our animal population in relation to the total human population has declined, while gardens and allotments, comparatively few a couple of generations ago, abound everywhere. It is now impossible to use farmyard manure on the scale the old gardeners used it, for gardens have increased and supplies of manure have decreased, and the need for more corn crops has forced farmers to convert grassland into arable, for which the home-produced manure is required, so that little is available for sale. This forces us to take stock of the position. How can we supply enough plant-food to replace the annual wastage through leaching and the necessities of plants? Fortunately nature helps us, for in most districts and in many gardens material capable of decomposition and therefore of supplying humus exists. For this purpose leaves from trees, grass mowings, and the green or dying refuse from any garden plants may be utilized to form humus and to give nitrogen. While it is true that farmyard manure contains everything necessary for the growth of plants, it is also true that the main elements are not always present in the right proportions. This was controlled in the old days by a good system of crop rotation, which, by allowing a crop to utilize the residue left unwanted from the previous one, made a rough balance. But in some districts there still are some supplies of farmyard manure available, although in small quantities. This should be used with the utmost economy.

One of the great advantages of the old system of using unlimited supplies of farmyard manure was the fact that soil so heavily charged with humus was impervious to drought, and that good crops could be obtained even in the worst dry weather. This shows that humus in some form must be incorporated in the soil annually or fertility will suffer increasingly and finally dwindle to nothing, and this is where a well-made compost heap of materials otherwise wasted comes in. If no farmyard manure can be obtained, compost can be used to supplement it – a plan which is excellent from every point of view. Indeed, there is nothing new in it, for on the great estates, in the past, all the fallen leaves from woods and pleasure grounds, together with hundreds, and in some cases thousands, of loads of grass mowings collected weekly throughout the season, were composted together with farmyard and stable manure. I have seen heaps containing thousands of loads and I cannot think of better material. But this supplies little more than the moisture-giving tilth, which provides humus with its high quota of nitrogen. The small amount of farmyard manure only partly supplies phosphates and potash, and, when compost is used alone, does so meagrely. Faced with this mineral deficiency, what are we to do? We fall back on so-called artificial manures for our mineral elements. Fortunately there are many good forms of phosphates and potash available, but these should not be used indiscriminately or with the idea that the use of a stated quantity will give stated results. If this were true gardening would be ridiculously easy and mechanical. But no! – fertilizers cannot operate in that way – there are far too many other factors involved. Some growers go as far as to say that certain crops require certain amounts of this or that element, but this takes no account of such factors as soil cultivation, humus content, soil temperatures – often dependent upon digging and drainage – weather conditions, times of sowing and planting, and innumerable details upon which success also depends. It is not the amount of plant-food in the soil which is the final determining factor, but the amount of food a plant is able to utilize, and for this good soil cultivation, which allows the plant's roots to penetrate freely, and attention to many cultural details, are of the utmost importance. The old cultivators, although wasteful in method, were correct in principle, for probably without knowing it they provided all the elements, in an assimilative form, ready for the plants to use, and as in their case abundant labour was available for frequent deep-soil cultivation the chief essentials for success were provided. We must therefore cultivate the soil deeply and well, add as much humus-forming material as we can get, with enough artificial fertilizer to make sure that our plants get enough minerals, and put our faith in attention to detail rather than in an attempt to get success from a bag of fertilizer. On heavy soils the necessary phosphates can be provided by eight ounces of basic slag per square yard, applied in autumn, and on light soils by four ounces of superphosphate per square yard applied in spring. Potash can be supplied by the application of two ounces of muriate of potash per square yard, applied in autumn, or one ounce of sulphate of potash applied in spring. Potash in a very soluble form can also be obtained from the garden bonfire, though this should be used to consume only rubbish which will not decay in the compost heap or which is diseased. Bone meal, which also supplies phosphates, is an excellent fertilizer in the absence of nitrogen supplied by humus, and to supplement it, if necessary, hoof and horn meal is excellent. Bone meal, which is slow acting, should be used in early spring and worked well into the upper layer of soil, four ounces per square yard being a good dressing, while hoof and horn meal, an excellent slow-acting nitrogenous fertilizer, should also be applied in early spring at the same rate. Dried blood, which is more readily soluble, is also a good supplier of nitrogen. It can be used between times during the growing season, at the rate of two ounces to the square yard, but in dry weather it must be well washed in with water. Nitrogenous fertilizers, such as nitro chalk, nitrate of soda, and sulphate of ammonia, all of which are quickly soluble in varying degrees, are best left alone except by the highly skilled or in special cases, for all are highly stimulating and leave no valuable residue behind.

If the land is well provided with the principal elements, then every attempt must be made to induce free growth, for without this growth and the consequent balancing root system the plant is unable to make full use of the plant-food provided. Lack of good soil cultivation and general neglect of fundamentals cannot be made good by lavish applications of fertilizers during the

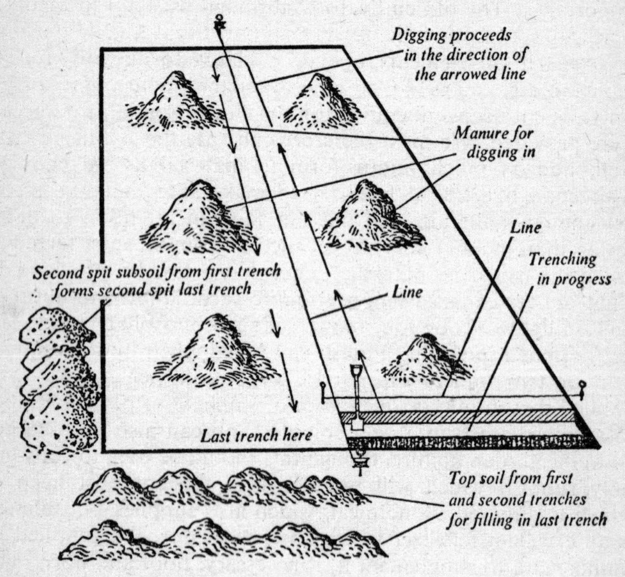

1. Diagram showing how to proceed with trenching so that carrying soil is reduced to a minimum.

growing season, but conversely, a strong, healthy plant, with an abundant root system, is capable of absorbing large supplies of food and sometimes may be fed artificially with great benefit because it has the machinery ready to utilize it. The healthy are often capable of absorbing rich materials, the weakly are unable to cope with it. Those who do not wish to try the separate plant-foods, or are afraid of their use, should buy a good compound fertilizer, which should be used strictly in accordance with the makers' suggestions – directions which are difficult to carry out because an ounce or two per square yard looks very meagre when applied. But what is the point of killing good plants for the satisfaction of feeling you have done something for them?

The cultivator's first aim is to make the physical soil conditions suitable for the reception of plants, for without good conditions much expensive plant-food may be entirely wasted. There are several methods of preparing the soil to achieve this.

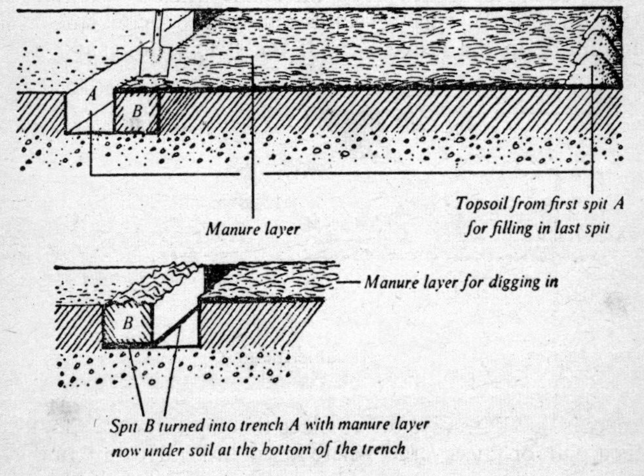

2. Single digging.

The first is by simple digging. The end of a piece of land is marked off with a line six inches from the end and the spit of land in front of the line, for its whole length, is dug out with a fork or spade, and taken by wheelbarrow to a convenient place at the other end of the plot, where the last digging will take place and where it will be ready for filling up the last trench. Then the line is removed and by working backwards, six inches at a time, across the plot, filling in the previous trench as the work proceeds, the whole plot is dug (Fig. 1). The fork or spade should be thrust into the soil to the full depth of the blade or tines, lifted slightly, and turned over, so that the soil is as nearly as possible turned upside down. At the same time a coating of farmyard manure or compost, previously levelled on the surface, is incorporated into the newly-dug land by the inversion of the spit (Fig. 2). On most soils a good sharp-edged spade is the most suitable tool, but on some types of stony land a five-tined fork meets less opposition and is much to be preferred.

The second method is by double digging, sometimes known as bastard trenching. By this method a strip two feet wide is marked off, and the soil all over the strip dug out to the depth of one spit, thus forming a shallow trench, the depth of the spit being equal to the length of the spade when thrust fully into the soil (Fig. 3). This top soil is removed to a convenient place for filling in the last trench. If the strip is long and narrow

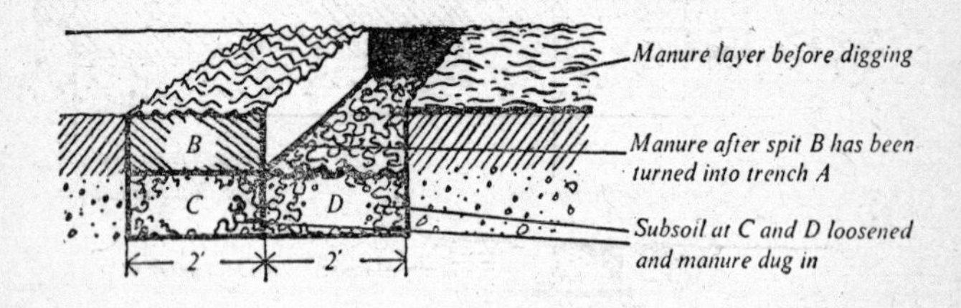

3. Double digging.

there is no alternative but to place this top soil on a spot – such as a path or grass verge, where it will be ready to fill in the last trench – as conveniently close as possible, but if the site is roughly square a lot of work with the wheelbarrow can be avoided by dividing the plot into two equal parts, digging one half at a time and arranging to finish at the same end as the beginning. In this case it is only necessary to transfer the soil immediately from the first trench to where the last trench will be. Then a layer of manure, taken from heaps previously placed in convenient spots on the site, is placed on the exposed bottom spit and dug in just as if it were a piece of top soil. After that a fresh piece is marked off and the top soil from it placed on the top of the first strip. The work then continues in the same way over all the site. Thus, although the position of the soil has changed, the top layer is still composed of top soil and no crude subsoil has been brought to the surface.

The third method is known as trenching, a term which generally implies cultivating more than two spits deep, although in some districts double digging, or bastard trenching, is also known as trenching. To many the term implies also that the bottom spit is brought to the top. As I have already explained, this system should never be practised unless the deep subsoil contains as much humus, and is in as good a physical condition, as the top spit – circumstances rarely found except in centuries-old gardens, in a few valleys where alluvial deposits are deep, and where there are silt deposits such as those around the estuary of the English Dee and in some parts of Lincolnshire. Those who have gardens in these districts are lucky, for the great majority of gardeners have to content themselves with subsoil which has never known exposure or the light of day and which should never be brought to the surface until the general condition of the soil is improved – a happy state so far ahead that the average man need not bother his head about it.

New owners of gardens and many gardeners of some experience are far more concerned with quick and attractive results, and there is no reason why these should not be obtained. Full trenching, or trenching more than two spits deep, should not be practised unless plenty of good farmyard manure or compost is available and unless the subsoil is capable of improvement in a few years or is of plastic clay, in which case disintegration assists drainage and therefore confers many benefits. Those with chalk, gravel, or flint underneath, with little organic matter, should content themselves with digging two spits well.

In full trenching there are two inter-related rules. One is that the soil, after trenching, must be in the same relative vertical position as it was, and the other is that as many trenches must be open at once as spits are to be dug in depth. Thus a strip is marked off, two feet wide, and the top soil taken to a convenient position. The second spit deep is dug out and taken to another convenient place, but not mixed with the precious top soil. The bottom spit, the third in depth, is dressed with farmyard manure or compost and well and deeply dug. Another two-foot strip is then marked off and the top soil taken away for filling in the top of one of the last two trenches. The second spit is then dug and lifted from the second trench to the first, after which it is dressed with farmyard manure or compost and dug again. Then the bottom of the second trench, i.e. the third

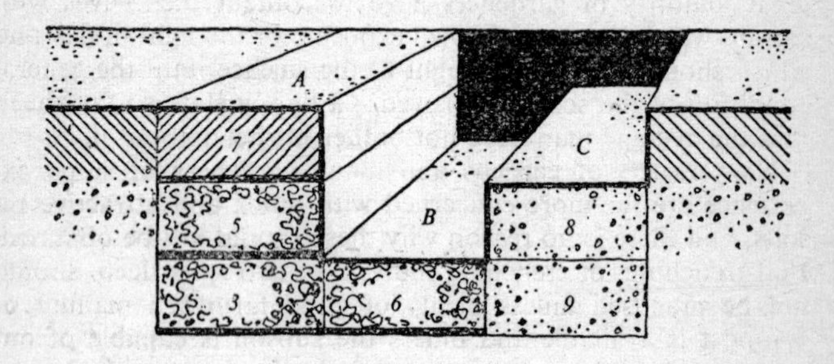

4a. Section showing plan of work on first three trenches, numbered for comparison with Fig. 4b. Spits 1, 2 and 4 are removed for filling in the last trenches.

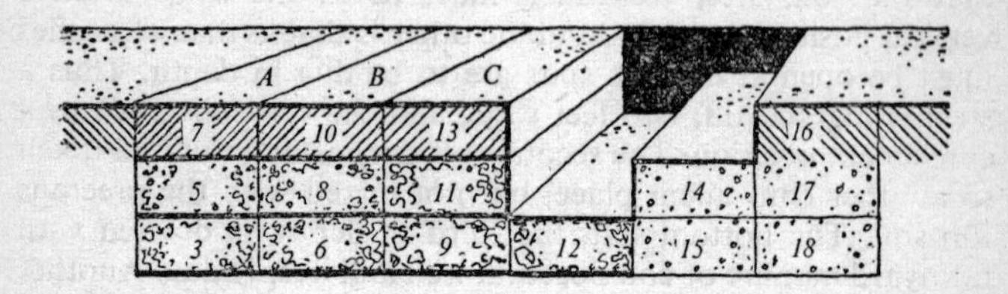

4b. Sectional diagram showing the work in progress with trench A completed.

spit, is dressed with farmyard manure or compost and well dug. A third strip, two feet wide, is then marked off and the top soil lifted to the top of the first trench, thus completing it with fresh soil which is still in the same relative vertical position, a feat which can be accomplished only by opening up a third trench. This process should be repeated, strip by strip, until the whole plot has been trenched, carrying on right across the piece of ground if it is narrow, or dividing it into two if it is roughly square, thus avoiding much laborious use of the wheelbarrow on ground that is soft, as it usually is when trenching is in progress (Fig. 4, a, b).

The newcomer to the work should look upon digging or trenching as a very pleasurable, health-giving recreation, not as physical drudgery which must be got over somehow. It is this last attitude of mind that leads to much misunderstanding and sometimes to a general dread and dislike of physical work in the garden, which is never wholly overcome. During the world wars many rushed on Sundays to their newly-acquired allotments or gardens, and with untrained muscles, and little knowledge of their tools, pulled and tugged and lifted until perspiration soaked their clothes and their bodies trembled with fatigue. Then they stood half stripped to recover. Next day they were all aches and pains and many found great difficulty in continuing the work. Some indeed had to stay in bed and many told me solemnly that they were never going to dig again for it gave them lumbago. Most of them, of course, were suffering from chill induced by getting much too hot and then suddenly much too cold, plus severe physical work to which they were not accustomed. That is not the way! No newcomer need fear anything of the sort if he takes ordinary precautions. To begin with, dig for only a short time daily and select a light spade or fork well within your capacity. Dig easily – do not tug and push in jerky, wasteful movements, but dig easily with your whole body. Use the weight of the body, the muscles of the arms and legs, as well as the body muscles – try to make every muscle of your body do its share. Dig with a gentle rhythm, dig steadily, and resist the little devil inside you which says 'You'll never get it done!' You will, very easily, and come to enjoy and even look forward to it. Go out into the street, watch an elderly navvy, and see how he uses pick and shovel. He lasts all day, and he works so easily, but he does a lot. Begin with an hour or so each day, perhaps only half-an-hour for some, and lengthen the period as your muscles become tough. In time you will feel a glorious hunger and a sense of physical fatigue which is wholly pleasant and will send you to sleep to wake refreshed.

Once I found an enthusiastic amateur friend with only his head and shoulders visible as he threw gravel out of a trench. There are demons like this in every district who believe that the deeper they dig, the better the result, and nothing seems to cure them. Do not listen to them! Use your head and learn how to be happy while digging. There is no reason why your garden should not be a place of joy.

Now about the compost which I have mentioned so often in this chapter. How is it obtained? It is simply the waste green-stuff from the garden or lawn induced to decay in a special way to obtain the best results. During and since the war we have heard a lot about compost heaps, but few realize that the practice of compost making is very old and that it was practised for centuries in the great gardens of this country. It is, of course, an invaluable product, and an analysis will show that, when well made, it is equal or superior to farmyard manure. But analysis is not everything – in manures it tells only part of the truth, for it does not necessarily follow that this substance of equal manurial value will give equally good results, and if there should ever be a choice between good farmyard manure and good, well-made compost, then the grower should choose the former without hesitation, for when used by the average person in the average small garden results are usually better. The great value of compost, however, must not be underrated, for, given enough of it, it is possible to grow good plants indefinitely by the use of compost alone. Indeed, I know several large gardens in the heart of the country, where farmyard manure could not be obtained, which were maintained in excellent condition by the use of decayed lawn mowings, long grass, and abundant supplies of leaf-mould, all obtained from the pleasure grounds and woods. In one particular case, where the pleasure grounds were very extensive, vast quantities of grass mowings, plus some leaf-mould, were, because of special difficulties, the only plant-food obtainable, and before the First World War the produce of that garden, both flowers and vegetables, was known nationally by the great number of prizes it obtained. It is true that in these cases the method of obtaining the compost was wasteful, for the material was simply put in large heaps and allowed to decay, but on the other hand some of the methods in recent years have become unnecessarily finicky and involved, and tend to deter gardeners from starting.

This part of the chapter is not intended to advocate shoddy work, or lazy, dilatory methods, but it must be remembered that most of the elaborate plans presuppose unlimited quantities of green material at one time, or at least enough to complete a compost heap, and in a well-regulated garden a large amount is never available at once. If there is then there is something radically wrong with the cultivator's methods. Like every job in the garden, this must be reduced to fundamentals, and all unnecessary work must be cut out. To elaborate for the sake of elaboration is just to waste time and energy. Be sane! Do not make gardening unnecessarily complicated – there are far better outlets for your energy in the garden itself.

And now for a simple plan. On a level piece of gravel, about five feet wide, start with a layer of green-stuff a few inches thick. On this place an inch or two of animal manure. Cover this with a layer of garden soil, an inch thick, and sprinkle upon this an ounce of hydrated lime, or chalk, or a handful of fresh wood-ashes, per square foot. If dry, sprinkle lightly with water, or, better still, with liquid manure or urine from a stable tank, if it should be available. Repeat the process until the heap is about four feet high. If animal manure is not available, use instead sulphate of ammonia at the rate of three ounces per square yard of bed, or nitro chalk at the rate of one-and-a-half ounces per square yard. Such heaps should be ready in about six months after completion. Any greenstuff capable of decay is suitable, but woody material, such as tree prunings and the like, must be reduced in the bonfire, and the ashes, which contain a valuable and soluble form of potash, collected as soon as cool enough and placed in a dry place for use in compost heaps or for applying direct to the land. Perhaps you will object that you have little time for these jobs and are unable to make even a simple compost heap for this reason. In that case dig a pit about two feet deep and heap the soil around the sides. Into this put all your green-stuff as it is available and use the rotten material when digging and trenching. It will not be made in the best way, but still it will be valuable humus. If, on the other hand, you have a large garden, and therefore a usable amount of vegetable refuse, and wish to go into the matter thoroughly, obtain a good book on the subject and find out all there is to know.

It must be admitted that the making of a compost heap is a slow process and to overcome this there are several proprietary articles now on the market, which, used according to directions, will shorten the period considerably, in some cases to a few weeks. If these are used, small quantities of refuse can be treated at frequent intervals and I have known some small growers who have used small bins or large boxes quite successfully.

Another valuable aid to cultivation is liquid manure, or manure water. One of the most valuable forms of this is the urine drainage from a stable, which in addition to the usual principal plant-foods contains also valuable growth substances. Cow-shed drainings also have their value, but as much antiseptic is used nowadays for washing down both animals and buildings this source of liquid manure must be suspect, for most antiseptics used for the purpose contain substances which destroy plants quickly. It should not be used without enquiry.

Liquid manure can be made by steeping a bag containing half a bushel of cow or sheep manure in a tub containing about fifteen gallons of water. The liquid should be diluted to about one third of its strength, by adding about two gallons of water to each gallon.

Soot-water can be made similarly by steeping half a bushel of soot instead of manure, but as soot supplies little more than nitrogen it should be used as an addition to the liquid manure and not as a substitute for it.

This chapter is intended to show how the garden can be put in good heart before operations start. The principles outlined apply to vegetable growing as well as flower gardening. I hope my readers will give it close study, for as a foundation chapter it is the most important in this book, and more than any other one on which success or failure depends.

·2·

Tools and Appliances

THE number of tools and appliances shown in ironmongers' windows, even in these austere times, is bewildering. Looking at them the beginner is apt to think that he will need a small fortune to equip his garden, but he can be reassured. While it is true that most of the articles displayed have practical value, it is also true that the beginner will need only a few tools at first, and he would be well advised to start with the necessary few and build up his stock of tools and appliances as the need for them arises.

From the first the importance of good tools must not be overlooked, for to buy inferior ones is sheer waste. A fork that twists or a spade that buckles under the first strain can be written off as waste, because even if restored to their original shape, they will twist or buckle again when next strained, and no one with a garden knows when that will be. The first essentials are a good spade and a first-class fork, for it is these that will probably be used more than other tools and upon them much useful foundation work depends. It is a mistake to buy tools too large or too heavy, for wielding them will lead to much unnecessary fatigue. Aim at buying something heavy enough for the job but handy enough to be manipulated easily and you will score over the fellow who believes that a tool which covers more ground will enable him to do more work. You will find that there are various patterns and shapes and that some cheap tools look almost exactly like those nearly twice the price. Choose a spade in which the blade follows the general line of the handle and which is only slightly curved. If, as with some makes, the blade angle is excessive, it will be found extremely difficult to thrust into the ground with the blade nearly upright, as should be done in digging. The handle should be U-shaped, like that of the spade shown in Fig. 5, for old hands will all agree that when used for a long period such a spade will be found easier to handle. The size known as No. 2 is the most convenient, and when buying it is wise to test the feel of the tool, for even the best makes vary slightly. The handle should feel right and the lower part should slip easily in the hand and be free from blister-forming lumps or rough-edged rivets. Buy the best procurable – it is the only safeguard you have. This policy, of course, is much cheaper in the long run, as a good spade will last for years if properly cared for. Unless the soil is abnormally heavy a fork with five tines or prongs should be chosen and should be of the best elastic steel. When struck or pulled, the tines should ring a clear note. The handle and general lines should be similar to those of the spade and the same faults and virtues should be looked for. It is even more important for a fork to be of good quality than for a spade, for I hardly know which is more exasperating – a tine which bends and remains bent or one which breaks off when subjected to a little extra strain.

Then you will need a shovel, and although the advice about a U-shaped handle and smoothness applies here, the blade should be curved well away from the handle so that the operator can shovel easily when in a stooping position. Judging by the shape of some of the inferior makes on the market I can only conclude that no one connected with their manufacture has ever attempted to use them, for to do so would almost entail lying on the shovel, and I have yet to see anyone who can wield a shovel very long in that uncomfortable position. While the edges of a spade should have no lateral bend or curve, those of a shovel should be slightly curved upwards, as it is meant for collecting and holding soil or rubbish. An inferior shovel is an abomination, for its operating edge will bend or roll over when it encounters obstacles, while the blade will quickly disintegrate and become like brittle paper.

Perhaps the handiest tool in the garden is the Dutch hoe (see Fig. 5), with which the soil surface may be improved and weeds prevented. After the heavier cultivation of autumn and winter the Dutch hoe is generally the first tool used in growing crops for loosening the soil, thus admitting air and by its frequent use preventing weeds from germinating. When buying such a light tool there is a great temptation to think that the wider the tool the more work it will do in a given time. Practice will soon teach you otherwise and you may find yourself cluttered up with something you will never use. So be careful !

Select a Dutch hoe well within your capacity, which you can twist and turn about according to the needs of the moment. For general purposes a six-inch Dutch hoe is the most handy, while a five-inch, or even a four-inch, will be found handy for special purposes, but at first one six-inch hoe will be enough.

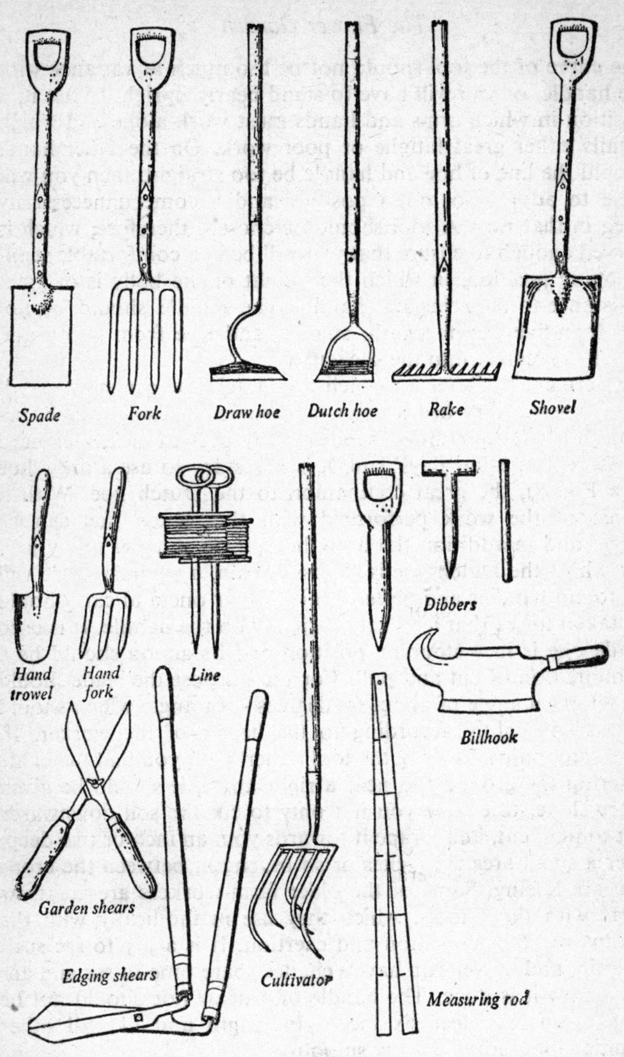

5. Garden tools.

The curve of the tool should not be too much at variance with the handle, or you will have to stand nearly upright to use it, a position in which arms and hands must work alone and which entails either great fatigue or poor work. On the other hand, should the line of hoe and handle be too straight, then you will have to adopt too low a position and become unnecessarily tired in that way. A tool should be chosen, therefore, which is curved enough to ensure that you will be in a comfortable semi-stooping position, in which the weight of the body is of great assistance to the arms and hands. The handle should be not less than five feet in length, smooth and free from knots, and fastened securely into the socket.

There are few soils on which the Dutch hoe cannot be used, but on some very heavy clays, and some clay soils which, because of an admixture of sand, rapidly become nearly as hard as cement in a few days' sun, it is necessary to use a draw hoe (see Fig. 5), the great companion to the Dutch hoe. With it much of the work performed with the Dutch hoe can be done, and in addition the draw hoe is valuable for many jobs for which the Dutch hoe is useless. Again, a six-inch blade will be found handier and better than a larger one and care should be taken to see that it is 'set' correctly on the handle. It is used while one is in a stooping position and its action should be a combination of cut and pull. For the purpose the blade should be set at an angle of about 60 degrees – an angle which should be varied slightly according to the height of the worker. If, when stooping and using the tool underhand, you find the blade entering the ground too near a right angle, it should be given more slope, to enable you not only to cut the soil downwards but to pull, cut, and scrape it towards you, an inch or two deep, over a small area six inches or so in length, between the crops you are hoeing. Some of the older farm-workers are great experts with these tools, which they use methodically with the minimum of waste action and exertion. It is a joy to see such rhythm, and if ever you have a chance spare time to see and admire how it is done. The handle of a draw hoe should not be more than four feet six inches in length and like all other handles should be perfectly smooth.

A good rake is a necessity. Most people have seen one, even if they have never used one, but few realize the importance of the tool. The heavy, cumbersome, hand-forged type, which looks as if it might have been made in the Middle Ages, should be avoided, and preference given to a lighter, cleaner-looking, slimmer tool of the American type, generally made of cast steel. This light and handy tool does not become clogged with soil or rubbish like the heavy, forged type with its thick, stubby teeth which, although of great durability, is difficult and irritating to handle. A tool which can be slung about quickly, and because of its lightness used at many different angles, scores heavily over the heavy tool with which it is impossible to obtain a really fine surface without also removing soil with the unwanted stones and rubbish. Do not buy too large a rake, as experience proves that one with twelve teeth is the most handy size. The handle should be smooth and a full six feet in length.

A good trowel (see Fig. 5) is indispensable. With it nearly all transplanting must be done. A five inch trowel, with a handle about four inches in length, is the best investment. The gadgety versions with long, slim handles, or long, narrow, tapering blades, should be avoided. They represent somebody's attempt to make work lighter, but are deceptive; generally they make work more difficult and tiring. The blade of a trowel should be of good steel and ring clearly when tapped. It is essential, too, that the handle should have a well rounded or somewhat flattened end instead of a rough point. A blister in the palm of the hand at the end of an evening's work may prove very unpleasant.

A useful companion to the trowel is a hand-fork (see Fig. 5), a useful little tool handy for pricking or loosening the ground before planting small enclosed or semi-enclosed areas. With handle complete it is generally about the same length as a good trowel and like that of the trowel the handle should be scrutinized closely before the tool is bought. The type made with three prongs, about five inches in length, is the most handy, and although those made with three flattened tines or prongs look the most attractive, the variety made with three round tapering prongs is more effective in use. Such prongs enter the ground far more easily than the flattened ones and thereby prevent much wasted effort.

The new cultivator will quickly discover the need for a garden-line (see Fig. 5), for there are few jobs connected with sowing or planting which can be done without it. For small jobs or short rows connected with pricking out in a frame or little nursery-bed a couple of short sticks and a piece of household string will suffice, but those who began gardening without advice and who made their first garden-line out of parcelling string, or by joining together odd lengths and sizes of unequal tensile strength, would readily agree that a stout, well-made garden-line is a great asset. A pieced-up string line, if stretched tightly enough for efficiency, generally breaks at a critical moment. To prevent this sort of thing purchase a length of line, with steel reel and plunger complete, specially made for garden use, and long enough for the longest dimension of your garden (sooner or later you will need the full length). A garden-line, to be valuable, must be dependable, as a good line generally is when new. But if it is constantly exposed to the weather it will not remain reliable, and it must therefore always be taken into a dry place immediately after use.

These are the absolute essentials, and with them the beginner will be able to manage. From time to time, as he goes along, the need for other tools will become apparent. It may be that grass becoming untidily long on the verges will call attention, and for rough paths the handy little tool known as a fagging-hook (see Fig. 5, Billhook) is useful. There are many types, some much too big to handle properly. A small, light one, in appearance something like a miniature scythe, should be chosen.

In most gardens a lawn-mower will be required sooner or later, and although in the case of an expensive item of this kind money may set the limit, a good make should be bought if possible. The small side wheel-driven machines are cheap and attractive and will do the job quite efficiently, but having no rollers, cannot be used to cut grass close to the edges. Strips remain, therefore, which these lawn-mowers can cut only by laboriously running them backwards and forwards at right angles to the verge. With a roller-driven machine, especially one of the modern ball-bearing type, such edges can be mown with ease, because two sets of rollers support it while it overlaps the edge. Possibly in this case the temptation to choose something too big is not so strong, as prices rise steeply with size, but for the man or woman with average strength a machine with twelve-inch cutting blades is extremely handy and because of its lightness the lawn can be mown much more quickly than when an over-large mower is used. However, there always will be odd spots and corners of lawn inaccessible to any mower and the grass on these must be cut by two-handed clippers. These are made on the same principle as scissors and the blades are ground in the same way. A pair with blades ten inches long, with foot-long handles, is a convenient size. These clippers are also used for the harder work of hedge trimming, and therefore good-quality steel is essential. As the blades are both curved slightly inwards, to ensure that the two cutting edges always meet under pressure, it is essential that they should not buckle or bend. Inferior blades, which often have quite a good appearance, are difficult to maintain in a keen condition and often buckle the first time they encounter thick grass or hard hedge shoots.

There are also long-handled edging shears (see Fig. 5), useful for cutting grass verges, which are easy to manipulate and quite efficient if of good quality. Their action is similar to that of hedge or grass shears, but by having their steel handles turned up almost at right angles and mounted on wooden handles several feet in length it is possible to stand in a semi-upright position to perform the job efficiently. It is even more important than with hedge shears that these should be of good quality, as long-handled edging shears are liable to encounter thick tufts of grass and sometimes lumps of soil which deflect poor blades and make them useless.

A good pair of well-sprung, light sheep shears, which are used with one hand only, will take the place of hedge or grass shears and long-handled edging shears for all grass-clipping purposes, but for hedge clipping they are useless. They tire the hand quickly unless one has much practice and therefore should be considered as odd jobbing or emergency tools.

As garden development increases with knowledge the ordinary two-foot pocket rule – an admirable appliance – will be found inadequate and a measuring rod will be needed. One can easily be made from a six- or ten-foot length of two-inch by one-inch batten. This can be made into a permanent measure by marking it off in pencil in six-inch lengths along the whole of its length, and afterwards making shallow channels along these marks with a fine-toothed saw. Such a rod will suffice for all ordinary measurements, even if they are lengthy; an architect's or surveyor's measuring tape, complete with case, is a luxury seldom needed.

After a year or two, when worn or overgrown edges need cleaning up, a crescent or half-moon edging iron is a great help. It can be used more accurately than a spade and after its use grass verges can be trimmed with the long-handled edging shears much more effectively and with a much cleaner appearance. Unless of good quality such a tool will be found difficult to keep sharp-edged, and, as much of its efficiency depends upon this, a good one must be chosen.

In recent years various weird-looking gadgets with many tortuous tines called hand cultivators (see Fig. 5), have come on the market. That they are useful cannot be denied, but as they merely scratch the surface it is doubtful if they do as much as a good Dutch hoe, and that less efficiently. For putting the final touches to an already clean bed, or to promote a dust tilth, they have their uses, but altogether they must be considered luxuries. Attractive advertisements which imply that the whole garden can be cultivated merely by dragging one or the other of these tools over the surface occasionally should be assessed at their proper value.

It is possible that occasionally and perhaps when first making a garden, a pickaxe will be needed. At the same time there may be a need for a small crowbar. Both of these tend to be expensive and many people get over the difficulty by borrowing, but the possession of such tools is an asset as they are generally needed at unlooked-for moments. Sometimes they may be picked up cheaply at a sale after large works are completed, but, if available, the back axle of a disused motor-car, suitably pointed by a blacksmith, makes an excellent light crowbar.

For flower gardening large dibbers (see Fig. 5), such as those used by the vegetable grower for planting cabbages, are rarely needed, but if they are a U-handle and shaft from any broken fork, spade, or shovel may be utilized. Such a dibber should have the operating end sharpened to a fine point. A dibber fitted with a permanent steel point which remains pointed and enters the ground a little more easily than a wooden one may be procured, but this additional expense scarcely seems justified for a tool which is used only very occasionally.

Smaller dibbers for pricking out and propagating cuttings will often be needed. When pricking out, a pointed dibber is used of a size proportionate to the seedlings. Thus, when tiny begonia seedlings are handled a dibber less than the size of a pencil will suffice, but when large, strong-growing seedlings are being transferred one roughly half-an-inch in diameter, and about six inches long, is more convenient. Whatever the size, these dibbers should be well pointed. They can easily be made at home from any convenient stake or piece of wood. Dibbers used for propagating cuttings should also vary according to the subject and may range in diameter from less than a quarter of an inch to something nearer half an inch in the case of thick-stemmed subjects like geraniums. They should be only slightly tapered, with the tapered points cut off square.

Stakes of various sizes are a necessity and their sizes may vary from tiny ones, nine inches or so in length, such as bamboo tips, to long thick stakes needed for weighty plants such as dahlias. For this purpose the heavy, square, gaudily painted ones sold by dealers, often of the dimensions of small posts, should be avoided. The dahlia border, or any other border for that matter, should exist for showing the plants, not as a kind of coconut-shy. To show up the beauty of foliage and flower, all stakes and appliances should be neutral in colour and as unobtrusive as possible. Approach your dealer and ask him to obtain some hazel stakes from the coppice. They are mossy brown in colour and do not offend the eye. They may be had in many lengths and sizes, but for tall dahlias they should be four or five feet long and at least an inch and a quarter in diameter. For sharpening large stakes a chopping-block and a chopping tool, known as a bill-hook or woodman's hook, are both needed, but sometimes stakes can be procured already sharpened in the woods.

The use of stakes implies the use of string for plant support. Thick, white, or violent-coloured string is nearly as intolerable as white or gaudy stakes, so buy either fillis string, which is soft in texture and restful in colour, or soft tying string of a green neutral shade.

One of the great pleasures in a garden is to be able to identify its occupants, and for this labels are necessary. People's ideas of labels vary tremendously and range from tiny ones, barely visible, to huge affairs that look like tombstones. Here again the appliance should be in proportion to the subject, small labels being needed for seedlings in pots and pans and larger ones for chrysanthemums, dahlias, and roses. For roses, and other permanent or semi-permanent occupants of the border, indestructible metal labels may be procured by giving a list of the names to your seedsman, and wooden labels, painted and unpainted, are available in all sizes from an inch or two to a foot long. These last better if the label is given a fresh coat of paint and the name is written in pencil while the paint is wet. If labels more than a foot long are needed, they may be cut from old packing cases or wooden grocers' boxes; a convenient width for sizes between one and two feet is one-and-a-half inches. The ends of such labels should be pointed.

Two knives are essential – one a big heavy pruning knife with a hooked blade, the other a small, light-bladed knife with a very keen edge, known as a budding knife. The pruning knife will do all the heavy work while the budding knife will be useful for taking cuttings, cutting string, and a multitude of small jobs for which a knife is required. In the case of the budding knife at least, quality is of great importance. A few odd earthenware saucers for seed sowing, perhaps a kneeling mat for the few weeds which must be destroyed by hand, some shallow boxes about two inches deep – known as seed-trays – for sowing seed and for cuttings, and a few flower-pots of various sizes, will complete the equipment until the need for more arises.

By the time the more important tools are procured the new gardener will have realized their value, but may not have realized the need for proper care. Tools which are put away covered with wet soil will quickly deteriorate, be difficult to sharpen, and rust away rapidly. The tool-shed, however small, should be clean and tidy, not a resting place for unwanted rubbish which will have to be cleared away sometime. Tools should be systematically hung on hooks or spikes and the small appliances and handleless ones placed on a convenient shelf or in a drawer. All steel tools should be washed or wiped clean every time they are used and then smeared with oil or grease. The discarded oil from a motor-car sump will answer admirably for this purpose and save expense. All stakes should be kept in sizes and bundled for convenience, while if no other place for them exists, labels may be stored in their sizes in small seed-trays or boxes.

Those fond of carpentry – and many gardeners are – can use odd half-hours for making labels, seed-boxes, cutting-boxes, small frames, and the like, and for this a small carpenter's bench in the tool-shed or garage is a great convenience. Wood can sometimes be bought as old packing cases from stores and grocers, and labels and boxes made at lesiure at home generally last longer than those bought ready-made.

The gardener should always have a note-book ready for use, for when his thoughts are centred on the garden, no stray idea should be neglected; it should always be recorded to be sorted and developed later on when definite planning is done.

Flower gardening is such a good hobby and so worth developing that every kind of assistance should be sought, and the tool-shed – and its small factory possibilities – should be considered as one of the chief aids, and studied accordingly.

Throughout this chapter I have emphasized the need for quality and I now do so again, for the most expensive article in a flower-garden is a cheap tool. With poor tools, you are condemned to delays and exasperation, which continue through the years – unless you are bold enough to cut your losses, throw out the offending articles, buy an outfit that will last a lifetime, and work in comfort. Such an outfit may have to be collected gradually, but it is worth it. There is little happiness to be obtained from rubbish.

· 3 ·

Laying Out the Small Garden of a New House and Re-designing an Old Garden

CONSTERNATION is generally the first feeling in the mind of the new house owner. Seeing the wreckage left by the builder in the garden he thinks, hastily, that never will he be able to conquer it. When he recovers, if he has no knowledge of horticulture, he either underestimates the amount of work necessary or greatly overestimates it, and feels appalled in consequence. I have known cheerful but over-optimistic beginners, who bustled in with such vigour that – mainly through their own undisciplined exertions – they became physical wrecks, and abandoned their gardens for good; and I have met many who, becoming pessimistic through lack of progress, have given up gardening, and vowed never to return to it. Both states of mind are equally bad and lead to much the same result.

Anyone who finds himself the owner of a new house has my sympathy, for conditions when the builder has just left are sometimes very bad. I ask the indulgence of any conscientious builder, who does more than clear up superficially behind him: what I say does not apply to him. It is a real delight to enter a new garden free of rubbish, but this is rare. Clay or other crude subsoil is often scattered about on the surface. Boxes tins, and buckets lie about. Scrapings from paint cans with the residue from distemper pails lie in little heaps. The deceptively rough top level is often made up of unused mortar, strips of glass, brickbats, and odds and ends of piping mixed in the clay, and the levels below cannot be trusted either, for the new gardener may find anything connected with building, from a rafter to a kitchen sink, buried by accident or by design. If his garden accommodated the workmen's huts near which the lime pits were sited and mortar was made, he often finds the pits filled up with rubbish in which nothing could grow, and in or on the soil innumerable lumps of mortar of varying sizes, including pieces of cement weighing hundredweights, which, setting hard after working hours, had to be disposed of somehow.

Finding all this, the average man can be excused if he fumes. It looks so bad that he longs to get rid of it somehow – anyhow

– and sow or plant something quickly to hide it. Anyone who reads the first chapter and reflects a little will see that success by this method is impossible. Even in this country, with its fairly equable climate and its frequent rains, plants cannot grow in such a medium. In such cases many earnest gardeners have gone on for years, subconsciously realizing that their lack of success was due to the soil, but not appreciating the basic reason for it. Often they attend lectures or gardening classes, read much gardening literature, use many bags of fertilizer – and all to no purpose. To those who think that this is the cause of so much disappointment I say: Stop your ordinary garden-operations early one autumn and set to work to clear out the ground systematically. It will pay a rich dividend. And if you are a newcomer, do likewise: make this the first job and continue steadily at it, however long it takes. It is the only way. Clear the surface first, then dig two spits deep and remove all rubbish, and look out especially for the most treacherous thing in the garden – broken glass – or it will be a curse for ever.

When you are not feeling too well, or are low-spirited for some other reason, you will be disheartened because the job is taking so long and the devil inside you insists that you will never finish it. But you will. Cast out the devil and carry on systematically. Study Chapter One in detail, and don't panic. If you do this and do not waste your strength in vain efforts, one day, much sooner than you expected, you will find that you have finished. Your reflexions will be pleasant too – the job was not half so bad as it looked. Apart from that glorious sense of achievement, you will realize that you have really enjoyed doing it, and, best of all, you will have the satisfaction of knowing that you have good ground work for cultivation. Within reason you can grow anything.

This all applies to the garden left in a rough condition, but there are others. There are gardens already made by builders who know little or nothing about horticulture and who pride themselves on the services they give to their clients. These gardens are sometimes worse than the others, because they are deceptive. There is a lawn which to the uninitiated looks good, and sometimes, to use the words of one builder, 'The garden has been landscaped.'

I knew of a pre-war estate finished in this way, complete with new roads, island shrubberies, and grass verges. All had been 'landscaped' – the same maddening repetition of shrubs being used in each garden and in island shrubberies at road junctions and bends. The roads, also constructed by the builder, and constructed well, had to have suitable running levels. These disagreed with the contours and, to make up the roads, soil was taken from any convenient place, including the front gardens. Each front garden and some back gardens were robbed of top soil, and to overcome the difficulty of restoring the garden levels, and to save a lot of excavation, the builder sunk each front garden, in some cases more than a foot, and made a bank on all its sides, connecting the flayed surface to the original levels by gravel paths and steep banks. The rough turf used, of little value for lawns, rested on gravel at the lower levels while the turfed banks were far too steep to be cut with a lawn mower. When finished, these quite extensive gardens were certainly attractive, but cultivators with a little gardening knowledge became very disheartened, for the starved grass almost disappeared in dry weather and the grass on the banks, whose roots were able to reach good soil, grew vigorously and had to be laboriously cut with shears. The attractive yellow gravel paths were also shams, for they consisted of an inch or two of gravel placed on the soil without foundation or drainage, and consequently, in winter, they became quagmires. One householder, a gardener of some experience, whose garden had been skinned down to the hard top of a twenty-foot gravel seam, had to remove turf and gravel and throw in innumerable loads of good soil before he could grow anything. Of the two, the rubbish-dump type is preferable to the falsely prepared, for whereas one can be put right by good method the other cannot be rectified without a quantity of good soil – so costly and difficult to obtain.

When the surface of a rough site has been cleared the cultivator must decide where the paths are to be, for these must not be accidental. A natural craving for variety makes many new gardeners – and some experienced ones – twist their paths into weird shapes without relation to where they lead. But a path or a road should lead somewhere; it should arrive at its destination in the easiest way. The path which by its curving doubles the distance is generally fussy, annoying, and in the end an eyesore, because points which protrude are trodden on. If you stop to look at the flowers in the border you trip over grass verges or blunder into the border itself. If the corkscrew path leads to a tool shed, then two steps have to be taken instead of one to fetch a tool, and if the compost heap is at the end of the garden – as it ought to be – then someone has to go twice the distance with the household refuse. If poultry or other livestock are kept, the same applies, and if there is no objective at the garden end, then the path is meaningless. In narrow strips of garden where the owner longs to do something to mitigate the monotony of long straight lines of fence, crooked or meaningless paths serve only to accentuate the trouble and are a constant source of irritation to the owner, who is often unaware that the fussy

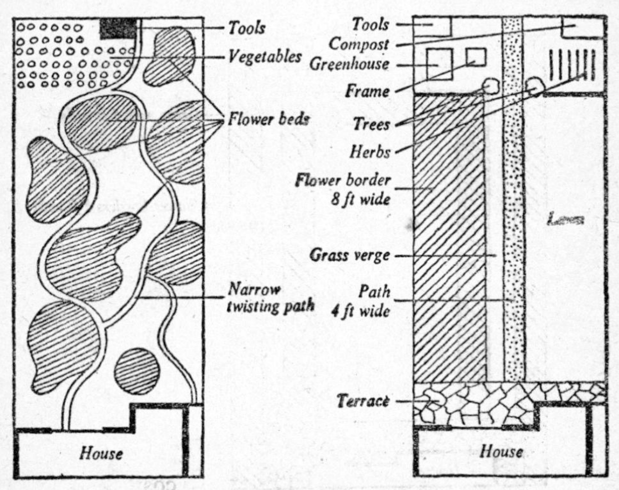

6. (Left) bad and (right) good lay-out.

path is responsible for the disgust he feels when he looks at his garden (Fig. 6).

If you own a narrow strip of garden with a summer-house at the end, you should make the path follow the general lines of the strip. This does not mean that the garden will be a set of dreary straight lines, for the borders can be broken up by plants of varying heights. If the garden is wide enough a path which follows the general lines of the boundaries is generally the most satisfactory; but it should be remembered that paths less than three feet wide are rarely successful, and that unless there is enough width, a double path uses up much valuable space and gives a bitty appearance. If a vegetable garden has also to be incorporated, such a divided layout is unsuitable, because the owner has to crop with many short drills or a few very long ones, and the difficulties of vegetable growing increase (Fig. 7).

Narrow strip gardens sometimes have a blank fence at the end, which, from the house, is unattractive. This can be masked by a summer-house with sides and front draped in creepers, by a trellis of light fir poles covered by climbing roses or creepers, or by the fence itself being covered in climbing roses

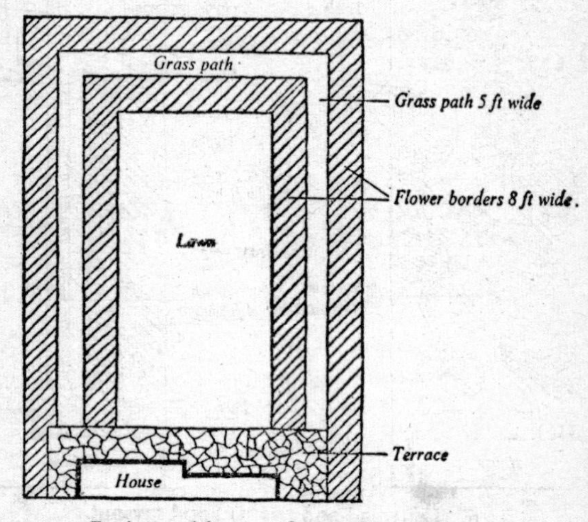

7. A good lay-out for a wider garden.

or creepers. Sometimes, too, a good effect at the end of the garden can be gained by the use of upright poles on which roses are made to climb, but these sometimes appear incongruous unless suitable roses on poles (pillars) are employed as part of the general layout. But there are other considerations. Often the end of the garden is needed for a compost heap or small livestock such as poultry and rabbits, and in every garden it is useful to have a small open space for stacking and sharpening pea stakes, bean rods and stakes of all descriptions; or it may be needed as the site for a tool-shed or garden hut. In such a case, the summer-house will have to be placed nearer the house and must be considered in connexion with a lawn, without which even a small garden is incomplete. But it is generally unwise to place the lawn directly outside a french window because footsteps falling repeatedly on the same piece of turf soon make ugly bare patches on the grass; so that the summer-house must be placed at one side or at the end of the garden, but must not interfere with the general layout.

Some form of hard wide path, or terrace, should therefore lie between house and lawn or house and summer-house or shed. The word terrace, formerly used to denote a flat platform above the level of the surrounding ground, is now also used to describe a level hard surface or path in front of or surrounding the house, and because of the general lie of the land this is often on the same level as the rest. Such a terrace should be of good hard material and should be large enough; six feet is the smallest practicable width, and if possible it should be eight feet wide or more. There should always be room for a few garden chairs and a table, because if the aspect is right, and the house is fairly well sheltered, a terrace like this is a pleasant place on summer evenings.

In most cases the terrace will be level with, or only just above, the level of the path; it cannot anyway be raised round the house higher than the damp course, but must be kept just below this mark, which is easily found, and this will ensure a correct general level.

Fortunate people in hilly districts, or on a slight slope outside a town, may have a partial or complete view of the countryside. This should on no account be blotted out; the distant view is precious, and should at all costs be saved. Sometimes a falling slope allows the view – it may be only a narrow vista between two houses or between house and tree – to be seen without obstruction, and in that case shed, summer-house, or pillar roses must not cut out the view, nor should fruit trees or flowering trees or shrubs be planted which would eventually block it out. Instead, the main path must be constructed to approach the view, and, from the house, give the impression that it continues indefinitely. Sometimes the end of the garden is on a higher level than the house and a path leading from the house might easily prove to be a channel for storm water. In such cases the main path must be diverted to the side of the house or flooding of the inside of the house may easily occur. Although drains are rarely needed in small gardens, in this case the provision of a drain capable of carrying away a large volume of water should be considered.

Some sort of frame for the view is necessary. I have seen a view framed by the trunks and lower branches of two tall ornamental cherry trees – and cherries are ornamental at any time, apart from the weeks they are in bloom, when few flowering trees surpass them. Their trunks must be long enough – a full ten feet – and as the lower branches sometimes have a tendency to grow downward it may be necessary from time to time to remove them. To make the most of the landscape you may need to lower the fence or persuade your neighbour to do so – if the fence is his – and protect the exposed part with wire netting.

Another effect, equally beautiful, can be gained by planting two slim cypress trees, one on each side of the gap. For this Cupressus Fletcheri is admirable because its body does not bulge too much as it grows; they should be planted one on each side, at least four feet from the edge of the path, to allow for natural expansion, even though this Cupressus is slim in proportion to its height. If you must have it still slimmer, this or any other Cupressus should not be clipped with hedge clippers, but should be cut back carefully with the knife about the end of April, just before the new growth begins, or during August. Two tall Cypresses, with perhaps a wrought-iron gate between, can also be used in short, square gardens to give a sense of distance, but the Cypresses must be slender and the gate must be attractive.

If the lines of the main paths are pleasing there is no reason why other paths should not be made leading from them, providing each path has a use, for to make a path for the sake of making it is always poor design. A path should either lead somewhere or have a definite use.

Before you reach this stage ask yourself what you really want to grow. Do you want to grow annuals, which are beautiful and simple, or delphiniums, which are regal, or perennial plants generally? Do you want to grow roses or early flowering chrysanthemums or any other specialized plant which would be unsuitable in a mixed border? Where is your greenhouse going? Take the greenhouse first: this should be near the shed and not too far from the house. It should be near a well-made path, for you will visit it so often, and when you have decided on its exact position, paths can be made accordingly. It is often better not to decide on the details at first, but to develop the main paths and let the others grow out of your new ideas.

Now about the construction of the paths. Start with the terrace. There is a choice of many materials for this: formal square or rectangular paving, crazy stone paving, plain or ornamental tiles, black Staffordshire bricks, ordinary red bricks well burnt for hardness, laid flat or laid on edge in a pattern. Small bricks of the Dutch and Belgian kind manufactured in a few kilns in this country make admirable paths. And then (I hesitate even to mention them) there are cement and asphalt. These both have splendid hard surfaces and will wear almost for ever; but they are hard to the eye. So appallingly hard are they that nothing looks right around them. Asphalt always looks wrong, even with a coloured surface, while cement, even when it is laid by an expert and coloured and adapted for the purpose, is still cement, and you can never forget it. Forget them and use something which, like a well-dressed woman, is never greatly in evidence.

First of all, study your house. I have seen bright yellow stonework all round a striking tomato-red house. What plant could be happy between tomato and ochre! I have seen, too, a muddle of lily pools, bird baths, rock pinnacles and crazy paving all crowded into the same little garden. Yellow stone will not be modified by exposure even in a whole generation, and bad design will always remain bad. Before you spend much money occupy the house a while and study its possibilities. If it is of red brick, cover some of its redness with suitably coloured creepers (of which more later). Then consider the possibility of constructing a terrace of red brick – possibly a shade darker than the house. If bricks to cover the whole terrace would be too expensive, lay grass on the terrace and brick paths through the parts leading to doorways much in use.

If you are content to have a terrace only and do not intend to smother the garden in stone, grey stone, either prepared or random, may be used. But if your house is stone, painted stone colour, or any shade of cream, any kind of stone can be used, including the bright yellow Cheddar stone, which, however, rarely looks so well as the restrained grey stone of the north. Try to obtain a material which will blend with your house and with your flowers, and, whatever you use, lay it on a good foundation.

Many people lay their stones or bricks direct on beaten earth and in some cases this is good enough, but if the paths are used for heavy traffic, after prolonged rain they begin to sag and squelch. Stones or bricks kick up and squirt a slimy black fluid on nylons and trousers, and once they have done so will certainly do it again after the next rain, as there is no cure but complete rebedding. Instead of risking this, make a hard foundation on which the paving can rest safely. Take out the soil for six inches, or better still eight, and if it is good soil, not contaminated by the builder, save it. Before filling in, get a long straight floor board and mount a spirit level on it. Then place the board and spirit level on builders' pegs, and make sure that the foundation is dead level according to the damp course, allowing for the requisite depth of the bricks or stone paving. Then fill in the hole to the right height with hard core material – broken brickbats, clinkers, stones from the garden, anything which is hard but allows good drainage – and put a couple of inches of fine material such as coal ashes or sand on top. Make dead level and on this lay the stones. Do not scamp the job but take a delight in making it just right, for if you do not you will suffer for it always. Use the spirit level and the straight edge repeatedly. If you are using squared stone there will be no difficulties with the edges, for which a line stretched on the outer edge will guide you, but if random stone or so-called crazy paving, find some pieces with straight edges to go on the edges and fit the more irregular and smaller pieces inside. With squared stone, the sides will be parallel, but crazy paving may vary in thickness and need bedding in separately according to thickness, bulges or hollows.

Probably the best form of crazy paving is the broken paving stones obtainable in some towns when stone pavements are replaced by asphalt. This is generally of a good grey colour and being uniformly flat can be laid with ease. Also, there is not much difficulty in finding pieces with a straight edge for the outside as there is with random stone from quarries. Take your time over this job. Laying crazy paving is fascinating but not easy. It is like a jig-saw puzzle but with no exact solution, and with weighty stones to handle. Although there is a great choice of stone, go for the broken paving stones, which are more satisfactory than any others.

But a word of warning. In the South-west and the West of England there are some very attractive cream and golden limestones, which flake out well for crazy paving and which, with a stone or cream house, look very well. Some of them, however, disintegrate easily after severe frost and if salt or some types of weed killer are used on them. So be cautious – a few enquiries beforehand may save much disappointment.

If you are fond of small rock plants, or the smell of scented thymes, lay the crazy paving stones on a layer of soil over the foundation and pack the interstices with soil for the tiny plants. But if the terrace is to be much used the stones should be set in cement carefully coloured to match. Setting in cement is also the most satisfactory method for squared stone, if it is to be used extensively.

Even when the house is built of stone, too much stonework is out of place; but, with tasteful planning, there are exceptions to this, which apply to small gardens which the owner cannot cultivate for lack of time. Such small gardens, if levelled carefully on flat or terraced levels, can be attractive if covered completely with paving squares designed with suitable small borders and beds. This type of small garden, with a well head, sundial or garden ornament in carefully chosen stone, may be expensive to lay out, but it costs little to keep up. I once saw a small ugly yard made into something restful and beautiful. The yard door was painted blue to match the house doors, and the drab walls of London brick had climbers trained over them. The floor was completely paved with square grey stone, except for side borders large enough to accommodate the climbers in comfort, while rock plants grew in well chosen places. The grey and blue shades harmonized well with the surroundings, and the climbers all toned in with one another. Homely-looking dull red brick can also be used for paving yards surrounded by red brick walls, and, as on the terrace or the path, can be laid flat, edgewise or in pattern.

Now for the garden path. Having decided where it is to go, study its width. If it is too wide, it will be costly and out of proportion in a narrow garden, and if it is too narrow, it will be little more than a useless ribbon. Few things look worse in a garden than a niggardly path. About four feet is the most suitable width for a small garden, and six for a wider garden, if there is enough room. Whatever the width, two people should always be able to pass or walk in comfort, otherwise edges and borders will be defaced, which is always noticeable, however beautiful the flowers around. If your paths are wrong, your whole garden is wrong, so study the question carefully.

On stony or gravelly soils, or where there is loose rock beneath, the paths may follow the general undulation of the land, but unless you are sure that water will not collect in the hollows, it is better to have a running level. This means a regular sloping line from the selected level on the terrace to the lowest point in the garden, or, in the case of two paths linked together by a third path at the end, two running levels from the terrace to two lower points, linked by the third path, at right angles, also on a running level if the two longer levels are unequal. This, in the case of short lengths, can be done by driving in a builder's peg, twenty inches or more in length, to the desired depth at each end, using the top of the peg to indicate the top of the finished path, stretching a cord tightly from end to end, and driving in, at intervals, pegs on which the straight edge may rest. Then excavate ten inches of soil – one good spit with the spade – and, if it is unspoilt top soil, save it for improving the depth of good soil on border or plot. As in the case of the terrace, place coarse brickbats, rubble, or clinkers six inches deep in the bottom, cover this with two inches of finer material and, if gravel is to be used, follow with two inches of binding

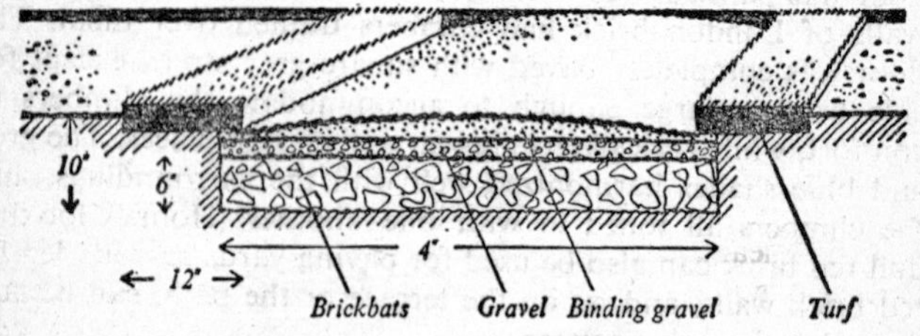

8. Section through a gravel path.

gravel (Fig. 8). Arrange for the top of the path to be convex – about an inch higher than the sides – when the path is complete. Where there are depressions not previously levelled fill them with soil to the required level before putting in the rubble, but ram in hard or the weighty rubble and gravel will sink and form depressions in the path.

People who do not want to spend a great deal on the path will generally use gravel, which, if laid as described, makes a very satisfactory and lasting path. But the surface must be of binding gravel, that is, gravel mixed naturally with enough yellow clay to make a hard surface after rolling. Half-inch granite or stone chippings which remain loose can also be used. These are laid flat, without a convex surface, and rely upon good drainage below to remain clean and porous. Generally, granite chippings are used in the north and west and gravel in the south and south-east. The material of the neighbourhood should always be used. (Fig. 9)

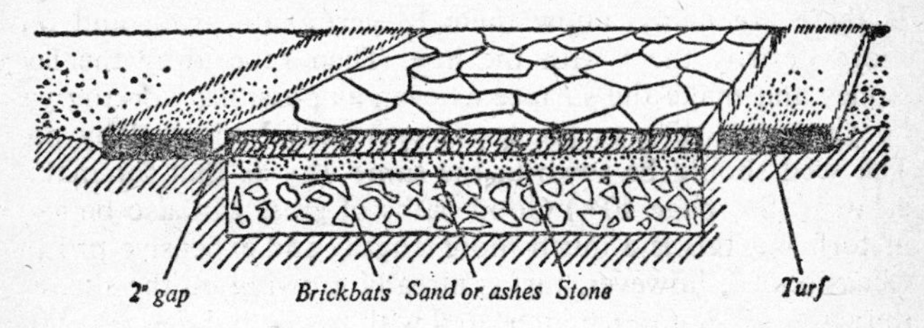

9. Crazy paving. Section through a stone path, showing 2-inch gap between stone and grass verge.

Some good artificial stone is now made in various colours, and some of it is quite attractive. Use this if you really like it; but, even at its best, I do not think it truly satisfactory – its very presence seems to be a constant reminder of artificiality.

The pleasantest of all paths and the easiest to make is of grass, but it cannot be recommended in all cases. On peat, with an impermeable subsoil, it quickly becomes a morass, and on clay, if it is used frequently, the surface will become impacted to a putty-like consistency, and grass cannot flourish on it. On some types of extremely light soils, the grass flies away in dust after a little hard wear, but it cannot be denied that on any soil when wear is not too great, four to six feet of green grass provides a restful satisfying setting equalled only by the lawn. Such walks will make the dullest vegetable garden look interesting, and I have in mind an old walled-in garden of about five acres with grass paths ten feet wide on which broad-wheeled pony carts were used to haul manure and rubbish. That garden was always beautiful. Even in winter it never looked hard and forbidding. Since I saw it I have advised the laying out of many small gardens on similar lines, and all have given great pleasure to their owners.

The procedure for making them is simple. If the soil is poor dig manure into the top soil and leave the subsoil alone. Wait until it is thoroughly consolidated and then tread it hard and thoroughly – every inch of it. Let it rest for a while, while you write to your seedsman and tell him your district, soil, and the number of square yards you wish to sow, and he will send you a suitable grass mixture. In the meantime, annual weeds will have germinated, so allow them to grow an inch or two high and then destroy them by hoeing shallowly with the Dutch hoe. If there are many, allow them to germinate again and once more destroy them with the hoe. Then rake away the large stones and make the surface as even as possible, working yard by yard according to the levels previously indicated by pegs. The seed should be sown in the same way as that for making a lawn. (See page 404.) Good paths of grass can also be made of turf, but this is a much more lengthy and expensive process. Occasionally, however, turf is already growing on the site, and miraculously not much interfered with by the builder. Economy alone will sometimes dictate the use of this; for treatment of it see the chapter on lawns (page 401).

This brings us to the difficult question of edgings – so important for appearance and general utility, for the soil in the cultivated borders must be kept in place. The grass path certainly scores here, for no other edging is required. I have seen many queer and diverse materials used for edgings, including broken plates in the Potteries. I have heard of knuckle bones being used – by a manufacturing butcher, no doubt – but I cannot imagine that rows of white bones, knuckle ends up, could be a very pleasing sight. Obviously weird edgings, which cannot remind one of anything beautiful, strike a jarring note where everything should be harmonious.

Edgings should fall into one of two categories. They should be utilitarian, in which case they should be invisible – or at least, they should not attract the eye immediately – or they should be beautiful, and therefore part of an attractive whole. Edgings matter a lot. They often decide whether a garden is to be attractive or irritating. Bad planning or design often give rise to a vague sense of annoyance in a place which should be restful and soothing, so study the question well. If room can be spared nothing is more satisfactory than a strip of turf a foot or more in width. This effectively contains the soil behind it and has a pleasant appearance. It is easy to maintain in good condition, needing only to have a light mower run over it once or twice a week during the growing season. Also it is as cheap as most things and much cheaper than some. If the paths are of gravel, verges of grass should be laid to overlap the gravel by an inch or two to prevent weeds from growing between gravel and grass, but if the paths are of brick or stone it is wise to arrange for the tops of turf and path to form one level and to leave a two-inch gap between turf and stone to facilitate easy clipping. (Fig. 9.) If this is not done you will have great difficulty in cutting the grass with clippers and, therefore, it will look untidy. An edging of grass is not strictly needed where brick or stone is used, but a green verge is an asset to any garden.

Growing plants are sometimes used for permanent or semi-permanent edgings. One of the best of these is the giant form of the sea pink, or thrift, Armeria Laucheana. This thrives almost everywhere, is particularly happy by the sea and flourishes in salt marshes. It is usual to plant clumps almost touching one another and divide and replant them every three or four years. This plant is perhaps more useful for the vegetable garden than for the flower garden, for the colour, a rather hard carmine-pink, would certainly clash with all the yellows and oranges so valuable in the border. Such edgings are not particularly easy to plant, for it is hard to find the true division between gravel and soil and to avoid damage when digging borders edged in this way.

In gardens in the south and west it is not uncommon to see the use of pinks. Used as a border they have the same disadvantages as sea pinks, but when in flower they have an attractive scent, and when not flowering their foliage is a pleasant grey blue. They are particularly happy on chalk, limestone, or where the soil is alkaline. Colour clashes can be avoided by the use of the white variety called Mrs Sinkins. But propagation is not easy. It is true that in the west of England it is possible to pull old plants apart, plant the pieces and obtain good results, but in the average garden in other parts this method fails and young plants must be obtained from cuttings or layers. (See chapter 26 on propagation.)

Nepeta Mussini, commonly known as Catmint, is also used in many places. This makes a very good edging, but as it grows tall quickly, it is inclined to outstrip in growth the occupants of beds and hide them. It can be propagated easily by division or cuttings and although the colour – a bluish grey – is not unpleasant, some people find the scent of flowers and foliage rather objectionable. Nevertheless, it is a popular plant and one which, because of its freedom of growth, is not likely to be discarded.

Box edging – in reality small clipped shrubs of box forming a miniature hedge from six inches to a foot high – must not be overlooked. It is an excellent edging and one which was used extensively in the past. In a garden surrounding an Elizabethan house – whether genuine or a modern copy – it looks exactly right, but for others it is not always suitable. Round some of the stone houses of the north and west it looks quite well, especially if the stone is weathered, but round the average modern house of bright red brick it seldom fits into the general surroundings, and, as it is costly, consider carefully before you use it. It is usually bought from the nurseryman at so much a yard run – the small shrubs being planted touching one another to form a continuous line. Careful clipping is necessary early each summer just as new growth begins. In moist districts, where slugs abound, all permanent growing edgings, except grass, have one special disadvantage – they harbour slugs; and box edging is the worst offender. But take heart. Since the introduction of slug destroyers containing Metaldehyde the slug menace is not so bad, so, if you prefer box you need not abandon the idea because of slugs.

Lavender, so useful for its perfume and the characteristic blue of foliage and flowers, although used in many gardens, can scarcely be considered a suitable path edging. It grows into quite a hedge – several feet in height – and is useful only for special gardens or for fragrant hedges in a spot where perfume is particularly wanted, so we need not consider its use as an edging for paths, especially as it is not really happy in some of the wetter soils. Santolina Incana, another grey-foliaged plant which does not grow quite so tall, forms a very good edging but sometimes proves rather expensive.

If you are interested chiefly in the usefulness of the edging, you can buy manufactured hard edgings which do not need renewal, and the best of these are edging tiles. They are made in a variety of shapes and colours, but preference should be given to those with a rolled upper edge, as neutral as possible in colour. They are made for utility, not for beauty, and should do their job as unobtrusively as possible. Their chief purpose is to form a boundary and keep the soil from tumbling over on to the paths, and they should always be sunk as low as possible. Fancy tiles with fussy points and scrolls should be avoided. The beauty of your plants should first attract the eye.

I once knew a man with a half-acre garden who spent all his spare time making unnumerable stepped terraces where only level ground existed. This could be done only by digging, and the garden became a series of holes and terraces held together by walls of huge flints, collected on the distant hillsides. All the flints were lavishly whitewashed. Chatting to him one day I asked him jokingly why he did it. His answer accounted for a lot. 'In my home (Switzerland) all our gardens are terraced and the stones are white. They look lovely there, so I have tried to copy them here. You do not understand.' I understood – but not in the same way. The Swiss gardens are on mountain sides where the sun blazes for many months, and the stone is part of the countryside. Often the only way to obtain enough soil is to terrace the mountain. Here, his site was flat, the soil was deep, and the garden surrounded by cleft chestnut palings, the artificial terraces were entirely out of place, their incongruity heightened by the ghastly white stones. He was recalling a place of beauty in what was nothing better than a madman's cemetery – a high price to pay for indulging nostalgia. I have seen, too, an ex-naval man who could not resist the use of paint, whitening the bricks he used for edging.

Bricks, if they are not too red, set well, either upright or diagonally, can make a useful edging. However, it is of little use to set either tiles or bricks in cement because the necessary digging of the ground on one side undermines and loosens them. Sharp-edged slates should be avoided, for if anyone falls on these it means a nasty accident.

There are, of course, many more materials which can be used for edging, including straight-edged wood and wooden shingles similar to roof shingles. These are now out of the question and, in any case, cannot be recommended because they are not durable, but one other deserves to be mentioned – Rockery stones. In a formal garden edgings of these have unattractive lines, are a general nuisance and take a great deal of labour to keep free of weeds – labour which anyone but a rock-plant lover will find niggling. But there are exceptions. If you have an irregular piece of ground on a hillside or any odd-shaped piece of land – perhaps backed by woods where regularity would be incongruous –

try irregular paths edged with weathered stone of varying width, with suitable soil interstices in which choice alpines are planted. The edges of these stones should overlap paths surfaced with chippings of material similar to the rockwork, and there should be an air of attractive informality about the whole thing.

To the lover of miniature plants, these narrow rock gardens offer scope for the almost daily attention which the rock plant enthusiast longs to give, for they can be given a few minutes, attention at almost any time. Care must be paid to the kind of plant placed immediately behind the rock edging and the probable appearance later of any plant placed in the background, for if the wrong plants are sited just behind the rock plants they will either hang over and smother them - which is bad - or they will have to be staked upright, looking gawky behind the small rocks, and completely spoiling the garden scheme - which is worse. Gardens with rock edgings can be extremely pleasing, but only those with some knowledge of natural rock formation, and of rock plants, should attempt to make them. It is not a job for the beginner.

This chapter would be incomplete without some mention of those with gardens of an acre or more who begin with slight or no knowledge. Such owners would be well advised to get hold of a competent garden architect or some horticultural firm with experts available, who can give valuable advice on the general lines the garden should follow, according to the surroundings; but that is where outside help should cease. It is true that detailed plans of layout and planting can be obtained and the whole garden mapped out to the last inch. But be cautious. Elaborately detailed and coloured plans can be very deceptive and the appearance of the garden after a few years very different to that visualized by the new owner. No two people see the same picture when they read a horticultural plan, which, unlike an architectural drawing, cannot be reproduced exactly and must leave much to the imagination.

Those who have gardens ready made for them miss the pleasure of seeing one develop. Knowledge grows with practice and a close association with plants, and daily living in a partly-developed garden is the best way to learn horticulture. Steady development over a series of years is the soundest, most satisfying, and most artistic way to proceed, for mistakes made in garden planning are difficult and costly to remedy, as well as a great waste of time.

· 4 ·

The Garden Frame

WITH the garden laid out and well dug, the new owner in his first season soon feels the need for some appliance for seed raising and nursing seedlings. Gardening articles talk about raising seed, and pricking out in a cold frame, and when his seed arrives from the seed merchant the instructions on many packets do too. Rarely does he know what a cold frame is, or why it is necessary, and as I shall mention one from time to time I will explain its structure and uses in advance.

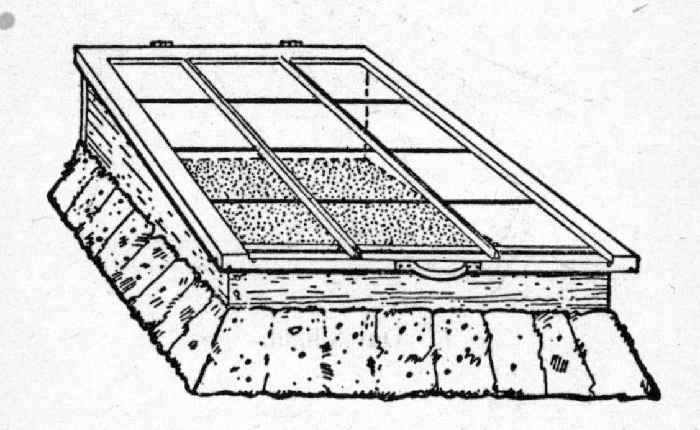

10. Simple wood frame, earthed at sides.

In its commonest form, a cold frame is a stout wooden frame, or box, on which is placed an arrangement which looks rather like a large sash window. This is known as a light. For the frame, stout wood is used – generally one and a quarter or one and a half inches thick. The usual standard size of each light is 6 feet by 4 feet and frames are built as single light units or in blocks of two or three. The front is constructed of one eleven-inch plank and the back of two eleven-inch planks, the side planks being cut to slope accordingly. (Fig. 10.) To prevent the lights from slipping sideways, dividers are placed between them – the side planks being fitted suitably with strips of wood to serve the same purpose. The side pieces and the dividers are grooved to allow rain water to flow to the outside, at the bottom, instead of dripping inside the frame. For the same reason the glass is overlapped, as tiles on a roof are laid, and thus, on the slope, rain water flows down outside the glass and sometimes condensed moisture flows down inside. Smaller frames, easier to handle and without obstructive sash bars, are known as Dutch lights. These are fitted with one large sheet of glass only 56 inches by 28¾ inches. (Fig. 11). Much lighter wood suffices to support these and both frame and lights can be moved easily from place to place, though the frame is composed of many units.

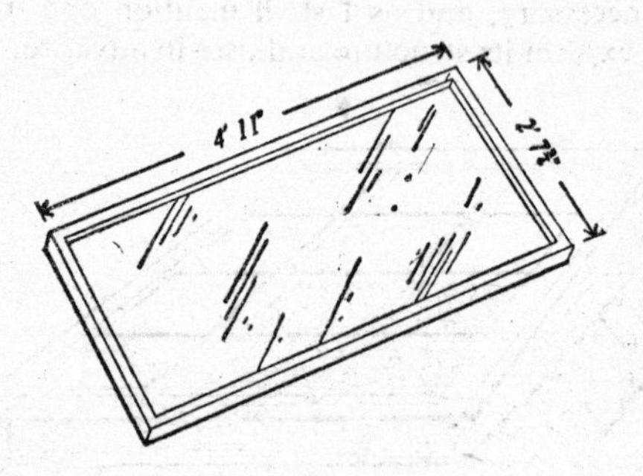

11. Dutch light.

Where there is need for it, and enough room to accommodate it, a span-roofed frame, constructed to take four or more Dutch lights, makes a very good substitute for a greenhouse, especially if a simple means of heating, as explained in chapter 22, page 299, can be arranged (Fig. 12).

If more elaborate or durable frames are wanted the standard size frames (6 feet by 4 feet lights) can be built of bricks or concrete; this is in every way better, and can exclude more frost than a wooden frame provided the top lights are suitably protected. These more solid frames are usually constructed with the tops of the foundations two feet or more below the ground level – the soil inside the walls built on these footings being excavated to form a deep brick or concrete pit. Such pits, filled with a hotbed (see page 50), may be used economically for many of the purposes for which a heated greenhouse is used,

12. Wooden pitched frame.

and an arrangement which allows the use of a little artificial heat in a snug glass-topped pit of this kind is a great convenience. It will readily be seen that if four or more standard lights are used to form a span roof, they form a good-sized glass-topped building, which can be used for a number of things we will deal with as this book proceeds. (Fig. 12). But these more elaborate arrangements are for the few; many people may have to use very simple appliances.

Do not despair about it. By excavating the soil – previously rammed hard – to form a pit, a very useful growing place can be provided if a light – Dutch or standard – is available. (Fig. 13.) You will have to stoop very low when attending to the

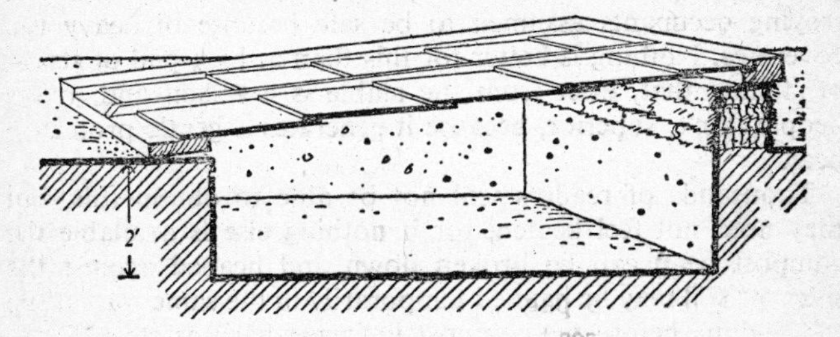

13. Earth frame-light placed over excavation in ground.

occupants of such a pit, but you will have the satisfaction of knowing that your seedlings or plants are tucked away from cutting winds, in a natural frame which will exclude many degrees of frost, if the light, the one part vulnerable to frost, is well protected. Simpler still is the little frame made of a shallow box with a large sheet of glass covering the top. (Fig. 14.) This, if you like, can be sunk in the ground for greater protection; then only the top of glass needs frost protection, unless it is extremely cold. I have seen a simple frame like this used successfully for the propagation of a large variety of cuttings, among them delphiniums, asters and phlox, and for raising many half-hardy annuals such as callistephus (annual asters), stocks, antirrhinums, and the like.

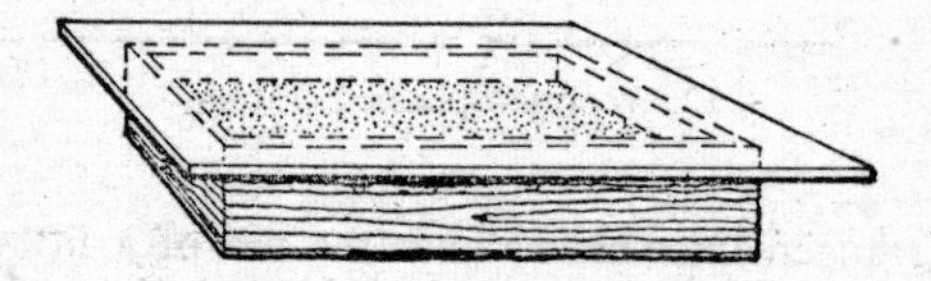

14. Shallow frame-glass on box.

Protection for both glass lights and the sides of frames may be needed suddenly when frost arrives with little warning, and should be available at a minute's notice. For this purpose nothing is better than the archangel mat – now, alas, seldom to be found – but any old bags, hessian canvas, or rick coverings can be used. For the sharp frosts of autumn or spring, covering the glass tops will suffice, but when prolonged severe winter frost arrives, the sides of wooden and brick frames must be buffered to prevent frost from penetrating gradually and destroying occupants assumed to be safe because of heavy top coverings. Nothing is better for this than a thick pad of straw, or, failing that, litter from the stable is excellent and, many people think, superior, because it generates a gentle protective heat.

Thousands of readers will not be able to obtain this, but they need not feel beaten, for if nothing else is available the compost heap can be broken down and heaped against the sides, or soil may be banked temporarily in the same way, if the job is done before the compost is frozen hard as steel. Every garden owner should look ahead for this and throughout the season save bags, hessian wrappers, or any household material adaptable for coverings. Garden waste such as pea haulm, the dead tops of annuals or anything of a strawy nature should be dried and stowed in a dry shed until winter. Successful conservation and a will to improve is often the chief difference between the successful gardener and the one for whom nothing ever goes right.

Years ago nursery gardeners, particularly in the extensive market-garden districts near Paris, used cloches (bell glasses) for protecting and forwarding early vegetables and salad crops. These cloches, often of true bell shape, but afterwards modified to straight sides, had a ball-shaped knob on top for easy handling. Sometimes cloches were used in conjunction with hotbeds, but their efficacy for forwarding purposes depended chiefly upon their ability to trap solar heat. As they were draught-proof, they did this effectively, but as they had no apertures for admitting air, they needed ventilating. For this purpose, they had to be propped slightly open at the bottom, and closed again several times a day to trap the warmth of the sun; this was generally done by the proprietor and his family, and can hardly be expected of the average householder to-day. Even weak rays of the sun would make the interiors of the bells heat quickly, and ventilation from the bottom would let the heat escape even more quickly; success with these appliances depended, therefore, on watchful attention.

However, in this country the name 'cloche' has been handed on to tiny structures of glass supported by wires, in a wide variety of shapes and sizes. The glass of these is held in place by metal clips loose enough to allow air to enter, and yet it gives protection and traps much heat. If additional ventilation is required, the glass forming the sides is sometimes cut an inch or two short to allow a continuous stream of air to enter. Cloches of this type can be fitted together to cover a continuous line and long drills of seedlings or growing plants – flowers or vegetables – can thus be protected or brought on. But even these sometimes need additional ventilation, which can be given by the removal or partial displacement of the top glass; otherwise, if allowed to become overheated for more than a short time, their sheltered occupants may grow soft and perhaps too spindly to flourish unprotected when fully exposed later.

In the days before greenhouses were common and the few existing ones were heated by flues which conducted and radiated heat from a furnace, frames with tops of oiled silk, parchment, and, later, glass, were heated by means of hotbeds. These were made of fermenting material in the form of the soiled straw used as bedding by the great horse population kept for transport in the cities. This, heavily impregnated with urine, and containing much excrement, was a cheap commodity brought out daily from the towns in vast quantities. When it was placed in a heap, it fermented and heated violently for several days, and when stacked carefully in layers and mixed with fresh fallen leaves would retain a gentle heat for several months. Hotbeds of this kind, if the materials are available, are equally valuable to-day, and if used intelligently provide a gentle moist heat superior to that provided by any heating apparatus. They should be put together much as a haystack is constructed, but need not exceed six feet in height. The fermenting material should be spread evenly, and in small quantities which should be thoroughly trodden as the work proceeds, otherwise sinking, owing to the decay caused by fermentation, will be uneven. Any sized frame can be used on hotbeds, but the larger sizes, such as the box frames with six feet by four feet lights, or the box frame fitted with Dutch lights, should have a hotbed underneath whose area exceeds that of the frame by at least two feet on each side.

But beware. The hotbed which gives of such a beneficent heat can also be very dangerous. A well-made hotbed can be deceptive. For some days after it has been made, if the litter has been thoroughly mixed with leaves which have not decayed too much, it will feel almost cool, even if built to some height, for the exposure to air necessary to mix thoroughly and the addition of cool leaves will have lowered its temperature; next day, and for a day or two afterwards, little more than a gentle warmth is felt. Perhaps with the lights in place there is a pleasant genial warmth. An enthusiast may then place seedlings or growing plants in the frame, thinking there could not be a more comfortable place; but he is mistaken. A well-made hotbed ferments very slowly, but from the time of making, increases in temperature until its maximum heat is reached. Sometimes the process is very slow for several days, but when fermentation has reached a certain pitch heat generates rapidly and a bed that remains comfortably warm for several days becomes so hot that you cannot put your hand in an inch or two deep for more than a few seconds. The excessive temperature alone would be too much for delicate seedlings, and in the process of fermentation and decomposition, dangerous gasses are given off which, though not very harmful to human beings if inhaled for only a short time, are fatal to growing plants. Many a gardener pleased with himself for having provided such snug quarters for his seedlings has found them, next morning or a day or two after, looking as if they had been scorched by a flame gun.

This can easily be prevented. All that is needed is patience and a plunging thermometer. Thrust the thermometer well into

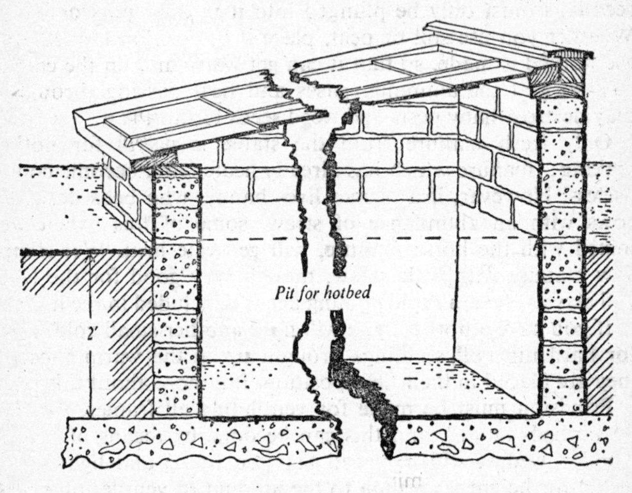

15. Brick-built frame with excavation for hotbed.

the hotbed, and note the temperature each day. You will find that it will rise gradually at first and rapidly afterwards. For a day or two a very high temperature will be maintained and then it will gradually decline. When the temperature of the hotbed has dropped to 80° F. the interior of the frame will register approximately 63° F. – a temperature just right for many floral seedlings and ideal for seed germinating. Because of this, the sowing of many half-hardy annuals must be timed to coincide with the hotbed decline in temperature. Wait for the proper temperature, when the heat is declining, and never place plants in the frame when the temperature is rising – even though it seems correct. The beginning of March is a good time to start a hotbed, which, if well made, should retain its heat for several months.

It is a good plan to put a six-inch layer of soil or peat all over the part of the hotbed inside the frame. If soil is used, pots or boxes used for seed sowing should be plunged in it up to their rims, and when they are removed seedlings should be pricked out direct into the soil, and followed by some vegetable crop when they are transferred out of doors. If peat is used, however, seedlings must only be plunged into it in their pots or boxes. Whether you use soil or peat, place it in position immediately the hotbed is made, so that it can get warm and, in the case of soil, so that the ammonia gases and heat passing through it may destroy many pests and weed seeds lurking in it.

Only fresh manure from the stable is useful for hotbed making; manure which has already heated and become cool is useless. However, if a farmer lives handy, who beds down his cows with an abundance of straw, some of this, when well mixed with the horse manure, will generate heat. Wet sloppy cow manure with little straw, though very good for the land, will serve only as a rapid cooling agent if included in the hotbed.

If you have a hotbed, you will need another small cold frame for hardening off seedlings brought up in the warmth before they are placed in their final position. But more about this later.

Provision must be made for ventilating all frames, whether on hotbeds or not, and this can be done by means of a large wooden wedge, which placed between frame and light is adjusted for height according to the amount of ventilation necessary, or by a stepped block which serves as a more rigid support. Cutting draughts of air – harmful to plants – can be avoided by inserting the wedge or block at the side of the light opposite the direction of the wind. This may be at the higher end, at either side, or at the lower end, if the frame has enough slope to allow the rain to flow away.

For some plants a frame placed in the shade is an advantage, but the shady spot chosen should never be beneath trees, which throw a shade too dark for most plants, and even for some weeds. Though most people do not realize it, there is something falling from deciduous trees at all seasons – small pieces of bark, bird droppings, pollen, showers of small dead flowers or catkins, the first-formed leaves which fall early in summer, more leaves during the following months, and the main fall of leaves which everybody sees. Twigs fall at all seasons. Pines shed their old needles, and evergreen oaks, besides casting a dense shade, shed leaves throughout the year. Water dripping from trees darkens glass, quickly destroys paint and loosens putty. It is true that debris can be removed from glass by frequent washing of it, but this labour cannot be justified in a garden where there are so many other pleasurable jobs waiting to be done. If you really want shade place the frame on the northern side of a wall or building, which, while protected from the direct rays of the sun, is in good light. Few will have to bother about this, as most frames are generally used for trapping and conserving light and heat.

The ground underneath a cold frame should be well drained. Gardens over chalk, gravel or rock, whether loose or otherwise, are generally porous enough, but soils of any type of clay, or on low-lying land, should be suspect. If it is found to be wet, the site chosen should be excavated about a foot deep and the hole filled in with rubble, stones, or clinkers, as advised for paths on page 38, the upper layer, on which pots will stand, being composed of two inches of finely-sifted ashes or sand. Unless frames are well drained, water given to plants in pots or boxes will collect and in a short time the bottom will be like a pond waiting to be cleared of mud.

Plant hygiene is important. The interior of a frame should be kept as clean as a living room. Weeds and dead leaves should not be allowed to collect and water must not be spilled, except on special occasions when damping down is necessary (this will be dealt with later on). If there is too much atmospheric moisture in a cold frame, from which, for lack of artificial heat, excess moisture cannot be expelled, many diseases – very difficult to combat under conditions entirely suitable for their growth – will make their appearance. The cold frame should not be the dumping ground for innumerable odds and ends and rubbish. Rubbish of all kinds is a breeding ground for disease and an excellent harbour for unwanted insects. To convert a cold frame into an auxiliary garden dustbin and attempt to grow plants in it at the same time is very unwise.

To the beginner, or those with little experience, the cold frame will be most useful for raising seedlings which cannot be grown outside and for the pricking out and the growing on of seedlings until the danger of frost has passed, when they can be planted in their summer quarters. For a time – perhaps a couple of seasons – this will suffice, but you will gradually discover many other uses for the frame which you can develop as your knowledge and skill improves. With a good cold frame, and skill and enthusiasm, you can beat the man with a good greenhouse, but who has poor methods and erratic and slapdash actions. I will say more about these developments in the cold frame later on.

Among the many uses of the cold frame there is one which deserves mention. A man with a very small garden who is fond of miniature plants – perhaps one of those owners who cannot have a proper garden, but is happy with a paved garden and his Alpines – will find a well-made, drip-proof cold frame very useful. In it he can grow and establish for years choice Alpines, which, although hardy, rarely survive, or are very unhappy, in the continuous drip of a six months' English winter. In large pans and suitable well-drained soil mixtures, colonies and clumps will last in good condition for years. For the busy man this type of horticulture is particularly attractive.

· 5 ·

Sowing Seed out of Doors

UNTIL they see aconites and primroses in spring, many people forget their gardens need seed, then they go hurriedly to the nearest shop which sells seeds and buy some, irrespective of quality, and get them into the ground somehow – anyhow as long as the job is done quickly. Then they feel better – atonement for the sins of omission has been made.

This is generally a mistake. There are seeds and seeds. Many people think that because seeds will pass a germination test they must be good, but this is only a small part of the story. There is the question of kind and variety and the reputation of firms known to gardeners for decades. Those well-known plant names, printed boldly on the packet, which, perhaps, also bears a vivid illustration, are no guarantee of goodness, for seeds are not manufactured. The best are grown with painstaking care in a climate which is not kind to seed growers. The worst are just seeds – grown and saved anyhow, although they bear well-known names. The plants of the best seedsmen are watched unceasingly. Men inspect them daily. The weak and weedy are pulled out. If any show signs of disease they are destroyed. When flowers begin to show colour they are scrutinized closely. Any plants which show deviations of colour and form, slight but noticeable, are removed – they are 'rogues' to be 'rogued out'. Only those which reach a high standard of health and vigour are retained, and out of these a very few plants of extra high stamina, great floriferousness and heightened colour are retained for stock – provided only that the pedigree is without blemish. Later, there are many other processes which only high-class seeds undergo. Is it any wonder that the best seeds cost a little more?

Compared with other costs inseparable from running a garden, the little extra is infinitesimal. It is obviously foolish to spend much money on laying out, tools, manures, labour and many small items, and risk it all to save a few shillings on seeds. Only the best are good enough.

Well before Christmas ask a good firm to send a catalogue. Nowadays, owing to paper restrictions, these are poor reminders of what they used to be, but even so to peruse a good catalogue beside the fire in winter is a great delight. My own recollection of catalogues goes back to the time I was a small boy. I was given the finely illustrated catalogue of a famous firm to cut out the pictures and make them into scrapbooks for children in hospital at Christmas. Those pictures made an impression on me I have never forgotten. The flowers appealed to me so much that I longed to work among them, and in due course, when I was older, I did. Even the abbreviated catalogues of to-day will give the garden lover much pleasure, and careful reading generally leads to the right choice.

If in doubt, describe your needs to your seedsman, who is well qualified to help. Advice and help are freely given. Send your order in as early as possible before the great rush for seeds begins, and when you receive them unpack and store in a cool dry place – never in a damp outhouse, or in the airing cupboard.

The sight of a neighbour sowing the first seeds in his garden is often infectious. Jack Jones coming home from work on the first fine Saturday afternoon of spring has only to see Bill Smith busily sowing seeds to go home and do the same himself. And others, later, seeing both of them sowing, hurry home and imitate them, and so it goes on. Bill Smith is a local gardening celebrity who wins a lot of prizes at flower shows and therefore – they argue – he must be right. But this reasoning has many flaws in it. Bill Smith's garden is on a slope and the soil inclined to be sandy. Jack Jones's garden is down the hollow where the clay subsoil prevents it from drying out. Bill Smith is a knowing one. He dug his garden in the autumn, and since then the elements have broken down the roughly left soil into friable mould – just right for seed sowing. Jack Jones's garden was dug only a week ago, when it was far too wet, and the drying wind has since converted the sloppy clods into lumps as hard as cement blocks, which will not dissolve gently until it rains again – unless a spring frost does the work a little quicker.

Gardening is not a game of rule of thumb but of calculated method and opportunism in its best sense. The time to begin the sowing of even the hardiest subjects is on the first occasion when there is good tilth. A good tilth cannot be measured or found by a chemical test, but anyone taking a little surface soil in his hand can test it for himself. When a tightly-compressed handful refuses to ball up, but falls to pieces again when released, there is a good tilth, and seed sowing may begin, provided the date is right for the subject chosen. As a general rule it is correct to start with the hardiest annuals only and rarely – very rarely – is it right to sow all kinds together. If a man takes a garden over late in the season or if, through force of circumstances, he cannot start at the proper time, he is forced to sow all his seeds very late and much at the same time, or not at all. But, if possible, sowing should be spaced out over many weeks and planned carefully, without stress, during the previous winter. A time table should be prepared as a guide, showing the subjects to be sown weekly.

But a word of caution. The list should be a guide only – not a time table to be obeyed rigidly. Time tables are dangerous. I once prepared one for a friend and found out afterwards that he sowed his onions in a deluge of rain and his early annuals in an April snowstorm – and snowstorms are not uncommon in April, even in the south. I should probably have known nothing about it except that the onions germinated badly, the annuals scarcely showed at all and a question of mine brought it all to light. When I expostulated, he replied that it was my fault as I had told him to do it.

Gardening is different to most things – it has no exact rules, but it is an absorbing recreation for the man of common sense. On the question of sowing dates, my advice is: Study your time table and use your discretion. Good tilth and good sowing conditions count before anything. If it is raining or snowing on the sowing date, wait until conditions are right again, and remember that it is better to be a day or two late than too early. In this chapter we are concerned not with what we should sow, but with the preparation of the garden and how to set about it.

First of all the ground must be level, a word which should not be confused with 'smooth', for, in the gardening sense, the two words are by no means synonymous. In a garden the level may be a dead level – which is rarely possible and hardly to be expected – or a running level – which is far easier to ensure in the average garden. If the ground was dug properly, according to Chapter One, then it should be level, but unless the cultivator is an old hand it seldom is. If it is not, it must be made so. Seed must be sown in small V-shaped excavations called drills, and if these drills are made on a switchback formation conditions along them are unequal, and seeds sown where drills follow depressions and hills are at a disadvantage.

For successful germination, seeds require moisture, air, and warmth. In a switchback drill, seeds on top of the slope are in soil which dries out rapidly in dry weather because of exposure and the extra drainage provided by the miniature hills, while those in the valleys may germinate. On the other hand, if the weather is wet, seeds in the depressions rot because the switchback formation forces rainwater to flow to the lowest level, and because too much soil moisture reduces the soil temperature; while those sown on the hills can germinate because of the moist conditions. Soil temperature plays an important part and often is the deciding factor in germination. The presence of too much water because of faulty land levels, bad drainage, or an

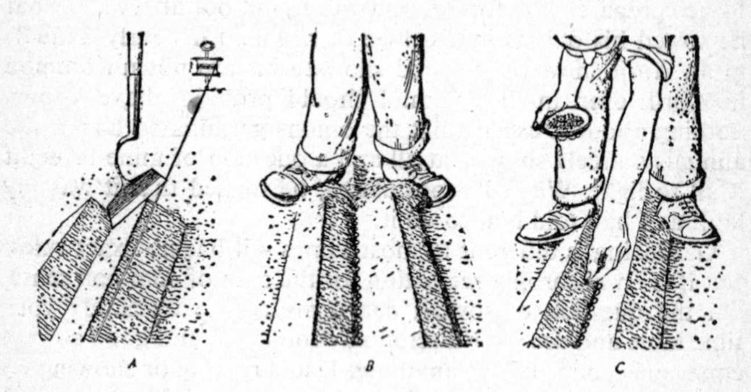

16. (A) Drawing a row; (B) Shuffling in soil; (C) Sowing seed.

intractable soil, always keeps the soil temperature low, and if sowing is attempted too early while the soil temperature is still low, seed – even that of the best quality and strength – cannot be expected to germinate. In digging, therefore, a level must be made an operation which becomes automatic with practice.

When a site has been dug badly, levelling can, unfortunately, be done only by taking soil with fork or spade – according to its nature – from the little hills and putting it into the valleys, a process which partly destroys tilth formed during exposure and, therefore, makes sowing and the conditions for germination a little more difficult. Then, having made a level, tread down the plot to be sown, and no more. Treading a plot for seed sowing should be done systematically to ensure that every superficial inch of the soil receives pressure from the feet. Running around anyhow is sheer waste of energy. Start on one side and keeping the feet parallel and close together tread firmly and evenly along a line, and go backwards and forwards making sure that no ground is missed. When finished, the plot should have a level roughened surface, stippled regularly with tiny hills. A rake should then be taken to smooth out the undulations and to remove large – and only large – stones.

Do not misunderstand me. Neither treading nor raking is meant to make a smooth impermeable surface. If by making your beds hard and smooth you shut out all air, your seeds will not germinate. With light flicks of the rake remove stones over an inch or so wide, and make the ground level with light backward and forward motions without dragging soil to the wrong places. Really it is not very difficult. The finished article will have a matt surface very much like a freshly tarred road sprinkled evenly with rather coarse granite chippings.

And now for drawing drills for the seeds. The idea is to make V-shaped excavations of a depth suitable for the kind of seed to be sown. Fine seeds need a shallow drill and large seeds a somewhat deeper drill, but we should never sow too deeply. In nature, seeds are cast on the surface by the bursting of seed capsules, but then nature does not expect every seed to germinate and, in fact, few seeds do. If the three important requisites for germination – moisture, air, and warmth – all be present (and they seldom are), then nature's germination is good, but in our garden we must have safeguards unless we are content to do a lot of work for nothing. So, by providing a drill, we go deep enough only to ensure regular conditions of moisture, enough air to enter the soil, and, with the air, warmth from the sun, unless we exclude it by compressing and plastering the soil surface.

Drills are made parallel at distances apart varying with the species, extensive growing plants being sown in drills spaced widely and smaller plants in drills spaced closely. The ultimate spread of the plant is allowed for by removing from the drills all but those which are spaced widely enough to admit full development. Newcomers to gardening may well ask: 'Why crowd seeds into drills when by scattering them evenly over the soil surface seedlings would have more room for development?' The answer is that seed sowing is not the last operation, and that after sowing seedlings must be thinned, perhaps staked, weeds must be removed, and the soil surface stirred frequently.

Nearly all soils are full of weed seeds – except that which contains no organic matter and is, therefore, inert and useless for plant growth. Generally it follows that very fertile soils contain more weed seeds than less fertile ones; and much of this seed is capable of lying dormant in the soil for many years and does not germinate until brought under the influence of warmth and air. It is one of the wonders of nature that weed seeds buried for decades – if not generations – germinate in great profusion when brought near the surface, and no-one seems capable of saying how long they will remain sound when buried. In many cases there are also the weeds which have lately been neglected, and consequently there must be easy access for dealing with weeds and for the necessary soil cultivation, so that the seedlings are not damaged.

Through the centuries gardeners have found that plants in drills, in spite of obvious disadvantages, offer the best means of access, and that broadcasting seeds is unsatisfactory except for narrow strips not more than four feet wide which allow a man to do weeding, thinning and soil stirring by reaching two feet on either side – the limit of comfort.

To ensure that the drills are straight and parallel a line is used and by using one of the pointed corners of a draw hoe – or one of the little triangular hoes sold for the purpose – holding this closely to the line and removing the soil to the right depth while walking backwards, the V-shaped drill is made. The soil displaced is heaped regularly at both sides of the drill; therefore a drill drawn two inches deep is in reality only one inch deep, a fact which should be remembered. The site of the next drill is marked off parallel to the first and the process continued until enough drills have been made.

Having decided what distances the drills should be apart from one another, it is a good plan to use the measuring rod at each side of the plot and mark off the drill sites by placing small stakes in the ground according to the number of rows decided on, thus doing away with the necessity of marking each row as the work proceeds. Do not prepare a lot of ground at once, even if conditions are favourable. Ground should always be left in its original winter state until it is wanted, for if reduced down to flatness it is liable to become caked and hard. This applies especially to some clay soils on which it is almost impossible to draw drills on ground prepared previously for sowing, and then subjected to heavy rain followed by hot sun.

If drills are made in advance they sometimes become so hardened by sun and wind that the roots of seedlings are unable to penetrate and so they die. Drills prepared beforehand on light soil occasionally remain in good condition, if moistened by frequent storms, but in dry and windy weather – such as we often have in spring – they dry out, and in neither the drill nor the covering soil is there enough moisture for germination.

Seed should always be sown thinly – a mere scattering is enough – but scatterings of seed at the bottom of a drill look so meagre that few can be persuaded they have sown enough – they feel quite unhappy about it. Sometimes, fortunately, there is only a small amount of seed and the seedlings emerge in isolated units, as they should. Unfortunately, however, there is often seed left over, so that a second lot and sometimes a third is poured over the original sowing, and the cultivator feels better. After a week or two of doubt he is first relieved, and then gratified to see a dense row of seedlings jostling one another out of the ground. This gratification is misplaced. The hedge of healthy seedlings quickly becomes a row of sickly invalids, for in the fight to obtain light and air all become hopelessly drawn, attenuated, and sometimes quite useless. Isolated seedlings, however, with plenty of light, air, and space for development, grow stockily, and not having to struggle upwards are able to develop laterally as well.

Now for the sowing. Some sow seeds direct from the packet, others use a canister with its lip bent to a v-shaped point, or one of the many gadgets now on the market for seed sowing. I doubt, however, if the old method of taking pinches of seed from a saucer with the finger and thumb, which regulate the flow of seed into the drill, can be bettered, especially for beginners who are able to see the contents of the saucer at a glance and therefore to regulate accordingly. (Fig. 16c).

The covering of seed is important. Watch a skilled gardener at work. When he has sown he straddles the drill and with a shuffling, forward motion with each foot alternately, covers the seed adroitly. It is the best method – everyone who sows seed out of doors should practise it. The soil is left in tiny irregular ridges, the top of each ridge marking the centre of the drill. These little ridges are then trodden down gently and the surface is again raked carefully with a light backward and forward motion which levels, but removes only sticks, rubbish, or large stones, and leaves the soil in its place.

The correct consistency of the soil after sowing is important because of the three essentials for germination – air, moisture, and warmth. If the soil is not compressed enough, too much air enters – especially if a period of drying wind occurs – and the seed is liable to lie dormant because the soil has become too dry. If it is compressed too much little if any air can enter, and the seeds fail to germinate because of lack of air and consequently warmth.

If you have a failure, do not rush away as soon as you discover it and write a nasty letter to the seedsman. A good seedsman's seeds are repeatedly tested, so look around and see where the fault lies in your methods. I have known many letters of complaint replied to by a gift packet of seeds to replace loss. Not once but on many occasions I have seen letters which have arrived from these same people. They were all more or less like this: 'Dear Sir, Thank you for the packet of seeds you sent to replace those which failed. They have come up splendidly. If you had sent me seeds like this at first I should not have had a lot of trouble for nothing.' In each of these cases, seeds from exactly the same parcel as those which failed were sent. It was not the seeds which were at fault, but the conditions, climatic causes, or the methods of the cultivator.

I truly believe that if the directions I have given here are carried out, my readers will run little risk of failure. Cold and wet are the chief enemies of good germination, and dryness of light soil the next.

This chapter is important, because success will depend on the observance of the principles set down in it. The basic rules should be studied closely; the minor details matter less. They are always in the hands of the cultivator – upon whom the final decision must rest.

· 6 ·

Bed or Border of Hardy Annuals

THE garden has been laid out, trenched or dug, and generally prepared, and the new gardener surveys a great bare patch. Even if it is a small garden it looks immense when he thinks of what is needed to make it the garden of his dreams. Even if he has not planned it on paper, in the mind there are already places allotted for perennials, roses, annuals, a patch of lawn, a piece of ground for sweet peas, a special place for some delphiniums, a corner for early-flowering chrysanthemums – and a lot more besides.

So far it is quite empty. What will it cost to make it into the ideal garden he has in mind? Even the most optimistic would not expect the bare patch to glow with flowers during the next summer. But no idea should be neglected and it is sensible to make plans, even though with more experience they are remade or modified many times; were it not for these, the final plan might never take shape.

While planning the beginner is, without knowing it, teaching himself. At first he sees things largely through the eyes of a flower show or a catalogue, without getting any clear picture, but when his plants bloom he sees them with more understanding. The catalogue is perfectly truthful in its descriptions, and the flowers are very much at their best in the glamour of the flower show; but they now convey something quite different, and he sees them as growing things, full of vitality and of life, and takes the first step towards sympathetic planning. But how is he to get over the time when he knows so little and cannot afford to stock his garden from the catalogue? The answer is simple: cover a good part of it with hardy annuals and experiment in a small way with other plants on the remainder of the site.

All the beautiful plants in the hardy annual group require simple treatment: the seed is sown direct on the flowering site, on ground prepared, and in drills made, according to the directions I have already given. They are sown in mid-spring, generally the second half of April, and some of them begin to flower within two months of sowing and, in an early season, before that.

Annuals are cheap, and can be grown in large numbers; but I advise the beginner not to fill the whole garden with them. Leave room in which to experiment. There is always something new to be learnt in gardening, and this is one of the greatest joys of it.

I regard annuals as the first step towards flower gardening. But do not underrate them. They are simple, can be grown simply, and do not cost much, but this does not imply that they are inferior or in any way to be despised. On the contrary, they include some of the most perfectly formed flowers known and almost every conceivable colour and shade is represented. They are particularly rich in flame, orange and delicate buff shades – shades often lacking in ordinary border plants – and shades of all the primary colours exist in hundreds. For making a border of deliberate design they are admirable, and for covering an odd piece of ground effectively and rapidly they are unsurpassed. Those who really cannot afford to buy other plants can cover the whole garden for a small sum, do so for several years with a fresh selection yearly, and will probably have a garden which everyone who sees it envies. So let us understand that we are using good material.

But how do we use that material? To take the seeds, drills should be drawn similar to those described in the previous chapter. They may be drawn in any direction and may be short drills running across the width of the land or long drills to run with the land. Generally, with few exceptions, they should be three inches deep, i.e. approximately one and a half inches when covered. The whole of the land to be sown with annuals, or as much as can be comfortably finished on the same day, if the site is a large one, should be covered with drills, spaced regularly one foot apart. Then with a stout stick, well pointed, small irregular lines should be traced, each to enclose a space of about two square yards on a large border, and about one yard on a small border. With the amazingly wide range of colours available those who are fond of colours and designs can have a wonderful time fitting in kinds and varieties into the jig-saw. There is not only an infinite variety of shades but an almost bewildering diversity of height, habit of growth, and colour of foliage, which means that in a well-designed border there is no need of flatness, monotony, or clashing colours. Soft shades only can be subtly blended, or a border made up entirely of vivid colours, with all soft shades omitted. In this

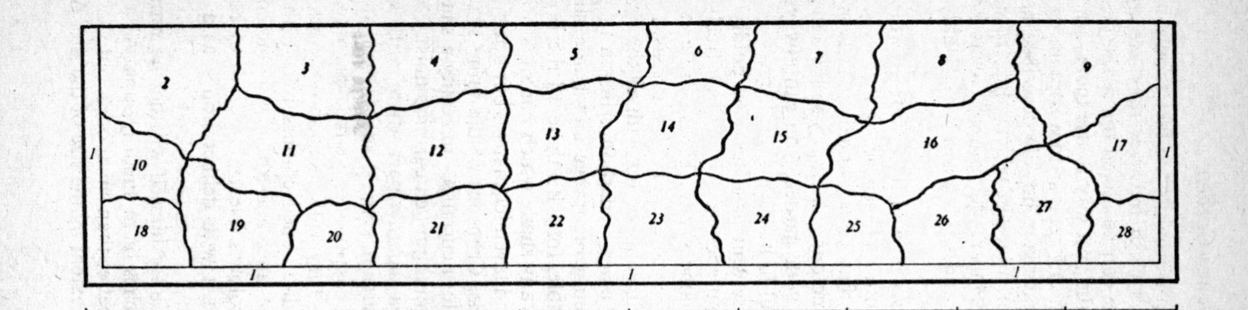

17. Plan for a border of Annuals, 12 by 50 ft.

1. *Allysum minimum*
2. *Lavatera pink*
3. *Scabious white*
4. *Larkspur salmon pink*
5. *Poppy double scarlet*
6. *Coreopsis tinctoria*
7. *Larkspur mauve*
8. *Lavatera alba splenden*
9. *Sunflower red or yellow*
10. *Godetia salmon pink*
11. *Cornflower blue*
12. *Chrysanthemum Annual mixed*
13. *Lupinus Haotwegii white*
14. *Godetia soft shades mixed*
15. *Clarkia elegans salmon*
16. *Cornflower pink*
17. *Lupinus mutabilis cream and pink*
18. *Nemophila insignis*
19. *Calendula orange*
20. *Candytuft mixed*
21. *Eschecholtzia buff*
22. *Viscatia blue*
23. *Lavia elegans*
24. *Rodanthe rose*
25. *Bartonia aurea*
26. *Linana mixed*
27. *Tagetes signata primula*
28. *Phacelia canpanulatra*

fascinating game for a winter's evening one fact should not be overlooked – certain colours clash however they are mixed. All shades containing orange can be mixed up, if the designer wishes, although this is not the best way to use them, but none of these shades will mix with any pink shades containing rose, or carmine (bear in mind that many flowers described as rose are often shades of carmine). Blues in which pink, rose, carmine, or red is not evident will mix readily with, or act as foils to, brilliant flames and oranges and settle down comfortably with the paler orange or buff shades.

Do not be in a hurry with a plan of this kind; it will affect your garden for several months. Remember that your garden is something to enjoy and that your annual border or plot should be a kaleidoscope of colour. Whether you have minutes or hours a day to spend in your garden, you can always find something fresh and beautiful in it.

For this you must plan. Use white sparingly but boldly – it is invaluable for splitting violent enemies. Use yellow freely with all the blues, orange and flame shades but separate it completely from all pinks, roses, carmines and carmine reds. Chocolate, crimson and maroon crimson will mix with all the oranges and will not clash with the blues – maroon crimson in particular brings out the full depth of orange and flame shades. Shades of cream are invaluable, for with these all the brilliant scarlets, oranges, flames and any shade which contains oranges may be divided. Lavender and lavender mauve, but not pinkish mauve, is also useful for this. Crimsons of the same shade as the old-fashioned crimson plush curtains – in reality a shade of carmine – and scarlets containing much carmine must join the carmine pinks and roses in a separate part where, with white, some of the paler shades of cream, some shades of blue and the whole range of rose – pale rose-pink, rose-red, carmine, carmine-crimson, and maroon – they will make a show as beautiful as any. Sometimes these full-blooded colours relieve the eye after colours of dazzling brilliance and are a welcome change from demure and delicate colours. Never be afraid of colour, splash it around, but splash it with deliberation – as a good painter does.

Each gardener must decide for himself whether he wants to splash colours in lavish patches or in small groups. As a rule, however, large patches are better than small ones, but their size should be governed to some extent by the size of the site. A plot from twelve to twenty-four feet wide can stand two- to four-yard patches and a border of less than twelve feet may have patches of a yard each. Niggling fussy scraps of colour, which express nothing, are unsatisfying and dreary, and even on a very small border very small patches should be avoided.

But there are exceptions. Some annuals are well fitted for use in narrow borders where the patches may be as small as a foot square, especially where a tiny border surrounds the house. There people unable to walk more than a short distance can enjoy fully the diversity and beauty of annuals simply by walking round the sunny sides of the house. There are other compensations for those unable to plan on a large scale. When small patches only are grown there is little risk of a bare patch appearing. Sometimes, even under the best cultural conditions, a patch of one kind or variety goes off, perhaps through disease or because slugs take a fancy to it in a wet season. This sort of thing seldom happens, but it can. In the irregular patched border if some misfortune occurs to the occupants of one patch, those in the surrounding patches take advantage of the extra room, develop accordingly and finally cover it. This is almost impossible in the case of very large patches. The size of groups varies with the gardener's taste, but annuals are particularly suitable for the small garden.

As for annuals on a large scale, only those who saw the former gardens of Sir Philip Sassoon at Trent Park, the borders of annuals at the R.H.S. Gardens at Wisley, and the masses of annuals to be seen in the seed grounds of our leading seedsmen, can realize their magnificence and unique suitability for effect. Some of the colours are extraordinarily lovely. At Trent Park, in particular, I remember the endless masses of colour shimmering in the sun, and it seemed inconceivable that they were created so simply and at such little cost.

Another case comes to my mind. Many years ago some noted gardens had been neglected and no provision had been made for the great borders, so to overcome the difficulty it was decided in April to make a show of annuals on borders which were fifty feet or more in width and half a mile long. On each side they flanked a semi-public road. The annuals were sown in great patches. Old and knowledgeable gardeners either shook their heads and looked wise or were scathing in their condemnation.

But they were wrong. A few varieties began to bloom early

in July and in August the whole length was ablaze with colour. The sight was unforgettable, and the fame of these borders spread while parties came from far and wide until they became numerous enough to be serious nuisances. In September most of the glorious patches were still in full bloom, and a number were quite good in October, for the soil was deep and good, and preparation, though late, very thorough.

Although all plants do better in the pure air of the country do not think that annuals are useless in smoky cities. Far from it. An old friend of mine who lived in one of the oldest parts of Camberwell – not one of London's brightest spots – had a long narrow garden, surrounded completely by high walls. This could only be described as a long back yard. The cat- and sparrow-ridden top soil, like ash in appearance and consistency, was useless, and had to be removed laboriously by being carried in baskets right through the house, for that was the only way out. Better soil collected from various sources was taken into the garden equally laboriously to replace the old.

I do not know what was underneath, but probably it was rubble, the result – so common in many districts of London – of refuse being dumped in swampy places. Under these appalling circumstances my friend began to garden, and the failure of perennials – most of which failed to survive the London winter of damp and darkness – made him try annuals. Though some of these never possessed the vigour of country-grown plants they were nevertheless a great success. The dingy back yard was entrancing each summer. Wherever there was space to place enough soil, annuals were grown. They were in beds, borders, narrow strips, buckets, tubs, and sections of hollow tree trunks. Climbing annuals were trained on strings and wires around the walls. Sweet peas and other tall annuals occupied odd spaces and seemed to invade the house itself. The whole was brightened by a vivid grass lawn, sown annually – for grass also would not stand the winter climate. It is true that the garden lacked form; my friend simply loved his annuals and they looked as if he had dumped them down anywhere, but with very happy effect. He greatly disliked all the full-bodied rose, carmine, and red shades, and by mixing all the other colours – which luckily blended or contrasted happily – he unconsciously created beauty where there was only ugliness before. He had a large family through which the fame of his garden spread, but the visitor's pleasure was curtailed by his not being allowed to set foot on the vivid grass – shaved perfectly twice a week. This was an idiosyncrasy he could not overcome.

The extensive beds and borders and the great variety of annuals cultivated in Hyde Park, Regent's Park, and almost every park, in London, including those in the poorest districts, also bear testimony to the suitability of annuals for smoky cities. In the City I have seen many little oases of grass and flowers, made by the sowing of grass and annuals in the spring. Nothing could be more refreshing than these, set amid depressing blackened buildings. In the great cities of the Midlands and the North, annuals are a boon to those in charge of the parks and open spaces who would otherwise have difficulty in finding bright colours in plants capable of surviving there. Annuals succeed under these conditions because all their growth is made during the best months of the year.

There are annuals for every purpose. Climbing annuals must not be forgotten, particularly the humble nasturtium which can be grown so easily. Some of these climbers are half-hardy and will need starting in frame or greenhouse – details will be given later on – and if these are used with other annuals which grow tall and are capable of standing alone, a wonderfully varied effect can be produced. If you prefer flat carpet-like patterns, you can produce these just as easily.

Now, what to grow? I readily sympathize with anyone unacquainted with annuals who, for the first time, tries to select them from a catalogue – they are bewildering in number and variety. Because of this I now give some extensive lists classified in several different ways. There is no reason why a new-comer should not order just what he wants, for the first year at least, and with the aid of these classified lists he will be able to fit what he buys into colour schemes and make plans of his own. There is little risk of a real howler being committed, for if the general rules laid down in this chapter are studied – particularly those which deal with discordant colours – and the classified lists are consulted, the rawest new-comer can go ahead with confidence.

Kinds and Varieties which may be grown as Hardy Annuals classified according to Colour and Height

The height is indicated in feet and climbers by 'Cl.'

WHITE AND CREAM SHADES

Tall

CHRYSANTHEMUM coronarium	3
Princess May	3
Double White	3
CORNFLOWER, White	3
HELICHRYSUM, Silver Globe	3
LAVATERA alba splendens	3
POPPY	
Giant Double, White	3
Giant Single, White	3
SALPIGLOSSIS, large-flowered, white with golden throat	3
SCABIOUS, Snowball	3
LARKSPUR, all sorts	2½ – 3
CHRYSANTHEMUM carinatum album	2½
Dunnettii, Double White	2½
GODETIA, Double White	2 – 3
NASTURTIUM, Tall, Pearl	Cl.

Medium

ARGEMONE grandiflora	2
CLARKIA ELEGANS, Snowball	2
LUPINUS Hartwegii, White	2
MALOPE, White	2
POPPY	
White Swan	2
Shirley, Double White	2
CALENDULA, pluvialis	1½
CHRYSANTHEMUM coronarium, Coronet	1½
inodorum plenissimum	1½
CLARKIA, White	1½
GILIA nivalis	1½
GYPSOPHILA elegans, White	1½
HAWKWEED, White	1½
JACOBEA, Double, White	1½
NIGELLA, Miss Jekyll, White	1½
SWEET SULTAN, Giant White	1½
CHRYSANTHEMUM coronarium, Dwarf Double white	1½
SALPIGLOSSIS, Dwarf, Creamy-White	1 – 1½

Dwarf

CANDYTUFT, Improved White Spiral	1
CLARKIA, Dwarf White	1
CONVOLVULUS minor, White	1
ESCHSCHOLTZIA, Ivory White	1
LINARIA, Snow-white	1
NASTURTIUM, Dwarf, Pearl	1
VISCARIA, Pure white	1
GODETIA, of sorts	$\frac{3}{4}$ – 1
RHODANTHE, White	$\frac{3}{4}$ – 1
ALYSSUM, Sweet	$\frac{3}{4}$
CHRYSANTHEMUM inodorum plenissimum, Bridal Robe	$\frac{3}{4}$
COLLINSIA candidissima	$\frac{3}{4}$
DIMORPHOTHECA, White	$\frac{3}{4}$
SWAN RIVER DAISY, White	$\frac{3}{4}$
VENUS' NAVELWORT	$\frac{3}{4}$
CANDYTUFT, Little Prince	$\frac{1}{2}$
ALYSSUM, minimum (Koeniga)	$\frac{1}{3}$
SILENE, Dwarf White	$\frac{1}{3}$

YELLOW AND ORANGE SHADES

Tall

SUNFLOWER, of sorts	3 – 10
CHRYSANTHEMUM coronarium	
Double Yellow	3
Golden Queen	3
COREOPSIS tinctoria	3
HELICHRYSUM, Golden Globe	3
SALPIGLOSSIS, large-flowered varieties	3
CHRYSANTHEMUM Dunnettii, Double Golden	$2\frac{1}{2}$
MARIGOLD, Double African, of sorts	$2\frac{1}{2}$
NASTURTIUM, Tall, Yellow	Cl.

Medium

MARIGOLD, Double French, Orange	2
BARTONIA aurea	$1\frac{1}{2}$
CHRYSANTHEMUM, Star varieties	$1\frac{1}{2}$
COREOPSIS	
Drummondii	$1\frac{1}{2}$
Coronata	$1\frac{1}{2}$
ERYSIMUM, Orange Gem	$1\frac{1}{2}$
LEPTOSYNE Stillmani	$1\frac{1}{2}$

LUPINUS, Yellow (Menziesii)	1½
MARIGOLD, Double African, Dwarf, of sorts	1½
RUDBECKIA, Golden Sunset	1½
SWEET SULTAN, Yellow	1½
SALPIGLOSSIS, Dwarf, Yellow	1 - 1¼

Dwarf

ANTHEMIS arabica	1
CALENDULA	
Orange King	1
Lemon Queen	1
CHRYSANTHEMUM coronarium, Dwarf double yellow	1
COREOPSIS, Golden Crown	1
DIMORPHOTHECA, of sorts	1
LAYIA elegans	1
LUPINUS, Dwarf yellow	1
NASTURTIUM, Dwarf, of sorts	1
OXALIS, Cloth of Gold	1
PLATYSTEMON californicus	1
TAGETES signata pumila	1
LINARIA, Golden Gem	¾
MARIGOLD, Miniature, of sorts	¾
ESCHSCHOLTZIA, of sorts	½ - 1
LIMNANTHES Douglasii	½
SANVITALIA procumbens	½
LEPTOSIPHON aureus	¼

PINK AND ROSE SHADES

Tall

CORNFLOWER, Pink	3
LAVATERA, of sorts	3
LUPINUS mutabilis, Cream and pink	3
POPPY, Giant Double	
Chamois-rose	3
Raspberry-rose	3
SALPIGLOSSIS, Large-flowered varieties	3
SCABIOUS, Large-flowered varieties	3
LARKSPUR, Tall sorts	2½ - 3
LUPINUS, Tall pink	2½
NASTURTIUM, Salmon Queen	Cl.

Medium

CLARKIA ELEGANS	
Double Salmon	2
Double Delicate Pink	2
GODETIA, of sorts	2
JACOBEA, Single, Bright Rose	2
POPPY, of sorts	2
SAPONARIA Vaccaria, Pink	2
CLARKIA, Double Rose	1½
HAWKWEED, Pink	1½
JACOBEA, Double, Rose	1½
SILENE, Armeria, Rose	1½

Dwarf

ACROCLINIUM, Rose	1
CONVOLVULUS minor, Pink	1
ESCHSCHOLTZIA, of sorts	1
LUPINUS, Dwarf Delicate pink	1
NASTURTIUM, Dwarf, of sorts	1
GODETIA, of sorts	¾ – 1
CORNFLOWER, Victoria, Dwarf Rose	¾
VISCARIA, of sorts	½ – 1
CANDYTUFT, Dwarf Pink	½
SAPONARIA calabrica	½
SILENE, of sorts	⅓ – 1
LEPTOSIPHON roseus	¼

CRIMSON AND SCARLET SHADES, INCLUDING CARMINE AND RUBY

Tall

COREOPSIS Atrosanguinea	3
HELICHRYSUM, Fireball	3
POPPY, Giant Double, Scarlet	3
SALPIGLOSSIS, Large-flowered varieties	3
SCABIOUS, Cherry Red	3
POLYGONUM, Ruby Gem	2½
NASTURTIUM	
Improved Lucifer	Cl.
Black Prince	Cl.

Medium

CHRYSANTHEMUM atrococcineum	2
CLARKIA ELEGANS	
Salmon-scarlet	2
Firefly	2
GODETIA, of sorts	2
MALOPE, Red	2
POPPY, Shirley	2
Orange King	2
Cardinal	2
CACALIA coccinea	1½
COREOPSIS cardaminifolia, Dwarf	1½
GYPSOPHILA elegans, Crimson	1½
JACOBEA, Double, Crimson	1½
SALPIGLOSSIS, Dwarf, Scarlet	1 - 1¼

Dwarf

CANDYTUFT, Improved Carmine	1
CANTRANTHUS macrosiphon	1
LINUM grandiflorum rubrum	1
NASTURTIUM, Dwarf, of sorts	1
VISCARIA cardinalis	1
ESCHSCHOLTZIA, of sorts	¾ - 1
GODETIA, of sorts	¾ - 1
COLLOMIA coccinea	¾
COREOPSIS, Dwarf Crimson	¾
ANAGALLIS, Scarlet	½
SAPONARIA, Scarlet Queen	½
VISCARIA, Dwarf Carmine	½

BLUE, MAUVE, AND PURPLE SHADES

Tall

CORNFLOWER, Blue	3
LARKSPUR, Tall sorts	3
LUPINUS, Tall dark blue	3
POPPY, Giant Double, Mauve	3
SALPIGLOSSIS, Large-flowered varieties	3
SCABIOUS, Mauve (Azure Fairy)	3

Medium

CHRYSANTHEMUM carinatum purpureum	2
CLARKIA ELEGANS, Purple Prince	2
GODETIA, Double Mauve	2
LUPINUS Hartwegii, Azure Blue	2
POPPY	
Mauve Queen	2
Shirley, Blue shades	2
XERANTHEMUM, of sorts	2
ECHIUM plantagineum	1½ - 2
SWEET SULTAN, of sorts	1½ - 2
ANCHUSA, Annual Blue	1½
COMMELINA coelestis	1½
CYNOGLOSSUM, Annual Blue	1½
GODETIA, Lavender Gem	1½
JACOBEA, Double, Purple	1½
NIGELLA, Miss Jekyll	1½
SALVIA, Blue Beard	1½
LINUM, Annual Blue Flax	1¼
SALPIGLOSSIS, Dwarf varieties	1 - 1¼

Dwarf

CAMPANULA loreyi, Blue	1
CANDYTUFT	
Lilac	1
Rich Purple	1
CONVOLVULUS MINOR	
Dark Blue	1
Sky-blue	1
CORNFLOWER, King of Blue Bottles	1
LINARIA, Mauve	1
LUPINUS, Dwarf Rich Blue	1
PHACELIA congesta	1
VISCARIA, Delphinium Blue	1
CORNFLOWER, Victoria, Dwarf Blue	¾
NIGELLA, Double Dwarf	¾
PHACELIA campanularia	¾
SWAN RIVER DAISY, Large-flowered Blue	¾
ANAGALLIS, Blue	½
CAMPANULA attica	½
NEMOPHILA, of sorts	½

General lists of kinds and varieties which may be treated as Hardy Annuals, giving colours, height in inches and approximate times of flowering from sowings made in April and in a few cases a little later

FOR FLOWERING FROM EARLY JUNE ONWARDS

CACALIA coccinea (Tassel Flower)	18	Vivid orange-scarlet
CHRYSANTHEMUM		
Carinatum atrococcineum	18	Deep scarlet
Burridgeanum	18	Flowers banded with white, crimson and yellow
Mixed Colours	18	Wide range of colours
NEMOPHILA		
Insignis	6	Bright blue
Grandiflora	6	Large bright blue flowers
Large-flowered Pale Mauve	6	Clear mauve, paler centre
PHACELIA ciliata	12	Lavender. Very free flowering

FOR FLOWERING FROM LATE JUNE ONWARDS

ANTHEMIS arabica	12	Yellow Daisy-like flowers
ASPERULA azurea setosa	12	Pale blue; sweetly scented
BARTONIA aurea	18	Large yellow St. John's Wort-like flowers
CHRYSANTHEMUM		
Morning Star	18	Soft yellow
Eastern Star	18	Primrose yellow, chocolate centre
Evening Star	18	Deep golden yellow
Southern Star (Eldorado)	18	Golden yellow, chestnut brown zone
Northern Star	18	Ivory White, sulphur zone
Coronarium, 'Coronet'	18	Combination of cream, white and yellow
Double Yellow	36	Bright golden yellow
Double White	36	Highly valued for cutting
Golden Queen	36	Large rich yellow flowers
Nivelli	24	Pure yellow. Valued for cutting
Inodorum plenissimum, Bridal Robe	9	Snow-white double flowers

CLARKIA pulchella, Double Rich Pink	18	Bright pink flowers, very double
White	18	Excellent for massing
COLLINSIA		
Bicolour	9	Lilac and white
Salmon Beauty	9	Delightful companion to Bicolour
Candidissima	9	Pure white. Charming as a front-line plant
COLLOMIA coccinea	9	Orange-red, star-like flowers
CONVOLVULUS MINOR		
Dark blue, Pink and White	12	In separate colours
DIMORPHOTHECA (Star of the Veldt) Very suitable for sunny, dry positions		
Buff Beauty	6	Profusion of flowers; buff-apricot
Apricot	12	Soft apricot
Lemon Queen	12	Lemon-coloured flowers, blue-black zone
Aurantiaca (Orange Daisy)	12	Deep orange
ECHIUM plantagineum	20	Purple-blue with rosy tint
Bright Blue	20	Pretty shade of blue
Blue Bedder	15	Deep blue. Compact and free-flowering
ERYSIMUM, Orange Gem	18	Deep orange
ESCHSCHOLTZIA (Californian Poppy) Very suitable for sunny, dry positions		
Red Chief	12	Rich red mahogany
Orange Prince	16	Bright orange; flowers extra large
The Geisha	12	Orange-crimson outside, deep golden yellow inside
EUTOCA viscida	12	Bright blue; very free-flowering
GAMOLEPIS Tagetes	6	Lemon-yellow; very free-flowering
GILIA tricolor	18	Lavender and white, with black throat
rosea	18	Rose-tinted flowers
nivalis	18	Snow-white; orange throat

GYPSOPHILA		
Elegans, Crimson	18	Rich crimson
White large-flowered	18	Purest snow-white
Muralis	9	Rose-coloured flowers
LAYIA elegans	12	Large yellow, edged white
LEPTOSYNE Stillmani	18	Golden yellow
LIMNANTHES Douglassi	6	Yellow and white flowers. Valuable for bees
LINARIA		
Snow-white	12	Pure white
Golden Gem	9	Golden yellow
Mauve	12	Rich purplish mauve
LINUM grandiflorum rubrum (Scarlet Flax)	12	Brilliant crimson-scarlet
Annual Blue Flax	15	Dainty pale blue
MATHIOLA bicornis (Night scented stock)	12	Lilac flowers
NOLANA grandiflora	9	Lavender blue; bell-shaped
PHACELIA		
Campanularia	9	Very showy bright blue
Viscida	12	Bright blue
Congesta	12	Mauve. Heads resembling Cherry Pie
Tanacetifolia	18	Pale mauve. Valuable for bees
PLATYSTEMON californicus	12	Bright lemon
SAPONARIA vaccaria		
Pink	24	Pink flowers borne in profusion
White	24	White; free-flowering
SHORTIA californica (Baeria)	9	Golden Daisy-like flowers
SILENE		
Pink Star	6	Plants covered with bright pink flowers
Pseudo-Atocion	12	Pink. Tall form of the preceding
VENUS' NAVELWORT	9	White Forget-me-not-like flowers
VIRGINIAN STOCK		
Crimson King	6	Crimson
White	9	White. Contrasts well with former
Yellow	9	Pale yellow, tinged with green

FOR FLOWERING FROM EARLY JULY ONWARDS

ACROCLINIUM		
Special Mixture, double and semi-double	12	Including white, cream, pale salmon-pink, and rich rose
Rose	12	Very dainty colour
White	12	Charming flowers
ANCHUSA		
Annual Blue	18	Pure blue
Bedding Blue (Blue Bird)	15	Pure blue; compact growth
CALANDRINIA grandiflora	18	Rose-coloured
speciosa	9	Ruby-coloured. Excellent for the rockery
CALENDULA		
Orange King	12	Double flowers of perfect shape
Lemon Queen	12	Clear lemon-yellow; double
Radio	12	Rich orange with quilled petals
Radio Golden Beam	12	Golden counterpart of the preceding
CAMPANULA attica	6	Violet-coloured flowers
Loreyi	12	Pale blue, shaded violet
CANDYTUFT		
Improved White Spiral	12	Pure white. Hyacinth-shaped spikes
Improved Carmine	12	Bright carmine
Dwarf Pink	6	Pretty shade of pale pink
Lilac Queen	6	Clear mauve or lilac
Little Prince	6	Snow-white flowers borne in profusion
CHEIRANTHUS Allionii, Lemon Queen	12	Attractive lemon-coloured flowers
CHRYSANTHEMUM		
Double White	24	Large double white
Golden	24	Large double yellow
CLARKIA ELEGANS		
Salmon-scarlet	24	Brilliant salmon-scarlet; double
Firefly	24	Vivid rose-crimson; double
Crimson	24	Crimson-scarlet; double
Salmon	24	Long sprays of double salmon flowers
Rose-pink	24	Glowing rose; free and double
Snowball	24	Pure white double flowers

CORNFLOWER		
Double Blue	24	Very freely produced
Pink	24	
White	24	
Victoria, Dwarf Blue	9	Neat compact habit. Deep blue flowers
Dwarf Rose	9	Rich deep rose
CYNOGLOSSUM		
Blue Gem	18	Blue Forget-me-not-like flowers
Annual Blue	18	Turquoise blue; very free-flowering
ECHIUM creticum	12 – 18	Soft red flowers
HAWKWEED, Pink, White and Yellow	18	In separate colours
LARKSPUR, Early-flowering Tall Rocket mixed	36	In mixed colours, double flowers
MIGNONETTE		
Giant White	18	White large-flowered strain
Red	15	Deep red. Immense spikes
Yellow	18	Golden yellow; free flowering
Cloth of Gold	12	Distinct yellow spikes; very showy
NASTURTIUM, DWARF VARIETIES. Nasturtiums do best in poor shallow soil and sunny positions		
Scarlet Queen	12	Dazzling orange-scarlet
Salmon-pink	12	Very free-flowering
King Theodore, Improved	12	Dark crimson
Cloth of Gold (Golden Queen)	12	Golden foliage; pure yellow flowers
Double Dwarf Fireball Gleam	12 – 15	Attractive vivid scarlet flowers
Double Dwarf Golden Ball Gleam	12 – 15	Intense gold; sweetly scented
OENOTHERA tarazacifolia alba	6	Large bell-shaped flowers, changing from pure white to rose

POPPY, ANNUAL		
Shirley Delicate Shades	24	Including salmon, apricot, peach, etc.
Dwarf Compact	12	Mixed colours
Orange King	24	Gorgeous orange-scarlet
Rose-pink	24	An even shade of rose-pink
Double Art Shades	24	New and unusual shades
SALVIA		
Blue Beard	18	Showy spikes of bright purple
Pink Gem	18	Long sprays of soft pink bracts
SAPONARIA calabrica	6	Small star-shaped pink flowers
SILENE		
Double Salmon-pink	12	A rich colour
Double Delicate Pink	12	Flesh-coloured flowers of great beauty
Armeria, Rose	18	Intense rose. Excellent for cutting
SWEET SULTAN		
Giant White	18	Superb pure white. Excellent for cutting
Mauve	18	Clear pale mauve
Rosy Mauve	18	Pretty shade of pinkish mauve
Splendens	18	Rich wine-red

FOR FLOWERING FROM LATE JULY ONWARDS

AGROSTEMMA coeli-rosa (Rose of Heaven)	18	Brilliant rose
ALYSSUM minimum	4	Dwarf plants covered with white flowers
Little Dorrit	4	Similar to preceding, but the plants are less spreading
ARGEMONE grandiflora	24	Poppy-like flowers with golden anthers
GODETIA, Tall varieties with flowers in long loose sprays		
Double Cherry Red	30	A beautiful rich colour
White	30	Glistening white flowers
Shell Pink	30	Dainty shell-pink variety
Rich Pink	30	Bright glossy pink
Mauve	30	Clear pinkish mauve
Crimson	30	Rich crimson

GODETIA, Dwarfer varieties with flowers in clusters		
Sybil Sherwood	12	Salmon-pink blended with orange
Kelvedon Glory	12	Deep salmon form of the preceding
Afterglow	9	Brilliant scarlet-crimson
Scarlet Queen	12	Intense crimson-scarlet
Pink Pearl	12	Pale pink overlaid on a white ground
Snowdrift	15	Pure white; very free flowering
HEBENSTRETIA comosa	18	Small white flowers; sweetly perfumed
LAVATERA (Mallow)		
Loveliness	36	Glowing rose-pink
Alba splendens	36	Large glossy pearly white flowers
STATICE spicata	12	Long spikes of puce-coloured flowers
Suworowi	18	Bright rose-coloured flowers with long spikes
SUNFLOWER, Small-flowered varieties		
Stella Red Hybrids	3 – 5ft	Bronzy-red strain of great merit
Stella	4 ft	Golden-yellow petals, small dark centres
Primrose Stella	4 ft	Pale primrose-yellow
Miniature	4 ft	Small golden-yellow flowers
SWAN RIVER DAISY		
Large-flowered Pale Blue	9	Pale blue, primrose centre
Dark Blue	9	Rich blue
Azure Fairy	9	Azure blue with white zone, dark centre
VISCARIA		
Rosy Queen	10	Brilliant carmine-rose
Pink Beauty	12	Pure rose-pink
Pale Blue	12	Pale china-blue
Fire King	12	Brilliant scarlet; very free-flowering
Pure White	12	Lovely white glistening flowers
Dwarf Blue	6	Large-flowered blue; compact strain

FOR FLOWERING FROM EARLY AUGUST ONWARDS

COREOPSIS		
Dwarf Yellow and Brown	12	Very effective
Crimson	9	Rich crimson. Plants very compact
Drummondii, large-flowered	18	Golden-yellow; chestnut-brown disc
Lemon Queen	36	Clear lemon-yellow; blotched crimson
Tinctoria	36	Yellow and brown; very showy
Atrosanguinea	36	Rich dark red
Marmorata	36	Chocolate and yellow striped
DELPHINIUM paniculatum	24	Annual species with violet-blue flowers
HELICHRYSUM, LARGE-FLOWERED, Well-known everlasting flowers		
Pink and Cream Shades	36	Refined colourings
Golden Globe	36	Clear golden-yellow
Silver Globe	36	Silvery-white flowers of perfect form
Fireball	36	Fiery-red flowers
MARIGOLD, DOUBLE AFRICAN, Best sown towards the end of April		
Dwarf Orange	18	Deep orange. Very floriferous
Dwarf Lemon	18	Clear lemon; flowers very freely
NIGELLA (Love-in-a-Mist)		
Miss Jekyll	18	Clear cornflower-blue
White	18	The white form of the preceding
SALPIGLOSSIS, LARGE-FLOWERED, Sow towards the end of April and in May where the plants are to bloom		
Dark Blue and Gold	36	Large, veined, funnel-shaped flowers
Light Blue and Gold	36	A pale blue form of the preceding
Brown and Gold	36	Very attractive variety
Golden-yellow	36	Effective colouring

TAGETES		
Signata pumila	12	Flowers bright yellow; very profuse
Golden Gem	12	Compact in growth

FOR FLOWERING FROM LATE AUGUST ONWARDS

CORNFLOWER, American	24	Beautiful pale lilac flowers
LARKSPUR, STOCK-FLOWERED, Tall-growing double-flowered strain		
Rosy Scarlet	36	Superb as a cut flower
Shell Pink	36	Pale pink; very beautiful
Blue	36	Rich violet-blue
White	36	A popular variety
Pale Mauve	36	Delicate lavender-mauve
Deep Mauve	36	Tones well with pale mauve and blue
LARKSPUR, SINGLE TALL BRANCHING		
Pink Pearl	30	Pretty salmon-pink shade
Rich Rosy Pink	30	Light graceful sprays
Single White	30	Very charming in the garden and useful for cutting
Mauve	30	
Blue	30	
MARIGOLD, DOUBLE AFRICAN, Best sown towards the end of April		Petals charmingly frilled
Giant Orange	30	Very rich colour; flowers of perfect shape
Lemon	30	Clear yellow; very fine
Pale Lemon	30	A pretty and delicate shade
MARIGOLD, SINGLE AFRICAN sow end of April		
Orange Beauty	24	Petals charmingly frilled
MARIGOLD, DOUBLE FRENCH, Best sown towards the end of April		
Tall Striped or Blotched	30	Yellow ground with rich brown markings
Tall Mixed	30	A combination of the best varieties
Orange Crown	12	Crimson petals surrounding an orange crown

MARIGOLD, SINGLE TALL FRENCH, Best sown towards the end of April		
Fire King	24	Bronzy-scarlet
Single French Mixed	24	Handsome flowers of various colours
MARIGOLD, SINGLE DWARF FRENCH, Best sown towards the end of April		
Legion of Honour	9	Clear yellow, blotched with brown
Diadem	9	Bright chestnut-red, margined with yellow
Star of India	9	Deep crimson, striped with golden yellow
RUDBECKIA		
Golden Sunset	18	Golden-yellow with chestnut markings
Autumn Flow	18	Golden-yellow ray florets; maroon disc
SCABIOUS (Sweet Scabious) DOUBLE LARGE-FLOWERED		
Salmon-rose Shades	36	Varying shades of soft salmon-rose
Coral Gem	36	Rich pink colour
Snowball	36	Large pure white flowers
Cherry-red	36	Beautiful rich glowing colour
Black Prince	36	Purplish-black; very free flowering
Mauve (Azure Fairy)	36	Pretty pale shade

FOR FLOWERING IN SEPTEMBER

CANTERBURY BELLS, ANNUAL		
Annual Pink, Deep Rose, Light Blue, Dark Blue, and White	24	In separate colours. May be sown on a reserve border, and later transplanted to flowering positions
EUPHORBIA marginata (Snow-on-the-Mountain) The seed is best sown in early May	18	Plant with attractive variegated foliage, broadly margined with pure white

List of Annuals suitable for temporary use to replace failures in Rock Garden, for temporary edgings, and for planting in suitable small spaces in crazy paving

ALYSSUM MINIMUM. The dwarfest Alyssum, forming a dense mat studded with small white flowers.

ALYSSUM, LITTLE DORRIT. Similar to the preceding, but less spreading. The flower heads stand erect. Height four inches.

ANAGALLIS (Pimpernel). Very free-flowering annuals of which there are two varieties: Large-flowered Blue and Large-flowered Scarlet. Height six inches.

CAMPANULA ATTICA. This annual blooms profusely over a long period. Charming violet-coloured flowers. Height six inches.

COLLINSIA, MINIATURE FAIRY. Attractive bushy plants crowded with Toad flax-like flowers in delicate mauve, pink and violet shades. Height six inches.

COLLOMIA COCCINEA. A free flowering annual with brilliant orange-red starry flowers. Height nine inches.

CORNFLOWER, VICTORIA, DWARF BLUE. Neat and compact. Carries a profusion of deep blue flowers. Height nine inches.

CORNFLOWER, VICTORIA, DWARF ROSE. Of similar habit to the preceding. Flowers rich deep rose; very attractive.

DIMORPHOTHECA, BUFF BEAUTY. A compact and early flowering Star of the Veldt, forming a dense mat twelve inches across, thickly covered with small buff-apricot flowers. Height six inches.

IONOPSIDIUM ACAULE. Known also as the Violet Cress. A charming miniature annual with pretty pale mauve flowers. Invaluable for rockeries and the paved pathway. Height two inches.

KAULFUSSIA AMELLOIDES. Excellent for rockeries. There are two varieties – blue and crimson. Height six inches.

LEPTOSIPHON HYBRIDUS. Tiny plants thickly studded with starry flowers in various colours. One of the most attractive annuals for the rock garden and paved pathway. The variety L. roseus bears brilliant rose-coloured blooms and L. aureus flowers of a bright golden-yellow.

LIMNANTHES DOUGLASSII. Bears delicately fragrant yellow and white flowers, much beloved by bees. Very free flowering. Height six inches.

NEMOPHILA INSIGNIS GRANDIFLORA. One of the best hardy annuals, charming in any position. Patches of these plants on the paved pathway look most attractive. Bright blue flowers. Height six inches. Nemophila atomaria bears white flowers with numerous black dots; height four inches.

SANVITALIA PROCUMBENS. There are single and double flowered varieties bearing pleasing yellow flowers. Very suitable for edgings and rockeries. Height six inches.

SHORTIA CALIFORNICA (Baeria). A very pretty hardy annual producing small golden Daisy-like flowers in the greatest profusion; height nine inches.

SWAN RIVER DAISY (Brachycome iberidifolia). A dainty annual with Cineraria-like flowers which are produced in abundance for a considerable period. Can be obtained in separate colours, such as azure blue, pale blue, dark blue, mauve and white. Height nine inches.

VENUS' NAVELWORT (Cynoglossum linifolium). Silvery-foliaged hardy annual with charming white Forget-me-not-like flowers. Height nine inches.

VENUS' LOOKING GLASS (Campanula speculum). A free-flowering and interesting annual. Obtainable in two varieties, purple and white. Height about nine inches.

A few of my readers, however, might like to start with small selections made for them. I have therefore selected three dozen of the best and most beautiful for their first attempt.

Thirty-six Good Varieties of Hardy Annuals

ALYSSUM. Minimum. Beautiful miniature Alyssum with small white flowers. Invaluable for edgings.

ANCHUSA. Bedding Sky Blue. Bright Forget-me-not blue Anchusa, carrying numerous well-formed trusses. Height eighteen inches.

BARTONIA AUREA. A showy annual with large yellow flowers. Height eighteen inches.

CALENDULA. Orange King. Enormous double orange flowers. Height about one foot.

CALENDULA. Chrysantha. Buttercup-yellow flowers. Height two to two and a half feet.

CHRYSANTHEMUM. Eastern Star. Deep chocolate centre and primrose-yellow petals. Excellent for decorative purposes.

CHRYSANTHEMUM. Carinatum atrococcineum. Fine deep scarlet flowers varying to a lighter shade.

CONVOLVULUS MINOR. Sky-blue. Height about one foot.

COREOPSIS. Drummondii. Large-flowered. Golden-yellow flowers with chestnut-brown centres, produced in abundance. Height eighteen inches.

COREOPSIS. Tinctoria. Showy yellow and brown flowers. Height three feet.

CYNOGLOSSUM (Hound's Tongue). Annual Blue. Beautiful turquoise-blue; flowers freely all the summer from an outdoor sowing in March or April. Height eighteen inches.

DIMORPHOTHECA (Star of the Veldt). Buff Beauty. A compact early-flowering variety growing only about four to six inches high.

DIMORPHOTHECA. Aurantiaca (Orange Daisy). Gorgeous orange flowers. Height twelve inches.

ESCHSCHOLTZIA (Californian Poppy). Scarlet Glow. Very rich scarlet-crimson double flowers. Height about one foot.

ESCHSCHOLTZIA. Aurora. Flowers delicate peach-pink and cream. Height about one foot.

GODETIA. Double Shell Pink. Height about two and a half feet.

GODETIA. Double Rose. Height about two and a half feet.

GODETIA. Dwarf Lavender. Small lavender flowers with white centres on dwarf bushy plants. Excellent for edging. Height eight inches.

GODETIA. Sybil Sherwood. Salmon-pink blended with orange, softened by a delicate white border. Height one foot.

LARKSPUR. Rosy Scarlet. Height about three feet.

LARKSPUR. Shell Pink. Height about three feet.

LARKSPUR. Mauve. Height about three feet.

LUPINUS. Hartwegii. Blue and White. Height two feet.

MARIGOLD. Double African. Giant Orange. Enormous flowers of perfect shape. Height two and a half feet.

NEMOPHILA INSIGNIS. One of the best of the hardy annuals. Bright blue flowers. Height six inches.

PHACELIA. Blue Beauty. Deep rich blue flowers with contrasting speckled silvery centres and primrose anthers. Height one foot.

RUDBECKIA. Autumn Glow. A most attractive variety; large golden-ray florets, contrasting well with rich dark maroon disc. Height eighteen inches.

SALVIA. Blue Beard. Showy spikes of bright purple bracts. Height eighteen inches.

SWAN RIVER DAISY. Mauve Beauty. Rosy-mauve. Height nine inches.

SWEET SULTAN. Giant White. Superb pure white flowers. Height eighteen inches.

SWEET SULTAN. Giant Delicate Mauve. Pale mauve outer petals with white centre. Very dainty. Height eighteen inches.

SCABIOUS (Sweet Scabious). Fiery Scarlet. Height three feet.

SCABIOUS. Mauve (Azure Fairy). Height three feet.

SCABIOUS. Dark Blue. Height three feet.

VISCARIA. Dwarf Blue. Compact bright blue strain. Height six inches.

VISCARIA. Fire King. Rich-scarlet. Height one foot.

Most hardy annuals will make a brave show under almost all conditions but nearly all will give better results with liberal treatment. There is an exception, however – the nasturtium. To give the superb show of which it is capable, it should be grown in the poorest soil. This does not imply that it does not give a good show under ordinary garden conditions – it does – but if the soil has been made comfortably rich for other annuals, so that they have a sturdy, self-reliant look, the leaves of nasturtiums become over-large and the leaf stems so long that the flowers, although borne freely, are smothered in the green. But sow nasturtium seeds on poor sandy or gravelly land, or on any land devoid of humus which bakes hard and dry in summer, and they will flourish until frost destroys them in the autumn. For covering a hot sandy bank on which nothing else will grow they are unequalled. Nowadays there are shades which blend with almost any garden scheme – except when rose and carmine shades are used – ranging from creamy white through numerous shades of buff, pink, flame, orange, scarlet, and crimson, including the blackest crimson.

Although nasturtiums do not need starting under glass and therefore are generally included in hardy annuals, the seeds should not be sown too early – the first week in May is quite soon enough. If sown before, the fleshy seedlings are easily nipped by May frost. The seed is large and, therefore, each should be carefully placed, by hand, six inches from the next in drills drawn as for other annuals. In the dwarf section the gleam varieties are greatly prized for their semi-double flowers and general air of opulence, but all in this wonderful family are brilliant. The tall varieties will make a flaming show if allowed to climb pea sticks in a border, or netting attached to a wall or fence, and I have seen them used with great effect for covering trellis work around a porch in summer.

Another annual which also dislikes high living and will give its brilliant best on a starvation diet is Portulaca, in reality a very dwarf succulent Mesembryanthemum, which is quite happy in a bank of sand. This useful plant, whose seeds should be sown early in May, needs no attention afterwards, for weeds rarely flourish in sand – they nearly always love fat land. Portulaca is also very valuable for use as a salad in times of drought when little else thrives.

There are many other annuals which luxuriate in good living but which can survive and make a good show in poor land in times of drought, but I must mention especially Bartonia aurea, a bright yellow species, and the many varieties of the dazzling Eschscholtzia, with their shades extending from cream to orange and through flaming scarlet to crimson; Convolvulus minor, a non-climbing small-flowered Convolvulus in several shades, and the semi-everlastings of fine form, Rhodanthe and Acroclinium – both in several varieties. There are not many true climbers which may be sown direct out of doors, but in addition to nasturtium, there are tall Convolvulus which twine prodigiously and Tropaeolum canariense, the canary creeper – a dainty yellow-flowered relative of the nasturtium – both of which do well from a late April sowing.

There are miniature annuals, too, especially suitable for the rock garden. Not that they displace perennial Alpines, however, for their chief use is in covering bare spaces after losses, or for making a good show for a season before the rock garden has got going.

It is important to mention the South African annuals, which are unequalled for brilliance and very beautiful. Of course, they are sun lovers, but, as most of them have come from high altitudes where in addition to sun there is much atmospheric moisture and temperate heat only, they succeed remarkably well in this country. Most of them can be sown with the hardy annuals, except the Nemesias, which should be treated as half-hardy annuals, but Nemesias and other South Africans like Dimorphothecas and Ursinias have a very remarkable quality – they grow very fast if sown during the summer, and from a sowing made in the open in June, without transplanting, all varieties of Nemesias and Dimorphothecas are in flower six weeks later, with Ursinia following shortly after. For these sun lovers the site must be open. There are several half-hardy annuals which can be treated in this way, but none responds so quickly as these South Africans.

I must not leave kinds and varieties without mentioning one other important matter. Those who start late can sow mixed annuals. They consist of mixed kinds as well as mixed varieties. Many people without experience begin with these, and, by choosing from the mixed, start to grow separate kinds and varieties the next season. With these mixtures I have seen waste land, unused patches in gardens, expanses of wild gardens, and all sorts of ugly places transformed. In the First World War hundredweights of this mixed seed were used to brighten up the war graves quickly.

In land which you suspect is infested with weed seeds, sow these mixed annuals in drills, but in fairly clean land broadcast the seed, which means simply scatter it evenly on the surface of the soil and rake in well afterwards. These patches of mixed annuals, which contain a wonderful variety of kinds and varieties in a wide range of colours, begin to flower early and continue late – generally well into November.

All the main families of annuals with their many varieties which can be sown separately in the annual border can also be bought mixed, i.e. in packets of mixed varieties – not to be confused with the mixed kind and varieties already mentioned. These can be included in the general plan or can be used in a jig-saw arrangement, all mixed. I once saw a border like this and found it restrained but satisfying. The vivid self-coloured patches one expects were missing, but the generous mixture of varieties in each family patch was beautiful in a delicate, old-fashioned way. The border reminded me of a slightly faded silk patchwork quilt, like those our grandmothers used to make.

I have said little about summer culture and really there is little to say. Most of the cultural part is done when the ground is thoroughly prepared in the autumn or winter, but there is an important matter which should not be neglected, and this is something few people do very happily – thinning. It always seems a shame to destroy tender seedlings. But it must be done. Luckily, annuals will make a show even if they are not thinned, but when they are thinned properly and each plant is given enough room the difference is remarkable. The procedure is simple but drastic. As soon as seedlings are visible use the dutch hoe between the rows to stir the soil lightly to admit air and prevent seedling weed growth. It should be used frequently – at least twice a week – to prevent successive crops of weeds from germinating. When the seedlings are big enough to handle comfortably, remove enough, by careful pulling, to allow those which remain to be spaced about an inch apart. When the growing seedlings have recovered from the check of disturbance and are sturdy, remove alternate ones, and as soon as they are large enough to escape the ravages of slugs remove all unwanted ones, leaving the remainder far enough apart for full development and close enough together to make a good show.

It is a little difficult for beginners to know the distance at which seedlings should be left, for their ultimate growth depends on weather conditions, the kind of soil, and many factors connected with soil preparation, but generally, in ground of average fertility, seedlings which grow a foot high should be left about six inches apart, and those which grow from eighteen inches to two feet should be left nine inches to a foot apart, with perhaps a little more room allowed for very tall plants. At these distances, with timely thinning, all seedlings will be either self-supporting or will support one another, but should any fall over or suffer from the effects of a gale, a few twiggy tops of pea sticks, interspersed, will support them amply without ties. Until the annuals have become dense, hoeing should be done regularly, but afterwards they are generally capable of choking out weeds without further attention, except for the occasional weed which can be pulled out by hand.

Now about autumn sowing. On well drained soils, and where there is shelter in the south and west, which includes South Wales and the South of Eire, a few annuals can be grown from autumn sowing. The best time to sow is in the first half of September. If sown before, the seedlings become too lush and succumb to the first hard frost, and if sown too late they almost cease to grow after the first impulse of germination and remain far too small to withstand bad weather. As the North-east wind is usually the worst enemy snow should be welcomed. Losses are bound to occur, therefore the seedlings should be only partially thinned in the autumn, and the final thinning should be left until it can be seen which are undamaged.

An autumn sowing is always a gamble with the weather, but if there should be losses there is ample time to sow again after they have been discovered. Given suitable weather the spring survivors of autumn sowing often make enormous plants which grow to a great height and give results far better than is usual with annuals. Those sown in the autumn, too, usually flower a full month earlier than those sown in spring. Not all annuals are suitable for autumn sowing, however, but the list given below includes all those with a reasonable chance of success.

Cornflower, all varieties
Larkspur, all varieties
Nigella, all varieties
Annual Chrysanthemum, all varieties
Calendula, all varieties
Scabious Annual, all varieties

Eschscholtzia, all varieties
Coreopsis, all varieties
Viscarias, all varieties

This list may not seem extensive, but as there are many varieties of most of the kinds mentioned the number is really quite large. A few of the kinds mentioned in this chapter are perennials, but as they give better results when grown as annuals they are included, as is customary.

Much more space would be needed for me to deal adequately with annuals, but I hope I have been able to give some idea of the pleasure which a well-designed annual border can give.

· 7 ·

The Hardy Perennial Border

A BORDER of perennials can be magnificent if boldly conceived, but only if boldly conceived. Half measures are seldom effective. Plants standing here and there in isolated misery have no place in the well-managed garden – even the garden of a beginner. Rather than subject them to such treatment, it is far better to cover most of the ground with annuals for a season or two while stock is being worked up on other smaller plots, not necessarily in full view. But let us begin at the beginning.

Perennial flowering plants are those which bloom each year but whose rootstocks do not die during the winter. Each spring they send up new shoots from the rootstocks and, therefore, they are called perennials to distinguish them from annuals which die after producing flowers and, sometimes, seeds. There are advantages and disadvantages in perennials. It is an advantage not to have to replant each year, but whereas the annual border can be thoroughly trenched or dug, and manure incorporated each winter, the perennial border cannot be treated in the same way, and because of this disadvantage, all sites intended for perennials should be thoroughly prepared by deep digging and by the liberal use of farmyard manure or compost.

Liberality and thoroughness is important because until the perennials reach the stage when replanting and dividing becomes necessary – generally after four flowering seasons – it will not be possible to work the ground deeply and all manuring must be done from the surface. But there should be a perennial border in every garden, for, despite the merits of annuals, none is complete without. It should never be tucked away, for this would be a gross misuse of valuable material.

Some perennials are magnificent. Their surroundings should, therefore, be the best that can be afforded. Many of them, too, are tall imposing plants which need a site where they can display their height fully and have room to develop freely; and this they cannot do unless the border or bed is generously proportioned. A slightly sloping site opposite a much-used room or french window is admirable, provided there is a patch of lawn between border and window, and a border on each side of a green path giving a vista which can be seen at any time from a favourite window is perhaps the most satisfying site of all, though only if the borders are wide enough to accommodate plants which need much elbow room to be fully effective.

A width of eight to nine feet is a minimum which cannot safely be reduced if a satisfying effect is to be secured. Therefore, even if the grass path is only four feet wide (this is a little narrow), a minimum width of twenty-two feet is required for the path and two borders, which, in many gardens, would swallow too much space. If this is the case one good wide border is better than two bad ones. It is useless to try to crush hefty plants – and some perennials grow very heftily – into cramped quarters.

If, when measured out, only a narrow grass path and flanking widths of six feet for each border are available, then put the path on one side and throw the two six-foot borders into one large border of twelve feet – quite a useful width. This may have the disadvantage of not running in line with the front door or french window; but a compromise can generally be arranged. Sometimes one end of a green path can be directed to a vantage point. If only the back of such a border can be seen, by a little skilful planning a selection of plants of less height – not necessarily of the same height or graded up like a house roof – can be planted at the vantage end to allow colour to be seen which would otherwise be hidden by the taller plants.

Perennials are not as simple to arrange in a border as annuals, since you must allow for diversities of height – and they range from a few inches to eight or ten feet – the great difference in flowering period – from spring to late autumn – and the immense colour range. To the average beginner, planning the perennial border looks so formidable that in many cases it is not tackled at all; which accounts for the jungle borders one frequently sees. Such borders give the owner neither pleasure nor a happy occupation, for knowing there is something amiss he is generally glad to get away and avoid them as far as possible, spending his valuable time instead tending plants he understands better.

Perennials are not really hard to group when their needs are understood, even though a full understanding cannot be acquired immediately. As a preliminary help, in this chapter I am giving a plan for a perennial border fifty feet long by twelve feet wide. Before studying this, obtain a catalogue of perennials from a good nurseryman; study the plants on the plan according to their catalogue descriptions, and note where they fit the plan. You will soon see that provision is made to plant flowers which bloom, in turn, from late April until the end of October, and will notice – perhaps with surprise – that flowering plants which together would make a great show are scattered in groups about the border. But this is deliberate, for if they were arranged otherwise, there would be long barren periods without flowers on large patches, following an equally large and arresting show of bloom, and the border is specially designed to prevent this by providing a display of flowers throughout the season, and not, in any section, to be colourful at one time and colourless at another. Closer examination will show that in addition to the timing of colours, the colours themselves have been arranged to give the best effect in much the same way as the annuals, but whereas annuals bloom at much the same time the colour scheme of perennials has to be arranged around those which are in flower together – probably in blocks scattered over the border and seldom close together. Finally, the question of height has been considered carefully. It used to be the custom to design perennial borders with the tall flowers at the back and others grouped regularly according to height, grading down as evenly as possible to some edging plant like Catmint or Santolina incana. Though effective in its way, this merely gave a splash of colour, for the flowers were planted too close together to be seen individually. In this plan I have tried to avoid such a crushed, regimented appearance, and to make the design of the border more flowing and unaffected.

Then there are the shorter plants. The suitable grouping of tall plants laterally, as well as back and front, provides spaces between where smaller plants can be grown effectively, and can be useful in hiding the naked stalks of tall plants which have lost their lower leaves. The border is thus given depth and richness, and the visitor has the excitement of discovering, when he looks closely, patches of unexpected colour.

When you have looked at plans and catalogues, you should, if possible, visit some well-known gardens or parks to see perennials in a well-designed border. The long double borders in a very fine setting at the R. H. S. Gardens at Wisley are splendid examples of good grouping, and satisfy those who are interested in rare plants as well as those who delight in colour.

Only a few will be able to visit Wisley, but the public parks in London, and in most large towns, nearly all contain borders of character. In some districts, too, there are large gardens where perennial borders are the main feature and where visitors are admitted, on certain days during the summer, on payment of a small sum devoted to charity. Seeing living plants with all their differing characteristics of foliage, habit, and colour is the best way of learning how to plan your own border, but even if this is impossible one season of experimenting with a few good plants will teach you a good deal.

And now to finish the job of planning. There are several large families of perennials which form the backbone of the border. Most of these are beautiful, colourful, and highly ornamental. Some of them have many varieties, which give great variety of colour and by flowering in succession ensure that their family is represented for a considerable time. The chief of these are delphiniums, lupins, Michaelmas daisies, phlox, and iris, but there are others with less varieties. Of these: campanulas, chrysanthemum maximum, helenium, helianthus, hemerocallis, kniphofia, liliums (bulbous), montbretia (hardy corms), paeonies, papavers, pyrethrums, scabiosa, trollius, verbascum, veronicas and others make good secondary selections. Many other plants have only a few varieties, and a large number are plain species, very similar to the first plant of the species cultivated in this country, or perhaps a native British plant collected from the wilds. Species under cultivation, although perhaps originally of one colour, sometimes begin to vary in shade, and it is these colour shades which, by selection, form the first varieties, or variations from the original. In some species, in time, colour breaks or mutations of a striking nature appear, and the plant breeder, by crossing these, evolves startling new colours – work which sometimes takes generations, during which vast numbers of plants which eventually prove worthless are produced and discarded in order to obtain a few which may interest the public: a costly business which explains why plant novelties are expensive.

Now for stock planting. Undoubtedly it is expensive to-day to buy enough stock for a border of importance, but there is good reason for this. During the war, nurserymen, in response to the need for food production, destroyed their stocks of flowers at great pecuniary loss, and grew vegetables, and when the war ended had to restock by propagating from small stocks which had somehow been preserved, and using unskilled labour. Nevertheless I advise all beginners to go to a good nurseryman and obtain the best. Scrounging for plants is not compatible with a good plan and very rarely produces a worth-while border, unless the person responsible is in a very fortunate position to acquire plants and has the necessary taste and skill to make a collection of scraps into a passable whole. Many people think that all they have to do is to chop up somebody's old plant and put in the pieces, or obtain 'slips', stick them in the ground and watch them grow. But they are soon disillusioned. They find they have either a lot of rubbish growing vigorously – for only the ruder species will stand such treatment – or an assembly of weedy nondescripts which refuse to develop into good plants in spite of time and patience.

The reason is easily found. The stock used by nurserymen is specially chosen for its vigour, all weak and diseased plants being rigorously discarded, whereas acquired parts of plants nearly always come from old plants fast dying in someone's border. In a nurseryman's hands propagation is supervised by experts and is suited to the kind of plant. Some are propagated by growth cuttings, others by root cuttings, and a few by division. When by division only, selected young growth from the outsides of the clump is used, the centre, generally composed of old and dying roots, being thrown away. However they are propagated, young plants are given adequate space in nursery beds and are tended carefully until lifting time arrives.

If the whole border intended for perennials cannot be filled the first season, fill a length of it from back to front and sow the remainder with annuals; or else fill the whole border with annuals and plant perennials in a less prominent part of the garden to increase stocks for planting in the border next season.

The best time for planting is in the autumn, but there is no reason why it should not be done at any time from October to March inclusive, provided soil and weather conditions permit. Be careful if, to save a valuable season, you have to plant in April. In this month, harsh east winds often have a drying effect on the land, especially if they are accompanied by frost at night, and newly-planted perennials may shrivel up unless they are given a great deal of water. This is often called madness, because it is thought unnecessary on heavy soils, but it is

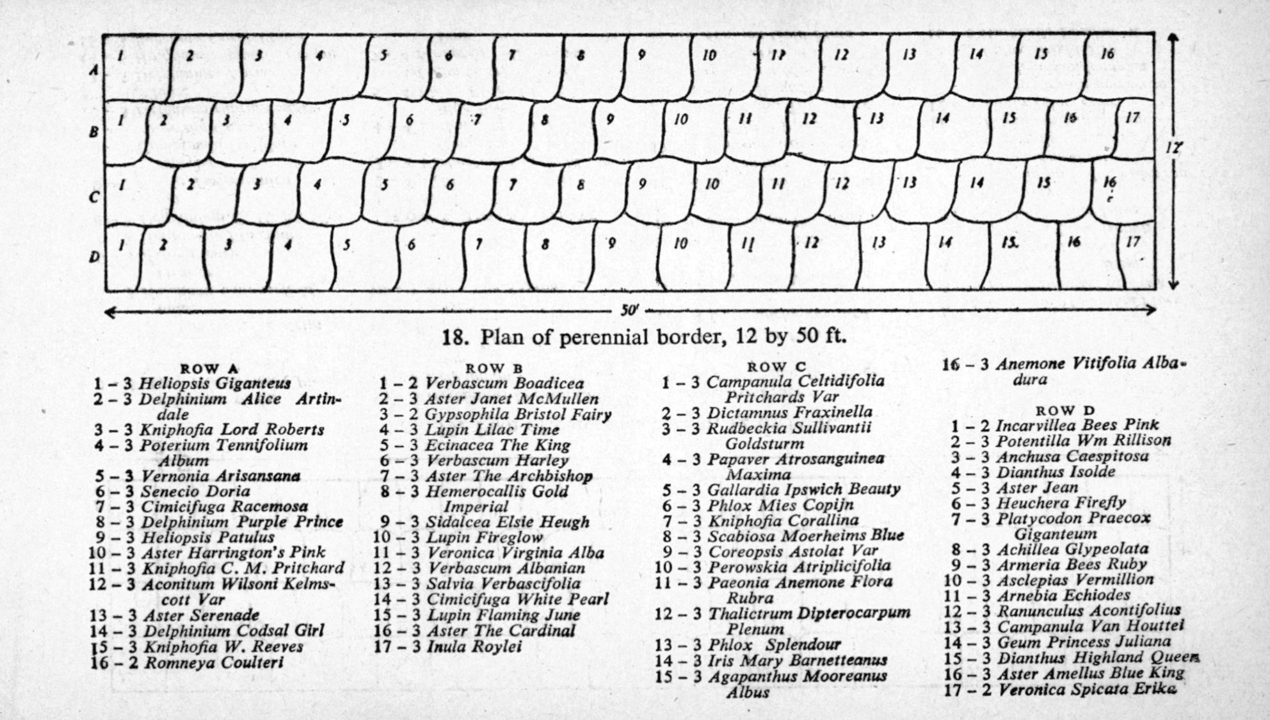

18. Plan of perennial border, 12 by 50 ft.

ROW A

1 – 3 *Heliopsis Giganteus*
2 – 3 *Delphinium Alice Artindale*
3 – 3 *Kniphofia Lord Roberts*
4 – 3 *Poterium Tennifolium Album*
5 – 3 *Vernonia Arisansana*
6 – 3 *Senecio Doria*
7 – 3 *Cimicifuga Racemosa*
8 – 3 *Delphinium Purple Prince*
9 – 3 *Heliopsis Patulus*
10 – 3 *Aster Harrington's Pink*
11 – 3 *Kniphofia C. M. Pritchard*
12 – 3 *Aconitum Wilsoni Kelmscott Var*
13 – 3 *Aster Serenade*
14 – 3 *Delphinium Codsal Girl*
15 – 3 *Kniphofia W. Reeves*
16 – 2 *Romneya Coulteri*

ROW B

1 – 2 *Verbascum Boadicea*
2 – 3 *Aster Janet McMullen*
3 – 2 *Gypsophila Bristol Fairy*
4 – 3 *Lupin Lilac Time*
5 – 3 *Ecinacea The King*
6 – 3 *Verbascum Harley*
7 – 3 *Aster The Archbishop*
8 – 3 *Hemerocallis Gold Imperial*
9 – 3 *Sidalcea Elsie Heugh*
10 – 3 *Lupin Fireglow*
11 – 3 *Veronica Virginia Alba*
12 – 3 *Verbascum Albanian*
13 – 3 *Salvia Verbascifolia*
14 – 3 *Cimicifuga White Pearl*
15 – 3 *Lupin Flaming June*
16 – 3 *Aster The Cardinal*
17 – 3 *Inula Roylei*

ROW C

1 – 3 *Campanula Celtidifolia Pritchards Var*
2 – 3 *Dictamnus Fraxinella*
3 – 3 *Rudbeckia Sullivantii Goldsturm*
4 – 3 *Papaver Atrosanguinea Maxima*
5 – 3 *Gallardia Ipswich Beauty*
6 – 3 *Phlox Mies Copijn*
7 – 3 *Kniphofia Corallina*
8 – 3 *Scabiosa Moerheims Blue*
9 – 3 *Coreopsis Astolat Var*
10 – 3 *Perowskia Atriplicifolia*
11 – 3 *Paeonia Anemone Flora Rubra*
12 – 3 *Thalictrum Dipterocarpum Plenum*
13 – 3 *Phlox Splendour*
14 – 3 *Iris Mary Barnetteanus*
15 – 3 *Agapanthus Mooreanus Albus*
16 – 3 *Anemone Vitifolia Albadura*

ROW D

1 – 2 *Incarvillea Bees Pink*
2 – 3 *Potentilla Wm Rillison*
3 – 3 *Anchusa Caespitosa*
4 – 3 *Dianthus Isolde*
5 – 3 *Aster Jean*
6 – 3 *Heuchera Firefly*
7 – 3 *Platycodon Praecox Giganteum*
8 – 3 *Achillea Glypeolata*
9 – 3 *Armeria Bees Ruby*
10 – 3 *Asclepias Vermillion*
11 – 3 *Arnebia Echiodes*
12 – 3 *Ranunculus Acontifolius*
13 – 3 *Campanula Van Houttei*
14 – 3 *Geum Princess Juliana*
15 – 3 *Dianthus Highland Queen*
16 – 3 *Aster Amellus Blue King*
17 – 2 *Veronica Spicata Erika*

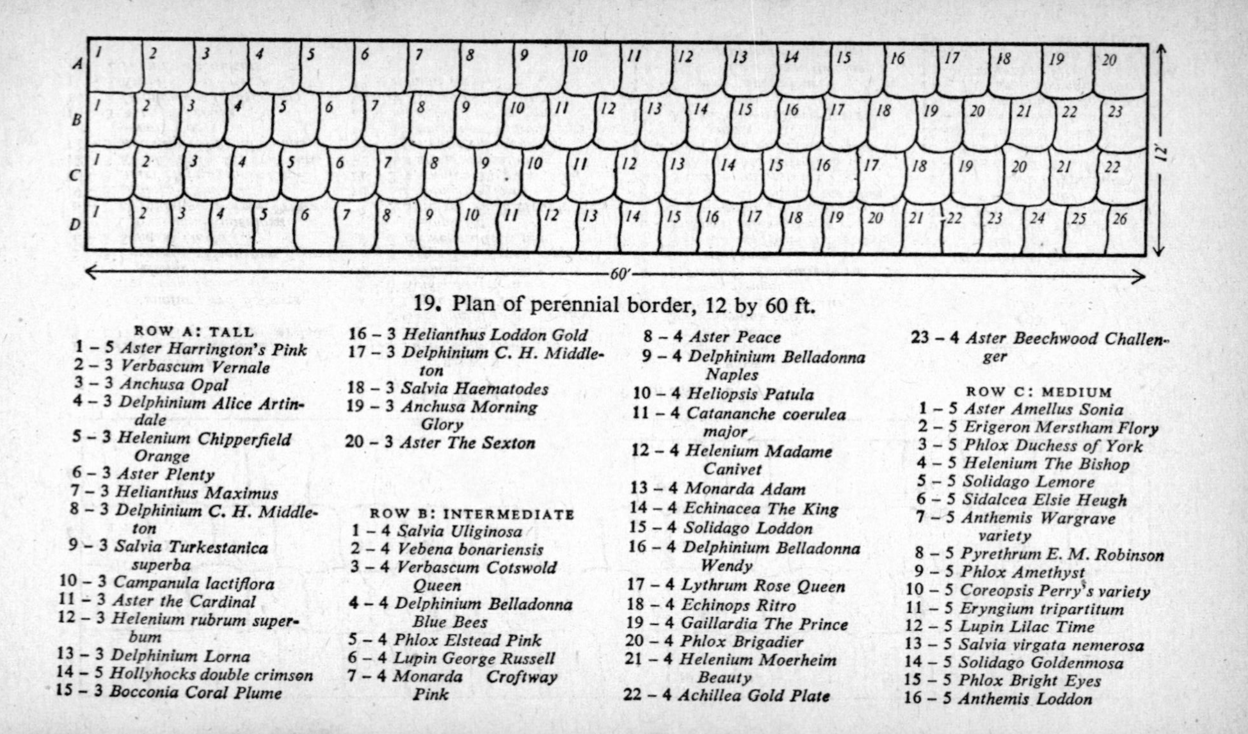

19. Plan of perennial border, 12 by 60 ft.

ROW A: TALL

1 – 5 *Aster Harrington's Pink*
2 – 3 *Verbascum Vernale*
3 – 3 *Anchusa Opal*
4 – 3 *Delphinium Alice Artindale*
5 – 3 *Helenium Chipperfield Orange*
6 – 3 *Aster Plenty*
7 – 3 *Helianthus Maximus*
8 – 3 *Delphinium C. H. Middleton*
9 – 3 *Salvia Turkestanica superba*
10 – 3 *Campanula lactiflora*
11 – 3 *Aster the Cardinal*
12 – 3 *Helenium rubrum superbum*
13 – 3 *Delphinium Lorna*
14 – 5 *Hollyhocks double crimson*
15 – 3 *Bocconia Coral Plume*
16 – 3 *Helianthus Loddon Gold*
17 – 3 *Delphinium C. H. Middleton*
18 – 3 *Salvia Haematodes*
19 – 3 *Anchusa Morning Glory*
20 – 3 *Aster The Sexton*

ROW B: INTERMEDIATE

1 – 4 *Salvia Uliginosa*
2 – 4 *Vebena bonariensis*
3 – 4 *Verbascum Cotswold Queen*
4 – 4 *Delphinium Belladonna Blue Bees*
5 – 4 *Phlox Elstead Pink*
6 – 4 *Lupin George Russell*
7 – 4 *Monarda Croftway Pink*
8 – 4 *Aster Peace*
9 – 4 *Delphinium Belladonna Naples*
10 – 4 *Heliopsis Patula*
11 – 4 *Catananche coerulea major*
12 – 4 *Helenium Madame Canivet*
13 – 4 *Monarda Adam*
14 – 4 *Echinacea The King*
15 – 4 *Solidago Loddon*
16 – 4 *Delphinium Belladonna Wendy*
17 – 4 *Lythrum Rose Queen*
18 – 4 *Echinops Ritro*
19 – 4 *Gaillardia The Prince*
20 – 4 *Phlox Brigadier*
21 – 4 *Helenium Moerheim Beauty*
22 – 4 *Achillea Gold Plate*
23 – 4 *Aster Beechwood Challenger*

ROW C: MEDIUM

1 – 5 *Aster Amellus Sonia*
2 – 5 *Erigeron Merstham Flory*
3 – 5 *Phlox Duchess of York*
4 – 5 *Helenium The Bishop*
5 – 5 *Solidago Lemore*
6 – 5 *Sidalcea Elsie Heugh*
7 – 5 *Anthemis Wargrave variety*
8 – 5 *Pyrethrum E. M. Robinson*
9 – 5 *Phlox Amethyst*
10 – 5 *Coreopsis Perry's variety*
11 – 5 *Eryngium tripartitum*
12 – 5 *Lupin Lilac Time*
13 – 5 *Salvia virgata nemerosa*
14 – 5 *Solidago Goldenmosa*
15 – 5 *Phlox Bright Eyes*
16 – 5 *Anthemis Loddon*

17 – 5 *Rudbeckia Sullivantii*
18 – 5 *Pyrethrum Kelway's Glorious*
19 – 5 *Phlox Lady Buchanan Jardine*
20 – 5 *Lupin Mrs Micklethwaite*
21 – 5 *Monarda Cambridge Scarlet*
22 – 5 *Aster Amellus King George*

ROW D: DWARF

1 – 5 *Aster Margaret Rose*
2 – 5 *Pink White Ladies*
3 – 5 *Anchusa caespitosa*
4 – 5 *Achillea Taygetae*
5 – 5 *Campanula Queen of Somerville*
6 – 5 *Armeria Bee's Ruby*
7 – 5 *Erigeron Elstead Pink*
8 – 5 *Geranium Wargrave*
9 – 5 *Gypsophila Rosy Veil*
10 – 5 *Geum Lady Stratheden*
11 – 5 *Veronica Wendy*
12 – 5 *Aster Snowsprite*
13 – 5 *Potentilla Gibsons Scarlet*
14 – 5 *Oenothera Missouriensis*
15 – 5 *Nepeta Mussini*
16 – 5 *Linum Six Hills*
17 – 5 *Geum Mrs Bradshaw*
18 – 5 *Gypsophila Bodgerii*
19 – 5 *Coreopsis verticillata*
20 – 5 *Ceratostigma Plumbaginoides*
21 – 5 *Achillea Cerise Queen*
22 – 5 *Lychnis viscaria splendens plena*
23 – 5 *Sedum spectabile Brilliant*
24 – 5 *Verbena Venosa*
25 – 5 *Viola cornuta purpurea*
26 – 5 *Aster Winston Churchill*

nevertheless sound sense, because the surface of newly-disturbed soil dries quickly under the influence of the elements, and the young plants are unable to reach the plentiful moisture below.

It is natural to be enthusiastic when an eagerly awaited consignment of plants arrives from the nurserymen, but do not open the container and scatter the contents around just to 'see what they look like.' Nurserymen pack plants away in their containers safe against any eventuality. Roots are wrapped in moss or some other moisture-retaining material and cased over with stout wrapping paper. Several of one variety are tied together in a package with a single label, and single items of one kind or variety are packed singly, each with a separate label. Together, the various packages are wedged tightly into the container and topped up with damp moss or wood wool.

Packed in this way they are insulated against the outer world and as safe as in the nursery plot. If they are delayed on the railway for a few weeks they will come to no harm. Also, if they arrive during a period of hard frosts they will not be harmed so long as the whole package is placed unopened in a cool shed or cellar – never in a heated building.

When they arrive in frost do not write straight off to the nurseryman and tell him he is a fool for sending the plants when the ground is as hard as a stone. He could not have lifted the plants if his own ground was hard when he sent them, and he cannot be expected to foretell the weather several days ahead. Put the package in a cool place and leave it there, still fastened securely, until you have milder weather. But even if they arrive in good planting weather do not leave them exposed to dry in the wind. Roots need moisture to keep them in good condition, and if exposed to the air for a day or two the plants will be checked, or may even die. A day or two's exposure to a stiff north-easter is enough to kill the choicest and perhaps all.

Opening packages in a hurry often makes you mix up varieties, for once the string holding the packages together has been cut it is extremely difficult to distinguish varieties apart, in spite of foliage distinction. Unpacking should be done systematically. The packages should be laid out close at hand – not on the planting site – in the order they appear on the plan. Each package should remain unopened until it is needed. Labels about a foot long – they are known as foot labels – should be prepared beforehand and extra labels should be placed nearby in case it is necessary to divide a parcel of plants in two. The name of kind and variety should be plainly written, thus – Delphinium, Lady Eleanor; and names will be more legible, and remain indelible longer, if written with a garden pencil on a surface smeared with white paint that is not quite dry. Garden pencils and labels can be obtained from seedsmen or shops selling horticultural goods. One package only should be opened at a time and its contents should be planted, according to plan, by starting at the top left-hand side of the plot in a position which has been previously marked out.

For planting, a good trowel should be used, holes being made with this to suit the root system of the plant. In each case roots should be planted to their full depth, the crown of the plant, with its dormant buds, being just below the surface. Some kinds, which retain a little foliage throughout the winter, should be planted with this just above the surface of the soil. Weak planting, which would allow a bird to pull out the plant, is bad, but brutally hard planting on heavy soils is worse. Each plant should be bedded in by the pressure of hand or foot firmly enough to withstand a pull by hand, but not hard enough to make the soil around it into a doughy mass which shuts out all the air. Generally, hand pressure suffices. Bear it in mind that the object is to make the plant comfortable, and not to plaster down the surface soil, and that therefore it is bad to tread on the surface of the unplanted part of the bed more than is necessary.

No planting rules govern the position of plants inside the marked patches, but grouping should be as informal as possible, the distances between the plants varying according to the subject. Small plants should be placed nine inches or a foot apart, and taller ones at distances according to height; delphiniums and hollyhocks need up to two and a half feet, and on good rich soil, where they are likely to develop well, can have more space given to them with advantage. To avoid losing them, labels should be put into position as the work proceeds, not left until it is finished. A good planter always tries to leave the ground trim and tidy as he plants – it saves a separate job – but if this cannot be done, the surface soil should be pricked up lightly with a small digging fork when the planting is finished, and loose soil at the sides should be spaded up so that the edges have a clean-cut appearance.

Planting perennials is a long-term affair which gives no immediate reward, and sometimes the gardener is disappointed at his first year's show. I well remember being called upon in a case of this kind. An enthusiastic amateur who could afford to do things properly had planted an immense border after very thorough preparation, and, with everything in his favour, there seemed to be no reason why he should not have a fine display for many seasons. About the middle of the second flowering season I was very surprised when he asked me to look at his border, as it had disappointed him greatly. I found a very scraggy looking lot of flowers in good ground which I knew had been well prepared. Greatly puzzled, after many questions I finally found out what he had done – he had lifted and replanted them after only one year's growth. When I expostulated, he told me: 'They made a poor show last season, so I thought there was something wrong, and dug them up and replanted them.' 'What, all of them?' I said. 'Yes,' he replied, 'I didn't mean to do them all, but when I had done the worst-looking ones I thought I had better go on – so I did the lot.'

Lifting and re-planting annually is the surest way to have a poor show of flowers in the summer. Perennials, even those under ideal conditions, flower sparsely the first season, while they establish themselves, but are magnificent in the second season and for several seasons afterwards if they are not disturbed. Plants, like humans, have their idiosyncrasies, and some perennials, like peonies and iris, like to remain in the same spot for a very long time. Indeed, peonies sometimes refuse to flower profusely until several seasons have passed, but when they flower they are so beautiful that they deserve a border to themselves, and neither they nor iris will give their best unless allowed to settle in peace.

It is often said that perennial borders need no more attention once they have been planted. Certainly they take little hard work, but some timely attention is necessary. After planting, and during the first growing season, little is needed beyond support and, occasionally, a light surface hoeing with a Dutch hoe. Once a fortnight is generally often enough for the hoeing, but if seedling weeds appear it should be done every ten days. A keen gardener will find Dutch hoeing quite a pleasurable job, and one which ensures that he penetrates into the inner part of the border, where he can see if any shoots need tying.

If support is needed let it be strong enough for the purpose but as unobtrusive as possible. Rows of white stakes, or, even worse, brilliant green ones, are unattractive and irritating in a garden. By all means paint your stakes or buy painted ones, but see that the colour is a neutral moss green. In some parts of the country unpeeled osier (willow) stakes can be obtained, and these – a neutral soft green in colour – are admirable for light support.

The wrong tying materials, too, can ruin the general effect of a border. Household string, packing cord, odds and ends of anything that will knot, are often used. Quite often these knots are left with long, unnecessary ends, which are almost as bad as large white stakes. Green twist, which is soft and not showy, is better, or ordinary fillis string – which is equally soft, much cheaper, and nearly invisible – is very good. Tie tightly enough for support but loosely enough to prevent constriction. Generally the tie should be loose enough to contain two shoots, although only one is enclosed.

When the border plants pass out of flower pause before any drastic cutting down is done. If the stem and foliage remain green, remove the dead flower heads only, allowing the remainder to die naturally before it is removed. Sudden drastic removal has a very weakening effect. A time will come when all old shoots need removal, and they should then be cut down as near as possible to the ground, which should then be lightly pricked with the fork, taking care not to damage or lift the plants in any way. If some well-decayed farmyard manure can be obtained, a three-inch layer (mulch) should be applied to the surface and allowed to remain all the winter. In the following spring the manure – which by this time will be advanced in decay – should be lightly dug into the spaces between the plants. Additional food may be given by sprinkling 4 oz bone meal and 2 oz hoof and horn meal on each square yard before digging.

Soon afterwards there will be a great transformation. Not having been disturbed during the previous winter the plants will grow fast and strong. But there will be too many shoots, so some must be removed. Most plants will give finer flowers and make a better show if they are allowed only five growths, but do not remove those that are not wanted all at once.

Remove them gradually until you have the right number left. For the first few weeks the border may look rather bare, but as the selected shoots extend and thicken you will see that there will be finer shoots than there were last season.

As time goes on many of the shoots – which have all the power of an unrestricted root system behind them – will branch out laterally. Phlox will develop very large heads with widely pipped flowers. Michaelmas daisies will branch until each shoot resembles a miniature fir tree. The original good soil preparation will now show its value and there is no reason why a border treated thus annually should not last for several years.

When the occasional season of drought arrives do not overlook the possibility that water may be needed. In short warm periods, drying out for a day or two will have no serious result, but when all the plants hang their heads dejectedly, day after day, the stems become woody, and afterwards, when rain arrives, are incapable of taking up a full supply of moisture. Apply water copiously before the harm is done, and try to saturate the soil to the full depth of cultivation. Driblets of water which moisten the surface only do a great deal of harm. If the soil on a border has become thoroughly dry, it is sometimes difficult to soak it evenly, and in such a case it should be given a second heavy saturation a few hours later. I need hardly add that a length of garden hose is a necessity, for watering with water cans is a dreary job, and takes up a lot of valuable time.

For those who want a good border, but find it impossible to proceed in the way I have suggested, there is another method – a very much cheaper way – that of growing perennials from seed. Although the choice is not so great, there are many kinds and varieties available. Raising perennials in this way is, I must admit, a gamble, but you may get many pleasant surprises out of it. You can expect hundreds of seedlings from a packet of seed, and when they flower not all of them will be good ones. But among them will be some which closely resemble named varieties and occasionally a real winner. Unfortunately, this method entails waiting, for not all seedling perennials flower in the season they are sown, and so a second season must elapse before the whole lot can be seen and selections made. Because of this, many people use the site intended for perennials as an annual border for a couple of years, while seedlings are raised in nursery beds in a less prominent place.

Sowing in April is advisable for most flowers, as this gives a long season of growth, but seeds of perennials can be sown at any time up to July or even August. They should be sown in drills just as annuals are sown, but when the seedlings are about an inch high they should *all* be pricked out into little nursery beds and spaced about six inches apart in each direction. It is important to prick off all seedlings, or, failing that, a fair sample of all, because sometimes the smaller ones, which are liable to be discarded, eventually develop into good plants. Each kind and variety should be carefully labelled.

Growth is usually very rapid and seedlings like delphiniums and lupins, which result from an April or May sowing, will flower in September. As they flower, good varieties should be marked by inserting a stake into the ground close beside them, and, if you like, they can be transferred to their permanent position, those which are not flowering being allowed to remain undisturbed until they flower in the following season, when further selections can be made.

As with annuals, labelling is very important, as, apart from the pleasure of knowing one's varieties, replanting, which eventually becomes necessary, is almost impossible if labels are missing, for the mixing of varieties cannot be prevented once a muddle has occurred. The labels chosen should be stout enough to stand an occasional kick or a blow from a hoe, and large enough to allow names to be written in a size legible from outside the border but not so large or heavy as to be offensive. Hoe the surface soil frequently and keep the border tidy. An untidy perennial border loses half its charm.

Thirty-six Good Perennials, excluding Delphiniums, Perennial Asters, Iris and Lupins

ACHILLEA eupatorium. Gold Plate. Large flat heads of yellow flowers; three and a half feet.

ACONITUM napellus. Spark's Variety. Dark indigo-blue; five feet.

ANCHUSA italica. Morning Glory. Bright blue; five to six feet.

ANTHEMIS tinctoria. Loddon. Orange-yellow, the best Anthemis; three to three and a half feet.

CAMPANULA persicifolia. Beechwood. Very large soft pale blue, a vigorous grower; three and a half feet.

COREOPSIS auriculata superba. Rich golden-yellow flowers, prominent crimson centre.

ECHINACEA purpurea. The King. Large flower of reddish-purple on long stiff spikes, a valuable acquisition.

ERIGERON. Merstham Glory. Rich deep blue, semi-double flowers; two feet.

GAILLARDIA. The Prince. Large flower, red and yellow; three feet.

GYPSOPHILA paniculata. Bristol Fairy. Very elegant form of the popular double Gypsophila; three feet.

HELENIUM autumnale, Chipperfield Orange. Orange-yellow; five feet.

HELENIUM. Moerheim Beauty. Large rich crimson; two and a half feet.

HELIANTHUS multiflorus. Loddon Gold. Glowing golden-yellow, double; six feet.

HELIANTHUS sparsifolius. Monarch. Bright deep yellow, large flowers; six feet.

HELIOPSIS. Gigantea. Rich yellow, large double flower; five feet.

HELIOPSIS. Patula. Chrome-yellow, frilled; four and a half feet.

KNIPHOFIA. Galpini. Orange; two feet.

KNIPHOFIA. Royal Standard. Yellow and red; three feet.

LYCHNIS viscaria splendens plena. Bright rosy-crimson, double; one foot.

LYTHRUM salicaria. The Beacon. Crimson.

MONARDA didyma. Cambridge Scarlet; three feet.

MONARDA. Croftway Pink. Clear pink; three and a half feet.

NEPETA. Mussini. Lavender-blue; one and a half feet.

PAPAVER. Mrs Perry. Terra-cotta orange; two feet.

PAPAVER. Salmon Glow. Large flower, soft salmon; two and a half feet.

PHLOX. Amethyst. Blue; three feet.

PHLOX. Brigadier. Bright orange-red; four feet.

PHLOX. Duchess of York. Soft salmon-pink; three and a half feet.

PHLOX. Spitfire. Salmon-orange; two and a half feet.

PYRETHRUM. Brenda. Bright cerise flowers of fine form borne on long stiff stems; two and a half feet.

PYRETHRUM. Kelway's Glorious. Glowing scarlet.

PYRETHRUM. Salmon Beauty. Good salmon-pink; two feet.

SCABIOSA. Clive Greaves. Violet-blue; two and a half feet.

SOLIDAGO. Lemore. A most striking dwarf Golden Rod. Broad, deep primrose flower heads; one and a half to two feet.

VERBASCUM. Gainsborough. Sulphur-yellow; three and a half feet.

VERONICA hybrida. Wendy. Bright deep blue, silvery-green foliage; one and a half feet.

Kinds of Perennials, most of which have many Varieties which may be raised from Seed

ACHILLEA, Double-flowered. The Pearl. Small double pure white globular flowers in loose sprays. Good for cutting. Height two feet.

ACHILLEA, Filipendula (A. Eupatorium). Golden Cloth. An improved form of this favourite old-fashioned border plant. Height three feet. Each stem with a large flat head of yellow flowers.

AQUILEGIA (Columbines). In variety.

ARABIS ALPINA. In variety.

CAMPANULA. In many species and varieties.

CENTAUREA, Montana. A Perennial Cornflower with large blue flowers.

CHRYSANTHEMUM, Leucanthemum. In variety.

COREOPSIS, Grandiflora. Produces large bold golden-yellow flowers during the whole of the summer months.

DELPHINIUM. In variety.

ECHINOPS RITRO (Blue Globe Thistle). Spherical heads of blue flowers on long stems.

ERIGERON. In variety.

GAILLARDIA. In variety.

GAURA LINDHEIMERI. Long graceful sprays of white flowers.

GEUM. In variety.

INCARVILLEA DELAVAYI. Large rich rose Bignonia-like flowers with deep yellow throats, produced in large trusses.

LINUM. In variety.

LUPINUS. In variety.

LYCHNIS. In variety.

MECONOPSIS. In variety.

MICHAELMAS DAISY. In variety.

NEPETA, Mussini. A form of this favourite edging plant, which comes true from seed. The attractive foliage surmounted by pale mauve flowers makes a pretty and lasting effect.

PAPAVER, Orientale. In variety.

POTENTILLA. In variety.

PYRETHRUM. In variety.

RUDBECKIA. In variety.

Coming between perennials and annuals, which will be dealt with in the next chapter, is a group known as biennials. There are not many in this group compared with perennials or annuals, but the few comprise some well-loved plants which most people like to have around them. These biennials are sown in early summer of one season and flower at much the same time in the following season. Some biennials are a little difficult to fit into general garden planning as they flower too late in the season to permit the site to be used for another crop during the same season, and when planting out in autumn this must always be remembered.

Perhaps one of the most important is the wallflower, so long grown in English gardens. This plant greatly dislikes transplanting; therefore, if a small site is found to suit it, seeds should be sown direct on the flowering site during July or early August. If, however, transplanting is necessary, seeds should be sown in a nursery bed out of doors in June. The wallflower is unhappy on acid soil; any soil acidity should therefore be corrected by using a little hydrated lime before sowing or planting. If possible, it should never be sown or planted after any member of the cabbage family because of its liability to contract club foot and because the previous crop has partially exhausted the kind of plant food needed by the wallflower.

It is usual to sow in drills, and if the seedlings are to remain on the site they should be only nine inches apart. When the seedlings are large enough, thin out gradually and leave the selected ones standing about six inches apart in the drills. If they are for planting on another site the seedlings should be pricked out about four inches apart in drills, which for the sake of cleanliness should be one foot apart. By hoeing frequently these nursery beds should be maintained free from weeds until a moist period in September occurs. But if September is warm and dry, it is advisable to wait until October, as wallflowers have much foliage, a poor root system, flag badly if transplanted in hot weather, and sometimes never wholly recover. Wallflowers are inclined to show many hardened woody branches after transplanting and to hide this partially and provide a better show should be planted in their permanent beds six inches apart in each direction. Sometimes stripiness in the blooms, said to be a virus disease, appears after a hard winter, but, although slightly disfigured, wallflowers retain their charming simplicity even when striped. The following are good varieties:

GIANT BLOOD RED	Deep red
GIANT ORANGE BEDDER	Orange and apricot
GIANT VULCAN	Deep maroon crimson
GIANT FIRE KING	Brilliant orange-scarlet
GIANT RUBY	Ruby red
GIANT YELLOW	Rich yellow

In addition to the above there are also early flowering varieties which include nearly all the principal colours. These are excellent for flowering on the site on which they are sown. Sometimes they start to flower in autumn and continue to do so all the winter if it should be mild. In many other districts they start to flower in February. A good selection is as follows:

EARLY FLOWERING VARIETIES

PHOENIX	Chestnut
YELLOW PHOENIX	Deep yellow
PRIMROSE PHOENIX	Primrose yellow
ORANGE	Early flowering counterpart of Orange Bedder
YELLOW, stained orange	The early flowering form of the old fashioned Wallflower

There is also a good double form usually sold as mixed, which comprises many beautiful colours as well as those accepted as wallflower colours, and an annual form which is interesting and uncommon.

Another old fashioned plant which never loses its charm is the Sweet William. It is invaluable for making a show in early summer and its modern colours are now quite startling. If sown at the end of May or early June and pricked out into nursery beds similarly to wallflowers it can be allotted its first quarters in early October. The following are very good.

SUPERB MIXED	
PINK BEAUTY	Salmon pink
SCARLET	Intense Grenadier scarlet
GIANT WHITE	
GIANT AURICULA-EYED	Bright shades
RICH CRIMSON	Deep crimson

Myosotis (Forget-me-not) should not be overlooked, for some modern varieties, when massed, give a sea of unforgettable bright blue. As an undercarpet for Darwin or May-flowering tulips it is perfect and it is equally effective when used for bedding alone. Although there is always a temptation to sow seeds of Myosotis when sowing other biennials in May or June, it is a mistake to do so as the fine large clumps thus produced become mop heads full of moisture in winter and rot in consequence. The smaller heads, resulting from a late July sowing, do not easily trap moisture, and therefore do not decay in winter. The following are recommended:

ROYAL BLUE	Vivid bright blue
ROYAL BLUE, Dwarf Strain	A dwarf form of royal blue
PERFECTION	A bright blue variety with multi-petalled flowers
LAVENDER GEM	A very fine lavender
ALPESTRIS VICTORIA	Dwarf azure blue
DWARF BLUE	A miniature blue variety about four inches in height

Another old-fashioned plant much improved of recent years is the Canterbury bell. Its June flowers sometimes overlap into July. Seed should be sown in May and the seedlings pricked out into nursery beds preparatory to being bedded out in early October. There are now some very good strains in blue, pink, and white in the well-known cup and saucer varieties. Those I give below are very good:

CUP AND SAUCER	Pink
CUP AND SAUCER	Pure white
CUP AND SAUCER	Blue
CUP AND SAUCER	Mauve

A simple plant from the woodland which will also do well in the open is the Digitalis (foxglove). In addition to the woodland form (known by most people) whose pink bells hang gracefully on one side of the tall spikes, there are now others which have flowers more beautiful, clothing all sides of the spike. In batches between shrubs they are wonderfully effective and for planting in shade where nothing else will flourish they are unsurpassed. Those I give below are worth a place in anybody's garden.

EXCELSIOR HYBRIDS	A delightful mixture of innumerable shades of pink, rose, mauve, purple, white, and cream on bloom balanced stems
EXCELSIOR WHITE	A remarkable variety with completely flower-clothed stems.
GIANT PRIMROSE	
GIANT APRICOT	
GIANT SPOTTED	

Polyanthus, which are true perennials, succeed best when treated as biennials, for they are at their best in the first flowering season. The seed should be sown thinly in boxes in late September or early October and wintered in the same boxes in cold frames. When spring arrives they should be pricked off six inches apart in drills one foot apart and planted in the flowering quarters in September or early October. They delight in rich, well-worked soil abounding in humus, and appreciate partial shade. The selection I give below is excellent:

SUPERB MIXED	Almost every imaginable colour except blue
GIANT WHITE	Creamy white
GIANT YELLOW	Rich yellow
BRILLIANCE	Vivid red and orange shades
CRIMSON KING	Maroon crimson
BLUE FLOWERED	Rich shade of blue

Primroses, in many shades, may also be grown in the same way.

Hollyhocks, also true perennials, are at their best if grown as biennials. Although they revel in good conditions nevertheless they are good drought resisters and continue to flower for many weeks.

Double daisies are likewise good when treated as biennials and others are the perennial arabis and the perennial candytuft, Iberis. All three should be sown in May or June, pricked out as advised, and placed in their permanent quarters in October.

· 8 ·

Delphiniums

THE delphinium of the present day is a magnificent plant. Its dignity, combined with a restful subtlety of colour, gives it a distinction possessed by no other plant. Its blue and purple, or perhaps mauve, spires tower above all other flowers in the border except the hollyhock, and although its colours blend with those of other perennials its distinctiveness makes a separate border imperative – if one can be found.

It has a long history. The name in Greek meant 'Little Dolphin', because the leaf and bud were thought to resemble the dolphin. Nearly two thousand years ago people thought its seeds had medicinal properties, its foliage stupefied scorpions, and the seed when cooked had insecticidal properties.

A plant something like the modern one was known about 1600, but the genealogy of the modern delphinium was almost unknown. Delphinium elatum was one of its parents, and two or three generations ago patient plant breeders began to convert this so far humble flower into the magnificent plant we know to-day.

The modern delphinium is happy on nearly all soils. It is said to have a preference for lime, but there is little authentic evidence of this, and there are many cases in which it is known to flourish on peat and sand as well as limestone and chalk. Like many other good border plants, although it will thrive in the worst conditions and make a brave show each season, it is seen at its best only when grown on deeply worked soil, heavily loaded with humus. It is particularly happy in a deep retentive loam.

As the modern delphinium is a hybrid, it does not breed true from seed, but has to be propagated vegetatively if good named varieties are required. Sometimes it is grown by division, but the best method is to propagate by cuttings taken early in the spring months.

Active growth starts early in spring, and a few warm days with a little sunshine in February are enough to induce fat shoots to emerge – often through melting snow. These should be taken with a heel of old wood attached, because the stems of delphiniums are tubular and roots are formed on the thin walls of cut tubes with great difficulty, if at all – hence the necessity for taking cuttings with a woody sealed-up heel. To cut these out cleanly it is necessary to bare the crown of the plant of any winter protection, and of the soil below it, so that the cutting can be made without undue injury. Insert the cuttings in small pots or boxes placed in a cold frame or a cool greenhouse, shaded from direct sunshine.

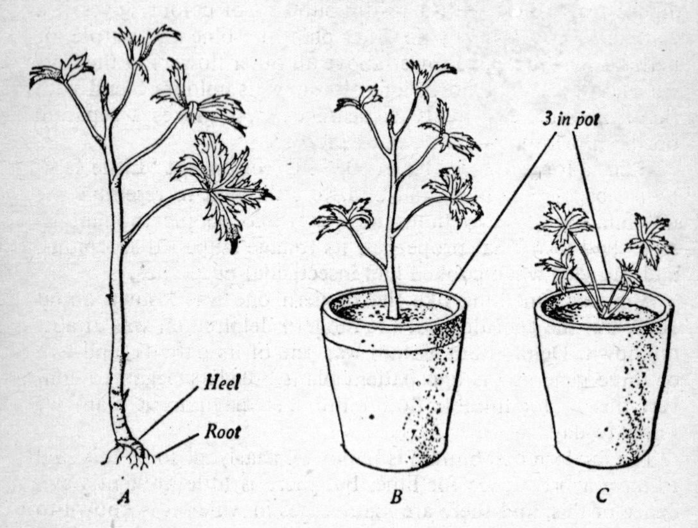

20. Delphiniums: (A) Good cutting; (B) Established cutting; (C) Seedling in pot.

Delphinium cuttings do not root quickly and it is generally six weeks or two months before they are rooted enough to handle again. More details of their propagation will be found in Chapter 26. When growth begins again after about two months, the cuttings should be exposed as much as possible to the air, because the delphinium is a hardy plant which should not be coddled. When the roots are two or three inches long, they should be potted separately, into pots four to five inches in diameter, and allowed to grow before being planted out in the open in early summer.

The soil for delphiniums must be thoroughly prepared and

deep cultivation is vitally important. It is true that delphiniums will grow and bloom well in almost any border, but magnificent spikes cannot be produced unless the soil is worked deeply and treated liberally. Incorporate quantities of farmyard manure or compost, and reinforce this with nitrogenous food which will be yielded up slowly throughout the whole of the growing season. If the nature of the soil will allow it, cultivation three spits deep is not too much for delphiniums, and each spit should have a liberal quantity of farmyard manure or compost. However, if the soil is shallow it is useless to dig too deeply; but take care to treat the upper levels as liberally as possible. At any rate the sub-soil should not be brought to the surface. In any system of trenching the soil must be replaced in the trenches in the same relative, vertical position. (See Chapter 1.) Also, as the work proceeds, 2 lb of bones, ground down to half-inch size, should be incorporated in each cubic yard, and when trenching is finished 8 oz of coarsely ground hoof and horn meal per superficial square yard should be well worked into the upper layer. This work should be done, if possible, during the winter or early spring months, although planting will not be possible until early summer.

As soon as the tops of flower spikes appear in their pots they should be carefully nipped, because, at this stage, the energies of the plants should be devoted to the building up of healthy crowns and a framework of roots. This careful nipping out must not be confused with cutting to the ground, as it is intended simply to divert the energy of the plant into other directions. The more healthy leaves that can be retained the better the root system will be, and care should therefore be taken to remove only the flower spikes and not the stems carrying leaves, which have manufacturing power.

It sometimes happens that a border cannot be made ready to receive the rooted cuttings as soon as they are fit to plant in summer. In such a case they should be planted in nursery beds until the autumn – a practice of nurserymen. However, it is much better to plant direct into the final position, as this avoids a check in growth, and because delphiniums are at their best during the second season after planting – to plant in nursery beds is to lose one season's growth.

Now about planting out. Delphiniums can exist in almost any conditions, but they should, if possible, be given plenty of room – two feet from plant to plant is not too much, and in rich soil in a good district three feet is better. At this distance, they can be arranged in clumps of three in a triangle or planted separately, but the system adopted should be well thought out beforehand and a planting plan prepared.

Luckily delphiniums do not all flower at the same time, and in planting care should be taken that those which flower together are not massed in any part of the border, or there will be bare patches at some time during the season. Take care, too, not to plant them in pent-house formation. The more the border is broken up with tall and short flowers the more pleasing it will be.

Planting must be done very thoroughly and firmly. The trowel is the best tool to use for this when plants from pots are handled, but plants in nursery beds which have established themselves by three or four months of growth will need lifting with a fork or spade and planting with similar tools. Loose planting is always bad, but hard planting can, in some cases, be worse. Planting should always be firm enough for good contact between roots and soil; it should prevent so much air from entering the soil as to cause excessive dryness and perhaps loss, and any curious bird from tugging out the plants. Hand pressure is generally enough, but sometimes, on light soil, foot pressure is needed. If planting out is done in early summer – say in the first half of June – it may be necessary to water thoroughly immediately after planting, but otherwise, if the soil has been well prepared, watering is rarely necessary. If it should be, water must be applied copiously or not at all – driblets do much harm.

In the early part of the growing season there is little work to do in the permanent border, though it should be hoed frequently – twice a week if possible. This has the advantage of creating a loose blanket of soil which effectively prevents the evaporation of moisture and precludes the possibility of weeds – a matter of great importance.

Labelling should be thorough. One of the attractions of a special border of delphiniums is identifying varieties, and visitors generally like to see the names for themselves. Everything possible should be done to prevent unsightly labels from catching the eye. Metal labels can be supplied by nurserymen or seedsmen which are unobtrusive, effective, and remain in good condition for many years. Wooden labels fifteen inches in length, two inches wide and about half an inch thick are quite effective, but if painted white they are obtrusive. This can be avoided by painting them black with a panel of white. Names can be made quite legible and will last much longer if written on a film of freshly-applied paint while it is still wet.

In the first year, delphiniums grown from cuttings cannot develop summer spikes as the tops are removed, but in late summer some secondary spikes appear. These should be removed also by nipping out their tops as soon as they are visible, as the plant at this stage should build for the future. When autumn comes, if there are any flowers on the secondary spikes they should be carefully removed, but the stems should not be cut down while the leaves remain green. Finally, when there is no greenness left, the stems should be cut close to the ground.

At the approach of winter it is a good plan to prick up the surface soil with a fork and apply a mulch of about three inches of well-decayed farmyard manure or compost.

The delphinium likes a wet soil, and even if water-logged it generally survives. However, wet soils often mean slugs, and slugs are extremely fond of delphinium shoots; in fact, in some heavy clay soil districts delphinium shoots are devoured as fast as they appear. However, since the discovery that Metaldehyde (Meta) is a very fine slug killer, no one need fear slugs, although, as under some conditions in the dead of winter it is hardly possible to apply Meta, it is wise to remove the soil from the tops of the crowns and to cover them with little conical heaps of sharp coal cinders, through which slugs pass with great difficulty. In spring these cinders should be removed and a dressing of slug destroyer given when the soil has been put back. A covering of ashes is also excellent protection against frost, which sometimes checks delphiniums in cold districts.

During the second season of growth in an established border, well-grown delphiniums will send up abundant shoots. Some may be required for propagating purposes and surplus shoots can be used to great advantage in this way, but if they are not, some kind of thinning is necessary if the plants are to be seen at their best. It is true that, left alone, sometimes two or three dozen spikes develop, and these, when in flower together, are unequalled for solid colour by any other border plant, but if you want good individual blooms you should thin the shoots to five at the most, and, if spikes are required for exhibition, three are ample. Some enthusiastic exhibitors thin their spikes to one, with the idea of getting one central giant spike, but sometimes this becomes malformed. One spike chosen from two or three is equal in size to one grown alone, and better in quality; therefore, two at least should be allowed to remain.

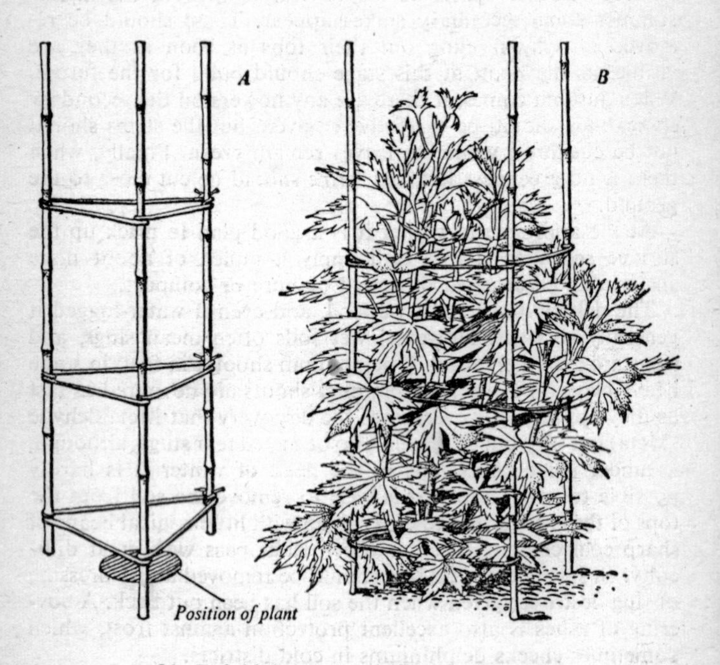

21. Delphiniums: (A) Staking; (B) Staked.

If you grow delphiniums to enjoy them while they are growing in the border, five spikes is perhaps the best number to leave.

A plant which grows so easily and has varieties which, when well grown, often reaches six feet, and sometimes nearly eight feet, offers much wind resistance, and spikes are easily blown out at the collar. Because of this, there must be some efficient system of staking. There are all kinds of methods employed.

Stakes must be firm enough to give adequate support to the stems, which are tubular, brittle, and fairly easily broken, but flexible enough to allow the plants to sway in the wind. If delphiniums are staked too rigidly the blooms may be snapped off by the wind. To get over this any stake used must be long enough to support the flowering part of the spike. Thin, tapering bamboo canes are excellent and with care they can be made almost invisible. Another good method is to thrust three or four tapering bamboo canes – painted moss green – into the ground around the spikes to contain the spikes inside with soft tying material. Sometimes thin stakes of steel or iron are used.

Many growers like to feed their plants during the summer, especially if they hope to exhibit them, but any feeding should be undertaken early enough for it to be absorbed for use during the season. Manures applied in large quantities during the last two or three weeks of growth, which are sometimes not available for the use of the plants until after the spike has ceased flowering, are not much good. Feeding should start early in May and be carried on until mid-June, and the application every fortnight of four oz of finely-ground hoof and horn meal per square yard is excellent. Quick-acting nitrogenous manures such as nitrate of soda, nitro chalk, or sulphate of ammonia should be avoided.

Delphiniums should never be allowed to become dry in the summer. It is often supposed that losses during the winter are due to excessive wet or frost, but generally, if there is no heavy rain in July and early August, the plants suffer without anyone noticing unless water is given copiously; the weeks following the first flowering period are usually the times they are neglected. In some hot countries delphiniums cannot be grown because of this summer difficulty.

When cutting delphinium spikes for show, remember that they are tubular and, therefore, liable to take up air instead of water. If the spikes remain off the plant, out of water, for more than a few minutes it is difficult to prevent rapid transpiration afterwards because of the air in the stems. In the few minutes after cutting, therefore, they should be placed in deep receptacles of water before they can absorb too much air.

If this is impossible, and after cutting the lower part of the stems contains enough air to prevent water from entering, the spikes should be held in deep water and part of the stem should be cut under water, so that air cannot enter the newly-cut part of the stem. If, after they have been cut and placed in water, spikes are put in a cool place for several hours, there is no reason why they should not be packed dry in suitable boxes, surrounded with greaseproof paper and with the lid tightly fastened to exclude air. Under such conditions even the most succulent spikes can be taken long distances uninjured. Some people prefer to prepare them in sheaves tied upright and placed in deep receptacles of water, but when packed in this way they are very difficult to transport.

The delphinium is not subject to many diseases, but sometimes mildew appears. This is not a crippling disease in the case of the delphinium, but is very unsightly. In districts where it is liable to appear the plants should be sprayed early in the growing season with a good colloidal copper fungicide, obtainable from any good seedsman, nurseryman, or sundriesman. This spraying should be repeated at intervals of ten days throughout the season.

Perhaps it is unfortunate that delphiniums flower early in summer, and people sometimes lament that during part of July and early August there are few blooms. But delphiniums send up a second crop of flower spikes in August and September which sometimes make a brave show. At any rate, seeds of annuals can be sown in spring, as long as enough room is left to allow you to stake the delphiniums later on. It is also possible – as will be seen in the next chapter in the case of lupins – to plant Michaelmas daisies with them for autumn display, and to use many brilliant varieties of perennials in the middle months of summer. These are only ideas; there are many schemes which will occur to the enthusiastic gardener after a year or two's experience; but with any scheme which involves intersowing or interplanting remember that delphiniums need more room than most other flowers.

Many people cannot give delphiniums the thorough cultivation I have advocated, but they are worth a place in the border under almost any conditions, and no one should do without them because he has not plenty of room. Good modern varieties are very numerous, and out of them I have selected twenty-four first-class varieties which are mentioned on next page.

Some of them are expensive, and if the price is too high send the list to your nurseryman and ask him to supply some slightly older varieties of a similar shade which will not be quite so expensive.

Twenty-four Good Varieties of Delphiniums

VARIETY	*Type*	*Eye*	*Flowering Season*	*Height*
Mauve:				
BLACKMORE'S GLORIOUS	Semi-double	Blue and Mauve	Mid	Medium
TESSA	Semi-double	White	Mid	Medium
Deep Mauve:				
W. R. CHAPLIN	Semi-double	Black	Mid	Medium
Violet-Purple:				
BRUTUS	Semi-double	Brown	Mid	Medium
SIR NEVILLE PEARSON	Semi-double	Black	Mid	Medium
Purple:				
BEAU NASH	Semi-double	Brown	Mid	Tall
Dark Blue:				
DUCHESS OF PORTLAND	Semi-double	White	Mid	Medium
LORNA	Semi-double	Brown	Late	Medium
Mid Blue:				
AGNES BROOKS	Semi-double	White	Mid	Medium
BLUE LAGOON	Semi-double	Brown	Mid	Medium
CHAS. F. LANGDON	Semi-double	Brown	Mid	Medium
GWLADYS SHARPE	Semi-double	Brown	Mid	Medium
MRS FRANK BISHOP	Semi-double	Black	Mid	Medium
WATKIN SAMUEL	Semi-double	Black	Mid	Medium
Pale Blue:				
CRYSTAL	Semi-double	White	Mid	Tall
ETONIAN	Semi-double	Black	Mid	Dwarf
Pale Blue and Pale Mauve:				
BRIDESMAID	Semi-double	White and Mauve	Mid	Tall
C. H. MIDDLETON	Semi-double	Brown	Mid	Medium
JENNIFER LANGDON	Semi-double	Black	Early	Medium
LADY ELEANOR	Semi-double	White and Mauve	Mid	Tall
Blue and Mauve:				
ALICE ARTINDALE	Double	—	Mid	Medium
LORNA DOONE	Semi-double	Brown	Mid	Medium

VARIETY	*Type*	*Eye*	*Flowering Season*	*Height*
Mauve and Pale Blue:				
CAMBRIA	Semi-double	Black	Late	Medium
Dark Blue and Mauve:				
PYRAMUS	Semi-double	White	Mid	Medium

All the Delphiniums I have mentioned so far in this chapter are hybrid varieties which descended from Delphinium elatum – generally called Elatum varieties – but there are other interesting ones derived from Delphinium belladonna. These are much dwarfer, lighter, branch freely, and are splendid for home decoration. Except that they rarely need any restriction of shoots their culture is in every way similar to that of their more hefty brethren. The colours blue and mauve dominate, but this section now includes a pink variety, 'Pink Sensation', said to be a hybrid between Delphinium belladonna and Delphinium nudicaule – a slightly tuberous half-hardy species. The shade of pink is very taking but quite distinct from the pink of other flowers, making it rather difficult to blend. However, this pink-flowered Delphinium is so good that it is well worthy of a sheltered corner of its own.

I give below a list of Belladonna varieties which includes 'Pink Sensation'.

Six Belladonna Varieties

VARIETY	*Type*	*Eye*	*Flowering Season*	*Height*
Mid-Blue:				
ORION	Single	White	Mid	Short
Dark Blue and Mauve:				
ISIS	Single	Purplish	Mid	Short
WENDY	Single	White and Blue	Mid	Short
Dark Blue:				
BLUE DRAGONFLY	Single	Mauve	Mid	Short
LAMARTINE	Single	White	Mid	Short
Pink :				
PINK SENSATION	Single	White and Pink	Mid	Short

· 9 ·

Lupins

THE modern lupin is delightful. It has a brilliant opulence and at the same time a dignity which few plants possess, and it has many varieties which are well worth planting together in a border of their own.

The lupin as we know it has only recently been developed. In the last two generations there have been great advances in horticulture, and in plant breeding more has been accomplished in a few years than in the previous three centuries. The evolution of the present-day lupin is one of the greatest achievements.

It is worth saying something about the history of the lupin. From time to time during the last two or three centuries many species were brought to this country from distant parts of the world. Many were of little value, but a few were worth cultivating, and of them Lupinus polyphyllus from Colombia proved the most useful. Only a few years before the First World War this was an undistinguished perennial, and the flowers of its few varieties, mainly poor blues and pinks, although showy, had little lasting power, the separate spikes being thin and weedy.

There have been many breeding experiments made with the lupin, but there are few records of its parentage. It is a leguminous plant with pea-like flowers on a long spike. For many years its spikes were exceedingly thin and the flowers were narrow in keel, wings, and standards, without the substance to give them lasting qualities.

Before the First World War there were several plant breeders in this country interested in lupins, and some new varieties were bred and distributed, but no noteworthy improvement occurred. Shortly after the armistice of 1918, when horticulture settled down again, lupin-raising took on new life, and the first so-called crimson appeared – Downers Delight. It could not be called crimson by any stretch of the imagination, but horticulturalists knew what was meant: at least it was a good red which marked a great advance in lupin raising. In addition, the flowers were larger and borne on strong spikes with much heavier bloom.

Before this the first good yellow, called 'Sunshine,' had appeared. This was said to be a cross between Lupinus polyphyllus and Lupinus arboreus, but whether it really was only the raisers knew. This was a good step forward, and from this time there were many introductions of good lupins, each of which, however, was only slightly better than the one before it; there was little fundamental difference.

In the north country a worker named George Russell made lupin breeding his hobby. He had a small garden and allotment in which he grew only lupins. He had little scientific knowledge, and relied mainly on acute observation and perhaps a little luck. Fortunately for him and the gardening world Lupinus polyphyllus crosses readily with other Lupinus species, and Russell procured a wide range of species, cultivated them in his garden and proceeded to cross them, if not indiscriminately at least very haphazardly.

He did so for many years. Most people laughed at him, and the results were meagre until one day he announced that he had bred a new race. Out of all the experiments, varieties had appeared with broad spikes, many flowers on each spike, and each flower a particularly fine one. Instead of the narrow pointed keel and meagre standards, lupins now had generous fat keels, large wings, and upstanding standards with a breadth which made them very much more striking than any lupins previously known. Yet few people were impressed. Several plant distributors were asked to see the new lupins, but most of them, though faintly interested, thought them of little value. But old George Russell persisted, and finally they were taken up by a well-known firm and distributed to every temperate part of the world where lupins could be grown. These, and the varieties which followed soon, ousted all the older varieties and gave promise of many striking varieties to come.

It is already a great plant with many good varieties. Almost every colour is well represented, including blue and yellow; only true scarlets and crimsons are missing, although there are many shades of pink and red. There are almost enough shades of all the represented colours to complete a colour chart, and in addition to self and partial self colours, some charming bicolours, in combinations not seen in any other plant. The self colours range from white to the blackest purple and from creamy yellow through every orange, flame and red shade – few species can show so many shades.

Lupins, once well planted, almost look after themselves. They will grow in comparatively poor soil, although – like some other species – they are at their best when grown in deep soil heavily loaded with humus, and they are at home in almost every type of soil, except where there is too much lime. They flourish in acid soils, but have a short life in alkaline soils. It is true that in soil that is only slightly alkaline they will flower well for one season, and sometimes attempt to do so during the next, but afterwards a gradual chlorosis attacks them, the foliage becomes pallid, and the plants die. Those who live on limestone or chalk or any alkaline soil cannot, therefore, grow lupins, except perhaps in their annual forms, which, though beautiful, are different from the perennials.

Lupins, which flower so generously, deserve generous treatment. Take the advice, therefore, that I have given so many times in this book – dig deeply, dig well, and incorporate as much farmyard manure or compost as possible. It would be difficult to prepare the soil too well.

Lupins are hardy in all but the most northerly or exposed parts of the British Isles, and like many other plants they are best established in the border in the autumn months, if possible. Stock should be obtained from a nurseryman. If enough can be procured to complete a bed or border in the first season, so much the better, but if not, get a few of the finest varieties at first and work up a stock afterwards.

They are propagated by division and root cuttings, but as this will be dealt with in Chapter 26 I will not deal with it now. Good plants should be sited generously apart in the borders, so that they will have space to show their beauty. On good soil, well prepared, three feet in each direction is not too much; two feet apart is quite a good distance.

The roots of lupins are fat, thong-like, and fleshy. Young plants should be planted with a trowel in much the same way as delphiniums, except that deeper and larger holes are needed to accommodate roots which are liable to snap if they are crushed into holes too small for them. Plant them firmly. No protection is necessary during the winter months, and in spring, if there are more than five shoots on a plant remove all weakly and unwanted ones to allow the others scope for branching development.

Some staking is necessary. Most lupins grow to a height of three to four feet, and some grow a little taller. They do not require such tall stakes as delphiniums, but they do need something to steady them from swaying too much in the wind, and to prevent them from being wrenched out at the base. Four light stakes of osier or hazel per plant, with a band of soft tying string around, will hold them securely enough, and there is rarely any need to stake each spike separately, although this can be done effectively and unobtrusively.

In the south, lupins flower early in June, and in the midlands and the north a little later. Their one failing – if it can be called a failing – is that they leave the border bare of bloom during the height of summer. However, much can be done to prevent this. Well-grown lupins make very large shoots which give not only large central spikes of bloom, but side growths with spikes

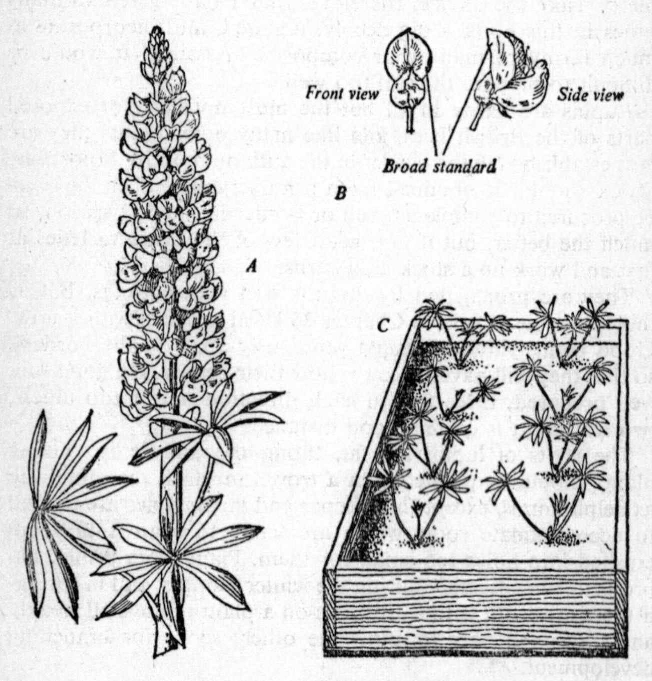

22. Lupins: (A) Modern lupin showing broad standards; (B) Detail of flower; (C) Seedling in box.

nearly as large. If the central spikes are cut away after their flowers have faded, high enough to leave all the side growths to develop, flowers can be expected for another two or three weeks and sometimes longer. When these side growths fade, the shoots bearing them should not be ruthlessly cut to the ground. Only the parts capable of bearing seed should be removed, thus allowing the plants to retain as much foliage as possible to balance the roots below and so maintain growth throughout the season. In August secondary flower spikes are thrown up from the crowns, and sometimes, at the end of August or early September, the lupin border is nearly as good in appearance as it was in early summer, though the flower spikes, of course, are slightly smaller.

Nevertheless, it is true that in a border with nothing but lupins in it a time comes in the summer when there are no flowers; but this can be overcome by planting some other flowers in the border. I have seen lupin borders gay with the perennial Phlox decussata, a family whose flowers give more flaming colours than those of any other border plant except the annual sweet pea. These can be planted easily between the lupins, especially if the lupins are sited rather widely apart – four to five feet instead of three feet or less. Perennial aster can also be planted and, taking up little room at midsummer, gradually extends as the phlox passes out of flower, and as the second crop of lupins dies away. Another good plan is to sow seeds of annuals between the lupins.

Lupins are at their best when planted in late autumn – an arrangement which allows the surface of the border to be left in a comparatively rough state in winter. If annuals are to be sown during April this weathered surface should be well worked down with a fork, drills drawn between the lupins, as advised in Chapter 6, and the seed sown in irregular patches in the ordinary way, except that small sites here and there occupied by the lupins must be missed. While the seeds are being sown the lupin shoots can almost be ignored, because at this stage they take up little room, and if the annuals encroach upon them later on, it is easy to thin them out enough to prevent the lupins from suffering. By using annuals which are not too tall, and in good colour combination with the lupins, it is possible to have a brilliant border for most of the summer. But many gardeners feel that lupins are entitled to a border of their own although they cannot fill it with flowers during the whole season.

Lupins which are happy in their soil and surroundings grow profusely and because of this, even in well-prepared soil, are liable to exhaust themselves quickly. It is necessary, therefore, to keep them well fed and well nourished. I have already stressed the necessity for allowing stems and foliage to remain in the ground as long as possible. Sooner or later these must be removed, but it should not be before they have lost all greenness. Then each plant should be cut down close to the ground, and the surface soil pricked up thoroughly with a fork and mulched with a three-inch dressing of well-decayed farmyard manure or compost – preferably manure. Applied in late autumn this will be much more decayed by early spring, when it can easily be forked into the soil after an application of 8 oz hoof and horn meal and 8 oz superphosphate per square yard. This should reinforce the food content for a considerable time and help the lupins to form stout upright and rigid spikes.

In cases where the soil is excessively light and easily dried out, it is wise to apply a mulch, just before the flowering period, of well-decayed farmyard or stable manure, or one of no value as manure but which will conserve moisture – such as chaff, dried grass mowings, litter from the stable, and the like. Many people dislike these mulches because of the difficulty of weeding effectively afterwards. I agree that they make weeding hard, but on some types of very light soil there is no other way to prevent moisture from evaporating. On medium and heavy soils, especially if they have been deeply dug and heavily manured during the winter, it is important to use the hoe frequently – twice a week if possible – and so create a blanket of dust to prevent moisture from escaping and thus being lost to the roots. For these soils the dust mulch is far better than any other.

Lupins need not be confined to the border. Many people with small gardens cannot make special borders and have little room for lupins in the perennial border; these can easily grow lupins in tubs or in boxes placed round the house. I have seen very effective use made of hollow sections of tree trunks filled with soil, and placed on path or terrace, with lupins planted in them. If lupins are grown in this way the soil must be liberally compounded. The base should be good loam from the meadow or good top spit garden soil mixed with half its bulk of farmyard manure or compost, reinforced with 8 oz hoof and horn meal per barrow-load of soil. It should be placed firmly in the receptacles and clumps of lupins planted during

23. Lupins – the result.

In the winter months no water is required, but in
drying out again takes place, water must be given
...ously and later, when roots begin to ramify, it may be necessary to water daily, and in hot weather twice a day or more.

Those who like lupins in the house can easily grow them in pots not less than nine inches in diameter. For this, clumps should be procured or lifted from the border and potted in soil similar to that used for tubs and boxes. If they are placed in a cold frame for the winter these may be very gently forced when spring comes – the extra heat gathered by the glass in a freely ventilated frame being enough. When they become too tall for the cold frame they can be taken from it to sunny sheltered positions and allowed to develop until the first flowers appear, when, after being staked to keep the spikes upright, the plants in their pots can be taken into the house, or placed in porch or veranda. Grown in this way lupins last for several weeks, provided they are not allowed to suffer drought and the rooms are not too hot.

Lupins are very effective when cut but have to be treated carefully from the moment they are taken from the parent plant. They should always be placed upright in water, and never laid on their sides after being cut or allowed to lean at an acute angle before being put in a bowl. This is because the tops of the spikes become upright at whatever angle they are placed, so that, unless great care is taken, by the time they are finally handled the spikes have assumed such grotesque shapes that they are almost unusable. When cutting, also, it is wise to place the flowers upright in water immediately, because the stems are tubular and liable to absorb air, which leads to rapid transpiration, flagging, and loss. Therefore, whether you are cutting them for the house or the flower show, the spikes must be perpendicular the whole time and special measures must be taken to ensure this, even if the containing receptacle has to be packed tight for transit – a matter which has given many nurserymen trouble in the past.

There is another species, Lupinus arboreus or the tree lupin, which, so far, has not been developed extensively and which has admirable qualities for growing in wild spots or in the border if the soil is poor sand or gravel. It can easily be established out of doors in the south of England, but is of doubtful hardiness in some parts of the north midlands and in the north. Grown in informal groups in the south it is magnificent.

A few years ago there were many such colonies around Canford Cliffs, where white and yellow lupins grew for miles in huge masses. Probably these came originally from a nearby garden, but their naturalization in Dorset shows the great possibilities of this species for wild gardens or poor soil where little else could grow. At Canford they were growing in sea sand dunes of apparently endless depth, and I have never seen finer lupins. There are only two varieties, yellow and white, which are equally good in every way.

Although Lupinus arboreus is a shrubby plant it can be grown from seed sown out of doors in April in much the same way as perennials are raised from seed, or the seeds may be sown under glass in February and brought on a little faster. In any case seedlings should be planted in their permanent quarters before they become too large, and as they spread extensively they should be stationed four to five feet or more apart – the gaps between being easily bridged in two or three seasons.

As I have said, there are many widely distributed species of lupins which are annuals. Some of these have been grown in English gardens for generations. There are quite a number which can be used instead of mixed annuals to fill up gaps between the two flower crops of the perennial lupin, and these can be found in the list of annuals I have already given. Their spikes are not as large as those of the hybrids of Lupinus polyphyllus to which we are now accustomed, but in their own way they are beautiful. Although they prefer good soil they will thrive on soil poor in humus and nitrogen, and are capable of making a fine show from July until frosts destroy them in autumn.

Nearly all perennial lupins grown to-day are of the Russell type, and I give below a list of twenty-four which should be satisfactory in most gardens.

Twenty-four Perennial Lupins

ALICIA PARRETT	Cream
BEATRICE PARRETT	Lavender Blue
BETTY ASTELL	Deep pink
BLUEJACKET	Lavender blue and white
CANARY BIRD	Canary yellow
CHARMAINE	Flaming orange and gold
CHERRY PIE	Cherry red and yellow

DAYDREAM	Peach pink and gold
FREDERICK PUDDLE	Glowing orange
FRED YULE	Terra Cotta and Yellow
FIREDRAKE	Cherry orange and Gold
GAIETY GIRL	Rose pink and yellow
GEORGE RUSSELL	Coral pink
GUARDSMAN	Rich Orange Red
HEATHER GLOW	Rich Purple
LILAC TIME	Lilac
LADY DIANA ABDY	Blue and white
MELODY	Carmine Red
RADIANT	Orange and Gold
RAPTURE	Rose pink and ivory white
SIMON HENRY	Cerise and white
TOM REEVES	Deep yellow
VELVET QUEEN	Plum purple
WHEATSHEAF	Gold overlaid pink

· 10 ·

Perennial Asters (Michaelmas Daisies)

IN many gardens the bundled faggots of Michaelmas daisies give little indication of the possibilities of this plant – so greatly improved of recent years. Like other very hardy plants they are often unappreciated, and people often dismiss them with: 'They are only Michaelmas daisies – they'll do anywhere.' Certainly there are few conditions in the temperate zone which they are not capable of enduring. Soil does not bother them at all – acid or alkaline, it is all the same. In chalk or peat, clay or porous gravel they will grow and flower, but always in proportion to the nutriment available. Through spells of drought on hot gravel they will live under conditions which would destroy most flowers, or cripple them for ever. They will continue to flower for many years in succession, even when continuously neglected, but if they are planted on rich deeply-dug soil and given the treatment they need they are magnificent.

Perennial asters are well worth a border to themselves, but are equally happy in a mixed perennial border, provided they have enough food and room to develop – a very important point. Although so well equipped to withstand hardship they can take full advantage of luxurious treatment and of richly fed soil. People often condemn them as garden plants because of their shabbiness, which is due to the deplorable conditions under which they are often grown. Badly treated, they have dried-up stems, as hard as hazel twigs, festooned with dead leaves and a few miserable flowers; well treated, the stems are green but hard enough to maintain a crop of large, healthy leaves from the soil level upwards, and the flowers, which grow profusely, are so much larger and finer than those of poorly-kept Michaelmas daisies that they look as if they might be new and improved varieties.

The first step, of course, is to prepare the soil; and it is impossible to do this too thoroughly for the aster. Few plants make such heavy demands on the gardener, but the results from plants grown under liberal treatment are so good that any extra trouble is justified. When the ground has been well prepared, as advised in Chapter 1, the use of some supplementary plant food should be considered. Asters need heavy supplies of nitrogenous food; you will not need additional phosphates or potash. A slow-acting nitrogenous fertilizer such as coarsely ground hoof and horn meal is excellent, for the perennial aster continues to grow for many months and, therefore, requires food for a longer period than many other hardy plants; and the nitrogen in hoof and horn meal, which is yielded up slowly, supplies plant food over a long period.

The best time for planting established plants from the nurseryman or divisions from one's own garden is the early autumn, but perennial asters can be planted at any time in the autumn or winter months when soil and weather conditions are suitable, and even if planting is delayed until late spring, fairly good growth will be made. If planting takes place at any time before Christmas hoof and horn meal should not be applied until early spring, to prevent the loss of nitrogen which would occur at a time of dormant growth, before the newly-planted asters could develop a new root system; but in the case of a spring planting, the hoof and horn meal can be added to the surface and well pricked into the border before planting – and this incorporates the fertilizer and prepares the surface for planting at the same time.

Asters vary in quality. At the top of the scale are the beautiful new and standard varieties listed by all good nurserymen, and at the bottom are the nameless flowers, which linger in odd corners for years, and are sometimes used for patching the border. These should be avoided. Under good conditions all perennial asters are capable of great development, but it is obviously foolish to cultivate a plant to its full extent, to admire its healthy leaves and stout stems, and ultimately to find that the flowers are disproportionately small, poor in form and colour, and useless for effect or cutting. Do not waste time and money in cultivating rubbish. Go to a good plant nursery and procure some young stock. These will look small and insignificant when you receive them in their dormant state and not to be compared with what you could take from your own matted roots or the clumps that a friend could give you, It seems impossible that such small plants will grow into the great flowering clumps – perhaps two feet across – of summer or early autumn.

A nurseryman's stock is propagated from cuttings taken in spring, potted after rooting, planted out in late spring or early summer in prepared ground, and allowed to grow under conditions of good plant nutrition for sale in the autumn and winter. Examination will show that beneath the slight soil covering there are several incipient buds surrounding a central stem – indeed, more than are necessary to ensure a fine plant in the next season and one that will respond fully to good culture. If, however, new plants cannot be procured, divisions of existing plants may be the only way of working up stock – for the time being. In this case, the old plants – and if they are really old they may be many feet across – should be carefully lifted

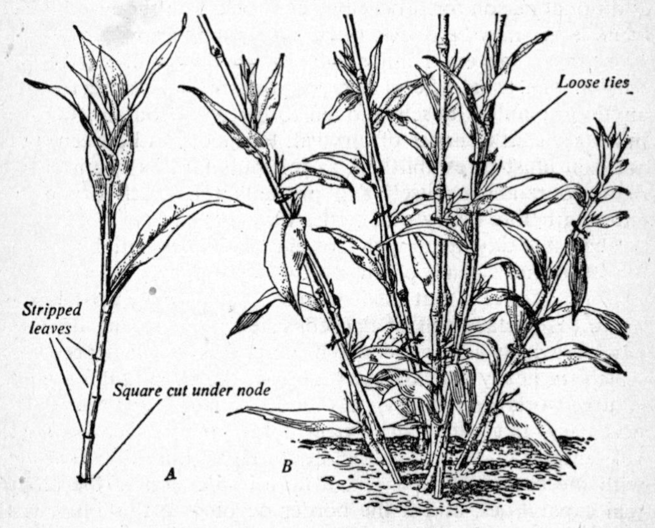

24. Asters: (A) Cutting; (B) Staking.

and divided into sizeable portions by inserting two digging forks back to back into the clumps and levering one against the other, forcing away portions for planting. If this is carefully done, small clumps will come away from the parent plant with their roots almost intact. Using a spade, though it is often recommended for this purpose, is wrong, as it cuts through roots and stems and everything in its way without discrimination. Such plants often start into growth badly in spring, but with the fork method damage is not nearly so great. Only selected good-looking portions should be taken from the outsides of the old clump, the old, woody, and sometimes dying

ing discarded. Large pieces are not necessary or desir- iece with untorn roots, which makes a comfortable handful, being the most useful size for a division.

Planting should be done with a trowel and as, under good cultivation, each plant will cover a large area in its first season, a distance of two and a half feet apart in each direction is not too much, three feet on very rich land, and in cases of thorough soil preparation, being almost imperative for a plant which can develop to cover so much ground. This, of course, is an additional reason for procuring new stock, as although the cost of novelties may be a little heavy, few plants are required, and stock may be very readily worked up during the following season. The usual rule of firm planting must be observed, for anything planted loosely enough to be tugged out by a casual pull stands little chance of survival. Firm contact between roots and soil must be established, as this puts far less strain on the plant to re-anchor itself and prevents too much drying air entering before heavy rain settles the soil.

The usual tidying up with trowel or fork is essential, not only for the owner's peace of mind – for untidiness in the garden is very oppressive – but also because such tidying up helps to make the surface soil of one consistency by closing up loose patches which admit too much air and levelling depressions, which, in heavy soil, collect water. At the beginning of spring routine work is not heavy, only an occasional light hoeing being necessary, but later, when growth becomes active, there is a very important duty. The bundles of growth usually associated with the perennial aster give a false impression of the plants' real capabilities, and if the border devoted to this plant is to produce plants to be enjoyed, another method must be practised.

So away with all bundling. From the first it must be recognized that no perennial aster needs more than five shoots for the development of its beauty and that the plants of most varieties give better results when four, and in some cases three, shoots only are retained; some indeed give excellent results when restricted to one shoot only. The shoots, when a few inches high, must therefore be restricted to three, four, or five according to variety and type, all other shoots being removed at the crown. Courage is needed to do this, for in the early stages of growth, aster shoots are thin, and after the removal of unwanted ones, those remaining look so dejected and forlorn that many who start to deshoot bravely have desisted suddenly, appalled at the skinny appearance of the stripped plants. Looking at them in this state it seems impossible that they could ever cover the generously allotted area. But they are well able to do so, for nature is a great leveller and with the full force of the root system driving hard, the intimate balance between root and top is soon restored, and as the balancing top growth is now forced into a few shoots instead of many, these quickly develop fat stems and large leaves of great manufacturing power. But left alone, even these would become a bundle, for the perennial aster has a natural tendency to push all its shoots upright, close together and crowding one another out, even though it stands in the centre of many unused superficial square feet.

To overcome this, all shoots – less one in some cases – should be tied separately to stakes thrust into the ground close to the plant, leaning outward from it at an angle of 45° from the upright or slightly less. In the case of a plant with three shoots, these should all lean outward and be spaced equidistant from one another. Four-shooted plants should be treated similarly, with three shoots trained to lean out and one trained upright in the middle. Five-shooted plants should have four shoots trained to lean outward with one shoot upright in the middle, and plants with single shoots should, of course, be trained upright. Some stout but not too heavy stakes are required, and, unfortunately, these will be much in evidence for a few weeks. Ugly white stakes and lurid green ones are an abomination. Stakes that are too stout and heavy are also unsuitable, for there is little weight to support.

Those in country districts are fortunate, for where there are osier beds stakes of one year's growth – discarded as being too large for basket making – are often obtainable. These, unpeeled, showing only their natural hue of soft moss green, are, if not invisible, at least not offensive, and as such osiers often approach five feet in length, they can be cut to any measurement to suit the heights of the different varieties. Their butts, which should be pointed for thrusting more easily into the ground, are generally seven to ten sixteenths of an inch in diameter – a most convenient size. In other country districts, hazel, ash and maple stakes can be procured from dealers who buy stakes of all sorts from the coppice. All these have a nice russet brown or grey appearance, which goes well with green foliage and is not obtrusive. Of these woodland products, hazel stakes, which are very straight and neat, and perhaps a little better in colour than the others, are the most suitable, and a butt diameter of half an inch or slightly less will give the necessary length with adequate strength.

Although there is still little difficulty in obtaining these in the country, it is always wise to order them in time, for stakes of this kind are selected while the work of coppice cutting proceeds. Small stakes are placed in one pile, stout stakes suitable for tomatoes in another, bean rods in another. Those with bushy tops are selected for pea stakes and shapeless sticks with various odds and ends go to make large and small faggots for burning. In towns, too, these stakes can generally be obtained from general dealers in firewood and sometimes from ironmongers who are also general dealers, but make your arrangements well ahead – stakes of this kind can seldom be found in stock. Although of good appearance woodland stakes are generally cheaper than those of painted deal or offcuts of other wood – so any trouble taken to obtain them is well worth while.

With the stakes in position and the growth tied loosely to them, in a few weeks results will be remarkable. Once balance between roots and top has been restored by sufficient leaf area a new impetus is created and astounding progress made. Stems thicken amazingly. Leaves grow large, dark green and leathery. Side shoots develop at every node, and as the lower ones easily maintain their lead, each main shoot soon resembles a miniature well-branched fir tree. Development proceeds fast until, at flowering time, plants with three or four shoots resemble three or four miniature, but well proportioned, fir trees completely studded with flowers.

Nowadays, the perennial aster gives a wonderful choice of varieties, for with the extensive crossing of the Novee Belgii and Novee Anglii sections new forms of great beauty have been developed. There are some nearly as big as annual asters (Calistephus), while others are mere buttons. The beautiful aster Ericoides at a distance looks like white heather, while other species such as Frikarti – said by some to be hybrid – Acris and others, strike further divergent notes equally effective in their own way. The shades between white and deep blue and purple are far too numerous to mention now and the many pink and red shades are increasing rapidly in number.

To the singles of true aster form must be added the beautiful double and semi-double forms which help to give the aster border a diversity undreamed of a generation ago. In addition there are the beautiful varieties of aster Amellus, which many consider the choicest of all. The members of this section are intermediate between the tall section and the true dwarfs. Their leaves are a little rougher in appearance than those of other types and their shoots, although well furnished, do not develop laterals as freely as the taller asters do.

As an autumn flower the aster is unequalled, and a few degrees of frost, which generally swoops with little warning in autumn, leave the majority unaffected. Some varieties begin to flower in August, and while, during September and October, a succession of bloom is easily maintained, there are others which continue until mid-November. The flowers, too, last long on the plant and attract bees at a season when few flowers are left for them to visit. For cutting purposes they are very light, decorative, and simple to manage, for the side growths are easily arranged and keep well in water if cut without the central stem, which is generally too woody to absorb enough water. Sometimes, after an exceptionally hot and dry summer, even the stems of the side growths become a little too hard, and consequently they soon fade, but by partially crushing the hard stems with a hammer before placing them in water, this difficulty may be easily overcome.

Some exception must be made in the treatment of all varieties of aster Amellus whose semi-dwarf shoots do not branch so freely and do not need stakes more than two feet in length. They are not capable of covering quite so much space, and therefore at least five shoots should be allowed to develop on each plant. However, it is wise to play for safety when staking all varieties and to use stakes too long rather than too short, for when the flowers approach their full development it is easy to nip off the unwanted parts of the stakes and to tie the tops of the shoots to them, so that they extend beyond the cut stake tops, which will then show hardly at all.

In addition to the kinds and varieties which need staking – and by this and suitable thinning are vastly improved – there is also a section of dwarf varieties which rarely exceed 12 in. in height and which need no support. Each makes a solid-looking ball-shaped clump smothered in blooms of various shades much like those of their taller brethren except that the flower stems are very short. They are charming for almost any purpose except cutting and well fitted to form an edging to the aster border proper. They are not too big for planting on flat shelves or large bare spaces on the rockery and, if lifted with a good ball carefully from a nursery bed, can be used to fill beds for an autumn display after summer flowers have faded. Unless the weather at lifting time is very wet, such a newly-planted bed should be heavily saturated with water. As a rule, plants treated in this way after a few days show little sign of having been moved.

Although so suitable for establishing in a border on its own, the perennial aster should never be omitted from the mixed perennial border, where its grace among heavier plants gives

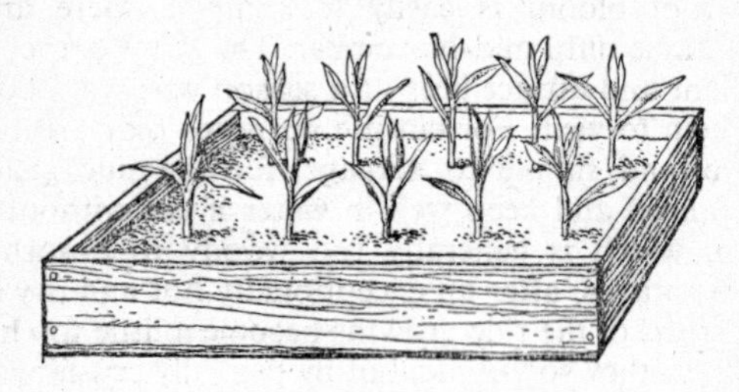

25. Aster cuttings in tray.

lightness to the whole. Its general colour tone, too, acts as an excellent foil to other autumn shades and prolongs the season of colour which fades all too easily as winter approaches. A well-grown aster is seldom in the wrong place, for there are few colours with which the blue, mauve and lavender shades will not blend, although the pink and red shades need careful thought before planting. Some of the modern shades of red are a great step forward, and it looks as if true scarlets and crimsons are now just around the corner. While some of the colours are difficult to reconcile with others, it should be remembered that many perennial asters bloom after their neighbours have faded, and therefore, a colour clash can be prevented; and that some of the new wine-red shades are so beautiful that a little juggling with colours and varieties on a plan in the winter months is well worth the trouble.

If a separate aster border cannot be made immediately, it is a good plan to procure some good varieties, allow them to become established, and then use them as a nucleus for propagating. Fortunately, most kinds and varieties reproduce easily. Plants established in the border for one season will throw up a quantity of shoots when spring arrives and these, severed when a few inches high, made into cuttings as described in Chapter 26, and placed in a cold frame, root readily in a few weeks. The emergence of these shoots varies with the season, but generally they are ready for propagation about the third week in April. As soon as the cuttings have developed enough roots they should be potted singly in pots three to four inches in diameter, placed in a cold frame, and hardened off by gradual exposure to the air, until, by the time they are well rooted, their tops have become hardy, when they can be planted in a nursery bed, about fifteen inches apart in each direction, or direct in their permanent quarters at distances apart suitable for mature plants. Few people have the courage to do this, for single-stemmed plants like these look scattered and lonely. But the plan is more than worth while. Established plants with three and four well displayed growths are beautiful, but the development of these single-stemmed skeletons into well-built conical specimens, each nearly filling the permanent space, is a revelation. Each should be staked upright with one suitable stake and quite early will develop lateral and sub-lateral growths of tremendous beauty – unique in perennial plants – when in bloom. This is, of course, provided that the site has been well and truly dug and manured as advised previously in this chapter, for the best of young rooted cuttings, merely stuck into shallowly dug ground without adequate plant food, cannot be expected to develop thus – they become merely sticky, starved, single-stemmed Michaelmas daisies, hardly worthy of a second glance. So beautiful and striking are asters grown well on single stems that some growers have become completely converted to the system and propagate annually to provide plants for a fresh bed each season, which, of course, allows them to recultivate the ground and enrich it with bulky humus-bearing manure annually.

The varieties of aster Amellus are not suitable for planting as single-stemmed rooted cuttings in permanent beds, as their habit of growth does not enable them to fill large spaces quickly, but there are some beautiful ones among them of an intensity of colour found in few other varieties. Their cuttings, however, do not strike so readily as others and may have to remain in the cold frame for several weeks longer to overcome this difficulty. Some growers place cuttings of aster Amellus in gentle heat, but as they can be propagated in cold frames, although a little more slowly, there is no necessity for this.

Of the many varieties now available, I give below a list of the most satisfactory, all of which should give much pleasure.

Perennial Asters

Twelve Tall Varieties

NOVAE-ANGLAE	
Harrington's Pink	Clear Pink; 4½ ft
NOVI-BELGII	
Climax	Light blue; 5 ft
D. M. Harrison	Deep rose; 5 ft
Crusoe	Soft mauve, tinged pink large flower; 5 ft
Gayborder Supreme	Rosy pink; 4 ft
Phyllis	Soft pink; 4½ ft
The Archbishop	Bluish purple, very good, large flower; 5 ft
The Bishop	Deep rose; 4½ ft
The Cardinal	Deep rose red; 4½ ft
The Dean	Bright rose, very large; 5 ft
The Sexton	Bright blue, large flower; 4½ ft
White Lady	Pure white; 5½ ft

Twelve Varieties of Medium Height

NOVI-BELGII	
Beechwood Challenger	Good clear red; 3½ ft
Beechwood Sunrise	Bright red, yellow centre, good; 4 ft
Colonel F. R. Durham	Double mauve; 3½ ft
Little Blue Boy	Bright blue, double; 2 ft
Little Pink Lady	Soft pink; 2½ ft
October Dawn	Lilac mauve; 3½ ft
Peace	Double, soft rosy mauve; 3½ ft
Plenty	Soft blue. The largest Aster; 4 ft
Gayborder Royal	Rosy crimson, one of the very best; 3½ ft
Barton Royalist	Deep rosy mauve; 3 ft
Lassie	Soft pink, large flower; 4 ft
Violet Lady	Bright yellow, violet eye, small flower; 3 ft

Six Good Pink Varieties

Lassie	Soft pink, large flower; 4 ft
Gayborder Supreme	Rosy pink, 4 ft
Harrington's Pink	Clear pink; 4½ ft
Phyllis	Soft pink; 4½ ft
The Dean	Bright rose; 5 ft
D. M. Harrison	Deep rose; 5 ft

Six Good Red Varieties

Beechwood Challenger	Bright red; 3½ ft
The Cardinal	Deep rose red; 4½ ft
Beechwood Charm	Rosy red
Beechwood Sunrise	Bright red, yellow centre; 4 ft
Gayborder Royal	Rosy crimson; 3½ ft
Winston Churchill	Rich red; 2 ft

Six Dwarf Varieties

Audrey	Pale blue
Blue Bouquet	Clear blue
Little Red Boy	Bright red
Margaret Rose	Rosy pink
Snowsprite	White
Victor	Pale blue

Six Varieties of Aster Amellus

Herman Lons	Pale blue; 2½ ft
Jacqueline Genebrier	Pale pink; 2½ ft
King George	Bright blue; 2½ ft
Mrs Ralph Woods	Bright pink; 2½ ft
Sonia	Clear pink; 2½ ft
Ultramine	Deep blue; 2½ ft

Some Species Worthy of a Place

Aster Acris	Clear bright mauve; 2 ft
Aster Ericoides	Dense masses white heath-like flowers; 3 ft
Aster Diffusus	White; 3 ft
Aster Cordifolius	Blue; 3 ft
Aster Frikartii	Pale blue; 2½ ft
Aster Vimineus	Blue; 2½ ft

· 11 ·

Hardy Border Carnations and Pinks

THROUGHOUT the ages, far back almost in the ancient world, carnations have been prized for their perfume, and the clear-cut border carnation has been valued for generations for its beauty alone, quite apart from the intoxicating fragrance of a number of its varieties. They are not so spectacular as many hardy plants, but nevertheless a good garden is not complete without a bed or border of these carnations, which never fail to charm.

Because of their perfume, symmetry, and exquisite markings they are essentially plants which should be seen close-to. They should not be put at the end of a long border or tucked away in a snug corner, but should be put in full sunshine near the house, where they can be appreciated fully. While it is true that border carnations revel in sunshine much hotter than is generally experienced in Britain, and that they do not object to long periods of drought, especially when near the sea, nobody in the southern half of England need fear for their hardiness – given the right treatment – and even in many northern districts border carnations often emerge from winter unharmed, especially in hilly country where a loose rock subsoil promotes good drainage.

Good soil preparation is of the greatest importance, but to carnations soil of great depth is not so important as it is to many plants. Neither is this plant a heavy feeder, for although it appreciates good humus it is able to exist and flourish on soils much too poor to give good results with free-growing border plants.

Drainage is all-important. Should the roots of delphiniums or Michaelmas daisies lie in soil a little too wet during a long winter, or if these, or most border plants, are planted on a retentive clay soil which releases water with great difficulty, little harm results, but the carnation cannot abide stagnant water, and if condemned to live in putty-like soil from which cold water cannot pass it frequently dies – a loss usually attributed to low temperature.

Unless for the purpose of drainage, the lower layers of soil for carnations need not be double dug or trenched, if this has been done previously. Instead, some decayed farmyard manure or compost should be worked into the top layer while it is being dug one spit deep. But if you want to grow carnations on a naturally wet soil then something must be incorporated to assist surplus water to pass out. It is comparatively easy to do this on the top soil, for here any material may be used which tends to create air spaces and is not otherwise harmful, and perhaps the most important is coarse grit. Years ago, it was possible to obtain this easily in the form of road sweepings from macadam roads, but since the introduction of tar spraying, even to unimportant side roads, this material has been suspect, for many by-products of coal tar are deadly to plant life. But grit from a gravel pit, sifted to about a quarter or three-eighths of an inch, is admirable material. Also crushed mortar rubble from a demolished building is excellent, and, to a lesser extent, broken bricks.

For this purpose too, good hard straw put through a chaff-cutter has been used with success, and I knew of one ancient cultivator, whose cottage garden was a bower of carnations in summer, who carefully kept his broad bean haulm, chopped it into three-inch lengths and worked it into his carnation borders before planting in early autumn. He explained to me that 'they were like a lot of little pipes to run off the water'. Stable litter free of droppings but containing much good straw is also useful. Fine sand, however, must be used with caution, for the combination of this with some forms of clay results in a concrete-hard substance in summer and a plastic mass in winter, and neither is good for growing carnations.

But all these are for the top spit. What do we do if the bottom is impermeable? If you want to grow carnations for many years the lower soil levels should be treated well, and some form of trenching is necessary. The best method is to trench as advocated in Chapter 1, and when the second spit has been removed place in the trench bottom six inches of broken brick rubble, clinkers, or stones, similar to those advised for the foundation of paths in Chapter 3, and replace both spits, taking care that the top soil is not put underneath. This will raise the level of the soil considerably – which in itself will assist surface drainage; but more thought than this must be given, for this drainage, although enough for the surface layers, will not dispose of unwanted water. Drainage of this kind, although valuable, does no more than provide a sump or pit to collect water from the soil above which will also act as a drainage pit for the surrounding soil; and this may easily lead to a rise in the water table and make the site wetter than before. Sump drainage is useless unless an outflow is provided for the collected water to escape, so a pipe outlet to a drain, ditch, or large soakaway, slightly lower in level, must be provided. Such a soakaway can be filled with brickbats, clinkers or any open material.

A friend of mine, who had great difficulty in growing carnations in some very intractable clay, solved the problem by excavating a great pit behind a hedge, filling it with faggots and covering the top with soil to resemble the surroundings. After draining his carnation borders with brick rubbled trenches, from these he led a line of land pipes to the pit which then received all the surplus water. This functioned successfully for many years but in time gradually became less effective because mud slowly choked it, so he cleaned it out and all was well again. Extreme measures of this kind are seldom required, for if only a slight slope exists a pipe line of land drains merely laid together butt to butt can be continued until it breaks the surface at a convenient point where collected water can flow out.

Although carnations can be grown on slightly acid soils they rarely give their best there. Instead they eke out a miserable existence and easily fall prey to pests and diseases. Perhaps it would be wrong to call them lime lovers, but they certainly thrive on chalk and limestone soils, possibly assisted in this by the good drainage usually associated with such soils. Unless lime is naturally present, or has been given artificially, it should be added – a dressing of 28 lb. per square pole usually being sufficient. More important than the quantity used is even distribution, to achieve which the lime should be finely powdered. Ground chalk and hydrated lime are good forms which should be applied evenly over the plot, but unslaked builder's lime may be used if it is easily obtainable in the neighbourhood. This should be placed in heaps and covered with moist soil to slake it, and when little volcanoes of fine white powder can be seen bursting through the soil covering, it can be distributed with ease. After slaking, lime not needed for immediate distribution should be collected and placed in a dry shed, otherwise if saturated by heavy rain it will become an awkward sticky paste. Care must be taken not to use lime at the same time as farmyard manure or much valuable nitrogen may be lost. Lime can be applied at any time, but it is better to apply it before planting if possible.

Border carnations can be divided into three sections, all of which are much alike in form. These are Selfs, Fancies, and Picotees. The first, as the name implies, are of one colour, according to the variety. Fancies have flowers with two or more colours flaked, splashed, and marbled on other colours. Picotees have one base colour with a narrow edging of another contrasting colour running round the edges of each petal. Nowadays, most of these have complete calyces which hold the

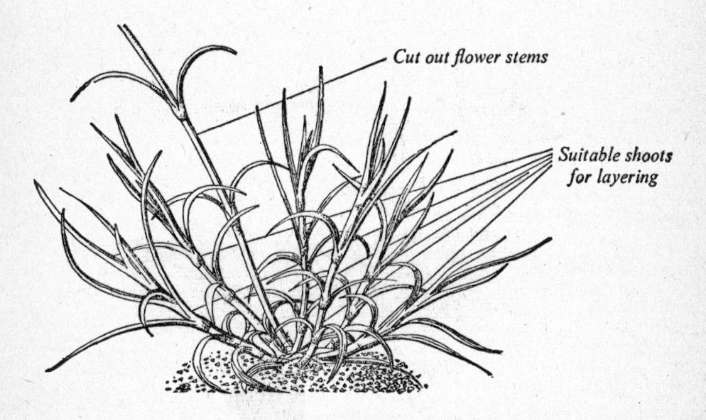

26. Carnation before layering.

petals firmly in position, but there are a few delightfully fragrant varieties known as Cloves, of which some of the older ones are very full-petalled and burst their calyces at several points – an untidy state which has to be corrected by small rubber bands. All these bloom only once a year, generally in July, and are propagated by layering, an operation which needs a little care and which is performed immediately after flowering. It is fully described in Chapter 26.

The fine soil surrounding these layers should be kept moist – if necessary watered daily – and in a month or six weeks the stems of the rooted layers can be severed from the parent plants, and with their newly-made root system and as much soil as possible carefully lifted with a trowel to be planted out direct into a bed or border prepared in advance or placed in small pots to be bedded out later.

Assuming that you intend to leave them undisturbed for two full growing seasons, they should be planted eighteen inches apart in each direction, in soil previously trodden firm but not unduly compacted. Some heavy soils will not need this treading, for their particles already lie too closely together – but you will be the best judge of this. Planting, however, must be done firmly; no plant should be loose enough for a casual pull to

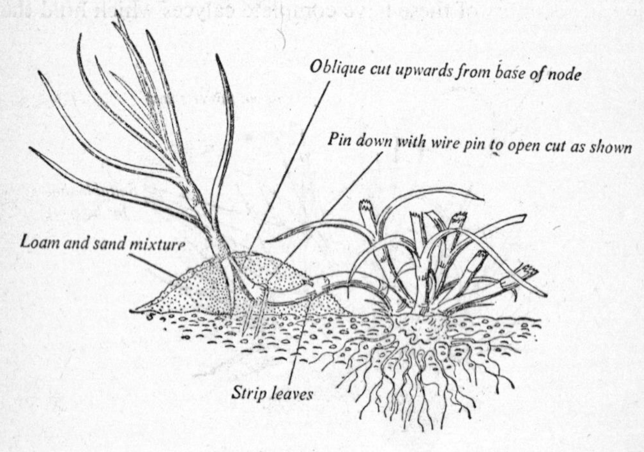

27. Layering carnations.

dislodge it, and carnations, if not planted firmly, will be loosened badly when rapid thaws, with their soil upheavals, overcome heavy frost. The earlier this is done in the autumn the better, for if the carnations are able to establish themselves while the soil remains warm, they will be far finer and give better results in spring.

During the winter, no attention is necessary except to keep the beds free of leaves, which, by collecting around the stems, may cause decay or harbour slugs. When growth begins in spring, stakes are needed, and for this unobtrusive hazel stakes or osiers should be chosen. Although the flower spikes on some varieties will attain a height of about two feet the spikes themselves are partially self-supporting; in most cases, therefore, stakes will suffice which, when plunged six inches into the ground, are eighteen inches above it. Loops of split raffia will serve to attach the spikes sufficiently firmly to the stakes and when, as summer approaches, buds can be seen, a decision about disbudding must be made.

Left alone, each spike would develop a number of blooms light and decorative in appearance, but rather small. With all lateral buds removed – the terminal bud only being allowed to develop – a fine bloom is produced, fit for the exhibitors' table, and if the grower wishes to exhibit, that is the way to disbud (as the removal of unwanted buds is called). But for the average man, who likes a show in the border and at the same time some blooms of good quality, there is a happy medium. This consists in removing the top lateral buds – which always seem to overcrowd and embarrass the central one – and those immediately below for about six inches, and allow buds, amounting to not more than five in all, to develop. This makes a very attractive compromise, either in the border or, if the flowers are picked, for the house.

As the blooms unfold and become heavy a few extra raffia ties may be needed to hold them upright, but the raffia should be split into fine strands and made to look as inconspicuous as possible; it is always a pity to spoil the natural grace of a well-grown plant by smothering it with wide bands of raffia or by giving it an ugly stake as companion.

Although carnations are not gross feeders they appreciate good treatment, and a little extra food at the right time is a great help. In spring when the lengthening flower spikes show distinctly above the winter growth a dressing of 4 oz. of bone-meal per square yard may be given. This is used chiefly as a source of nitrogen and phosphate, but on very poor land, where the nitrogen store is likely to be low, this can be supplemented with 2 oz. of coarsely ground hoof and horn meal per square yard. The latter, being in large particles, is a slow-acting nitrogeneous fertilizer which yields its supply of plant food slowly and over a long period, and nothing more will be required for the season.

Weeds which choke the foliage and rob the roots of carnations of their sustenance should never be tolerated, but if the Dutch hoe is plied regularly once a week there should be no weed problem. Weeds – really plants in the wrong place – can be frightful eyesores among carnations, which, because of their slow growth, have little fighting power.

After flowering, the old spikes should be removed cleanly down to a point where the first growth begins, and then it will be seen that the layers of last year have grown into large plants with six to perhaps a dozen spreading shoots. These can be left intact if it is proposed to carry on the bed for another year – a

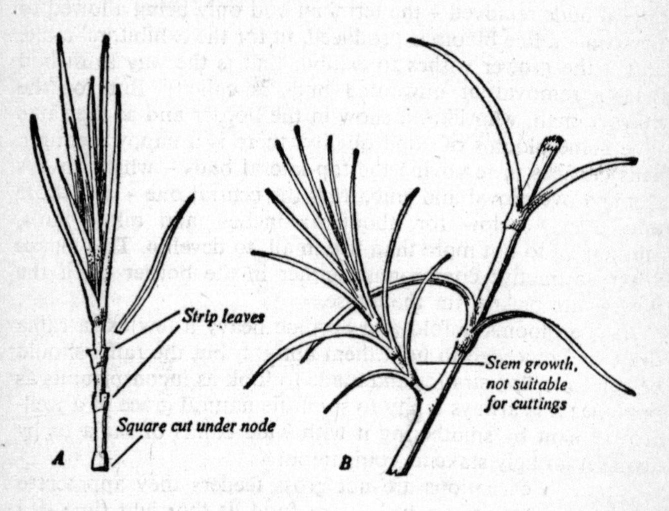

28. Carnations: (A) Suitable and (B) unsuitable for cutting.

method which gives excellent results in quality and a big show at the same time. If necessary some plants can be layered, but the removal of the rooted layers will give a very patchy effect. For stock purposes, it is generally better to grow a few plants separately in a place not so much in evidence and to leave the main bed or border alone to flower without disturbance during the second season, or, if room can be found, to use two beds and, by replanting one each season, ensure a good two-year-old bed with its masses of bloom annually, in which case the older bed can be utilized for propagating each season. Few really worth-while plants give such a good return for very little trouble as the border carnations, but often this is not realized until a bed of undisturbed two-year-olds comes into bloom.

While fully appreciating improvement and the symmetrical beauty of many of our moderns, I must confess to a real love for the old Crimson Clove. Although its flowers have untidy petals which tumble out of the calyx, it has a lurking beauty and an unforgettable heavy perfume. I should always grow it. This old-fashioned variety is not always obtainable and is not included in the list 'Clove Varieties', none of which burst their calyces.

Nowadays there are innumerable excellent varieties, some of them very much alike. From these I have made selections from each section which should prove satisfactory in most districts.

Twenty-four Good Self-coloured Varieties

ADONIS. Bright carmine pink of perfect form. The lovely, brilliant flowers carried erect on stiff stems.

ANTIQUARY. Handsome bluish lilac of fine form and strongest border habit.

ARCHIBALD DOUGLAS. Fine large scarlet.

AVALANCHE. Snow white, of the finest exhibition form. The stems of this variety are perfectly rigid. A flower of great purity.

BADACHRO. Bright Neyron rose; large broad petals and fine form.

BLACK PRINCE. Fine dark crimson, of giant border habit. The flowers are of perfect form, the petals solid and thick.

BLAVEN. Flesh-apricot. A well-formed flower of fine border habit.

BOOKHAM GRAND. Clear crimson. The flowers are of perfect form and symmetry.

CHORISTER. Soft apricot. A beautiful and dainty variety.

COWSLIP. Clear yellow. Good form and extra strong growth.

ELLIOT DOUGLAS. Large slate-grey.

ENDYMION. Beautiful bright rose-pink. Flowers well-formed of medium shade.

FIERY-CROSS. Brilliant scarlet. Of perfect exhibition form, and strong border habit.

FLAMBEAU. Deep apricot or Lincoln red.

GREY DOUGLAS. Large heliotrope-grey of fine form.

INDUNA. Clear crimson. Of exhibition form; a magnificent border variety.

KING CUP. Sulphur yellow, fine.

KINLOCH. Rose-madder, an attractive flower.

LENT LILY. Large yellow of strong border habit.

LOCHNAGAR. Fine large dark crimson.

OBERON. Deep rose-pink of fine form.

PARA HANDY. Brilliant scarlet. The flowers are well-formed and of good size.

PROSPERO. Violet old rose.

SNOWY OWL. Dazzling white. Large flowers are held on wire-like stems.

Twenty-four Fancy Varieties

AFTON WATER. Soft pink, flaked deep rose.

ARGOSY. Perfect form. Clear yellow ground, edged and marked brilliant scarlet.

AURORA. Bright yellow, heavily edged and striped brilliant carmine violet.

BENACHIE. Apricot, heavily edged and marked heliotrope. Beautiful and fascinating.

BOOKHAM DREAM. Pure white heavily marked scarlet, large perfectly formed flowers.

BOOKHAM GRACE Pure white, edged and striped brilliant geranium scarlet. Large flowers carried erect on wire-like stems.

DOUGLAS BURN. Snow white, marked with bright Garnet Lake stripes.

DUNCAN KNOCK. Lavender grey striped bright rose. A robust border variety.

EDENSIDE GLORY. Rich apricot, heavily suffused pink, perfect flowers on stiff stems.

EDENSIDE PRIDE. Pure white, edged and marked brilliant scarlet; flowers of exquisite form.

FANCY FREE. Magnificent form. White marked with pale Delft rose.

GOSHAWK. Bright sulphur-yellow edged and barred carmine-violet.

HIDALGO. Buff-yellow, edged and marked heliotrope.

HORSA. Apricot ground, heavily marked scarlet.

KESTREL. Yellow ground, edged and striped deep cyclamen-purple.

MARY MACLEOD. Buff apricot, heavily edged and suffused rich pink.

MARKSMAN. Orange apricot, edged and striped rosy pink.

MRS. HAUKSBEE. Pure white, lightly marked rosy-pink.

PAINTED LADY. Straw-yellow, flushed pink, heavily edged and marked delicate grey.

SELBORNE. White, heavily striped and edged rich deep crimson.

SURREY FANCY. Buff-apricot, edged and striped soft rose-pink.

THELMA. White, striped and edged salmon pink.

TONY WELLER. Yellow, heavily striped and edged crimson.

VIRGINIA. White, heavily marked soft pink. Rigid stems.

Some Clove Scented Varieties

AILSA CLOVE. Pure white heavily marked ox-blood crimson, fine form and size.
BLACK DOUGLAS CLOVE. Glowing Chrysanthemum crimson.
BOOKHAM SPICE. The finest white Clove.
CAMROSE CLOVE. Soft shell-pink
CARMINE CLOVE. Bright crimson carmine.
DAINTY CLOVE. Lovely soft salmon pink.
EMPRESS CLOVE. Violet-blue.
FIONA CLOVE. Fine scarlet.
MERLIN CLOVE. White, marked purple.
MOTLEY CLOVE. Reddish pink ground, evenly striped ox-blood red.
PERFECT CLOVE. Glowing deep crimson.
SPARKLING CLOVE. Salmon-red.
VINOUS CLOVE. Dark Burgundy.

Six White Ground Picotees

EVA HUMPHREYS. Purple edge.
FAIR MAIDEN. Rose pink edge.
GANYMEDE. Broad edge crimson.
PATRICK. Light purple edge.
LIDDINGTON'S FAVOURITE. Light rosy scarlet edge.
E. M. WILKINSON. Red edge.

Six Yellow Ground Picotees

TOGO. Heavy crimson edge.
FIREFLY. Crimson edge.
SANTA CLAUS. Medium purple edge.
MARGARET LENNOX. Heavy rose edge.
MRS I. I. KEEN. Medium rose pink edge.
THISBE. Heavy edge scarlet.

Now let us deal with pinks. When I was a boy village gardens in the south-west were gay with pinks each summer. They were everywhere. They sat on old walls, invaded banks, and hung over rocks. Cottage gardens were smothered with a disorderly fragrant mat of them. In Dorset villages nestling between chalk hills they grew in vigorous abandon. Varieties were many. There were selfs and patterned ones both double and single, small varieties with wispy petals and fat bursting doubles, all heavily perfumed. Many of these varieties are lost, but they were healthy then, and who knows how long they had survived? They throve so amazingly because they were growing in the right soil and were left alone to fend for themselves.

In those days few cottagers were garden-minded. Sometimes they stuck in a few plants, given them by a neighbour, into an odd corner and perhaps chopped up a patch of pinks to make room for them, but usually the pinks were left to grow year after year without disturbance, for no one thought of clearing the flower gardens for reconstruction – only patches were cleaned a little at a time with long intervals in between. When starting a fresh patch of pinks old plants were pulled apart and pieces with several shoots were pushed in the ground. Generally they grew, but nobody was in too great a hurry, and if the fresh patch took a year or two before becoming fully clothed, it mattered little. Sometimes some of the more knowledgeable tore off single shoots with heels attached, called pipings, and these grew more readily, but the cottagers at least never thought of making cuttings with a knife. As the knowledge of gardening spread, people began to dig their gardens to grow more variety, and the pinks – perhaps a little despised – unable to stand so much disturbance suffered in the process.

Pinks are charming friendly subjects worth growing for their perfume alone, and there is a place for them in most modern gardens. Although many of the old-fashioned varieties are lost there are still some good ones existing, and many modern ones, for people have rediscovered their worth. They should be planted in a spot where they can be left alone for some years, for if allowed to grow and spread naturally they do not acquire the woody bareness so often seen in plants harried to death in the mixed border. If allowed to grow in suitable spaces left on crazy paving they form dense rounded mats, provided, of course, they are clear of the trodden track. In dry walls from which there is no excuse to eject them they are particularly happy, and are almost equally happy on dry stony banks and on sunny patches of rockery which are otherwise difficult to clothe.

There is no need to adopt the 'tear-off and push-in' methods of our forefathers, for pinks root readily from cuttings. These are taken with a sharp knife just after their flowers have faded (full details will be found in Chapter 26). They root readily in a cold frame, or a box covered with glass, if shaded from direct sunshine, but need careful ventilation to correct the tendency to damp off which accompanies a humid atmosphere. When rooted, it is sometimes convenient to place each one in a three-inch pot before planting out of doors, but for this ordinary garden soil will suffice if a little sharp grit is added and, in lime-deficient districts, a little crushed chalk or hydrated lime – not more than a pound to each bushel of soil. Although they are so much at home in paving, dry walls, and other well-drained situations, they can be grown well in any bed or border – the general directions for carnations applying to pinks also. While, of course, there could be no objection to the making of fresh beds annually, there is no need to clear out beds after the second season's flowering, as the preceding pages have shown. The single varieties are neat-looking and do not burst their calyces, but most double varieties tend to spill over, a matter which disbudding does not improve; this, therefore, need not be practised. Most varieties are not more than a foot in height. All are hardy.

Sweet Scented Pinks

COLE TIT. Blush-rose, centre carmine-purple. Serrate.

CROSSBILL. A very pretty Appleblossom flower, centre and base of petals rich crimson.

DABCHICK. Peachblossom pink, centre carmine. Deeply lacinate.

DIPPER. A large bold flower; Appleblossom pink, with centre of blood red. Serrate.

LAVEROCK. A fine large flower, soft rose-pink; centre clear deep red.

MARVEL. Rich rose-opal, maroon centre.

NIGHTJAR. Lilac-pink, centre and picotee edge of deep red.

REDPOLL. Rich pink smooth petals with deep red centre.

SERIN. A bright flower, Mallow purple, rich red centre.

WHITE QUEEN. Pure white, frilled edge.

WOODLARK. The old type of laced pink, White edged crimson.

WOODPECKER. Pale salmon, maroon centre.

This is not all. In addition to carnations and pinks, somewhere midway between the border carnation and the pink comes an extensive range of interesting hybrids known as Allwoodii. According to the raiser they are half pink half carnation, a statement well supported by their appearance, for certainly they combine the grace and beauty of the carnation with the general thriftiness of the pink, and carry a delightful perfume also. Unlike the border carnation and the pink, which have definite flowering periods, Allwoodii continue to flower as long as climate permits – generally from early summer until November fog arrives. Some of the varieties are tall, produce freely blossomed stems, and are very good for cutting.

The blooms of Allwoodii are very like small, well proportioned carnations, the petals of which, however, do not stray from their calyces. Of about the same height as border carnations, their flower spikes need the support of light stakes, otherwise they become bent, untidy and of little use for cutting. Undoubtedly they are worthy of a good place in the garden where, apart from staking, they are very little trouble. Their general culture follows the same lines as that of carnations and pinks. There is a wide range of colours including a few old-fashioned shades now rarely seen in pinks.

In addition to the usual means of propagation, border carnations, pinks, and Allwoodii can be grown from seed, and border carnations grown in this way give excellent results. It must be remembered, however, that vegetative propagation is necessary to retain named varieties and colours because, in the main, carnations do not breed true from seed. If you do not mind a small proportion of singles among the doubles, and like a sweeping range of colours and shades, then carnations raised from seed will prove excellent. Seed can be sown at any time during spring or early summer, the earlier the better. If a greenhouse with a temperature of 55° F. is available, sow in February; if you have a cold greenhouse only, sow in April, and if no greenhouse at all, sow in a cold frame in June. Full directions for sowing will be found in Chapter 23.

All seed should be sown thinly, but carnation seed particularly so, otherwise the smaller seedlings, which generally give the best colours and types, are crowded out and lost. To make sure that none of these small seedlings is discarded every one should be pricked out into boxes immediately it is large enough to handle, or if this would provide too many, the contents of the pot can be divided into two and all the seedlings in one half pricked out irrespective of size. The operation of pricking out is fully explained in Chapter 24. Some growers sow more seed han is necessary, and select the fattest and most vigorous seedlings, only to find at flowering time that a large proportion have given single flowers.

Carnations of all kinds are capable of recovering from much check, but the difference between checked and unchecked plants is so much in favour of the latter that the pricked-out seedlings should be established in their permanent quarters as soon as they become four inches high, before there is any likelihood of their being checked and hardened by starvation. The general culture for carnations should be followed, but as seedlings are so much more vigorous than plants vegetatively propagated a slightly greater distance from plant to plant should be allowed. They grow with astonishing vigour and by the autumn sometimes develop into great clumps of foliage with twenty or more shoots, all of which flower during June and July of the year following sowing. And what a joy they are ! In contrast to the thin and sometimes delicate stem of the named varieties they are bold massive sheaves of bloom, nearly two feet across and almost self-supporting, but a few light stakes around each clump, to support a string on which the outer blooms can lean, is an advantage.

A good strain of seed will provide a glorious medley of colours – selfs, fancies, white grounds and yellow grounds, with only a small proportion of singles. But singles should not be despised, for even old and experienced growers, when they see a really good single, love to see the form and colour in a way which is not possible in a distracting flurry of petals. For this reason some people like to put the singles in a bed by themselves, perhaps in a favourite corner near a window – a method easily carried out if seed is sown in February. There is then little difficulty in potting up the seedlings early and allowing the first flower spikes to develop and flower during the first summer after sowing, thus allowing the segregation of singles and doubles and perhaps the elimination of a few whose form and colour do not satisfy.

By sowing annually the biennial system can be practised just as it is with plants from layers, and, apart from the intrinsic beauty of seedlings, there is always the possibility of finding a winner which can be perpetuated by layering. In any case there will be many hardly distinguishable from the named varieties, with the added advantage of the rude health and initial vigour which seedlings possess.

Good seedsmen also offer splendid strains of pinks which can be grown very easily in the same general way as carnations. They, too, are very satisfactory, but only provided you take the important precaution of buying only the best – advice which is by no means costly. These remarks also apply to

Allwoodii, which give a remarkable range of colours when grown from seed – a form of culture which many people prefer.

There is yet another type of carnation which should be in every garden, known as the annual chabaud or marguerite carnation. This is grown from seed and flowers freely five or six months from the time of seed sowing. It is not really an annual, but as it does not always prove hardy in this country it is usually treated as a half-hardy annual. Apart from the fact that it is a carnation, with all the romance associated with the name, it is a magnificent bedding plant which, in August, September, and October, will furnish a lavish display of bloom and fill the air with delicious fragrance. How long the unbroken sequence of bloom would continue can only be conjectured, for excessive damp brings the flowering period to an end in November, but if climatic conditions permitted, I have little doubt that a flowering season of more than six months would be possible – an estimate partly borne out by the success of the plant when it is lifted from the flowering bed in October and placed in large pots protected by a greenhouse with enough artificial heat to exclude damp only. Treated thus, I have seen marguerite carnations in full flower at Christmas, giving an amazing display. There is a tremendous range of colours, including yellows, and the blooms, most of which have fringe-edged petals, greatly resemble the carnations seen in the shops. Such a good all-round plant can be forgiven for its habit of calyx bursting – to which a few varieties are addicted; it has so many other good points to offer.

To obtain as long a flowering season as possible, sow your seed early if your greenhouse will give you a night temperature of 55° F. Failing this, wait until the sun warms up the greenhouse in April, when, by closing the ventilators and bottling up sun heat in the afternoon, enough warmth can be obtained to maintain a comfortable temperature during the night. If you are without a cold greenhouse, utilize a frame, or even a glass-covered box, to germinate seed and forward your seedlings.

In the early stages, the general treatment should be similar to that for seedling carnations of all types, but the marguerite carnation will thrive in a little more warmth than the others, and because of its rapid and extensive growth should be planted in soil more heavily enriched with farmyard manure, or compost, than is usual for carnations generally. If treated specially, this plant is far hardier than is generally thought, and under good management, in early summer, I have seen tumbling masses of flowers produced by plants which have wintered out of doors, and I remember a particularly fine display in the summer of 1947 following one of the worst winters for centuries. This method can be carried out, with reasonable hope of success, in dry districts in the south and south-east where the soil is well drained, and in the south-west only where drainage is good and the annual rainfall not high. For this, defer sowing until May and treat the seedlings in the usual manner, but by full exposure endeavour to produce hard thrifty seedlings to plant in their permanent quarters as soon as they are large enough.

Because, in this case, the object is to obtain durable plants, the soil should be well drained and, although not too poor, should not have been dressed with farmyard manure or compost for a year. The usual precautions about lime should be taken. In such a bed the young plants should not be watered during drought, except after planting, for if hot weather should harden the stems a little more than usual, so much the better – the chances of survival are much greater. Those which survive will grow into clumps of astonishing dimensions from which an almost inexhaustible supply of fragrant blooms can be taken for many months. Good strains can be obtained to colour and as mixed.

There are a few other types of carnations and pinks with which there is no need to deal in this volume, as they are of little use to the average gardener, but there are many people, accustomed to seeing beautiful carnations in shops, who would like to grow some like them. These are known as perpetual carnations, and flower more or less all the year round. Except in a few very favoured districts they are not hardy, or they are only hardy enough to stay alive, and therefore, as they cannot give their best out of doors, they must be grown in a cool greenhouse. Given suitable conditions their culture is easy. Information on the culture of this type of carnation will be found in Chapter 22 on the 'cool greenhouse', with other interesting subjects.

· 12 ·

Sweet Peas

THE sweet pea has romance. About two hundred and fifty years ago the monk Cupani sent from Sicily some seeds of a new plant to a friend in this country. It was an insignificant weedy annual which had blooms of crimson or purplish crimson colour, unattractive but fragrant. Noticed by few at the time it gradually became listed in seedsmen's catalogues. For many years it was regarded as an ordinary tall annual for the border, but about a century ago there were florists who saw grace in the sweet pea and began to study its variations. As so often happens, under the influence of good cultivation other colours appeared, and soon there were bi-colours and many well-defined self colours, but the flowers were tiny and their short stems gave them little decorative value.

Towards the close of the last century, Henry Eckford, fascinated by the sweet pea, began to experiment. Others were also probing the possibilities of this plant, but Eckford was generally a little ahead of them. After many years' work he raised a new race of giant sweet peas known as 'Grandifloras' and increased the colour range so tremendously that almost every known colour was represented in many shades and, in addition, the Eckford varieties retained the characteristic perfume of the species. By this time the sweet pea was undoubtedly a beautiful plant and many experts considered little further improvement possible.

So important had it become that in 1900 an exhibition and conference was held at the Crystal Palace to mark the bicentenary of its introduction, and many thousands of blooms were presented in good condition. It was a great event – few knew how great – for it soon became whispered about that a new and startling break in sweet peas existed. In the gardens of Earl Spencer in charge of Silas Cole had appeared a large pink variety, infinitely more beautiful than any previously seen, which had wings and standards heavily flounced and frilled. It seemed that nature had lavished so much material on the flowers that they could be held together only by being heavily pleated and waved.

The new variety was called 'Countess Spencer'. In the hands

of another raiser a similar variety appeared, and it is said that a third also existed, but Cole's variety was much superior and became the forerunner of the modern sweet pea. Progress was not easy. Countess Spencer failed to breed true and several years of hard work were necessary before the new sweet peas came to stay, but when they did they quickly ousted Eckford's creations, which are now almost unknown.

Most people know the modern sweet pea by appearance. It is truly the queen of annuals. From no other annual is it possible to cut flowers at the end of May and continue to do so until September, as in many districts is easily possible with the sweet pea. It is a plant which loves very rich, deep, moist soil and much atmospheric moisture, but greatly dislikes high overhead temperatures, which seems very strange as it originally came from the warm climate of Sicily. It is explained by the fact that in Mediterranean islands germination of annuals takes place in early autumn, growth is made during the mild winter when frost is scarcely known, and most annuals come into flower in spring and quickly produce seed when the great heat of summer makes further blooming impossible.

Although the sweet pea loves cool soil it can be grown successfully in almost any soil in the United Kingdom, but in districts where late spring or early summer drought occurs it is inclined to go out of flower a little more quickly. In some districts in the south-west and west of England it is magnificent, and in Scotland it is often in full flower at the end of September, largely because both soil and atmospheric conditions are cool and moist.

It is, of course, possible to grow sweet peas by very simple means, but when grown haphazardly or without much care, the results bear no comparison to those from plants cared for throughout a long season of growth. To deal with the sweet pea adequately entails an autumn sowing, and this should take place at mid-September in the midlands and north and early October in the south. In boxes of John Innes Compost No. 1 seeds should be dibbled in one inch deep and one and a half inches apart in each direction. These boxes should then be placed in cold frames which should be closed until germination has taken place. It is wise, when sowing the seeds, to sow mousetraps almost as freely as the seeds, because if there are any mice within miles they always manage to find sweet pea seeds, however well protected, and by the time the trouble is discovered much valuable time has been lost. It is important either that the soil used for sowing should be very moist or that the seeds should be watered in immediately after sowing, after which no watering of any kind should take place until the seedlings can be seen emerging through the soil. Driblets of water at this stage are extremely harmful and often the cause of trouble attributed to bad seed.

In the southern half of this country and in many districts of the midlands and north the sweet pea is hardy unless rendered

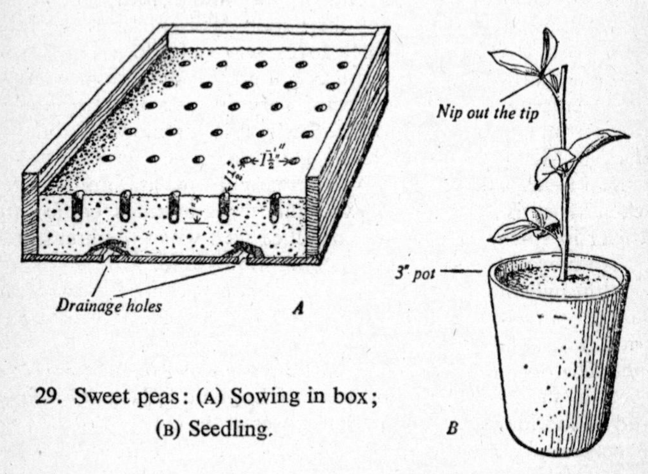

29. Sweet peas: (A) Sowing in box; (B) Seedling.

tender by treatment. It is therefore important to treat the seedlings as hardily as possible throughout the winter growing period. After germination, lights should be taken from the cold frame and the seedlings exposed to the air freely, at all times, except in torrential rain or very severe frost. At first there is some risk in this exposure because sparrows and other small birds delight in the tender tips of sweet pea shoots, and it is therefore wise to stretch fish nets over the frame for protection. When the seedlings are further advanced this trouble usually ceases and total exposure can be practised.

As soon as the seedlings have made three pairs of leaves their tips should be nipped out and the seedlings encouraged to form basal growths needed for future development. The sweet pea, unlike the culinary pea, does not build a good plant from the original leader, as this dies away gradually as the plant advances and developing side shoots take its place. The central shoot, whether stopped early or removed afterwards, is therefore of little use after the seedling stage.

When the seedlings have made a little basal growth after stopping each should be potted up singly into a three-inch pot filled with John Innes Compost No. 2 and placed in suitable cold frames. It is unwise to group pots closely together; instead, they should stand with rims one to two inches apart so that each seedling has abundant light, air, and room for development. They should remain in the cold frames until the end of February, or perhaps a little later, when they must be hardened off by exposure outside the frame preparatory to being planted out of doors at the first possible opportunity.

And what of the soil? The sweet pea when well developed is a most extensively rooted plant, and it is not uncommon for a plant growing ten to twelve feet in height to have a great network of roots equally long – an indication that the soil must be dug deeply, thoroughly, and well enriched with farmyard manure. These extensive roots branch and rebranch into an ever extending system of feeding roots, each of which acts as a kind of mouth. In growing a plant so equipped one should never forget the intimate balance of nature. If soil preparation and attention to detail permit development of extensive branching and rebranching roots, it is also possible to have a stem and leaf area corresponding in development and extent, and it follows, therefore, that the greater the root system the greater the plant will be, and, therefore, the more sweet peas will be borne.

The time for soil cultivation is in the late autumn or early winter months and when trenching deeply in the way described in Chapter 1 the surface soil should be left as rough as possible, and not moved until it is time to start operations in the spring. Generally, if good farmyard manure or compost is available no other fertilizer is necessary, but in cases of heavy soil where only a little bulky manure is available it should be supplemented by 4 oz. Basic Slag and 2 oz. Kainit per superficial square yard applied in the autumn, and on light soil 4 oz. superphosphate and 1 oz. sulphate of potash per superficial square yard applied in the spring, about a fortnight before planting out.

Before this stage is reached it is necessary to erect a framework of stakes capable of supporting this free growing, extensive plant – so likely to offer considerable wind resistance. Sweet peas grown in the way I suggest often reach a height of twelve to fourteen feet with leaves five to six inches across, and sometimes more. Plants closely hedged together at this height and with great leaf area are liable to be swept away during July and

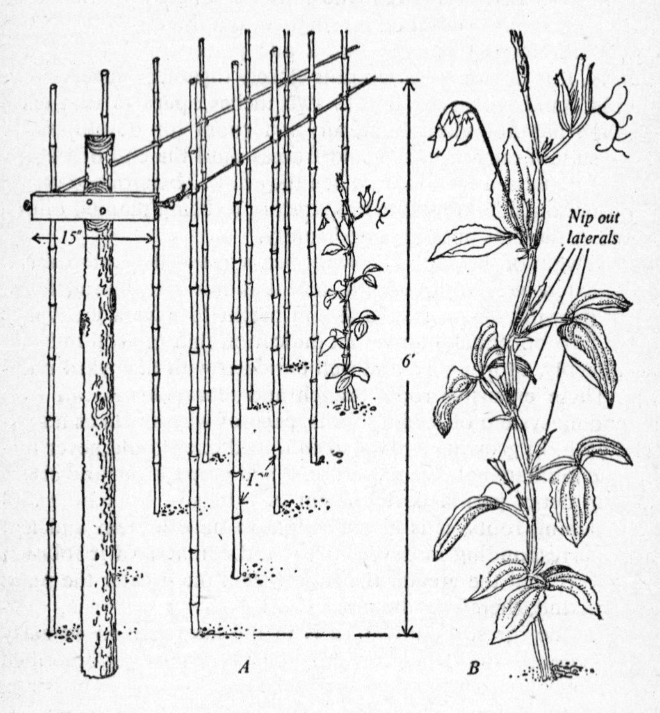

30. Sweet peas: (A) Staking; (B) Dealing with sideshoots.

August unless rigid supports capable of withstanding great pressure are afforded. To achieve this posts ten feet high are erected at each end of the row, sunk firmly three feet in the ground. To each post is attached a spreader about a foot wide and at each end of these spreaders wires are strained tightly from post to post. To the wires are attached bamboo canes, or any suitable slim rods or stakes, thrust into the ground to keep them rigid at the bottom and spaced six inches apart along each side of the double row. Thus the seedlings form a double row with a hollow centre something like a hollow wall of bricks. If well grown, seedlings sometimes have considerable leaf area when planted out, and although by that time they have more than one shoot, all should be tied to the stakes immediately after planting to prevent damaging friction caused by buffeting.

The root system of the sweet pea is unlike that of most plants except the culinary pea. At planting-out time roots may be several feet long, freely provided with lateral and sub-lateral extensions, white and of the diameter of parcelling string. If handled with reasonable care they are not easily broken. They are often found wound in tight coils around the base of the ball of soil when it is knocked from the pot at the time of planting. Because of this many good growers unwind them at the bottom and shake them quite free of soil before planting them extended like fruit tree roots in a spreading hole, which cannot always be made conveniently with a trowel. Others say that this treatment is harmful and that the ball should be planted intact, as knocked from the pot, irrespective of the wound-up roots. Controversy has long raged around the point, but experience proves that shaking-out is best for light soils, partial shaking out for medium soils, and no shaking out for the intractable clays which are in the minority.

The time of planting is also a debatable point. There is no doubt that in the milder parts of the country the sooner sweet peas are planted out the better, and in such districts it is often possible to plant out in the latter half of February. It so often happens that in the last few days of the month there is a period of tilth-promoting drying wind when it is possible to plant out in comparative comfort – an operation which sometimes becomes impossible later in the wet and windy days of March. In almost any district, if the soil is light, no opportunity to plant out should be lost; on the other hand, one should not attempt to plant out by date, as to do so might lead to total loss or crippling. Only when good tilth makes it possible to erect framework, wires, and stakes without converting the surface soil into a plastic mass should this work be attempted.

In some districts planting is not possible until mid March and in others the end of March; growers should sow their seeds a little later in the autumn in these parts to prevent seedlings becoming too forward before spring weather conditions permit planting. With some close clinging clay soils there is generally a brief period in early spring when the surface soil, reduced by the elements into a fine powder, is ideal for planting, and if this opportunity is missed sometimes a chance does not again offer for many weeks, while seedlings starve and languish. Conditions matter far more than dates for planting. If the earth cloys – keep off.

After planting, little top growth will be observable for some weeks – sometimes five or six – but the grower should not become anxious about this, for roots form steadily in spite of adverse weather. Generally growth begins apace about mid April and plants appearing dormant in one week may grow rapidly in the next. At this stage it becomes necessary to start the gradual thinning of shoots. It is unwise to do this in one operation as sparrows, slugs, and other enemies take their toll, so shoots should be reduced gradually until only one per plant is left. These selected shoots should be attached loosely but securely to the sticks with raffia, fillis string, or soft green twist. Hard string or wire is generally undesirable, although there are wire clips on the market sold especially for the purpose which often take longer to attach than it takes to tie string.

All ties should be made loosely enough to permit expansion, because the main stem, which at this season is about one eighth of an inch in diameter, will later on closely approach half an inch. Each shoot, as it grows, should be treated as a single cordon – in much the same way as a tomato – all laterals being removed as soon as they appear. It is important not to allow lateral shoots to become large because the stopping of any plant should be to divert plant energy into the desired channels; and to allow extensive growth, only to remove it afterwards, is a gross waste of plant energy and a check to the plant at the time of removal.

During May growth is generally steady and the labour of tying not very great, and buds appear towards the end of the month. At first there will be only two or three on each spike, all of which should be allowed to develop for use in the house. In their development there is no strain on the plant unless they are allowed to form seed pods, which, of course, strain it greatly. If spikes are cut regularly before they approach the seed-pod stage, no strain will occur and there will be blooms available for the house almost daily.

In June growth is very rapid, and towards the end of the month if the weather is hot and humid they may easily make one foot to eighteen inches of growth each week, which may necessitate tying securely twice weekly. This is not laborious but enjoyable, and it gives one time, while working, to appreciate the beauty of growing plants. During such periods of active reflection one is able to study the intimate habits of varieties and form opinions which are useful later on.

Ground cultivation in the spring to summer period amounts to little, but it should entail hoeing at least once a week – twice a week is better. This, of course, prevents weeds from germinating and at the same time, if the weather is dry, creates a dusty blanket of soil through which moisture evaporates with difficulty. In dry weather anxious growers often wish to give water, a wish which should be restrained unless circumstances demand otherwise, since sweet pea growing depends not on water applied during the summer months, but largely upon thorough ground cultivation during the autumn and attention to detail throughout the whole season.

Provided the soil has been deeply prepared and contains enough humus, water is rarely necessary. If, however, ground cultivation cannot be thorough and the land is known to be deficient in humus, watering may be necessary and some form of artificial mulch should follow it. The best mulch is the natural dust mulch created by the hoe, but in dry land, in excessively hot weather, a time comes when evaporation has exhausted so much moisture that there is little left to conserve and something must be done. In such a case water should be applied thoroughly, copiously, and checked from rapid evaporation by a protective mulch. Undoubtedly the best mulch for such soil is well-decayed farmyard manure, but if that is not available a mulch of any light material, such as chaff, dried grass mowings, stable litter, or even clean straw, all of which effectively hinder moisture from escaping, should be applied.

Then there is the question of feeding during the summer. A wide range of newspapers and periodicals often contain advertisements for sweet pea fertilizers. I cannot say these have no value but I can say that applied at the wrong time their value is mostly psychological. The application of these often makes the grower feel better because he imagines he has assisted his plants, but generally these preparations are applied too late for the plants to use them effectively. Most of these fertilizers are compound manures of some value, and in cases where the soil is uncommonly poor, and if they are used strictly in accordance with the maker's instructions, they do good. Unfortunately in many cases the prescribed dose, when applied, looks so meagre that the grower feels dissatisfied and applies another which, he argues, cannot harm – it appears so little. In the case of compound manure this is sometimes true – but if the grower uses quick-acting nitrogenous chemicals there is much trouble in store for him. Lulled into the belief that because such substances are quickly soluble the plant can utilize them immediately, he applies a further dose. A few days later he inspects his plants expecting miraculous results, but there are none. He forgets that although this nitrogenous fertilizer may be rapidly soluble it is impossible for a plant to utilize it immediately. One might just as well expect a child, ill fed from infancy, with little flesh on an ill-boned frame, to become suddenly big-boned and lusty after a few days of rich food – the analogy is much the same. Dissatisfied with progress, such a grower often applies a third heavy dose and a week or so later becoming desperate applies yet another and then trouble begins. Flower stems lengthen gawkily – topped with miniature blooms. Disease comes quickly. Blooms become bloodily streaked and splashed with alien colour. The plants collapse, quickly turn brown, and in a few days die.

Quick-acting manures of this kind are valuable but should be avoided by all except those with expert knowledge. If really necessary they can be used with advantage provided extremely small doses are applied. Half an ounce of nitrate of soda per superficial square yard is a normal dose but almost invisible after application – hence the trouble to which such a dressing leads.

The sweet pea differs from most florists' flowers – the rose excepted – because blooms cannot be saved for a day or two, and kept in good condition, until enough are collected; its blooms develop daily and far too quickly for mass collection. From the time a spike is placed in water its top bloom expands, intensifies in colour and becomes more lustrous until it reaches its zenith. When expanding, its colours become purer and its silken sheen brilliantly iridescent – a happy condition in which it remains sometimes less than half an hour, after which, although still attractive, it slips slowly and surely into a far less shimmering beauty. This must be remembered by all potential exhibitors.

On the day before the show, spikes should be cut at about 11 a.m., if possible when quite dry and in sunshine. They should never be cut when wet with dew or rain, although this is not always avoidable. Neither should they be held in the hot hand for friends to admire. Instead, immediately they are cut, they should be placed in receptacles of water previously placed near-by. The spikes selected should have the bottom blooms in good condition with the top blooms half expanded – neither more nor less. If more advanced than this the bottom blooms are in danger of collapsing before judging takes place, if less, the top bloom will remain weak in appearance, undersized, lustreless and poor in colour which – as the top blooms of sweet peas usually prove the deciding factors – would be bad.

When cutting, only blooms which come up to standard should be selected and these should be tied in bunches of twenty, their stems immersed deeply in water, and while in their receptacles taken immediately to a cool semi-dark shed, room, or cellar. Here they should remain for at least two hours or until they have taken up as much water as they are capable of absorbing. After this the bunches should be taken out of water, each wrapped completely in white tissue paper, and packed closely into boxes lined with greaseproof paper to exclude as much air as possible. The bunches should be packed tightly enough to prevent movement in transit and loosely enough to prevent the blooms being crushed. The packed bunches should be heavily overlapped with greaseproof paper and the lid fastened down tightly enough to prevent the ingress of air. If cut, prepared and packed in this way sweet pea blooms may remain cased for forty-eight hours without deterioration provided the boxes remain air-tight and are not exposed to the sun or placed in heat for more than a short time.

Blooms which, by necessity, are cut when wet with rain or dew must be dried if possible. For this, the spikes should be thinly arranged in wide-necked receptacles of water which should be taken to a warm room where a brisk current of air can circulate freely. A heated greenhouse with all ventilators and doors thrown open answers the purpose admirably. This may delay packing for several hours and upset plans later on, but sweet peas packed when wet are generally found to be almost useless when unpacked.

A grower who goes to a show knowing these facts about bloom growth is able to act accordingly. If the weather is cooler than is seasonable he should unpack the flowers and immediately place them for the time being in vases of water. If possible he should stand the vases containing them in a warm place to accelerate bloom expansion. On the other hand if there is extremely hot weather which will lead to over-rapid expansion, he should allow the blooms to remain packed for two or three hours longer and when unpacked select a cool place to delay expansion as much as possible.

At most shows vases are provided and to make the most of his blooms the grower should pack these vases closely with reeds cut level to the top. Into these reeds the sweet pea stems are stabbed after being cut wedge-shaped for greater convenience. Reeds used in this way display sweet peas efficiently, but in doing so absorb much water needed by the sweet peas; to prevent the water falling to a dangerous low level, more must therefore be poured into the vase from time to time until the time of judging. The blooms are displayed, facing the public, close enough together to enhance their colour value, but well spaced enough to stand out boldly.

Show schedules usually ask for a vase of sweet peas or a number of vases of sweet peas, each not to *exceed* a stated number of stems. This, of course, should be noted. If the schedule says that each vase must contain a definite number of stems, then the exhibitor must comply, but if it states that the vase should not contain *more* than a stated number it is not necessary to exhibit the maximum number – a point worth noting. If not more than twelve stems are called for, it is a great pity for a man with eleven good blooms to include one defective bloom to make up the number, for this will greatly lower the standard of his entry. Do not forget to fill up your vases immediately before judging starts, because after it has started you can, of course, do nothing.

In most districts sweet peas grown in the way I have suggested give long-stemmed blooms for exhibition, or for the house, from early June until mid August, and even in warm districts they usually persist in good condition until the second or third week in July. Towards the end of this period, if allowed, they reach a height of twelve to fourteen feet, which for many people makes them difficult to manage. Apart from this difficulty, long bamboo canes or bean rods are expensive and not easy to procure. To overcome this it is possible to use sticks six or seven feet in length and to lower the plants almost to ground level, tie them horizontally across the stakes, and turn the tips upright again.

This operation, known as layering, is quite simple. At the

time of planting, six sticks are left without plants being placed by their sides. As soon as the plants begin to grow out of reach they should be carefully lowered. One at a time they should be taken down, tied across the unused canes near the soil level and their tips turned upright again at a much lower level. The first one lowered should be attached to the first vacant stake and the remainder should follow in sequence on both sides of the double row until the full number have again been attached to the stakes. When all have been layered their tops should not be more than eighteen inches above ground level.

In a season when sweet peas are forward it is a good plan to layer before blooming starts, as layering sometimes leads to the temporary production of crooked spike stems. From the cultural point of view, it is doubtful if layering suits the plants better than continuous upright growth, but it does do away with several handicaps, including the use of tall steps or a kind of movable scaffold by which to reach the tops.

There is no annual or other garden plant to compete with the sweet pea for continuous indoor decoration, but many people do not want to cultivate in this way, and need them for garden decoration only. To ensure the best display seed should be sown in September or October, and the seedlings treated well during the winter and planted out at the first opportunity in spring as carefully as if they were grown for cutting. The only cultural difference is that seedlings for garden decoration should not be disbudded but allowed to grow naturally. They are effective if planted in clumps of six or eight and allowed to climb on tall pea sticks placed in the ground in sufficient numbers for the plants to cling, but not thick enough to look heavy. A variation of this is to obtain larch thinnings from the woods with the side branches shortened to about eighteen inches on each side of the central pole. If these are planted upright and the sweet peas are allowed to cling naturally to them, they form an unusual garden feature, and sometimes develop into tall columns.

Sweet peas can also be planted in a line to form a dense hedge, and for this, if good plants are available and the soil is treated well, they should be planted one foot apart, and staked immediately with tall bushy sticks. In the moist atmosphere of the west I have seen hedges ten feet high and nearly five feet thick dense with bloom.

Where autumn sowing is impossible a less elaborate method is to sow in shallow boxes in January and February, using the soil and methods as advised for autumn sowing. The boxes should be placed in a slightly heated greenhouse and after germination removed to a cold frame for the seedlings to harden off. Like autumn-sown seedlings these should be planted in their permanent quarters at the first favourable opportunity but direct from the germination boxes. In Scotland and in some northern districts these early spring-sown seedlings sometimes succeed better than those sown in the autumn.

There are still simpler means of growing this accommodating plant by sowing seed in the open, as culinary pea seed is sown, at the end of February or March, and even as late as mid April, seed sowing direct on the flowering site can still be practised, but unless the soil is exceedingly good and the district very moist the results can scarcely be good. In some parts in the west, north-west and in Scotland, sweet peas often flower gloriously at the end of August and September when grown in this way, though this method usually proves unsuitable for the south-east. However, seed is expensive and to sow enough to ensure good germination and to offset loss caused by mice, slugs, and birds sometimes proves costly and ends in failure; and therefore, people who practise this method usually sow cheap mixtures of sweet peas which when in flower have little value. Late sowing out of doors should not be undertaken unless no better course is possible.

Sweet peas can also be grown very well in large tubs or boxes, and I remember a terrace in the Italian style on which large tubs containing orange trees were placed each summer with other tubs in which sweet peas were planted. The orange trees, of course, were permanent and were housed during the winter, but the sweet peas were planted annually in the tubs. For this form of culture good autumn-sown plants should be placed in tubs filled with a compost consisting of good loam and farmyard manure in equal parts and enough coarse sand or grit to ensure free drainage. The tubs must have holes in the bottoms for drainage and the need for timely copious watering should never be overlooked.

Sweet pea varieties are innumerable. Sensational Spencer varieties are still being raised. Many beautiful forms are likely to appear and from the wealth of those already available I have selected the following:

1. White	ALBATROSS
2. Cream	CREAM DELIGHT

3.	Cream Pink	LOYALTY
4.	Almond Blossom Pink	MRS R. BOLTON
5.	Salmon Pink on Creamy Buff	PRINCESS ELIZABETH
6.	Orange Cerise	CYNTHIA DAVIS
7.	Cerise	MOLLIE
8.	Scarlet	AIR WARDEN
9.	Crimson	CRIMSON EXCELSIOR
10.	Lavender	MRS C. KAY
11.	Mauve	ELIZABETH TAYLOR
12.	Blue	STYLISH
13.	White ground Pink	MONTY
14.	White ground Picotee	TELL TALE
15.	Cream ground Picotee	RECONNAISSANCE
16.	Bi-colour Pink	GAIETY

In addition to the above there is a race of early-flowering sweet peas valuable for blooming under glass. The seeds of these should be sown in boxes during August and the resultant seedlings, when large enough, placed in eight-inch pots, instead of being potted singly. Two seedlings should be accommodated in each pot. From sowing time until frost threatens in October a cold frame is enough for their temperature needs, and after this because they are not hardy, they should be taken to a cool greenhouse capable of excluding frost. Free ventilation is essential and high night temperatures are harmful – 45° to 50° F. in mild weather and the exclusion of frost in severe weather being all that is necessary. In sunny districts flowers appear in February but in cooler parts of the country form a little later. The plants do not grow very tall and the blooms are of the Spencer type. There are not many varieties and these are usually sold under colour descriptions. Early-flowering sweet peas supply a few good blooms under glass at a time when others cannot be induced to flower.

Between the early-flowering varieties and the tall Spencers is a new type called Cuthbertson raised in the United States. In height it is about midway between the two types already mentioned, its flowers are larger than those of early-flowering sweet peas, and some varieties equal the size of the tall Spencers whose flowering period they forestall by a month. Few have yet been seen on this side of the Atlantic, but it can be said that when treated in the ordinary way in winter and planted out with known late-flowering varieties their behaviour is equally satisfactory. When available for general use they should be a great acquisition.

Finally, there are the Cupids. These are dainty plants which grow only a few inches in height and need no artificial support. Flowers are profusely borne but are too short-stemmed for decorating the home. If treated in the same way as their taller relatives and planted out early in spring in well-prepared ground they are excellent for massing in beds and borders. Provided dying blooms are removed regularly to prevent the formation of seed pods Cupids are able to produce blooms to the end of the summer. There are many colours and shades suitable for blending with other flowers, but Cupids are so individual that they deserve a bed or border to themselves, where they can be enjoyed without distraction.

You will enjoy growing sweet peas. Probably no other plant will respond so generously to your efforts.

· 13 ·

Early-Flowering Chrysanthemums

IN the hands of the scientific plant breeder there is apparently no end to the development of any amenable species and this seems especially true of the chrysanthemum. Its culture in other lands goes back thousands of years, though, of course, there is little record of this. Since its introduction to England in 1764, at various times it has been pronounced nearly dead, played out, or at the end of possible development. But not a bit of it! The played-out chrysanthemum has never been healthier or more popular. Never in its long history has it given such a range of types and colours in multitudes of good varieties which begin to flower in July and cease in the following March.

Of these, it is the early-flowering section with which I must deal in this chapter, a section represented by a quantity of beautiful straight-stemmed varieties of many types from the tiny ones, whose charm is in their lavish sprays, to the opulent beauties which, in August or September, have the size and attractiveness of the exhibition types of November, but are grown without protection, in a simplicity which was unthought of only a few years ago.

Early-flowering chrysanthemums require simple but generous treatment. It is not only the astonishing new types and varieties that have contributed to their modern success; cultivators have discovered that the elaborate stopping and hardening processes of the past were not only unnecessary but actually deterred growth. Nowadays there is far less back-aching and finicky work in growing early-flowering chrysanthemums; all that is essential is liberal treatment and the avoidance of check at any stage of growth.

Almost every specialized crop grown in the garden is dependent upon good land cultivation – deep digging and liberal manuring – and the chrysanthemum is no exception; indeed, it is doubtful if any plant in the garden makes better use of deep, moist, humus-charged land. When well grown, its development is so great and its complex root system – ever greedily spreading – so enormous that it is capable of absorbing great quantities of water and with it the plant foods it so much enjoys, which, because it is big and healthy, it is able to use in ever greater quantities as its roots and leaves extend.

Do not think, however, that the chrysanthemum is fastidious and will grow only under luxury conditions – that would be wrong. There are few plants more adaptable. I have seen it giving good results on almost every type of poor land. It will survive neglect and recover nightly when growing under the worst conditions of drought and in the end give usable flowers. Between the two extremes of poor dry soil and rich suitable soil the early-flowering chrysanthemum will respond according to conditions and treatment, but the response is always generous and sometimes surprisingly good.

Although it is in so many respects a tough plant there is little satisfaction in doing the least possible for it and hoping for the best. A grower should never forget that sound methodical work becomes a pleasure, while the line of least resistance often degenerates into monotonous drudgery. I have no hesitation in saying that to all who cultivate chrysanthemums thoroughly the plant's abilities will come as a revelation – unless, of course, they know them well already.

Let us begin at the beginning. In autumn, when frost threatens or perhaps has already blackened the few remaining blooms, all stakes and supports should be removed and old growth cut away. It is hard on the plant if this is suddenly removed to ground level; therefore leave some six inches of stem above the ground. Before you begin, look round and if you see any weakly plants do not cut them, but lift them with root and top growth intact and burn them. Disease often lurks in the unhealthy plant – perhaps a virus disease, and contact with a knife or other tool is a ready way of infecting many healthy plants. If a virus-affected plant, too, is placed with the others, aphis, perhaps unsuspected, may easily affect them all.

All plants free of disease should be carefully lifted with a fork and reduced in size by shaking away some of the soil clinging to the ball. All sucker shoots springing from below soil level or long shoots on the remaining part of the stem should be removed. The cut-down plants with their roots are now known as stools. Next, take them to a frame which has a hard bottom, pack them closely together in this, shake a little fine soil between the roots and cover them over completely with two inches of finely-sifted soil. Old potting soil reduced by means of a sieve answers admirably.

Although capable of withstanding a few degrees of frost the early-flowering chrysanthemum is not quite hardy. The frame will therefore need protection during severe weather, for which stable litter, straw, or several thicknesses of sacking are useful; I once remember seeing a five-inch layer of peat spread all over glass frames with good effect. In long, severe spells, however, it is well to remember that it is possible to exclude frost through the well-protected top of a frame and admit it through the unprotected sides, so that in really bad weather some bulky material must be heaped against the sides of the frames to insulate them as thoroughly as the top. For this purpose litter and straw are easily handled, but decaying leaves or soil can be heaped against the sides in an emergency.

In mild weather plenty of ventilation and cool treatment is desirable, but it is a great convenience if the stools can be accommodated in a frame in which there is a little artificial heat, either hot water pipes or electrical heaters, not to give the stools daily warmth during winter – they do not need it – but to exclude frost during severe weather and in early spring to induce the stools to produce fresh cuttings which will be needed in February.

Some growers pack their stools into boxes so that in January they can remove them easily from cold frame to greenhouse, but an overcrowded greenhouse is no place for chrysanthemum stools, so, unless a good open position is available on a bench where they can be sprinkled with water occasionally, they are better off in a cold frame which can be kept nicely warm, if need be, by closing the lights early in the afternoon and thus bottling up solar heat.

The choice of cuttings is important. The large fleshy sucker-like shoots which appear during the winter are almost useless. They should be removed as they appear. True, they make good Irishman's cuttings (shoots with roots already attached), and grow away readily at first, but they rarely make a satisfactory plant in the end and it is the end which matters. The best ones are the fresh shoots which spring up together, taken when about three inches long and inserted in boxes or pots of sand or sandy soil. Further details of this will be found in the chapter on 'Propagation', Chapter 26.

The pots or boxes containing the cuttings can be taken to a slightly heated greenhouse or to a cold frame, but in each case should be well watered with a rosed can to provide enough moisture and to settle the cuttings in their sandy beds. In either place the cuttings will flag and those in the greenhouse will flag horribly. But do not be alarmed at this. Cuttings going through this phase are not good to look at, and so there is

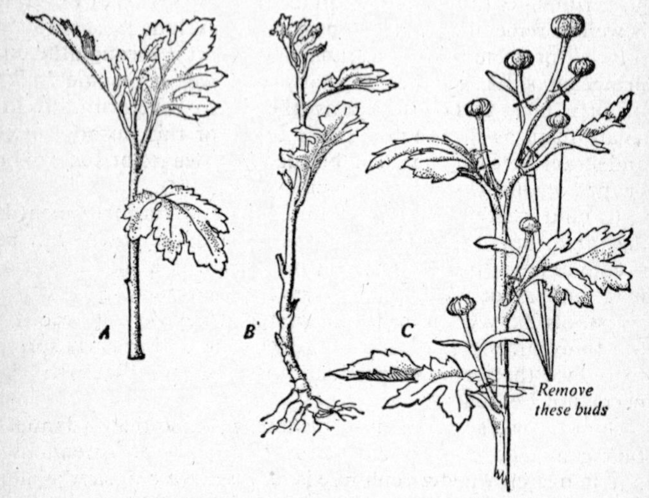

31. Chrysanthemums: (A) Suitable cutting; (B) Unsuitable cutting; (C) Disbudding.

often a feeling that something must be done for them. Generally it has the effect of inducing the person who feels pity to seize a rosed can and sprinkle them heavily with water – treatment which if continued will cause a large proportion of them to decay.

Flagging can be stopped or prevented by placing the cuttings in frames which have little air space or in a shallow box covered by a sheet of glass. This box could be placed in greenhouse or frame, whichever is to be used, but this is scarcely worth while and is very laborious, because in a frame in which there is little enough air space to check transpiration sufficiently to prevent flagging, moisture collects rapidly on the glass undersurface, and unless this is wiped several times daily the water begins to drip, and this can be damaging enough to cause heavy loss. After a week or ten days, flagging usually ceases and at the end of three weeks or a month stiff and perky cuttings show signs of new growth.

To grow early-flowering chrysanthemums successfully not only must check be avoided, but they must be encouraged to grow steadily at all times so that their stems can thicken and lengthen as much as they can before they are planted out. Our forefathers believed that good blooms could not be obtained unless stems were hardened until they were as unyielding as hazel twigs, and to achieve this hardening rooted cuttings were placed in small pots which, for a few days, suited them well. But the chrysanthemum has a densely matted root system with such abundance of rootlets that its appetite for food is enormous; and it was therefore not long before plants became pot-bound, in which condition they sat and starved until planting-out time came. By this time they were tall, thin, and their stems were so hardened that it became necessary to cut them down to within a few inches of the ground to obtain fresh shoots, often not more than two or three per plant, making it necessary to

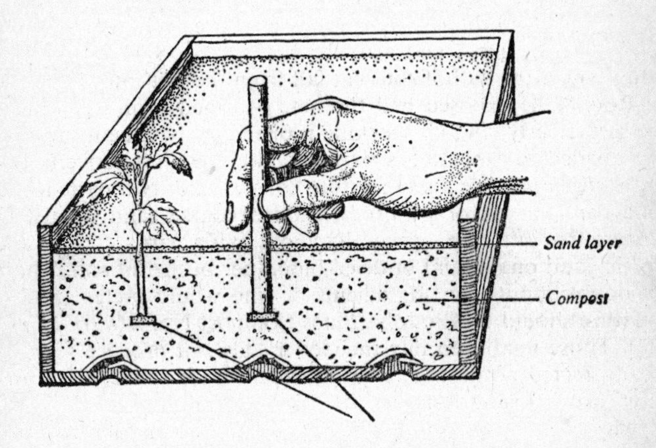

32. Chrysanthemums: planting cuttings in box.

stop all shoots again before plants of reasonable proportions could be formed.

Nowadays, it is recognized that this system resulted in a great waste of plant energy and that if a chrysanthemum is not checked at any time it is enabled to produce much more with less effort. To this end, therefore, the rooted cuttings, fast becoming plants, must be treated liberally and given a free root run that they may grow unchecked and with vigour in the important period between being rooted and planted out – a time when they are made or spoilt.

Let us, therefore, consider the best way to handle them with this end in view. The aim is to permit or induce plants to develop the maximum amount of stem growth possible, so that from this they may produce the greatest number of shoots – technically known as breaks – and at the same time maintain them in manageable condition for planting out. This may be done in two ways – planting in boxes or in soil placed in a cold frame. The best type of box is known as a seed tray, and can be bought at any good seedsman's or horticultural stores. Its dimensions are approximately 14 inches by 9 inches by 3 inches. Boxes of similar dimensions can be obtained in various depths, but for this purpose the three-inch depth is the most suitable. If the cuttings have been rooted in pots it is an easy matter to turn the pot upside down, place the hand underneath, with the fingers between the rooted cuttings to prevent them falling out or being damaged, and give the pot a rap on box or bench, after which the ball of soil will fall from the pot into the hand.

Round the exposed ball the newly-formed root system will be seen clearly, and by breaking it open the rooted cuttings can be divided and planted separately, twelve going conveniently into each box. Use a soil mixture consisting of two parts loam, one part leafsoil or peat, and enough coarse sand or grit to ensure free drainage – generally about half a part suffices – and to this add one pound of dried blood per bushel of soil. Those in doubt about their ingredients or who would prefer another mixture should try the John Innes Compost No. 2 (see Chapter 22). Those unable to mix their own soils can procure soils already mixed according to this formula from nurserymen and horticultural sundriesmen.

The little plants should be spaced evenly in four rows of three and the soil pressed in moderately firm but evenly about the roots, and the boxes should then be placed in a cold frame, after being watered sufficiently to saturate every particle of soil in them. At this stage no chrysanthemum should be coddled in heat, protection from frost being all that is necessary. For a few days after the transference, ventilate cautiously by tilting the lights a few inches only. About ten days later, however, when roots have rambled into new soil and tops stiffen, tilt the lights as high as they will go for safety, and when the plants are well acclimatized remove the lights altogether and replace them only on nights when frost threatens. If a cold frame is used without boxes it should stand on a hard bottom on which three inches of soil have been placed. Into this the rooted cuttings should be planted firmly four inches apart in each direction. Subsequent treatment is, of course, the same as when rooted cuttings in boxes are accommodated in a frame.

There is a vital precaution to observe. Early-flowering chrysanthemums should not be allowed to become dry at any time, and they are liable to become so as they grow and expand, especially in those blustering days of spring when cold wind tempers sunshine. To let them become dry for a day or two is the quickest way to harden and check them, a condition which results in fewer shoots and much smaller blooms. Generally they need water daily and sometimes twice daily to keep them uniformly moist, a state in which they make lush but sturdy growth, fit for planting out at the first moment when danger of frost has passed.

Each grower of these charming and useful chrysanthemums should endeavour to plant in rich soil – as rich as it can be made with ordinary resources. Those who have deep loam or loam approaching brick earth or clay are indeed fortunate, for such soils, if well enriched with humus, give truly remarkable results. Fortunately it is simple and pleasurable to observe, before planting, the rules I have given. Most cultivators can do so with ease, for the duties necessary are no more than simple attention to timely detail, with an avoidance of coddling or fuss, but where the soil is in question, the matter is, to some extent, not altogether in the cultivator's hands.

But he can do much. It is understood that he cannot transform poor gravels, sands, or chalk into rich deep loam, but by deep digging and the persistent incorporation of farmyard manure and any form of humus he can do much to reduce the handicap – a handicap shared, of course, by every occupant of the garden.

Because few plants will survive so much neglect as chrysanthemums is no reason for placing splendid plants in soil lacking enough food – instead, the soil treatment should be the best possible. By raising fat sturdy plants half the battle is already won, and the other half is in soil enrichment. If the soil is naturally good and the advice given in Chapter 1 followed, little supplementary food will be required, but on naturally poor soils, even though well treated, and on soils of better quality which the cultivator has not been able to treat well, additional plant food must be given.

On the very good soils 6 oz. dried blood per square yard applied about ten days before planting will give a splendid start, and little, if anything, more will be required throughout the season, but poor soils should be dressed with 4 oz. superphosphate, 8 oz. hoof and horn meal, and 2 oz. sulphate of potash per superficial square yard. Soils which come somewhere between these two extremes can have these quantities halved if it is thought desirable, but there are few soils within the poorer categories which would not be improved by the full dressing because good plants with a well-built root system are capable of using much food.

In a lime-deficient soil a dressing of not more than ½ lb. hydrated lime per superficial square yard might be applied, but as the chrysanthemum gives its best in slightly acid soils the average garden soil will not need this addition. All manurial dressings should be scattered very evenly on the surface and lightly pricked into the soil surface with a fork, and as in this case there is no need either to dig deeply, or to turn the soil over; a mere surface pricking or scratching with the fork will suffice.

Chrysanthemums brought up hardily can withstand a few degrees of frost; when ready, therefore, they should be planted out without delay. Usually, well-grown plants, bedded out in boxes and frames, develop sufficiently to plant out by mid April, and if at that time there are no frosts at night there should be no hesitation about planting out in any district in the south midlands, south and south-west, unless the garden is in a depressed frost pocket or on a very bleak exposed site. Even then it is debatable whether the plant would suffer more by planting out in doubtful weather conditions at a stage of growth when no deterioration, hardening, or starving had taken place than by planting in perfect weather conditions after starvation had occurred. In doubt of this kind I would always bed out when the plants were ready, except, of course, when there was hard frost or falls of snow – April conditions we have known in this country which happen only rarely.

Whether for a display in the flower garden, border, or bed, or for planting in the kitchen garden for cutting only, early flowering chrysanthemums are more satisfactory if placed fairly close together. Fourteen inches apart in each direction is a good distance, because sited thus their shoots eventually occupy all the space above ground and so support one another. When transferred, the plants, with their four-inch balls, should be lifted carefully from boxes or beds and placed in their new quarters with as little root disturbance as possible. For this a small hand fork is a convenient tool with which to make a hole slightly bigger than the balls of the chrysanthemums and so facilitate planting.

Roots should never be pushed into a hole too small to accommodate them comfortably; they should rest easily in a space large enough to permit soil to be placed round their roots without injury. Chrysanthemums should always be planted firmly and, unless heavy rain threatens, the soil around them should be well watered in with a rosed can or a hose – if convenient, immediately after planting. This provides enough moisture to support them until new roots grip the soil, and closes up any unnecessary air spaces resulting from planting. It is an excellent plan to fasten each plant to a stake before watering.

Stakes are important, for they have to take the weight of the plant in high winds and last throughout the flowering period. While stout enough for its purpose a stake should not attract attention, and one of hazel about ¾ in. in diameter is perhaps the most satisfactory. With a foot thrust into the soil, about two inches away from the stem of the plant, it should stand a good three feet above the soil level. To this stake the plant should be attached with raffia, fillis string or green twist, tightly enough to prevent strangulation and loosely enough to allow for stem expansion – a distance of one inch between stake and plant stem after the tie is in place usually proving satisfactory.

There is a rooted belief that good early-flowering chrysanthemums cannot be grown successfully unless 'stopped' many times – meaning by this a periodical pinching out of the tips of the shoots. Nothing could be further from the truth. Belief in this practice has spoilt many a promising batch of plants by inducing or compelling them to produce a much larger number of shoots than they could comfortably support; this results in a large number of poor blooms. Instead of being stopped to make it produce more shoots, nearly every early-flowering variety should be encouraged to grow stoutly until the break bud

– the first one – appears. This is then removed, but by that time from ten to a dozen shoots, and in some cases many more, have broken out from the stout main stem and are already several inches long.

This is the only stopping necessary for early-flowering chrysanthemums, except in the case of one or two odd varieties. But it should be noted that varieties vary greatly in their habits, for while some, when well grown, begin to break (shoot out) close to the roots, other varieties do not begin to do so until they are a foot or more in height, when shoots are produced in abundance and in ample time for flowering at the right period. Any attempt at early stopping or stopping more than once not only spoils the grace of the plant, but results in thin blooms of poor quality – sometimes without even the doubtful compensation of quantity.

For the average person who requires blooms for the house all naturally developed shoots should be allowed to grow, but chrysanthemum growers become very enthusiastic and sometimes wish to exhibit. To produce show blooms, from three to five shoots only should remain, the unwanted ones being rubbed out when quite tiny. The selected shoots must be looped carefully to the central stake with soft tying material as soon as the need arises, for without the protection of other shoots they will be far more vulnerable to the wind.

With some varieties of late-flowering chrysanthemums stopping and disbudding is managed otherwise, but this is dealt with in Chapter 28.

During summer, chrysanthemums growing in good well-treated soil will need little attention. For the first few weeks after planting a regular weekly or twice-weekly hoeing with a Dutch hoe should be given, but as growth becomes liberal this will not be needed, for the side shoots develop so densely that, for lack of light, weeds cannot grow at ground level, and therefore, from midsummer onwards, hoeing is necessary only round the outer sides of the beds, or on paths between the beds where chrysanthemums are grown for cutting.

Good and well-prepared soils will suffer little from drought, but when this is long continued water should be given generously, for it is wrong to take advantage of the chrysanthemum's capacity to exist. The effect of persistent drought is to harden stems, prematurely check growth, and produce a small hard bloom of poor development. A dressing of 4 oz. dried blood per square yard, applied before watering, often gives an additional fillip and helps to maintain a correct nitrogen balance, as there is always a risk of nitrogen loss when several heavy waterings are given. To prevent this loss as far as possible, only enough water must be given to saturate the full depth of cultivated soil. Less than this is sufficient; more than this results in the wasteful leaching of valuable food constituents. To test soil, when in doubt about moisture, an auger is an excellent tool, for after screwing this into the ground to the right depth it can be withdrawn with soil particles embedded in the screw, thus enabling the operator to test the sub-soil moisture accurately.

From the middle to the end of June, according to the district and variety, buds will appear at the shoot terminals. At first, just one or two buds will be seen, but lengthening shoots will show terminal buds surrounded by smaller buds and beneath these other buds appearing from each leaf axil, sometimes for a foot or more down the stem, measured from its tip. To appreciate the fully-developed beauty of the modern early-flowering chrysanthemum all buds, except the terminal bud, should be removed as soon as they are large enough to handle by rubbing them out carefully with the finger and thumb.

This is called disbudding or stripping down and should always be done as early as possible. To allow unwanted buds to become big, necessitating removal with a knife, entails a great loss of plant energy leading to malformed or undeveloped blooms. It is not enough only to remove unwanted buds surrounding the terminal bud, for the removal of these alone tends to send more energy into buds remaining at a lower level which, in consequence, grow very quickly, surround the centre bloom and not only smother its beauty but rob it of energy needed for development. Disbudding, or stripping down, must be thorough to be effective.

But there are other varieties whose blooms grow in graceful strays and whose true beauty can be seen only when they are allowed to flower without bud restriction. These, in the early stages, are treated just like their somewhat stouter fellows, but finally they need no disbudding or stem stripping. They should be left alone to flower as they please. Although they do not possess the size and dignity of the disbudded varieties, many of them are nevertheless delightful. For late summer and autumn colour they are unique, and make an attractive bed on the lawn or perhaps near the windows where colour is so much appreciated. For all decorative purposes they are light, graceful, and rarely out of place. For a dinner table under artificial light, or for filling large bowls for hall or lounge, they are invaluable.

Pests and Diseases

The best way to combat pests or diseases is by good culture, and when this is given the cultivator has little to fear. As this is fully dealt with in Chapter 32, I will not say more about it here.

In addition to the true early-flowering chrysanthemums which flower by 1 October, out of doors, unprotected, there are several other types some of which are said to be hardy and which bloom in the open during the autumn and early winter months. One of the most useful of these is the Korean, a hardy type reputed to have originated in Korea. The flowers are single and there is a great colour range of excellent named varities. It is said that they will remain in the border and give good results year after year, much like a hardy perennial, but undoubtedly they give their best if propagated annually and treated similarly to early-flowering chrysanthemums.

Mention must be made also of a dwarf race somewhat similar to the Korean but smaller in bloom and dwarfer in habit called the Lilliputian. These also are hardy but the hardiness is like that of chrysanthemums seen in cottage gardens for generations – a hardiness vulnerable in a season of excessive frosts. The Lilliputian should be treated in much the same way as the Korean.

The number of chrysanthemums which can be grown out of doors is now very large and to aid cultivators to make a good selection I give below some of the most reliable in each section.

Eighteen Early-Flowering Chrysanthemums for Exhibition

BRONZE:	Bill Riley
	Leader
	Tosca
	Westfield Bronze
PINK:	Brenda Talbot
	John Woolman
	Sylvia Riley

PURPLE:	Purple Ray Zenith
RED:	Balcombe Brilliance Red Flare Red John Cooper
WHITE:	Brumas Snow Princess White Wings
YELLOW:	Brighton Yellow Doreen Yule Yellow Triumph

Fifteen Early-Flowering Chrysanthemums for Cutting

BRONZE:	Chatsworth Merrydew Eamonn Andrews
PINK:	Daydream Sweetheart New Princess Peach Blossom
PURPLE:	Zenith Ronald
RED:	Red Flare Balcombe Brilliance
WHITE:	Brumas Cotswold White Serenus
YELLOW:	Delightful Harold Park Yellow Wings

Fifteen Early-Flowering Chrysanthemums, including Anemone-Flowered varieties for garden display to be grown in sprays undisbudded

WHITE:	Cotswold Gem Snowfall P White Bouquet P

YELLOW:	Yellow Wendy
	Golden Gem
	Mosquito P
	Golden Sweetheart *
	Yellow Bouquet P
PINK:	Sweetheart *
BRONZE:	Wendy
	Firedrake
	Sparkler
	Winnie Avemy
	Royalty
	August Red

* These varieties have many other colour sports. P: Pompon varieties.

For exhibition, sometimes it is necessary to study stopping times a little more closely and for those who wish to do so I give a list of stopping dates.

Variety	*Date stopped*
CHATSWORTH	25 May
MERRYDEW	N.B.
EAMONN ANDREWS	15 May
DAYDREAM	1 June
SWEETHEART	N.B.
NEW PRINCESS	20 May
PEACH BLOSSOM	7 June
ZENITH	15 May
RONALD	N.B.
RUBY	N.B.
RED FLARE	N.B.
BALCOMBE BRILLIANCE	N.B.
BRUMAS	25 May
COTSWOLD WHITE	N.B.
SERENUS	15 May
DELIGHTFUL	N.B.
HAROLD PARK	30 May
YELLOW WINGS	20 May
BILL RILEY	20 May
LEADER	1 June
TOSCA	14 June
WESTFIELD BRONZE	24 May

Variety	*Date stopped*
BRENDA TALBOT	20 May
JOHN WOOLMAN	25 April
SYLVIA RILEY	N.B.
PURPLE RAY	20 May
ZENITH	15 May
BALCOMBE BRILLIANCE	N.B.
RED FLARE	N.B.
RED JOHN COOPER	15 May
BRUMAS	25 May
SNOW PRINCESS	25 April
WHITE WINGS	20 May
BRIGHTON YELLOW	1 June
DOREEN YULE	25 May
YELLOW TRIUMPH	20 May

Where the break bud had appeared – the plant thus making a natural break – this is indicated by the letters N.B.

· 14 ·

Pansies and Violas

PANSIES have an old-world grace and charm which few can resist. Their quaint colourings, velvety appearance, and the puckish faces they assume, fascinate many people who often feel very disappointed at the results of their own efforts to cultivate them – perhaps in an elaborately kept garden.

There is a strong underlying reason for this. It is not mere coincidence that pansies grow to perfection in the tiny gardens of old cottages in sheltered villages. Such villages often sit comfortably in a lap between hills. The soil is generally rich alluvial mould which has slipped to the bottom of the hillside and the gardens themselves, cultivated for centuries, have surface soil rich in humus. Often such gardens have an old apple tree or two, giving partial shade, and are cool, moist, and sheltered by wall or tall hedgerow. This combination gives the pansy what it needs – cool, moist soil rich in humus, a little shade in hot weather, and protection from cold, harsh and drying winds. We must heed these facts.

The garden owner should never attempt anything and everything because of good results in somebody else's garden – it would be foolish. Even in this small land of ours, which offers countless opportunities for good gardening, soil and climate vary tremendously, sometimes in gardens only a stone's throw apart, and this must be considered. If your garden is windswept and the soil poor, it is no place for pansies – in such a case wait until you can provide some shelter; but if you are favourably situated there is no reason why you should not grow pansies for many months. However, if conditions are borne in mind, and a suitable spot is selected, a very large number of garden owners can grow pansies successfully, though it must be admitted, sadly, that they are rarely suitable for the new garden unless it is sited on some rich old market-garden soil or on naturally rich land. In gardens established for a few years with permanent vegetation around there is generally a spot where a few can be grown if it is remembered that, although pansies appreciate shade in very hot weather, in the main they are sunshine lovers and their chief need is rich cool soil.

In spite of their soft and somewhat succulent appearance they are far hardier than appearances suggest, and hard indeed is the winter that wrecks them. It is true that the thaw in March, 1947, found them badly bruised and shaken, as it did many flowers generally considered hardy, for that winter was one during which even native English yews were blasted; usually there is little to fear on that account.

The pansy has suffered to some extent because, in the minds of many, spring is the time for seed sowing; and generally it is. But there are exceptions. If the pansies are intended for summer flowering in the same season then spring is the right time to sow – if seed is germinated in a greenhouse. For the average person, however, it is better to sow in summer to produce a plant of the right strength and size to stand the winter. For this, sowing should be adjusted to circumstances. If the seedlings are too small when autumn planting time arrives, probably they will not be strong enough to survive; if too large they will be battered by wind, look sickly after frost, and perhaps collapse in May before flowering.

We must seek a suitable time, therefore, which will fit with the soil and climate of the garden. In our calculations we must remember that the soil is warm in summer but that gravelly and sandy soils are generally much warmer than clay soils which retain much moisture. On the warmer soils, the end of July or early August is not too late, for medium soils mid July is a good time, and from mid June to the end of June excellent for the heavy soils. At these seasons no protection is necessary and coddling should be out of the question, but a protected spot where wind can be baffled is a great advantage, for persistent winds dry the soil and lead to a condition which sometimes results in irregular early growth after the seed has sprouted – a kind of malting process.

The simpler the job is made the better. Select a little patch, carefully draw drills two inches deep and about ten inches apart, sow the seed thinly, carefully cover with soil, make moderately firm and rake the surface level. On light soils annual weeds, such as the annual nettle, invariably germinate before the pansy, so in case it should be necessary to hoe between the rows before germination is complete, mark the end of each row with a small stake thrust into the ground – a wise precaution to take at any time and by running a line from stake to stake make it easy to destroy the germinating weed seeds between the lines by hoeing, without danger to the crop, thus leaving a two-inch band, representing the top width of the drill, untouched by hoe or other tool. Annual weed seed, of course, will also germinate in this narrow strip, but with the chief competitors removed from the middle of the rows the position will

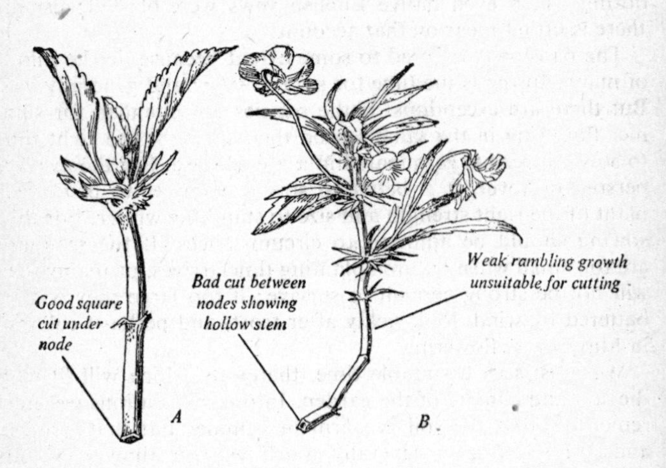

33. Violas: (A) Good and (B) bad cuttings.

not be nearly so bad. Afterwards it will be quite a simple job to pull out by hand the offenders in the drills and thus give the true occupants breathing space and room to develop.

If the soil is not thoroughly moist at sowing time water should be given, and to germinate seed in dry weather the best method is to water the drills before the seed is sown. By the use of a long-spouted light watering can, used without a rose, it is easy to pour water along the bottom of the V-shaped drill; a method which will save time, and afford ample moisture for germination, as the seed will have direct contact with moist soil.

When the seedlings can be handled comfortably, they should be bedded out. Again allot a place where it is sunny but not draughty or windswept. It should be a level site, too, for watering may be necessary. Sometimes a small portion of the vegetable garden is admirable as the deep digging and heavy manuring with farmyard manure – so necessary for vegetable production – produces soil heavily charged with humus; ideal for pansies and the like. If this cannot be found then try to enrich the ground which must be used – not with fresh manure, but with well-decayed farmyard manure, compost, or some form of decayed humus.

Not much is needed, as deep digging is not necessary, so a little well-decayed farmyard manure or stable manure, a few barrow loads of well-decayed leaf soil, some compost, or even some fresh granulated peat will suffice. The latter, of course, is excellent, but, in a case like this, its full benefit is obtained not for the immediate crop but for the one which follows, because peat decays slowly. In the south of England, at least, good soft humus is always the answer for pansies. Whatever material is available should be well forked into the soil, which should then be trodden firmly all over, once only. To traverse it more than once would be to produce impacted soil which checks growth but moderate firming by treading prevents over-exuberant growth and assists the plants to grow steadily, sturdy and healthy.

From the seed bed the seedlings should be carefully lifted with a hand fork to preserve as many unbroken roots as pos-

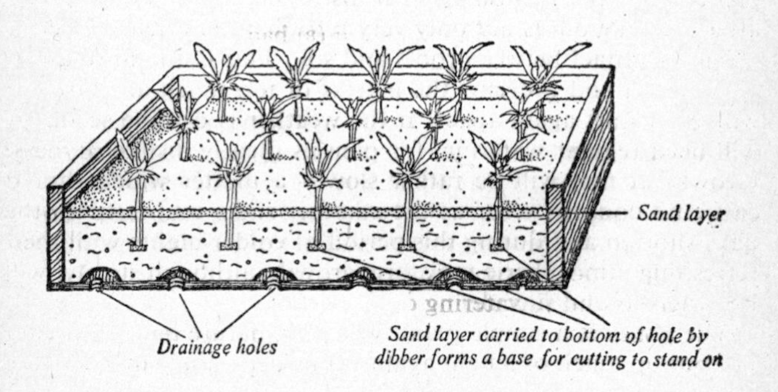

34. Violas: Cuttings in tray.

sible. No plant should have its seedlings forcibly dragged from the soil and the succulent pansy least of all. Neither should pansies be allowed to be exposed unduly to the drying influence of wind and sun. To prevent this, a few only should be lifted at a time, and these should be kept covered with an old cloth, a piece of light sacking, or – the old countryman's stand-by – a rhubarb leaf. Four inches apart in each direction is a good distance for pricking or bedding out. For this pleasant job some old hands make holes in the soft soil with the first finger, but the average man will get on better if he uses a dibber cut from a piece of stake three quarters of an inch in diameter and sharpened to a blunt point. With this in the right hand holes are made of a depth to suit the roots, the seedlings being held in the left hand, the roots lowered to their full extent and the soil carefully pressed close round the roots and stem firmly, but not firmly enough to bruise the stem. Seedlings should always be bedded or pricked out (terms which mean the same) only a little deeper than they grew in the seedling bed. They should never be buried up to half their length or have their leaves smothered indiscriminately with soil.

The bed may be made to any length, but not more than four feet in width, so that all seedlings on either side of the bed are within easy reach of the hand – a matter of importance later on. They should be watered immediately after pricking out, for even though the soil is comparatively moist, fleshy-leaved plants like pansies soon suffer if disturbed and a good soaking after pricking out is not only very refreshing but helps to make efficient contact between roots and soil. This is an aid to quick root action and prevents the ingress of too much air. Growth will soon start again apace. If the weather is dry the seedlings will need regular watering, for pansies greatly dislike dryness. Growth at first will be rather slow – a matter which should cause no concern – for as the summer sinks into autumn the days shorten and during this period of colder nights with their refreshing atmospheric moisture, growth, although steady, will be generous and succulent.

The pansy is a simple plant, which by nature and habit cannot put up much of a fight against intruders; the pansy nursery bed must therefore not become choked with weeds. The growth-promoting conditions so beloved of pansies in the late summer and autumn are also ideal for annual weeds, which, unfortunately, grow much faster than pansies. Pansies allowed to remain obliterated by a dense growth of weeds – if only for a very short time – become so bleached and drawn in the unequal struggle for light and air and so weakened in constitution that they rarely recover fully. Then flabby growths, sometimes feet in height, have to be cut back to within a few inches of the ground, and a cut-back pansy is a poor thing compared with the happy compact type of plant allowed to live a suitable life without ever-encroaching neighbours.

So, from the first, weeds must be kept under. Tiny Dutch hoes only two or three inches wide can be bought, and if these are fitted with short wooden handles like those of household shovels, very useful hand hoes – to be used with one hand – can be made. With a little practice, you will find it easy to hoe between the rows of seedling pansies and between the seedlings in the rows, whether they are pricked out opposite each other or diagonally, the few seedling weeds remaining being easily removed with the finger and thumb. It is a bad plan to wait for weeds to appear before starting, for if at that stage a week of wet weather occurs at the end of it weeds can be so big that hand-weeding with all its disruption has to be resorted to and, apart from the disadvantages to the seedlings, few people really like hand-weeding – in any case a non-productive occupation that wastes time.

Begin with the tiny hoe, therefore, only a few days after pricking out, and repeat regularly, at least once a week – twice a week being much better. Friends who do not understand the principles involved may laugh at you for hoeing for nothing; but do not mind them; you will have cut out completely the possibility of weeds, and that is something to be thankful for.

Instead of using a tiny hand hoe some people like to stir the soil between the seedlings with a forked stick, an operation which if performed often enough is as good as hoeing. In both cases the object is the same, to disturb the surface soil, to prevent weed seeds from germinating, to create a good tilth between the seedlings, and, in dry weather, to create a dust blanket and thus prevent evaporation.

In September the seedlings should be placed in their permanent quarters in soil treated as described previously in this chapter. The leaves and stems of well-grown pansies are succulently snappy and bent stems and broken leaves will result from rough handling; therefore handle them as carefully as possible when lifting. However, do not misunderstand this charming plant, which, although soft in appearance and easily bruised and broken, is capable of withstanding long and severe frost; this careful handling helps it to do – it is the drawn and battered plant that comes through the winter badly.

35. Pansies flowering outdoors.

When lifting, use a trowel to dig out the seedlings carefully with as many intact roots as possible, and with a good ball of soil attached – a double handful of ball, knit closely by roots, is not too much to move to the new site. Place each carefully in a flat shallow box or tray as it is lifted, and, when full, carry it carefully to the new site, taking care to remove the seedlings from the box or tray in the same order as they were placed in it. To receive them, make a hole a little larger than the ball of soil so that each can be placed in the new bed without crushing or breaking the root, plant slightly deeper than the old level, make moderately firm, and tidy up.

Pansies scattered forlornly over a wide area rarely look their best, so plant closely enough to ensure that when fully grown they nearly touch one another, so that the bed appears completely covered. For this nine inches apart in each direction is not too close for vigorous development and good effect on the poorer lighter soils; this distance may be increased to one foot apart in each direction on heavier or naturally richer soils.

Pansies generally have few enemies, but in town areas they

36. Pansies flowering indoors, face to the light.

are sometimes attacked by sparrows. Sometimes bird scarers have little effect and if this is so, an old fish net stretched tightly over the bed, supported on forked stakes a foot high to prevent the net from sagging or dragging on the seedlings, is by far the best remedy. Fortunately the need for this rarely occurs.

During the autumn months when pansy growth is most rapid, the hoe should again be used frequently, but from the time of planting into flowering quarters a larger hoe can be used with ease, one of 5-in. width being the easiest to manipulate (the fellow with the widest hoe seldom does the most or the best work). When, at the beginning of winter, wet days occur, it is time to leave off hoeing, not to start again until a sunny day in early spring. In winter, beyond keeping the bed or border free of fallen leaves, no attention is needed.

As May approaches, summer and autumn-planted pansies, in good soil and conditions, begin to flower freely, and if treated with care will continue to do so for many months. They will flower for a short time and continue to exist under nearly all conditions, even though they are very neglected, but if the beds are hoed regularly and all old fading flowers removed before seed pods can develop and if, during really hot weather, an occasional soaking of water can be given during the evening they will continue to bloom splendidly. When forced into flower rapidly by a spell of heat during July or August, the blooms are much smaller; this is quickly rectified by the coming of the shorter days and cooler nights of September, when large and thickly opaque blooms develop again. But to achieve this, it is important to prevent seed pods from forming, because if only a few of these develop they will soon cause flower production to cease. Pansies, however, are well worth any extra trouble, which, after all, amounts to little more than a few pleasant duties such as all garden lovers enjoy, and the reward given by the successive appearance of many softly-shaded flowers is something not to be forgone lightly.

All pansy lovers, however, cannot start sowing during the previous summer; but if they have a greenhouse or frame they can sow early and obtain seedlings which will flower freely during the summer of the same year. If the greenhouse has a little heat and a night temperature of 55° F. can be ensured, a start can be made in February by sowing seed thinly in pots, pans, or boxes – whichever is available – and by pricking off the resulting seedlings into shallow boxes of John Innes Compost No. 2 sited about three inches apart in each direction, as soon as they are large enough to handle comfortably. Full directions for this are given in Chapter 24.

After pricking off, the seedlings should be watered carefully, but without allowing them to suffer from drought at any time, cultivated in the greenhouse until mid April, thence transferred to a cold frame, and gradually hardened off by a daily increase of ventilation until, finally, the light or glass covering is removed preparatory to the seedlings being planted out at the end of May. After this, their treatment should be in every way similar to that necessary for plants wintered out of doors. People who have no artificial heat in their greenhouse should wait until the latter half of March before sowing, while those with only a cold frame should wait until an April sun gives enough heat for quick germination. Even they, however, will gain much time and have a crop of blooms for late summer and autumn. For all seedlings resulting from late sowings, the treatment after planting out into the final quarters is the same as for those wintered outside.

Twelve Varieties and Strains of Pansies

PERFECTION. A strain with a great variety of colours, shades and markings
FIRE BEACON. Wallflower-red, flushed orange
ULLSWATER. Blue with blue-black blotch
CRIMSON QUEEN. Red counterpart of Ullswater
BLACK PRINCE. Glossy black flowers
PEACOCK. Peacock blue, maroon and crimson
LORD BEACONSFIELD. Purple violet and mauve
LARGE FLOWERED.

White
Yellow
Bronze
Pale Blue
Purple

Allied to the pansy is the viola, or tufted pansy, a charming plant which blooms even more freely than the pansy. Generally the blooms of violas are smaller than those of pansies, but not always; there are some violas as large as some pansies, but whereas all pansies have three or five blotches of another colour or shade on the petals, those of violas, although perhaps of several colours or markings, have no distinct deeper blotches. In habit the viola is much more freely branched and its flowers are produced abundantly. There was a time when to secure violas true to colour it was necessary to propagate them from cuttings, and although this is still true of many good varieties there are reliable bedding strains which breed true to colour and type which can be treated in every way similarly to pansies. Violas, however, will endure more sun and thrive under much harder conditions than pansies, and, although they appreciate very good soil conditions, can be planted with safety in soils and situations useless for pansies. In sheltered districts they begin to flower in February, and during a very mild winter will sometimes bloom throughout the whole of the dull season if planted in a sheltered place. The following good varieties breed true from seed: –

GIANT WHITE
GIANT YELLOW
APRICOT
PRIMROSE

PERFECTION	Mauve
BLACK KNIGHT	Glossy black
ADMIRATION	Deep violet
PURPLE QUEEN	Rich purple
BIZARRE	Violet purple and apricot

Violas have been cultivated for centuries in this country, and there are many self and fancy varieties which can be reproduced only vegetatively – from cuttings. These are usually taken in September, and consist of healthy growth extremities two or three inches in length which, after suitable preparation, are inserted in shallow boxes of John Innes Compost No. 1 placed in a cold frame, or on a bed of similar soil compost placed about two inches deep on the floor of a cold frame. For more details on the propagation of cuttings see Chapter 26. The cuttings should be spaced about three inches apart in each direction, and to prevent excessive transpiration the frames should be closed until root action has begun. Whether the cuttings are being rooted in a soil bed or in shallow boxes no attempt must be made to coddle them, and the temptation to place boxes of cuttings in a warm greenhouse must be stoutly resisted, for violas are unhappy in artificial heat.

As soon as cuttings no longer flag and a little fresh growth can be seen, throw the glass coverings wide open daily whenever weather conditions permit, and replace them only in soaking rain or severe frost. On rainy days the light or glass covering should be propped open with a suitable block of wood (see Chapter 4), but in prolonged heavy frost the frame should be closed, and the light and sides given the protection of a covering of bags, litter, straw, or even peat, for although the viola generally proves hardy when established out of doors in the south, newly-propagated plants are not capable of withstanding great cold. When spring arrives gradually harden off by progressively increasing ventilation and finally by removing the glass coverings altogether, preparatory to planting out at the end of March or in April. Subsequent treatment should be much like that given to pansies, for the viola, too, loves cool moist positions and humus-laden soil, but it can also endure harsh summer conditions and will often flourish and continue to flower in prolonged drought, even when growing in soil of little holding value. Those who need propagate a few plants only and who have neither greenhouse nor cold frame will find a box covered with glass equally satisfactory. (See Chapter 4.)

The violas cultivated in this country can be divided roughly into three types: bedding violas, show violas, and smaller ones suitable for rockeries or small borders. Some bedding varieties can be grown from seed and cuttings, while others can be grown from cuttings only. The so-called alpine group, i.e. those suitable for rockeries, include some species which can be reproduced from seed and varieties of these species which must be raised vegetatively. Show violas are grown very extensively for show purposes only in some northern districts and among them are many quaint and fascinating varieties. Some are pencilled while others are splashed and striped with vivid colours laid on a pale colour base, and yet others have coloured picotee edgings much like those of a picotee carnation.

Twelve Varieties for Bedding, to be propagated from Cuttings

ADMIRATION	Good deep purple bedder
BULLION	Free flowering bright yellow
IDEN GEM	Early, deep blue, bushy
JAS. PILLING	White, edged lavender
J. B. RIDING	Fuchsia pink
MAGGIE MOTT	Early, free flowering mauve, scented
MOSELEY PERFECTION	Clear golden yellow
MRS MARRISON	Mahogany suffused pink
PICKERING BLUE	Best sky-blue, early, free flowering
PRIMROSE DAME	Primrose, very free
SUE STEVENSON	Violet, yellow centre
W. H. WOODGATE	Early, free blooming, china blue

Twelve Varieties for Show Purposes to be propagated from Cuttings

ADA JACKSON	White, edged mauve
ANNIE HAMILTON	Purple, top petals pale blue, pale blue patch on side petals and on middle bottom edge of lower petal
DOUGLAS UPTON	Pink with reddish purple centre striped purple
HARRY MERRIFIELD	Large yellow
JOHN FELSTEAD	Large very deep purple

LESLIE KEAY	Pale cream, edged purple
LOIS MILNER	Deep cream, edged blue, upper petals shaded blue
MARY HATTON	Very good dark purple
MILTON BEAUTY	Dark reddish purple, lighter towards edge
MRS J. CAIRNS	Deep purple, edge of top petal striped light blue
RUNNYMEDE	Pale yellow, belted blue
SUE STEVENSON	Violet, yellow centre

Among the alpine violas there are Viola cornuta and its varieties, some of which closely resemble cultivated violets of the Princess of Wales type. These are often sold on the streets of our cities as sweet violets, which they closely resemble in every respect when bunched closely, except in perfume. There are also Viola gracilis and its varieties and a number of other charming species. All alpine species and varieties, including all the smaller species, can be propagated similarly to the larger bedding and show types, except that, being smaller, cuttings can be placed more closely together, and when planted out can be accommodated in little crannies between small rocks or planted generously in flowing drifts on banks, or between large rocks, provided there is enough depth of soil to maintain them in good health.

Their adaptability is remarkable, for they will often flourish on sunbaked rocks in the south and grow in extravagant beauty on rocks dripping with moisture in the north, and, in a different way, be equally happy in both positions, or indeed in any. The advice given to keep pansies free of fading flowers and, therefore, seed pods, applies with even greater force to all types of violas, which, because of their greater freedom of flowering, are much more likely to become exhausted if neglected. Suitable species and varieties for the purpose are:

Species and Varieties suitable for Rock Culture

VIOLA Gracilis	Purple
Clarence Elliott	White
Major	Violet blue
Alpina	Purple
Aetolica Saxatilis	Bright yellow
Arkwrights Ruby	Mahogany red

Cornuta	Rich violet blue
Jersey Gem	Bright blue
Purpurea	Purple
Mauve Queen	Pale mauve
Lutea splendens	Bright yellow
Nigra	Dense purple black

There is yet another interesting section of the family known as violettas, the first of which was said to have resulted from a cross between Viola cornuta and Viola Blue King. In size they are intermediate between Viola cornuta and the bedding violas. There are many charming varieties, including some very fine bicolours, and all are suitable for edgings, rock gardens, and for planting in the interstices of little-used paved paths. They are propagated in the same way as bedding violas. The following is a good selection of varieties:

Twelve Varieties of Violettas

BLUE TIT	Purplish blue self
BUTTERCUP	Bright orange yellow
DELIGHT	Creamy yellow flushed deeper tones
DUCHESS	Primrose yellow, margined deep lavender
ENID	Bright yellow
IVORY	Ivory white
GOLDCREST	Deep yellow, edged lavender blue
LITTLE DAVID	Cream
PICOTEE	White, edged and flushed lavender
QUEEN OF THE YEAR	China blue, sometimes flecked with white
TOM TIT	Bright mauve blue
VIOLETTA	White, lower petals flushed yellow

· 15 ·

Lilies

FEW would deny that lilies are the aristocrats of the hardy garden. They like woodland, with its chequered shade, and the moisture of the valley. Undergrowth does not deter them, indeed for most species it is an advantage, and when in congenial surroundings all they ask is to be left in peace to flourish and multiply. Cost alone might prevent their being used to fill the bed on the lawn or the border where a change is needed; which is as well, because with a few exceptions lilies are not fitted by nature to be bedding plants in the usual way.

Lilies form a varied and extensive family whose members have been gathered from many parts of the world. Most of them are hardy and although some lilies come from countries much hotter than ours they are accustomed to endure colder winters, probably because they are protected from frost by a thick covering of snow. This also applies to some species and varieties known as greenhouse lilies, which are rarely happy out of doors because our summers are not warm enough, or our warm summer period is too fleeting – the latter factor is often the deciding one.

There are exceptions to this. There are few horticultural rules which are not broken, and rules for lily culture are frequently upset – generally because of local conditions. Thus it is that on the west coast of Scotland, where the influence of the Gulf Stream is felt and where the rainfall generally trebles that of the south-eastern counties, Lilium auratum, the golden-rayed lily of Japan, flourishes magnificently – even better than it does in its native home, according to collectors and travellers.

This points a moral. In this country lily culture is dependent upon local conditions of soil and climate as well as on conditions of atmosphere. Not everyone can grow lilies, or at least all lilies, and this is not necessarily because of inattention, neglect, or faulty cultural methods, but because climatic conditions are not congenial. Before any lily planting is attempted, therefore, surrounding conditions, as well as those in the garden itself, should be studied.

There are a few lilies happy in almost any good garden, but these are the exceptions, with which I will deal later. The majority of species and their varieties require shelter from cutting winds, particularly from the north and west, partial shade, or shade during part of the day, good drainage, constant moisture at the roots, much atmospheric moisture, protection from spring frost, when shoots and leaves are immature, and, last and by no means least, soil abounding in humus. It is apparent immediately that the owners of many small gardens cannot supply these requirements, and therefore, they must be content to grow lilies which succeed everywhere. Luckily there are a number of these.

Despite the obstacles I have outlined there are many people with new houses, and some with old, who have either ideal conditions or, with slight alteration or adaption, could make them so.

Between the two world wars many thousands of houses were built on what was formerly coppice or woodland. Generally, trees and undergrowth were left – mainly because of the expense of clearing – only enough being removed to accommodate foundations and give the builder working space and room to dump materials. Sometimes, indeed, most of the original coppice and a big tree or two were left standing, to the consternation of the new owner, who felt unable to deal with them. Some such owners after the labour of years managed to remove them, but most gave up in despair. There were many such cases in widely scattered parts of the country.

A similar procedure is still being followed, sometimes to accommodate prefabs, and all who have houses in such a position, before wasting money and labour in attempts at complete clearance should see if it is possible to make an informal garden leaving trees and undergrowth, which have taken many years to mature, and using them as the framework of a natural garden, with lilies as a permanent feature. If not in a swamp – and few houses are so placed – such a setting is nearly perfect. Often in a woodland there is a thick top layer of leaf soil humus – which lilies love. The coppice or trees give welcome shade and provide shelter from wind, and the soil can be prepared for lilies accordingly. Possibly some of the coppice will need removal – a simple matter compared with wholesale clearance – but before starting, the site should be considered thoroughly. Woodland lilies are not happy in dense shade; therefore informal beds made by clearances must not be under the canopy of a huge tree or where undergrowth would smother them.

Lilies in such a situation would suffer not only from lack of light but often also from lack of water, for a well-foliaged tree can shed, to its outer perimeter, nearly all the rain which falls. In such an informal situation, line and measuring rod must be forgotten and beds made in clearances between the shade perimeters of trees, as informal in appearance as possible. If there is any choice between a gentle slope and the bottom of a gully choose the slope, for the deep depressions of valleys – even small ones – are often waterlogged frost traps.

Study the soil. If layers of decayed leaf soil exist then there is little to do but stir the surface soil deeply with a fork, but without delving too much. Do not on any account bring the subsoil to the top – the informal garden is no place for trenching or working in the way the formal square should be worked. Stir in the leaf soil many times until the top soil is as light as the ashes of a wood fire. If no top layer of humus is naturally present add leaves, leaf soil, peat, or very well decayed farmyard or stable manure – never fresh manure. Here and there in the clearances group a few low growing shrubs according to the list given later in this chapter.

Now let us see how to plant. Lilies are bulbous plants with loosely-scaled bulbs sometimes many inches in diameter. The scales have no outer covering like those we know as Dutch bulbs, but are brittle, sometimes protruding, and, if exposed to the air, quickly perishable. Lilies are propagated by scale cuttings, bulbils which form in the leaf axils of some varieties, by seed, and, if left alone in congenial surroundings, multiply rapidly by natural bulb increase.

Bulbs of flowering size can be purchased of most kinds and varieties, except some greenhouse kinds and varieties from China, Japan, and the Himalayas which cannot be imported at the moment. It is wise to begin with bulbs – most good nurserymen supply them. Because of their scale structure, their rapid loss of water when exposed, and consequent shrinking, lily bulbs should not be left open to the air a moment longer that necessary. Bulbs of most varieties are available in late autumn, but a few are ready earlier. Generally, if from a British source, they have fleshy roots attached. Plant them as soon as they are received without exposing them beforehand. Because they lose water so rapidly, and to prevent breakage, nurserymen pack them in some soft moist insulating material such as peat, sphagnum moss, leaf-mould, or a mixture of all of these. If bulbs cannot be planted immediately it is better to allow them to remain in the moist package for a few days rather than expose them, but bulbs should not be kept wrapped too long or they may develop bleached shoots which rarely recover when planted.

With few exceptions most lilies like deep planting, so with a small spade make holes six to eight inches deep – the latter depth being better – for large bulbs. In any case arrange that after planting at least four inches of soil rests on the top of the bulb. Although lilies are so fond of moisture, if the soil is heavy and the bulbs lie in stagnant moisture they are inclined to rot; therefore, unless the soil is sandy or very well drained, place a handful of coarse sand for the bulb to rest on at the bottom of each hole.

In cases of bad drainage, pipe lines and soakaways might be arranged as advised for carnations in Chapter 11; indeed on some soils this might be the only way to make lily culture possible, but an intermediate step between a handful of sand and full drainage is to place a small shovelful of stones beneath each bulb or beneath each group of bulbs – a simple operation which carries with it some risk of forming a sump to hold water. Some experienced growers aver that planting the bulbs on their sides will assist in preventing decay in wet soils, but I doubt if there is much in this theory as the scales would be wet in any case. However, undoubtedly it is a good plan to surround and cover each bulb with sand before replacing the soil.

Imagination should be given full play – lilies are planted to stay. They should not be dug up and replanted annually or on any biennal or triennial plan, but should remain happily established for ever; when planting, therefore, they must be given room to multiply through the years and generally to form part of the surroundings. This entails siting them some distance apart, eighteen inches from bulb to bulb not being too much. Groups should be irregular in outline and fit the surroundings in shape.

The new grower should not feel disappointed if yearly results are not consistently good. It is true that if bulbs of flowering size are procured a good show of bloom can be expected during the first season after planting, provided they were planted in autumn without undue delay, but in the next season spikes will be smaller and blooms fewer while bulb splitting multiplication takes place and tiny bulbs develop – eventually to reach flowering size. Then in the course of several years each bulb will be come a colony and colonies meeting in informal groups will make a brave show annually, provided no chopping down of growth occurs or that blooms are not cut with long stems to decorate the house. For house decoration it is better to plant a few flowering-sized bulbs in an odd corner annually, because the slaughtering of stems and foliage is an ordeal established lilies should not be asked to endure.

With one exception – that of Lilium candidum – lilies resent being moved when in growth and even Lilium candidum is not improved by the process and sometimes fails to flower in consequence. Occasionally an odd bulb or even a batch of newly planted lilies will signify their resentment at being moved by remaining dormant for one season. Generally this is mistaken for total loss and if the site is not abandoned it is dug over and something else planted or sown. Usually this is a mistake as, left alone, in the following season a fat shoot emerges showing no sign of debility but appearing all the better for a season's rest. To guard against mistakes in circumstances of this kind and for many other reasons the position of each bulb planted should be marked, by thrusting a slim but strong bamboo into the ground close to the bulb. With this in permanent position, should a bulb fail to shoot, it is an easy matter to scrape away the soil carefully to find out if it has decayed. Should it be found sound, although without a shoot, then it should be allowed to remain undisturbed to develop normally in the next season. The stake would also serve to support the shoot if lightly looped to it with raffia.

In the countries to which many kinds of lilies belong, winters are severe, but spring comes abruptly, without the period of alternating weather conditions we understand here, which includes the late spring frost so damaging to young growth. While the bulb is dormant and covered safely with soil and snow it remains unharmed, but in this country of comparatively mild frosts lilies are sometimes damaged, not in the cold season, but when May frosts arrive with their unwelcome return to winter, and these are often sufficient to cripple leaves and shoots already well advanced. For this reason some light cover must be provided.

In the case of lilies this has few complications, for lily shoots delight in pushing their way through undergrowth, provided it is not too dense. Light protection of any kind also assists to conserve ground moisture and the humid atmosphere lilies enjoy so much. In districts where the bracken fern abounds, this, heaped lightly over the planted bulbs to a depth of fifteen inches, provides protection from wind and frost, and prevents the soil from drying, while not being unsightly in a woodland setting, but straw, although less pleasant to the eye, is equally effective.

A top growth of annuals is satisfactory if seeds can be sown in September to provide cover before the nipping frosts of May. For this, cornflower, Blue Nemophila insignis, or Phacelia campanularia are excellent, while at the same time providing a ground veiling of blue which, like that of the bluebell, fits so happily into a woodland scene. Many people have overcome spring frost difficulties by planting low shrubs, which, pleasing in themselves, help to build up the wild garden landscape while affording cover for the lilies between or, in some cases, underneath their branches. There are many suitable shrubs and in the list below I give a selection which should satisfy. Not all of them are evergreen – but this is not as important as it might appear, for the protection needed is very light and even a thin veiling of criss-crossed branches checks the descent of all but the worst frosts, which fortunately occur seldom.

Some Suitable Dwarf Evergreen Shrubs

Andromeda polyfolia, Arctostaphylos Uva-Ursi, Bruckenthalia spiculifolia, Daboecia cantabrica, Danae racemosus, Daphne Cneorum.

Erica (Heaths) in variety; Gaultheria nummularioides, G. procumbens; Hebe (Veronica) amplexicaulis albicans, H. Buchanani, H. carnosula, H. Colensoil, H. decumbens, H. glaucophylla, H. Godfreyana, H. Hectorii, H. pimeloides, H. pinguifolia, Kalmia glauca; Lavandula (Lavender) dwarf varieties; Ledum latifolium, Ledum palustre; Leiophyllum buxifolium; Mitchella repens; Pachysandra axillaris; Pachystima myosinites; Pernettya mucronata.

Rhododendron hippophaeoides, R. impeditum, R. fastigiatum, R. intricatum, R. orthocladum, R. cantabile, R. scintillans, R. ferrugineum, R. racemosum, R. calostrotum, and R. saluenense. Santolina chamaecyparissus; Sarcococca humilis; S. ruscifolia; Skimmia fortunei.

Dwarf Deciduous Shrubs

Berberis Thunbergii, B. Wilsonae, Caryopteris Clandonensis, Ceanothus Gloire de Versailles, C. Marie Simon, C. Topaz,

Ceraostigma Willmottianum, Daphne Mezereum, Hypericum Androsaemum, Philadelphus microphyllus, Potentilla fruticosa and varieties.

Sometimes the woodland site, although otherwise perfect, has soil not overburdened with decayed vegetable matter, and, if so, any addition must be designed to build up humus and so create soil and atmospheric conditions so thoroughly congenial to the planted lilies that they will increase with natural fecundity. In such cases mulches of leaf soil, scarcely decayed, or fresh granulated peat applied in early spring several inches deep, can do nothing but good and at the same time afford much protection from frost, especially if on those May evenings when the sky clears suddenly, and the temperature drops rapidly at sundown, this mulch is adjusted, by heaping, to cover the vulnerable stems. This affords complete protection and does not injure because it can be restored to its old mulch level when frost danger has passed – generally by 19 May, although in the centre of England and in the north frost is sometimes a trouble in early June.

There are many lilies which are quite happy in the occasional shade of the woodland and the following list gives a good selection.

Lilies for the occasional shade of the Woodland

Lilium Bolanderi
distichum
Grayi
giganteum
Hansonii
Henryi

Lilium Horsfordii
Leichtlinii var. Maximowiczii
tsingtauense
Wardii
Willmottiae

Although lilies, in the main, are woodland flowers, it would be wrong to classify them sharply or place them in definite categories, for many which seem to belong to one category will thrive equally well in another. Thus it is that some sun-loving lilies noted for their love of light will also be happy in partial shade, but there are some eminently fitted for sunshine, and therefore suitable for planting in the open border. Even these do not require full or continuous sunshine as a necessity but will succeed equally well in partial shade during a part of the day according to the direction of the sun. Dense shade, of course, would be unsuitable, but so it would be for the shade loving lilies, therefore, sun loving lilies may be planted in any garden which has sun for a goodly part of the day but not in a garden from which sun rays would be completely curtained by the heavy tops of forest trees. These are the lilies for the open garden:

Lilium aurantiacum (croceum)
bulbiferum
callosum
candidum
dauricum
Davidii
elegans
Humboldtii var. magnificum
japonicum
leucanthum
myriophyllum
pardalinum

Lilium carniolicum
chalcedonicum
columbianum
concolor
pomponium
pumilum (tenuifolium)
regale
Sargentiae
speciosum
testaceum
tigrinum
umbellatum
Wallichianum

All the above lilies can be used to form part of a scheme for the perennial border, provided they are not likely to be disturbed. However, in borders of this kind where much surface forking is done there is grave risk of disturbance and injury. If this is avoided and space is allowed for expansion then these lilies are happy. The success of the great clumps of Lilium candidum and Lilium croceum in the cottage gardens of the south and west is mainly owing to the fact that little is done to the borders.

Not all lilies are tolerant of lime. It has been said that certain lilies are lime lovers, but this is not quite true, for even Lilium candidum – the one which succeeds in alkaline soils before all others – is equally happy in a well-drained sunny site free of lime. There are, however, a large number which are tolerant of lime, and therefore those who live in the South Downs or the limestone of the west need not do without lilies.

Lilies for Lime-free Soils

Lilium Bakerianum
Hansonii
Horsfordii
japonicum
Leichtlinii var. Maximowiczii

Lilium medeoloides
neilgherrense
nepalense
rubellum
Wallichianum

Lilies Tolerant of Lime

Lilium amabile
- aurantiacum (croceum)
- Backhouse hybrids
- Brownii
- cernum
- chalcedonicum
- concolor
- Davidii
- davottiae
- Hansonii
- Henryi
- leucanthemum var. chloraster
- longiflorum
- marhan

Lilium bulbiferum
- callosum
- candidum
- carniolicum
- Martagon
- monadelphum and vars.
- pardalinum
- Parryi
- pomponium
- pyrenaicum
- regale
- testaceum
- umbellatum Hort.

The above list gives a fine selection. It is fortunate that some of the most showy lilies as well as the most popular are tolerant of lime, and that these, in the main, are sun-lovers.

It is quite possible that many people with small suburban gardens, who have no woodland, possess a border a little too shady for perennials, and, if so, such a border, which is of little general use, might become an ideal lily border. In it could be planted a few choice shrubs such as acers, azaleas and small rhododendrons, some hardy ferns, of which there are many suitable, and perhaps a few hardy ornamental grasses. From the beginning such a border should be laid out and regarded as a permanent home for lilies and other flowers which enjoy some shade, and it has the great advantage that it does not need annual expense. Shrubs and plants recommended are:

Shrubs

Acer palmatum varieties

Ferns

Onoclea sensibilis
Adiantum pedatum
Polypodium phegopteris
Osmunda regalis
Polypodium dryopteris

Grasses

Stipa arundinacea
- calamagrostis

Lyme (Elymus) arenarius
Festuca glauca
Stipa pennata
- splendens

Miscanthus sinensis var. variegatus
Miscanthus var. zebrinus

37. Lilium tigrinum, growing in pot.

There are many lovers of lilies who possess neither woodland nor suitable border, but in quite a small area have a cold frame or perhaps a cold greenhouse. They have no need to despair, for with some pots, suitable soil, and some good bulbs, they can have a most interesting show. With the protection of a cold frame and greenhouse they can grow almost any kind and variety of lily, as most of the principal requirements, including humidity and shade, are under control. At this stage I must not go into the matter more deeply, as the subject will be dealt with in Chapter 26. Although the lilies which can be treated in this way are almost innumerable those with little experience will find the following varieties most easy to handle:

Lilium candidum
regale
tigrinum and its varieties
croceum
formosanum

Any of the above lilies when grown in frame and greenhouse can be taken into the house to develop as their buds begin to open, and some will fill the air with fragrance for several weeks. After flowering they should not be neglected, but should be taken out of doors and watered regularly until their foliage dies, when they can be transferred to the open or, if no suitable place exists, given to a neighbour with a good garden. Lily bulbs are rarely of any use for pot culture during the second season.

The owner of a heated greenhouse can do rather more, because he is able to lengthen the season of growth. He can cultivate the aristocrats of the lily world which flower in early autumn, as well as being able to force others gently into flower at odd seasons. Few plants force more easily than lilies, provided their principal needs are catered for. As in the case of those grown in the cold greenhouse and frame, fuller information will be found in Chapter 26.

For greenhouse culture, however, one variety of the large white trumpet lily, Lilium longiflorum, sometimes known as the Lent lily, deserves special notice – the variety or sub variety of that species grown in St Helena. This is a sturdy lily which, grown in a country where the seasons are opposite to ours, arrives here at the end of May. If bulbs are potted up immediately they are received and placed out of doors, they require

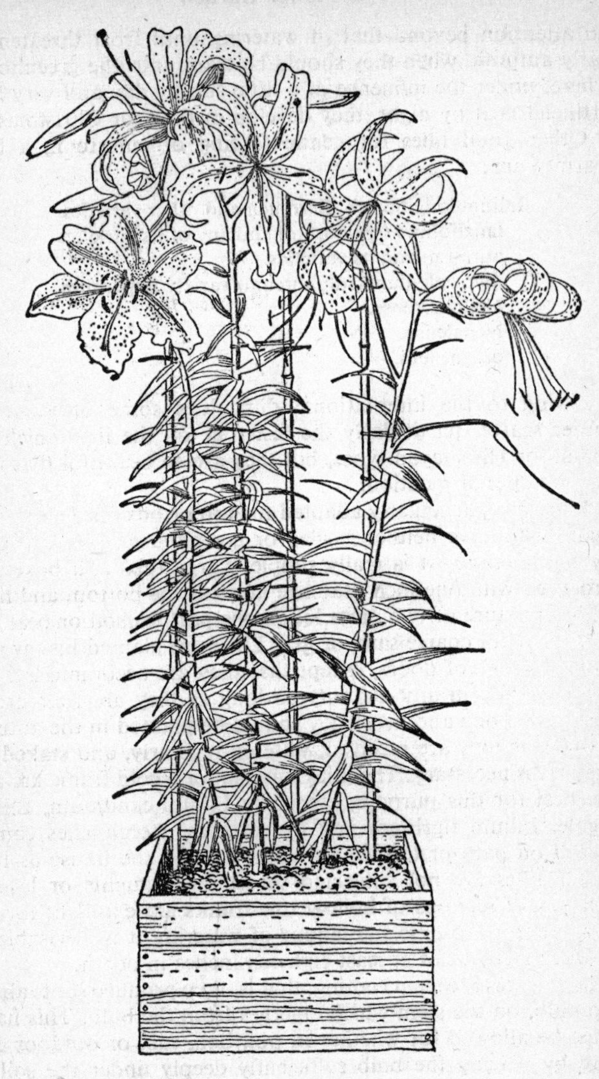

38. Lilium tigrinum, growing in box.

no attention beyond that of watering until frost threatens in early autumn, when they should be taken into the greenhouse, where, under the influence of a little sun by day and very little artificial heat by night, they develop in time for Christmas.

Other good lilies for gentle forcing or culture in a little warmth are:

Lilium longiflorum, Bermuda and other varieties.
lancifolium (speciosum) and any of its varieties.
auratum and its varieties.
myriophyllum (sulphureum) variety Superbum.
Neilgherrense.
Nepalense.
ochraceum.

Owing to the international difficulties some of these are rather scarce, particularly the last four on the list, which are Indian or Himalayan types, but they are so beautiful that they deserve special mention.

Lilies are particularly adapted for tub or box gardening, and many who have neither garden or greenhouse can grow them by this method. It is really simple. Large tubs and boxes are procured with one-inch drainage holes at the bottom and filled with a mixture of two parts loam, one part leafsoil or peat and half a part of coarse sand or grit. Lilies are planted just as they would be out of doors, except that they are accommodated in a tub or box in any quantity so long as they are four inches away from one another. They should be planted in the autumn as soon as they are received, watered regularly, and staked for support if necessary. The lilies suitable for a cold frame are also the best for this purpose, especially Lilium candidum, Lilium regale, Lilium tigrinum and its varieties. Receptacles can be placed on path or terrace anywhere around the house as long as the lilies are not subjected to cutting draughts or lashing winds. Cut sections of hollow tree trunks are excellent for the purpose, and to ease the labour of watering it is advisable to procure receptacles at least eighteen inches in depth.

Some lilies are stem rooting, that is, they produce roots above the bulb, on the stem which emerges from the bulb. This habit must be allowed for whether in pot, box, tub, or outdoor culture by placing the bulb sufficiently deeply under the soil to allow the stem roots to enter. This should make little difference, because most lilies should be planted deeply enough in any case, but I mention it because some authorities recommend that lilies in pots should be planted with their bulb tips level with the soil surface – a condition which is foreign to the habit of lilies.

The following are stem rooting lilies:

Lilium auratum and its varieties.
speciosum (lancifolium) and its varieties.
longiflorum and its varieties.
tigrinum and its varieties.
Hansonii.

· 16 ·

Gladioli

THE gladiolus is a sun lover. Although it comes from the sunny South African mountains or the warm moisture of Central Africa it is nevertheless happy in this country. For several centuries gladioli species attracted botanists and plant breeders, so that when the present century began varieties of sterling garden worth existed, but few would deny that modern developments are startling and some of the latest varieties of incredible beauty. They greatly enrich our gardens.

Although varieties of the modern large-flowered hybrids vary slightly in their habits, their complicated ancestry has given them few fastidious habits, so that almost every variety can be planted with prospects of success.

The gladiolus is usually classed with bulbous plants, but it is really a plant with a corm, that is, the bulbous portion, instead of having a number of fleshy sheaths overlying one another – as in an onion – is a flattish, solid mass which provides sustenance to the growing plant until fresh roots are formed to take over the work gradually.

In common with other plants of mixed heritage, gladioli thrive in almost any type of soil, but, like most highly cultivated hybrids, they reveal their capabilities only when planted in deeply worked soil well supplied with the principal elements and heavily charged with humus. In many chapters in this book I have stressed the necessity for deep cultivation and the liberal incorporation of farmyard manure and compost, not as a short-term policy, or an expedient to perfect some special plant, but as a yearly habit, so that all soil may become good enough for any crop, and developed specialities like delphiniums, sweet peas, and gladioli, all of which can be grown under poor conditions, can thrive and reveal glories rarely seen by the average grower – in the end, with little trouble.

In the average small garden, the kitchen and flower gardens often overlap, which is one of the reasons why I so often advocate that the site of the onion bed should be changed yearly instead of much good farmyard manure being wastefully incorporated into the same site – something beloved of exhibitors. If trenching and manuring can be undertaken for the onion bed alone, by rotation, all sites in the garden are eventually benefited, and I cannot imagine any better preparation for gladioli, which delight in mellow soil, than the preparation given to the onion bed during the previous year.

This perhaps is fortunate, for gladioli, with all their flaming beauty, are not ideal bedding plants. They each produce only one spike of flowers, with perhaps a couple of lateral spikes, but the flowers face mainly in one direction, and at planting time it is impossible to tell which that will be, so it follows that in any bed or border a large proportion of spikes will show their sides, at various angles, or a flowerless green back. Because of this, gladioli are better for cut-flower purposes than for garden decoration, although it must be conceded that when planted thickly and seen in the mass, in spite of the disadvantages I have named, whether mixed or in separate colours, they make a glorious show. For the home they are ideal, because when cut with the first bloom half expanded one may expect a fortnight's delight in any room which is not unduly hot.

For cutting purposes, gladioli are often included in the perennial border, where they make a good show. Some people like to include them in beds of annuals or to relieve the flat appearance of formal beds on the lawn, but the noble gladiolus standing apart from its fellows, dejected and alone, looks incongruous, and such surroundings serve only to accentuate its one-sided appearance, do little to enhance its beauty, and, by isolating it, call attention to its faults.

Although not the only good site, the kitchen garden is the ideal place for gladioli, and if this is in a position where the brilliant varied colours, of which there are so many, can mingle happily in the same line of sight with those of the annual or perennial border, so much the better.

Gladioli are not hardy, and therefore cannot be permanent occupants of any site, but must be planted yearly. It is true that during an exceptionally mild winter they sometimes survive, but, except in the sheltered south-west and in favourable districts in the south, this seldom happens, and with such choice plants the risk is not worth while. Gladioli, therefore, may be sandwiched in between any other two crops in the kitchen garden or in the flower garden with the full knowledge that the site will become available for any treatment in the late autumn. If a well-tilled site is not vacant in the kitchen garden, or one of similar preparation in the flower garden, an open site should be

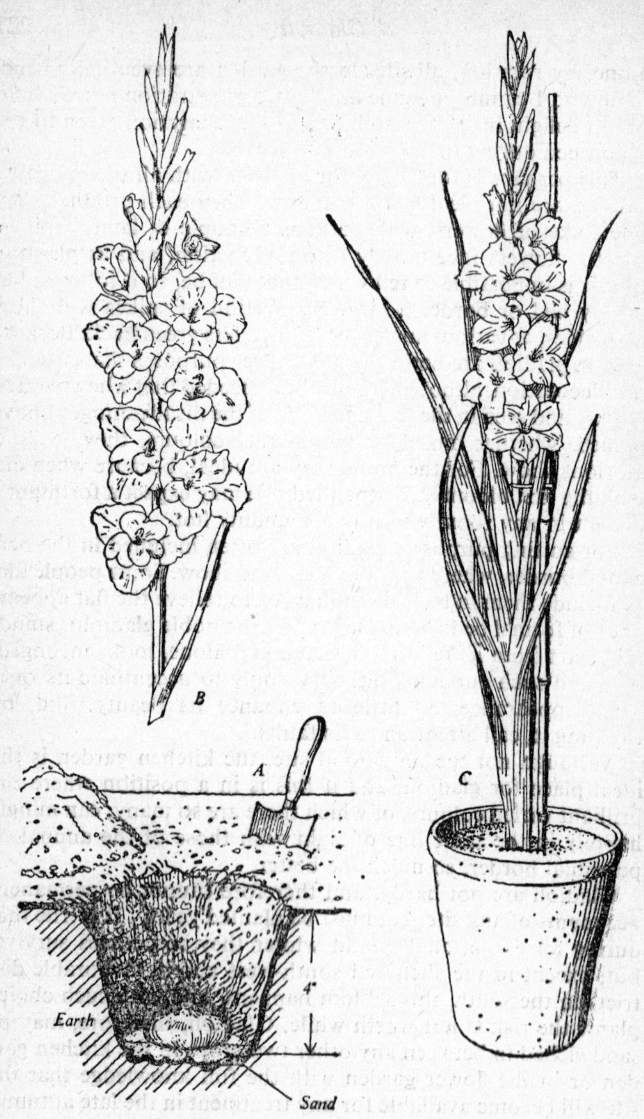

39. Gladioli: (A) How to plant a corm: sectional diagram; (B) Gladioli in flower; (C) Gladioli grown in pot

prepared by trenching or double digging (bastard trenching) as described in Chapter 1, but for this farmyard manure must be well decayed, and if abundant compost is available it is preferable to fresh manure, which does not suit gladioli.

Gladioli do not mind a little shade, although they give their brightest colours when in full sunshine; neither do they object greatly to drought, except that spikes are shorter, and flowers more closely packed on the stems and lacking in substance, but they love, and need for perfection, a cool moist soil. There they can produce foliage in plenty, thick sturdy spikes, long enough for the most impressive decorative purpose, and to demonstrate the peculiar virtues of the variety.

But the cool soil should not be a swamp – it should be well drained. There are few plants produced from corms which can exist in stagnant moisture or in ill-drained sour soil. Lime is not a necessity and slightly acid soil is tolerated, but the sourness of an undrained swamp is too much for gladioli as, indeed, it is for most cultivated plants.

It is well to begin with fresh corms. These can be procured from any good seed or bulb merchant in the winter months or early in spring. Planting may take place at any time between mid March and mid June when soil and weather conditions are favourable. In favoured southern districts, if soil-penetrating frost is no longer expected, planting may take place in mid-February, but the golden rule of keeping off the land when it is wet and sticky applies with great force to gladioli planting.

There can be a wide choice in the spacing of gladioli. While the corms can be planted almost touching each other in rich land, and if a massed display is required, better results are obtained if they are sited one foot apart in each direction; but between these extremes corms can be sited at any distance according to soil, climate, and circumstances. For this purpose, do not use that deceptive tool, the big D-handled dibber, for it leaves holes beneath the corms which, whether filled with water or air, would be bad in this position. For the average garden, where the soil is in fairly good condition, six to eight inches apart in rows sited one foot apart is a good distance. Holes should be made with a trowel and the bases of the corms placed flat on the soil at the bottom of the holes. Shallow planting is undesirable. It leads to rapid growth above the ground before the danger from frost has passed and insecurity in the wind, and, as the corm for the following year is produced on the top of the old one, the plant is greatly handicapped in producing this and the surrounding tiny cormels. There should be four inches of soil on top of the corms after planting is complete – to plant deeper would put too great a strain on the plant and possibly retard the flowering period.

Whether they are needed for cutting or garden decoration the time of planting is important. By planting at intervals the flowering period can be lengthened and flowers ensured until the coming of frost. However, it should be remembered that a delay of a fortnight at planting time does not guarantee a similar delay in flowering and that as the season advances the number of weeks needed for maturity is correspondingly shortened. Thus gladioli may be planted in mid-June, three months after the first planting time, but these plants will not flower as late as three months after, but probably five or six weeks after those planted in March. In the north, planting late is almost useless because cold nights arrive before stems and buds can develop, but in mild districts, where early autumn frosts are not expected, planting in July is permissible; indeed, if cold frames are available in which the gladioli can be grown in soil beds and arrangements made to elevate the lights on a wooden framework above the tall growing spikes, some wonderful blooms can be secured at a time when few people have them.

By planting a stated number of the same varieties each week, a succession of blooms can be secured in mild districts, from mid-July until early November. This is possible only if the corms are well cared for before planting. To allow them to give off their moisture slowly in hot shed or greenhouse during spring and early summer is to risk total loss. If the corms survive such treatment they are dry, possess scanty vitality, and hold little reserve food in store for supporting a shoot and growth – which in the warm earth of midsummer is rapid – until a fresh root system forms. Instead, corms required for late planting should be housed in a cool, dry, dark place, and if cold storage can be found whereby they can be kept in a temperature of 45° F. so much the better. Such corms emerge at the end of the period hardly shrivelled, little smaller in size, and with no tell-tale shoots like those on corms forced into growth in a high temperature before being planted.

When planting in loose shifting soil it is a good plan to draw a large drill with the corner of a hoe and plant, with a trowel, at the bottom of this U-shaped depression. Later, when growth is vigorous and as the spikes emerge from the centre of the sheath formed by the spear-like leaves, the soil previously drawn out can be returned to the drill to hold the stems more firmly and – if the garden is not windswept – do away with staking except for a few varieties weaker in the stem than others.

During growth, the stiff pointed leaves of gladioli, always thrusting upward, can compete with other plants better than most, but it is unfair to make them compete with weeds. It is true the foliage is spear-like and that it can thrust vigorously, but it is rather narrow and the leaf area not great. It follows, therefore, that although gladioli are able, in most cases, to keep their heads above the ever-encroaching weeds, they are weakened in the process, and weeds must be more than kept under – they must be prevented from appearing. After a mild winter, an infestation of weeds often begins in the period between planting and the appearance of growth – a time when nothing can be done – but this can be prevented by lightly forking all the surface soil before planting, or, if the tilth is powdery and good, in which case it is a pity to destroy it, hoeing every square inch carefully with a Dutch hoe before starting to plant. Afterwards, as soon as shoots are big enough to discern in the rows, hoeing should be done regularly, twice weekly if possible, so that weeds cannot germinate. This is far more important than might appear, for the annual nettle, which seeds when only an inch or two in height, and the annual grass, poa annua, which seeds when not much taller, are able to mature seed unsuspected.

If weeds are tolerated, not only do they hamper top growth, but they rob the legitimate crop of its sustenance, as well as entailing a useless waste of labour in removing them if they are allowed to become large, or if a rainy period prevents hoeing for several weeks after such weeds have obtained a foothold. Half a day's hoeing at the proper time – before weeds appear – will often prevent several days of back-breaking hand weeding. Working in a jungle of weeds wet with rain can never be a pleasant experience, but if rain should continue, a neglected site must be cleared sooner or later or the crop is irretrievably ruined.

Now we come to watering. Although gladioli will withstand drought so cheerfully no one can truthfully say they are improved thereby, and on many soils, in spite of good soil preparation, a time comes during a hot summer when watering becomes imperative. If drainage is good, gladioli will revel in hot sunshine, a humid atmosphere, and much moisture at the roots, but to create these conditions watering must be thorough. Driblets of water to the top soil, where evaporation is rapid, do harm by encouraging roots to the surface which are only to be destroyed by hot sunshine. Soil moisture conditions should be uniform, day by day, to be effective. Water, slightly chilled for preference, should be applied copiously enough to saturate the soil to the full depth of cultivation. But much of the labour in applying water is lost unless steps are taken to check evaporation, for the sun filches away moisture very rapidly in times of drought. Although the garden is well cultivated dust mulches are of little use in severe drought on soils of thin or porous gravel; and, therefore, a moisture-retaining mulch must be applied. If plant food can be given at the same time so much the better, and for this dual purpose there is nothing better than a four-inch layer of well-decayed farmyard manure.

Some growers like to water lightly after applying this to make liquid manure from the mulch available to the roots immediately. This is an excellent plan, but the second watering should not be too heavy or much of the valuable liquid may be washed away in the drainage, and so be lost to the plants. Horse manure, free of straw and not over-fermented, makes a good manurial substitute, and if neither this nor farmyard manure is available, a protective mulch of straw, chaff, cavings, stable litter, or peat will do much to check evaporation, if nothing else. However, one should not be over hasty in mulching, for from the day a mulch is applied normal hoeing ceases.

Often the weather changes quickly after a mulch is laid, and seedling weeds quickly appear. If the grower does not take action at this stage, he will eventually have an incipient jungle, which, in wet weather, will saturate him to the waist whenever he wants to cut half a dozen spikes. So, after rain, as soon as the mulch is partly dry it must be stirred – not so gently that seedling weeds are merely moved on a raft of manure from one damp site to another, but with vigorous blows with a five-tined fork sufficient to break up the mulch. This is a tedious job perhaps, but one by no means as bad as that of hand-pulling fat succulent weeds nourished on rich manure. Neither will this manure moving take so long. The tyranny of hand weeding is iniquitous – it is labour which gives no return.

Now we must think of support. Whether to stake or not is an often debated point. It is admitted that on some windswept sites there is no other course; otherwise the plants will be buffeted, the flower edges torn, and the spikes wrenched from the corm, which, if corms are planted shallowly, can happen after a few gusts on a windy site. When planting has been deep or precautions have to be taken to mould up the stems, there is little to fear, provided there is a little protection from wind. Staking never improves gladioli; indeed, it often makes naturally stiff plants appear ugly, and, as in the case of delphiniums and other plants, it can be a dreadful snare, for if not done properly, instead of making plants immune from wind it makes them vulnerable to it. Again I say that the natural hazel or coppice stake is the least conspicuous, and, for this purpose, a stout osier makes a good second. However, as with delphiniums, stakes should be long enough to support the tops of the spike as well as the stems or the first sharp gust is liable to behead the spikes or bend them to the point of uselessness. Green twist is good tying material for gladioli, but fillis string is almost equally good and nearly invisible. Raffia, which for gladioli would have to be used without splitting, shows itself a little too much – tying material should not attract the eye.

It is perhaps unfortunate that the lower blooms of a gladiolus spike pass away quickly in all but the best weather. In hot weather they fade swiftly, and in persistent wet their edges decay and become raggedly marked and shredded. Keen exhibitors, taking advantage of the one-sided flowering habit, make wooden protectors in which to enclose the spike. These are like three-sided boxes of wood, with open front and the back attached to a stake long enough to enclose entirely the full length of the spike. Each protector is about two feet in height, six inches deep, and six inches wide mounted upright on a stake of suitable height. One end, the top one, protects the tip, but the other is omitted to accommodate the spike. Thus the flowering part of the plant is protected on three sides and gets light on one side only, and on this side a small curtain is fitted on pairs of hooks, one on each side about two inches apart. As the buds develop into blooms the curtain is drawn up to shade them or protect from bad weather. Some growers fit the front of the protector with a sheet of glass, which excludes much cutting wind but needs adjustment for ventilation at the top, and also with a curtain for shading the blooms from the bottom upwards. By the use of this appliance, which prevents the lower blooms from passing away quickly, it is sometimes possible to obtain many pairs of blooms, in good condition, at one time.

As gladioli face in one direction they lend themselves to exhibition work, but many keen growers are puzzled about the time of cutting and method of handling. If protectors are used the difficulty is partly solved, but if not there are other methods for obtaining good results. Four days before the show selected spikes are cut on which the second bloom of the bottom pair is about half expanded. The stems of these spikes are then plunged deeply in receptacles filled with water which should be taken to a shed or room where the light enters from one side only, and placed on bench or table with the flowering side of the spike facing the light. In summer days of average temperature this leads to the production of a pair of blooms daily. On the day before the show, therefore, there should be eight blooms expanded in good condition and then packing should take place.

Gladioli are packed in single layers laid in light boxes, the heads of the spikes being placed at each end and the stems of the spikes from one end resting between the stems of those from the other. Both sets of stems are securely fastened down midway along the box with a cleat. Before packing, the box should be well lined with greaseproof paper arranged so that after packing the blooms can be well covered with paper on top. The lid should be securely fastened to exclude air. Next morning, in the heat of the show tent or hall, another pair of blooms will open and sometimes two pairs. However, in very hot weather it would be well to cut spikes three days before the show instead of four. Careful packing and handling is necessary throughout as gladioli are easily bruised.

Because of this tendency some growers attack the job from another angle. The day before the show spikes are cut, in full sunshine if possible, but with two or three pairs of blooms expanded. They are then laid deliberately on the hot ground – to wilt. After about an hour when they are becoming soft and flexible they are packed in boxes without being placed in water beforehand. When taken from the boxes they are, of course, soft and withered, but when placed in water quickly recover and begin to develop more blooms. It is a very convenient, trouble-saving method which could be adopted in necessity, but I much prefer the slow method which entails care throughout and does not stop at any time.

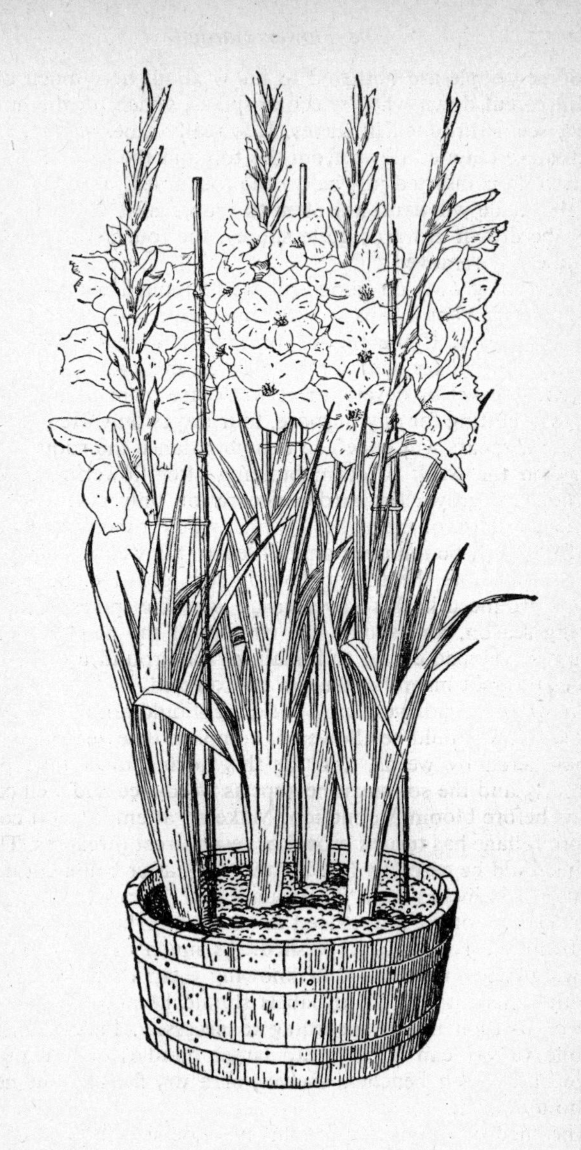

40. Gladioli growing in tub.

Some people are bothered to know about how much of the plant to cut down when selecting spikes, which, to the uninitiated, seem shrouded in leaves. It is really quite simple. If the leaves are counted down from the top and the point and edge of a knife is inserted just below the fourth leaf a little pressure on the blade will cause the stem to snap easily. The spikes can then be drawn upwards quite simply, the four leaves adhering being easily removed.

Gladioli, grown on good soil well supplied with moisture, develop excellent corms – sometimes better than the parent corms planted. If the fullest corm development is to be expected, their spikes, with all their leaves, must not be cut down to ground level or development will cease from that moment. If, when cutting for any purpose, four leaves only are removed, sufficient spears will be left to counterbalance the roots and so carry on the work of corm building after flowering time. If gladioli are grown for garden decoration only and no spikes are cut, the top of the spikes – which would otherwise produce seed – should be removed and all leaves allowed to remain intact to promote the fullest development possible. Sometimes corms produced in this way send up very fine spikes in the following season, and should the climate of the neighbourhood permit developed corms to remain in the ground undisturbed, spikes of great magnificence can be expected.

Gladioli which have ceased to flower should not be neglected. Instead they should be allowed to complete their seasonal work unhampered by weeds, and for this hoeing must take place regularly and the soil must be kept as weed-free and well cared for as before bloom production. Make no attempt to lift corms before foliage has turned brown or severe frost threatens. Then, each should be carefully lifted with a fork after being cut down to about six inches from the ground level. They should be tied into bundles of six and placed on shelves or benches or hung up from the roof of a cool shed. As much of the charm in growing many varieties is in knowing them or being able to identify them, tough tie-on labels should be attached to each one or to each bunch according to necessity. Large numbers of one variety can be tied into larger bundles or laid out in large batches on benches, shelves, or a dry floor – but never without a label.

The shed or room used for this purpose should be cool and airy and no attempt should be made to dry off the corms rapidly. For this reason a heated greenhouse is generally unsuitable, although a cool greenhouse, with slatted benches through which air can circulate freely, may be an advantage in a very wet autumn, especially if a little artificial heat is available to dry the atmosphere and assist in ripening off the outer skins of the corms. Generally, after about a month or six weeks of this treatment, unwanted outer husks will part from the corms without difficulty; however, nothing should be taken away except what parts easily from the corm. The cleaned-off corms should be laid in single layers on boards or laid out on shelves in a cool, airy, but frost-proof building until planting time again arrives.

All the above is intended to apply to the modern larger-flowered varieties which are hybrids of many species and of which a list will be found at the end of this chapter, but there is another set of hybrids derived mainly from Gladiolus primulinus. This species was discovered in 1902 in the district close to the Zambesi falls where there is much atmospheric moisture. It was about half the size of the gladioli then in commerce, golden yellow in colour, light in appearance, and highly decorative. It differed from other gladioli because its top petal curved downwards and gave each flower a hooded and somewhat demure appearance. In its original state it was fascinatingly beautiful and its use as a parent has given rise to innumerable attractive varieties, most of them of great beauty. It is said by raisers that many large-flowered varieties of to-day owe their colour and much of their beauty – although not their size and stature – to this parent, but enough remain which show the true dainty primulinus characters to warrant a separate list. This I have not given, however, as losses during the war years have not yet been made up sufficiently to warrant distribution again.

In addition, there is a small family of early flowering gladioli which are hybrids of Gladiolius colvilei. Except in very sheltered places in the south and south west they are not hardy. In their habits they differ from all the gladioli I have already described as they need autumn planting – not later than October. They grow about eighteen inches high, are light, dainty, and highly decorative. If potted early and brought on gently in a slightly heated greenhouse they flower early in March and April. They prefer well-drained soil but must not be allowed to become dry when growing or the flower spikes become blind. The best known variety is a white one called 'The Bride', but sometimes there are coloured varieties with sharply blotched petals available.

ATLANTIC (M). Brilliant Coral red florets. A good exhibitor's variety. Slightly taller and stronger than most.

BENJAMIN BRITTEN (M). Light rosy mauve with faint bluish throat. Medium height. A distinct addition to the colour range. Outstanding.

CIRCE (E). Richest salmon closely approaching orange. One of the most pleasing varieties. Medium height.

DEVOTION (M). Creamy sulphur, with scarlet and yellow falls. Deeply frilled. An attractive colour combination. Medium height.

DR FLEMING (M). Deep shell pink at edges paling to a primrose throat. Well frilled. A perfect exhibition spike slightly under medium height.

GOLD RUSH (M). Deep golden yellow florets placed well on long strong willowy stem. One of the best of the yellows.

HELEN EAKEN (E). Cream with slight greenish sheen, deeper falls. A good spike of medium height.

HENRI DE GRIEVE (M). Rich salmon orange florets well placed on a good spike. Medium height.

HUAHINA (M). Soft golden orange florets on strong stem of medium height. A distinct addition to the orange shades.

JE MAINTIENDRAI (M.) Bright orange scarlet suffused chestnut florets on strong tall stem. Slightly above medium height.

JO WAGENAAR (M). Velvety orange scarlet florets on spikes slightly above medium height.

LA FAVOURITE (M). Orange scarlet with lighter throat. Excellent in every way. Medium height.

PACTOLUS (M). Primrose, flushed crimson with large scarlet blotch in throat. One of the most attractive. Medium height.

PERPETUUM (M). White with delicate pink flushings. Bold florets, well placed on strong stem. A little above medium height.

POLYNESIE (M). Bright salmon pink with lighter centre. Slightly frilled. Well placed florets on strong stem of medium height.

RAVEL (M). Light violet blue with crimson marked throat. One of the best in the blue section. Medium height.

SALMANS GLORY (M). Sulphur-white, scarlet blotch in throat. Bold florets on long strong stem slightly above medium height.

SKYMASTER (M). Primrose, flushed strawberry with deeper throat. A perfect exhibition spike. Medium height.

SNOWFLAKE (M). Pure white. One of the best of the white varieties. Medium height.

SPOTLIGHT (M). Bright yellow with scarlet blotch. Very outstanding. Medium height.

TOBROEK (L). Very dark velvety maroon. Heavily frilled. A very beautiful variety.

UNCLE TOM (M). Deep velvety chestnut crimson florets on long, strong but slender stem. Medium height.

WEDGEWOOD (L). Violet blue with deeper throat and falls. The strongest blue variety. Very large.

WELTWUNDER (E). Light yellow with crimson throated florets. First class in every way. Slightly above medium height.

Letters in brackets after the name, represent the season of flowering, i.e. Early, Medium, or Late.

· 17 ·

Violets

SWEET VIOLETS are greatly loved. In Victorian and Edwardian times they were fashionable wear for most occasions. They would be found in boudoir and cottage parlour and generous bunches were sold in the streets for a penny.

In Cornwall great areas were devoted to their culture, and in some southern counties violet fields were quite common, especially in moist districts. The First World War disrupted the violet industry and decimated the acreage of plants – food was more important. Between the two World Wars there was a partial revival and once more violets came on the streets, but not for a humble penny. The Second World War was disastrous for violet growers, as most of the revived Cornish acres were sacrificed for food, and, to a great extent, still are – hence the high price of violets to-day, which gives a great impetus to their production in private gardens.

The sweet violet, a relative of the pansy and viola, is not quite hardy in most districts, or rather, its measure of hardiness, which generally permits it to survive, does not allow it to give its best. To produce fine flowers it needs protection during the winter months. It is true that on Cornish slopes and sheltered coves, as well as in wind-shielded fields along the south coast, it receives no protection, but this is a different matter. When exposed to cold and damp it merely survives the dead winter period and is able to put forth only a few short-stemmed blooms in spring, but given the protection of a cold frame the sweet violet is able to give a wealth of long-stemmed fragrant blooms from September to mid-April, and few plants can do as much.

But let us look at the plant. It is a perennial which reproduces itself by runners much as a strawberry does. Unlike those of a strawberry these runners are active at all times but grow most during spring and autumn. Spring is the best time to begin propagation. By lifting a clump it is found that a number of runners, in all stages of growth, surround a central crown. These runners can be easily detached from the parent crown and utilized to produce a new stock of plants, which, because of the initial vigour possessed by a newly-rooted plant, are able to give far finer flowers when rooted separately than when rambling wildly while still part of a matted plant. Some runners are found already rooted and these can be utilized as they are, but there are many unrooted ones which should be treated to produce roots and form plants of flowering size by early autumn.

The stems of runners which have a head of leaves should be severed to form cuttings with about three inches of stem below the head. These stems should be stripped clean of all incipient leaves and put together to form a batch for propagating. Violets can be propagated out of doors, but can be rooted far more quickly in a cold frame and in a manner to send them on their way with better prospects. Supposing a frame is available, it should be placed on a hard bottom on which a few inches of soil has been placed. John Innes Compost No. 1 is suitable, and finely-sifted; sandy soil well enriched with leafsoil or peat is ideal. Into this the cuttings should be firmly inserted, four inches apart in each direction, and well watered in. After insertion the glass lights should be placed on the frame and kept tightly closed so that, by denying fresh air, transpiration from the fleshy leaves can be checked and consequently rooting effected earlier.

Some shade should be given on sunny days. Throw a rush mat, hessian canvas, or any thin material available on the glass light, but remove this shading during dull periods. Alternatively the glass can be painted with a thin solution of distemper, or,

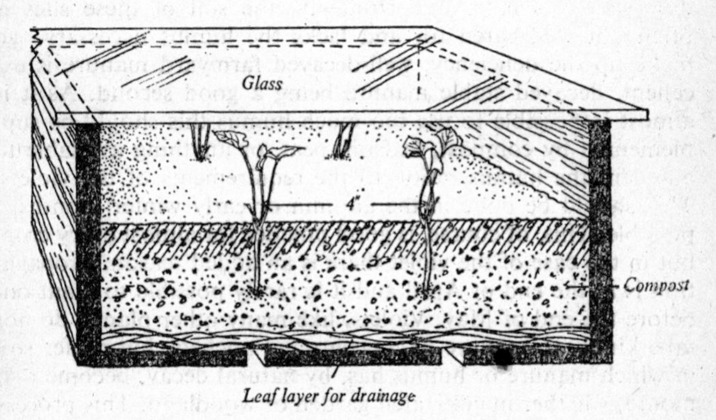

41. Violet cuttings in glass-covered box.

in an emergency, some clay water, which, although not permanent, gives sufficient protection from the sun's rays to prevent scorching; but any substance sprayed or painted on in solution should be sufficient only to temper brilliant light and not enough to obscure or darken totally.

After about three weeks rooting begins and new leaf growth appears. From this stage, ventilation of the frame should start and continue progressively until the light is removed altogether, when, after a few days, the rooted cuttings will be ready to bed out into their summer quarters.

The cultivated sweet violet is a woodland plant closely related to, or descended from, the small sweet violet of the hedgerow or wood. It delights in partial shade and much moisture, and revels in rich humus. In folds and pockets in hedgerow or wood where leaf deposits deepen yearly you will find the sweet violet, and similar conditions must be reproduced if you wish to obtain the length of stem and the size of bloom which the cultivated violet can give.

An old orchard, where the trees are tall and without dense leaves, is an ideal place, or any similarly shaded spot in the garden. The shelter given by a plantation of bush apples and pears is also good, and perhaps one of the best places is a border on the north side of a wall warmed by the sun in early morning and in late afternoon only. Such semi-shaded positions are generally moist in soil and atmosphere and reproduce the conditions violets love. Unfortunately, the soil of these sites is often not well cared for and lacks the humus necessary. To make up the deficiency, well-decayed farmyard manure is excellent, decayed stable manure being a good second. As it is almost impossible to use too much humus this should be supplemented by compost, leafsoil, peat, or anything available to augment the humus ration to the requirements of the violets. This should be done in the autumn or early winter months if possible. This, of course, is good practice for almost every crop, but in the case of the violet there is an added reason. Propagation is at the end of April and it is rarely possible to plant out before the end of May. Violets, like many other plants, do not take kindly to manure in concentrated pockets, but prefer soil in which manure or humus has, by natural decay, become rich mould, whether in cultivated garden or woodland. This process is greatly accelerated by frequent forking which mixes the ingredients well, makes the soil lighter, and keeps the site free from weeds at the same time. Soil, liberally manured and enriched with humus in the autumn months, and frequently forked during the spring, is so improved that it is almost unrecognizable when planting time arrives. After such treatment it will possess the rich lightness and tilth usually associated only with prepared potting compost, and is ideal for violets.

The rooted cuttings should be lifted carefully from the frame with a fork and planted on the new site with a trowel. Planting deep enough to ensure that the new crown of the plant sits comfortably into the soil should be practised. Firm planting is desirable. Fifteen inches from plant to plant is a good distance to permit growth expansion and to facilitate working operations during the summer.

Violets in spring and summer should never suffer from lack of moisture; their foliage should be bathed in dense atmospheric moisture and their multiplying roots should always penetrate into wet richness. A season too wet for most other crops suits them admirably. Real success with violets depends on two main items – humus and moisture, the former being of little use without the latter, and a little shade being an additional benefit. It is not a flower which can be cultivated by half measures – if indeed any worth-while plant can be; therefore, if no rain falls, water frequently and copiously, enough to ensure a heavy volume of atmospheric moisture always rising from moist soil. This advice may surprise some of my readers, accustomed to seeing violets relegated to some odd corner of the garden where they just manage to exist. There they give only a few short-stemmed blooms, not much superior to those of the woods – deliciously scented perhaps, but not a patch on the long-stemmed beauties, as large as Viola cornuta, which may be produced by better methods.

Under congenial conditions of soil and moisture growth flourishes luxuriantly. Side shoots, which would become runners, soon emerge. All these side shoots should be picked off immediately they appear or each plant will soon become a mat of stringy runner growth – unmanageable and unwanted. Instead of this, the whole of the summer energies of the plant should be devoted to the building of stout healthy single crowns, ever thickening in stem and becoming larger in leaf growth, because, from this central stem – which, with its bunch of spreading leaves, becomes a crown – violet blooms are produced all the winter. Under good conditions, growth may be unbelievably rapid, entailing the necessity of removing all side shoots weekly – an effort which is well worth while – for leaves, many inches across, are produced on stems long enough to permit the single-crowned plants to cover the ground, even though they are liberally sited. Large leaves of great manufacturing power lead to violet blooms of corresponding size.

Such generous treatment is greatly to the liking of annual weeds. These must be suppressed, or, better still, prevented. The advice I have given in nearly every chapter – to use the Dutch hoe frequently – must be given again, for I know of no better method for preventing weed growth. But it must be timely, regular, and frequent. Twice a week is not too much. Surface hoeing on loose weed-free tilth can be rapid, almost without fatigue, and an enjoyable job. It has many advantages, not the least of which is the opportunity to inspect plants frequently, to observe growth, to note idiosyncrasies of varieties, and to store in the mind interesting facts for the future. Weeds are man's natural enemies and the mind of the cultivator is at peace if he feels he has beaten his foes.

In the cool dewy nights of August, growth accelerates rapidly, and for a month or so the succulent growth needed for success continues. About mid-September the crowns should be lifted to their winter quarters – the cold frame. Before this is attempted it is good to tread between the rows and around the plants carefully, thus systematically to consolidate the soil for better transplanting. On this occasion lifting is a much bigger job – it must be done with a spade. With this tool, cut the soil down into square blocks, each with a plant at the centre, lift carefully with the spade, place on tray or barrow, and transfer to the cold frame. There, in prepared compost, make suitable holes to receive the blocks, and then transfer them with as little disturbance as possible. Although these clumps are lifted thus with large blocks of soil containing the roots, the compost to which they are transferred is important.

It should be realized that when they are again well established they possess a far-reaching humus-hungry root system for which a rich rooting medium should be provided. Compost consisting of half loam and half leafsoil with enough sand to ensure free drainage is excellent, and, if necessary, peat can be used as a substitute for the leafsoil. Prepared garden compost can easily take the place of both peat and leafsoil, and, if the necessity arises, good top soil can be used if loam is not obtainable. But if it does exist, nothing is better than an old hotbed which, if chopped down with the used top-soil layer included, can be turned a few times to form an ideal mixture, retaining moisture and providing humus at the same time.

Despite great care, some of the soil on the carefully cut blocks from the open falls away with handling, and although the violet roots may remain undamaged they need congenial soil, which, to a violet, is more important than to most plants. Good spacing for the large-flowered sweet violet is fifteen inches apart in each direction – in the frame as well as out of doors. After firm planting the compost should be saturated with water, sufficiently to ensure that the subsoil is penetrated, for it may well be that another subsoil watering will be unnecessary before the season ends. Dry subsoil in violet frames often leads to unhealthy conditions and to a puzzling debility which people seldom blame on deep soil dryness, so the first watering must be sufficient to ensure that water pours out of the foundations of the frame. Few plants succeed when sited over a dry subsoil even though the top soil is reasonably moist – the violet least of all. It is a condition seldom found in nature and one which the violet would probably never encounter in its natural home.

This copious watering refers to the time of planting in frames in September only; later in the season the water supply must be handled skilfully and carefully; but of this more later.

With the decreasing sunshine and waning light of September, shading of any kind is unnecessary and growth starts again apace. Runners are again rapidly put out and with them some blooms. Both runners and blooms should be removed regularly, the former to force the plants to grow only from single crowns, and the latter not only to take advantage of fragrant flowers for the house or to wear – and many people still wear them – but also because withered blooms quickly decay and form plague spots from which disease spreads even more readily than from decaying leaves.

Dead leaves, too, should be removed regularly together with all leaves from trees which blow into the frame as autumn advances; indeed, to keep violets growing under the hygienic conditions necessary to produce winter blooms all the plants should be examined and dead leaves removed once a week without fail throughout the winter season. True, this is something which does not happen to violets in the wild state, but the wild violet blooms late in spring only, and the aim of the violet cultivator is to gather blooms continuously during autumn, winter and spring; hence conditions which predispose to good health are necessary.

After planting in September the frame lights are not needed for protection then, but when October frost and fog chills the air they should be placed on the frame. But not to be closed. It is good to make a rule never to close the frame completely by shutting down the lights except in the most severe frost; in all other weather, the lights must be held open by blocks or wedges to allow a free current of air to pass through the frame at all times. To achieve this, it is not sufficient to insert blocks at the top at the highest end of the frame only; instead, the lights should be lifted alternatively top and bottom to prevent the formation of pockets of stagnant air in any part of the frame.

During exceptionally good days in winter – and they sometimes occur – it is very beneficial to the violet plants to remove the lights altogether, and an exceedingly good plan, which amounts to necessity in the neighbourhood of big cities, is to clean the glass of all filth occasionally, by washing it with a cleansing fluid and swilling down afterwards with clear water.

As the days grow short, dampness of the air increases, and there are many short days with too many hours of bad light. During this depressing period little if any water is required, and whereas in the summer the great aim is to keep roots and atmosphere as moist as possible, in winter the reverse applies. In the dark days the violets cannot make use of water in air or soil, and if subjected to too much at the roots or in the atmosphere are likely to get damping-off disease. This is the chief reason for free ventilation, dry atmosphere, and the frequent removal of dead leaves and blooms and, of course, any weeds which appear. The weekly plying of a small Dutch hoe, adapted for use in one hand, will preclude the possibility of weeds and maintain the surface soil in a healthy well-aired state.

Cultivated violets are, of course, much more vulnerable than their wild brethren, and in very severe weather need protection. This in the absence of rush mats or hessian coverings might be anything available – stable litter, old sacks, straw, or anything handy being pressed into service. In an emergency leaves, leafsoil, peat, or even a covering of soil will protect them, and if a wooden box frame is used the comparatively thin wooden sides need protection as much as the top. Unfortunately, disease flourishes in a stagnant atmosphere. No covering must remain on an hour longer than necessary, therefore; instead, when thaw occurs, it should be removed, the frame again freely ventilated, and all dead and dying leaves removed speedily.

As the days lengthen growth starts again and becomes active, and blooms are produced in profusion. Those of February and early March are exceedingly good, but as April days become longer and sunshine and warmth force the plants to flower rapidly the blooms decrease in size and quality gradually, until

42. Clump of violets lifted for planting in frame. Root contained in block of earth.

by mid-April – coincident with the time for propagation – they are small and far less beautiful.

Violets can be grown in the cold greenhouse as well as the cold frame, and anyone who has an unheated house unoccupied during the winter might well consider its use for violets. For this culture, propagation and summer treatment are the same, and the plants when lifted in blocks of soil should be planted in the soil floor of the greenhouse in compost previously prepared in the same way as that for a cold frame. Winter treatment is also similar to that of a frame, and ventilation, which in a greenhouse is sometimes less effective than in a frame, must be carefully studied: at no time should the house be closed except during severe frost.

Violets do not succeed in the heated greenhouse unless artificial heat is used sparingly in severe weather and sufficient only to prevent the temperature dropping below freezing point. In this case, violets in pots or boxes do well and flower freely during the dead season when blooms from the cold frame are not so plentifully produced. However, any attempt at hard forcing by artificial heat leads to dire results, both in visitations of pests and incidence of disease, about which I will say more in Chapter 32.

The variations in large-flowered sweet violets are not great and there are not many good varieties. The pick of these, which are reliable in most districts, I give below:

Princess of Wales	Purple blue. The largest single violet
Lloyd George	Purple blue, pink centre. Semi-double
Princess Beatrice	Bright mauve blue
Czar	Reddish purple. The most free flowering violet

There is a very large-flowered variety not included in the list above – Governor Herrick. This has tremendous vigour, produces large purple blue blooms in great profusion, and is much easier to cultivate than any other. But it is scentless. As I cannot imagine anyone wishing to grow violets without perfume I have deliberately omitted it. This variety, which because of ease of culture is grown extensively for marketing, disappoints many town dwellers who buy bunches and then find them without fragrance. Viola cornuta, which has no pretence to perfume, is equally attractive.

All I have so far written in this chapter refers to the large-flowered sweet violet, all varieties of which are single or semi-double. But another race exists, the Neapolitan violet, whose members are collectively known as Parma violets, and all of these are double. The propagation and subsequent treatment of the Parma violet is similar to that of the large-flowered sweet violet, except that as it is not a woodland plant it does not object to sunshine in summer, provided it is well supplied with water. However, during the summer it is difficult to restrict any variety of this flower to a single crown, as it naturally divides into a number of crowns, which together make a clump. If runners are shortened regularly to conform to this clump results are very satisfactory. The foliage of the Neapolitan violet is much smaller – possibly only a third of the size of the cultivated sweet violet; it is also paler in colour and much smoother. When well grown, the fully double flowers are more than an inch in diameter and exquisitely scented. Many people prefer them to the more lightly built blooms of the large sweet violet. The following are good varieties:

Duchesse de Parma	Lavender Mauve
Blue Patrie	Blue
Marie Louise	Mauve Blue
Comte de Brazza	White

Let no one reading this chapter imagine that violets cannot be grown without the aid of a frame or greenhouse. They can, and successfully, but not to such perfection. If you have no frame or greenhouse, propagation must be on a prepared bed in the garden, sheltered as far as possible from cold wind and shaded from too much sunshine. The summer culture should be as I have already advised, but when September comes a suitable sheltered site should be found. Here we must copy nature. The violet, when growing wild, is found not only in deep pockets of humus, generally derived from leaves deposited by the wind in a hollow where there is shelter from cold north and east winds, but open to the south and south-west where it enjoys spring sunshine. Therefore, to make cultivated violets comfortable out of doors a sheltered site must be sought. This can be a narrow border by the house where walls around collect sun heat by day to radiate comforting warmth by night, or a site where shrubs or woodland give shelter. It must be remembered, however, that whereas in the summer the cultivator should try to keep violets as cool as possible, in the winter, when they are planted out of doors, the opposite applies. Warm corners must be found – but only for winter and the spring flowering period.

Many people manage to protect the plants by placing over them shallow bottomless and lidless boxes covered with sheets of glass, and some do so by using glass cloches. Both methods demand a little attention because such coverings, unless they are ventilated freely, and their glass is given a daily, or twice daily, wiping to remove surplus moisture, are liable to predispose damping off, and therefore, unless attention is given regularly, violets planted in sheltered corners are better unprotected.

I have already mentioned that, at the time of propagation in spring, some runners are found already rooted, and if a summer site was prepared beforehand these can be planted out direct without further preparation. This is the simplest way to propagate, but, unfortunately, I must say that these labour savers rarely do as well as plants from newly-made cuttings, which are more sturdy and do not straggle as do those rather long runners rooted in advance of severance.

Violet culture, to be successful, demands a little care and trouble, but the result, in so much fragrant beauty, is well worth the effort. Few, indeed, are those who do not enjoy growing violets.

· 18 ·

Dahlias

THE dahlia, now such a striking part of the autumn landscape in parks and gardens, is one of our most accommodating plants. It is from Mexico and was first heard of in Europe through an article published in Madrid in 1615, when it was called the Acocotli. As so often happens when new plants are discovered, nothing was heard of it again for some time, but in the 18th century Nicholas de Menonville reported having seen bushes with aster-like blooms which had stems six feet long and leaves like those of an elder tree. This created a wonder plant legend which led to the sending of seeds, in 1798, to the Botanical gardens in Madrid.

We do not know whether these seeds were taken from wild species or from cultivated plants, but the Abbé Cavanilles, probably sensing a good plant, named it after Andreas Dahl the Swedish botanist. However, the dahlia came to this country through the Marquis of Bute, who, when British Ambassador in Madrid in 1798, sent some seeds to this country.

As the seeds came from a tropical source it was assumed that the new plant needed great heat. The fact that its natural habitat was in the mountains was overlooked, and consequently plants raised from this seed languished in hot greenhouses, where they became almost useless and were certainly not appreciated. Some authorities say that a species called Coccinea was grown in a Chelsea nursery by a John Fraser early in the 19th century, but there is little evidence of this. We do know, however, that Lady Holland reintroduced the dahlia in 1804, since when it has been grown in this country without a break.

Again we do not know whether this seed was from a true wild species or from cultivated plants, but it is believed that the dahlia was grown in Mexico for many years before it came to this country. The seed might therefore easily have come from domesticated plants. However, in the early days of the glass house no plant was very popular unless it required great heat, and the persistent belief that the dahlia required the hottest of tropical treatment nearly ruined it and prevented its development for many years. Finally, however, its requirements became known, and when it was realized that another border plant, ridiculously easy to grow, was available, plant breeders began to experiment and distribute varieties.

About 1812 a good deal of enthusiasm was created because the first double-flowered dahlia was raised in Belgium and this quickly gave rise to several forms which developed on the lines of show or fancy dahlias, i.e. circular, tight-petalled balls something like the show and pompon dahlias of to-day. The general habit of the plant was almost unnoticed, as in those days flowers were nearly all shown with paper collars around their necks and in tubes stuck in boards, in the same way as carnations, roses and chrysanthemums used to be exhibited. Because of this fashion, stems were of little account, and the border value of the dahlia still remained small, as blooms dangling on limp stems were hidden in a mass of foliage. It is not very remarkable, therefore, that the dahlia, although favoured by exhibitors, made little progress as a garden plant, and it was not until the formation of the National Dahlia Society in 1870 that real progress began.

At first, varieties of the ball-shaped types were the only ones which were really popular. This continued for some years until a variety of a new type was introduced, which, because of its spiky appearance, was called a cactus dahlia. Multitudes of cactus varieties followed, but with very ineffective stems. The virtues of the dahlia as a border plant were almost forgotten while breeders confined their attention to blooms alone – the more spiky they could be bred the better. Even to this day, some cactus varieties are inclined to hang their heads, but with other types this great defect has been well overcome.

Gradually, however, as the merits of the dahlia became known the cactus type gave way to looser, larger varieties on the one hand and on the other to small decorative forms which in time developed into the sturdy varieties we now know. Nowadays all good varieties hold their heads boldly above their foliage and all have the stiff self-supporting stems which have helped greatly in making the modern dahlia so popular. So valuable has the dahlia become in its transformed state that it is doubtful if another plant exists to-day which, once planted in the border, gives so little trouble. All it requires is some good soil, a stake, a tie or two occasionally, and sufficient water to keep it going. It can withstand drought and terrific heat provided it is given enough water, and while it does not give a bad account of itself on poor soil it is magnificent in good soil and well cultivated.

As it comes from the mountains of Mexico it resents great heat during the early stages of growth, but is quite unable to stand frost. Possibly in some of its native districts a few degrees of frost are registered during the winter months, but as it reproduces itself vegetatively it is furnished with thick tubers, which, hidden beneath a few inches of soil, were probably sufficiently protected. As many people know, if we have a mild winter dahlias left in the open sometimes survive without protection, and a knowledge of this shows what treatment they should have and has some bearing on propagation.

The dahlia, when fully grown, has a number of thick tuberous roots, many of which are six inches or more in length and several inches in thickness. They are not formed on stolons like potatoes, but all converge on a central stem, and if, when winter approaches, they are lifted intact, the stem is removed as near as possible to the converging tubers, and without mutilation they are placed in a cool moist shed or frost-proof cellar they will pass through the winter without difficulty. In this the dahlia resembles the potato, because tubers keep well in a moist frost-proof place and badly in a dry place, even if it is cool. Most people know that the best potatoes in winter come from moist clamps in the open, and if one had quantities of dahlias clamp storage would be admirable. But for the average person a cool moist shed from which frost can be excluded is the ideal place. Most troubles connected with dahlia storage are caused by putting tubers in too warm and dry a place, which leads to a continuous loss of moisture, until little life remains when spring arrives.

The easiest way of growing the dahlia is to plant the stools intact, just as they were lifted in autumn, which can be done in the open about the middle of April. This is a rough and ready method which will give fairly good results, but which cannot be followed yearly because of the gradual deterioration of the tubers. A large stool after planting will give a plentiful growth of shoots greatly in excess of those needed to build a plant. These shoots must therefore be reduced to two and for the best results one is better.

Planting should not take place before mid-April or shoots will emerge before the danger of May frost has passed. After disbudding, the selected shoot will need the support of a stake, and it is a good plan to drive the stake into the ground before planting and to plant the tuber close to it, thus preventing the risk of driving the stake through the tuber and mutilating it.

Dahlias grown from old tubers will sometimes bloom much earlier than those propagated in other ways, but the flowers generally are not so good, and, except that it is a time-saving method which all can adopt, this system cannot be recommended for the best results. However, a variation of this, and

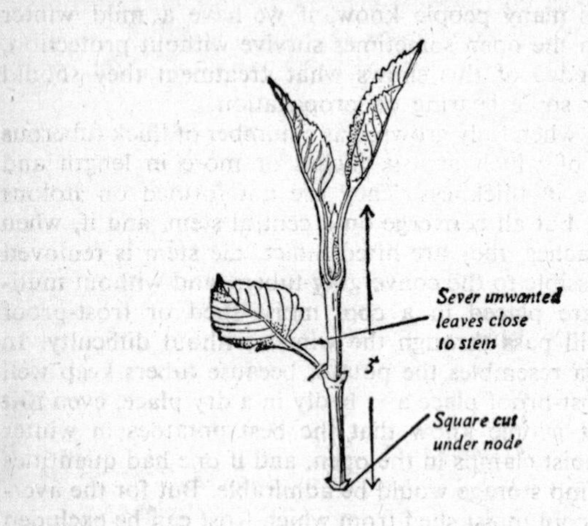

43. Dahlias – cutting.

one which generally gives better blooms, is to sever the tubers carefully from the central stem and to plant each one separately. But, although good plants and blooms are obtained from plants which survive, losses are inevitable. It is not a method to recommend for the flower border, but one suitable for dahlias which are planted in the kitchen garden to provide blooms for cutting and prevent the partial mutilation of plants when they are at their best in the flower garden.

The modern method of propagation is by cuttings. Stools of the previous season are placed in gentle warmth in February. If there is a quantity of stools they can be accommodated on the greenhouse bench, covered in advance with three inches of leafsoil, peat, or fine soil from the garden. On this bed the stools are placed with tubers interlocked to save space, and soil, leafsoil, or peat trickled between and placed above to keep them moist and covered to the depth of one inch. Years ago, propagation was always undertaken in high temperature, but it is realized now that too much heat has a weakening effect upon the cuttings while roots are forming, and that, therefore, a temperature of 60° F. should not be exceeded or growth will be thinly drawn and weakly. Shoots are taken for cuttings with a sharp knife when about three inches in length, and, in spite of modern methods whereby growers propagate cuttings without trimming or other preparation, I still prefer to cut the shoots square just below a node and trim off closely all leaves which are in the way.

Cuttings should be dibbled in firmly into small pots filled with a mixture of sifted loam and sand in equal parts. A square-ended dibber should be used so that a hole is made with a flat bottom on which the base of the cutting rests firmly. After insertion a cutting should be so anchored in the soil that it can be tugged gently without being displaced. Cuttings should be well watered immediately after insertion.

Prepared and dibbled in in this way cuttings will take root on a greenhouse shelf or bench if necessary, but dahlias, unlike geraniums and chrysanthemums, resent flagging at any time, and as they flag and, therefore, transpire in the atmosphere of the ordinary greenhouse it is a better plan to place them in a glass propagating case. Sometimes this can be made by putting a small garden frame on top of the greenhouse bench, or, if a few cuttings only are to be rooted, a box about nine inches deep with three inches of peat on the bottom and a sheet of glass to cover the top will answer admirably. In a tiny frame of this description there is one drawback – the collecting of moisture on the under side of the glass. This leads to dripping, which can be prevented by turning the glass – thus placing the dry side underneath – several times a day. Such propagating cases prevent transpiration and promote freshness. Cuttings root in about ten days, after which they should be stood outside the frame or box in the ordinary atmosphere of the greenhouse to become a little harder before being potted separately.

Pure loam and sand used for propagating contains little plant food. Rooted cuttings should therefore not remain in the propagating pots a day longer than necessary. They should be potted firmly in three and a half inch pots with John

Innes Compost No. 2, in which they should go ahead. A temperature of 60° F. suits them admirably, and if on cool nights the temperature of the greenhouse should drop 5°, or even 10°, little harm would result. Slow, steady progress is much better than rapid growth, which usually leads to attenuation and impaired constitution. For the same reason, pots should always be stood several inches apart so that the plants can expand laterally in a normal way, instead of being forced to fight for air and light and to become lengthened and enfeebled in consequence.

During propagation, before roots have formed, some shade is necessary. This is easily given by spreading a newspaper over the propagating frame on sunny days, but from the time enough roots have formed no shade is needed. During spring the greenhouse becomes gradually warmer because of the increase in solar heat; it is necessary, therefore, to increase ventilation daily so that air is freely admitted regularly to prevent growth being too rapid. Also plants, like humans, need fresh air for good health.

Where a greenhouse is only slightly heated and the temperature does not greatly exceed 55° F. at night, dahlias can be propagated and should be entirely satisfactory but take a little longer to root. Sometimes, indeed, these prove better than those propagated in a higher temperature.

I fully realize that many people may need simpler methods; indeed, some will have only a few to propagate, possibly not more than a dozen. Such people could put a few dahlia stools, or perhaps one only, into a box of soil and place it under the greenhouse stage, should there be no room on top. In this case, the shoots, obtaining only partial light, could not be quite as strong and healthy as those raised in full light, but probably they would be sufficient for the purpose, and no reason exists why they should not root satisfactorily in a small propagating case such as I have described.

The treatment of dahlia plants after potting is important. The dahlia is a great feeder and responds generously to good feeding, but this can be overdone and if so the dahlia becomes lush and too flabby for practical use. Plant food should therefore be used with caution. Because of this, nitrogenous plant food, or plant food of any description, should not be added to the John Innes Compost, which is sufficiently well balanced to support the plant until it is repotted. The young dahlia should be encouraged to grow sturdily and be potted on immediately it has enough roots.

It is not uncommon for dahlias potted early in the season into three and a half inch pots to remain in them starving until bedding-out time. Consequently they become too hard, seriously checked, and unable to reawaken progress for many weeks after being planted out, and so as much as six weeks' growth can be lost out of the restricted dahlia season. This form of check should be prevented by potting on the young plants immediately they are ready into five or six inch pots of John Innes Compost No. 2. This produces well-balanced plants without undue early hardening and prevents flowering check – a condition very common when plants remain in small pots too long. After this final potting the plants should be returned to the greenhouse, with a night temperature of 55° F., where they should remain until hardened off at mid-May by being placed in a cold frame and afterwards in the open air, preparatory to being planted on a prepared site at the end of May.

Dahlias love an open site. Not that they will not grow where there is a little shade, but when so doing they are not able to give their best, as they do not obtain enough sunshine to supply their manufacturing needs. Select the best open position, therefore, so that they may flower early and continue until the frost.

I have already said that the dahlia will endure poor soil, and while this is true it is also true that few plants respond to good treatment as generously as it does, though many modern hybrid plants respond to a lesser degree. The soil should be fully worked and farmyard manure or compost should be incorporated liberally. This should be done in the autumn or early winter months – if only for the sake of consolidation. Dahlias grow wildly in rich soil which is loose, and produce masses of foliage with few flowers; whereas the same soil sufficiently consolidated might produce plants which gave firm, bright blooms on stiff, healthy, self-supporting stems.

However, there is danger in this. At a meeting I once emphasized the necessity for firm soil, and later in the season I was asked to give advice to someone whose dahlias refused to grow. The soil was a heavy plastic clay to which farmyard manure had been added liberally, the plants had been raised splendidly, and there appeared to be no reason for lack of progress. However, in the end I found out that the grower had taken my words far too seriously and to consolidate his soil had rammed it with a heavy rammer, not once, but many times. Consequently the fine-textured clay was so impacted that enough air could not enter, and this and the inability of the roots to penetrate prevented growth.

Let no one reading this imagine that good dahlias cannot be grown unless the soil is very good, because almost any well-worked garden soil, whether peat, sand, chalk, clay, or alluvial mixture, can be made fit for the dahlia. Digging or trenching should be in accordance with the depth of soil and crude subsoil should not be brought to the surface. On the poorer soils it is almost impossible to use too much farmyard manure or compost. On the rich loams and clay soils much less is required. On poor sand or gravel soils where minerals are usually deficient it is excellent to supplement farmyard manure or compost with 4 oz. Super Phosphate and 2 oz. Sulphate of Potash per superficial square yard applied about a fortnight before planting.

Distances for planting vary tremendously according to the type of dahlia. There are now decorative types six to eight feet high which build big bushes, while there are others which grow only a foot or eighteen inches high. One must not be misled into thinking that all dahlias which produce giant sixteen-inch blooms are proportionately big – they are not. Some huge blooms come from comparatively small plants, perhaps not more than three feet in height, whereas some of the small decorative varieties are borne in profusion on great bushes which require much room.

Luckily, for many reasons, the dahlia is not a permanent occupant of the border. It has to be lifted each season and this gives the grower time to study varieties, heights, habits, and many things which assist him to plan for the next season. Thus mistakes may be rectified.

Before planting any dahlias – or before propagating – their descriptions must be studied from a catalogue and their approximate height noted. If height should be given as four feet, in good soil it will probably exceed four and a half feet; on the other hand, on poor soil it may not reach the stated height – soil must be allowed for. With regard to siting, some of the bedding varieties which grow only fifteen to eighteen inches in height should be sited about fifteen inches apart, the free flowering decorative varieties should be six feet from their nearest neighbour, and the large decorative varieties sited four to five feet apart. Very definite rules might be misleading – it is a matter which the dahlia enthusiast can decide for himself after he has decided what varieties he will grow.

Blind planting, however, which is seldom worth while, may lead to dire results, and it is always wise to keep very full notes of heights, spreading capacity and various details as they occur to the grower, so that adjustment can be made when planning for the next season. Dahlias, like potatoes, are known to vary their habits in different gardens.

When fully grown or approaching that stage, dahlias develop heavy foliage which is easily torn away by wind. They must therefore be supported efficiently. Unfortunately dahlia stakes must be stout, and before they are covered with foliage are offensive looking. Stakes which are neutral in colour should therefore be found if possible. Any garden would be ruined by the use of the large square stakes, painted a vivid green, usually sold as dahlia stakes. Coppice stakes, capable of affording good support, sold by dealers as tomato stakes, are far better. In colour they are usually grey green or brown, and therefore not quite so obtrusive. While a stake about one and a quarter inches in diameter will support the biggest dahlia, smaller varieties, whose height should be noted beforehand, should be staked accordingly. Bedding varieties rarely need stakes as they are planted closely and when in full growth support one another.

All stakes should be driven into position when the ground is free from encumbrances, in preparation for planting. It is usual to attach the main stem of the large growing types direct to the stake as the plant grows, a method which suffices if done efficiently. However, there are some large decorative varieties of balloon-like habits of growth, for which a central stake only is not enough and which need several light stakes surrounding the bushes and tied to the foliage with bands of green twist or raffia. A variation of this is to use thin steel rods which, if not too tall, are almost invisible. However, if dahlias are grown for cutting only, in some part of the garden where appearance is not so important, almost any method of support which effectively holds heavy growth can be used.

Dahlias which have been grown well throughout sometimes develop large dimensions, and if blooms of high quality are required from these some stopping and disbudding is necessary, especially with the large decorative varieties. These are stopped by nipping out the tip of the central stem when it is eighteen inches high, and if blooms are required for exhibition only three of the resulting lateral shoots should be retained. All buds on these three, except the terminal one, should be removed with all lateral shoots which develop below the bud, so that the three stems become three single cordons, each topped with a large bloom. With everything in their favour such blooms sometimes approach sixteen inches in diameter, with stiff umbrella-like stems two to three feet in length, rigid enough to be self-supporting when placed in large vases. If, however, a display of blooms is preferred, five or six shoots might be allowed to each plant which should be disbudded similarly. In this way a glorious show can be ensured of large blooms free from the suspicion of vulgarity.

Dahlias in all sections, except the dwarf bedding varieties, are improved if treated thus, as the treatment enable blooms to stand unhampered by foliage, which, in this country, is generally produced too freely.

Dahlias needed for show are best cut in the forenoon, if possible, when quite dry. Immediately after cutting, to prevent unnecessary transpiration, all unwanted leaves should be stripped from the stems, which should be immersed in receptacles filled with water previously placed in position nearby. Sometimes, as in the case of delphiniums, there is difficulty in inducing tubular stems to absorb water and in such cases they should be held deeply under water and severed again, while in that position, to prevent air being taken in. Generally, however, most of the trouble with transpiration is due to allowing fleshy leaves of large area to remain on the stems. Dahlias keep well in fairly cool rooms, but, like many other flowers, will not last long in hot dry rooms, especially if overburdened with leaves.

In addition to plants raised from cuttings and tubers planted from the parent stool, there is another form of tuber known as the pot tuber or pot root. This results from a late rooted cutting which, potted once, is allowed to remain in the pot all the summer. Of necessity it starves, but in doing so it forms a small tuber suitable for sending by post or abroad by Air Mail and is very useful to the ordinary enthusiast with few resources. Most nurserymen will supply it. When tubers are received they should be potted into pots three and a half inches in diameter in March or April and grown just as if they were propagated from cuttings. From one of these tiny tubers a shoot quickly emerges capable of developing into an extensive plant. In many gardens where the soil is light and poor they are preferable to freshly rooted plants as they offer more resistance to bad conditions. They are also useful for planting direct out of doors about mid April, but as they are small they are easily lost; hence the necessity for placing all stakes and labels in position first and planting by the side of the stake and label, so that the identity cannot be mistaken and location cannot be overlooked.

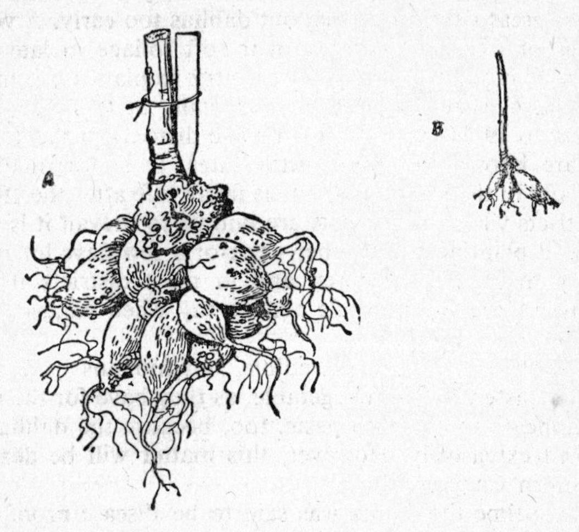

44. (A) Dahlia showing tuber formation after one season's growth. (B) Dahlia pot root.

Dahlias can be grown in yet another and very fascinating way – from seed. They do not breed true but nowadays they generally prove true to type, and the grower can expect a wonderful display in practically every shade of colour known in dahlias. It should be remembered that all novelties are raised initially in this way, but as they cannot be reproduced from seed the varieties to be perpetuated have to be propagated vegetatively. Seed should be sown in pots or boxes of John Innes Compost No. 1 about mid-February in a temperature of approximately 60° F. or slightly lower, if needs be. Seedlings grow rapidly after germination and quickly need potting into three and a half inch pots without intermediate pricking out. John Innes Compost No. 2 is suitable. Afterwards seedlings are treated in the same way as plants raised vegetatively and finally hardened off by exposure preparatory to being planted out of doors at the end of May or early in June. Seedlings possess initial vigour denied those produced vegetatively, and therefore they must be expected to develop with much greater rapidity and to attain greater size and status.

There is a general warning which it is well to give. Although growers should be anxious to plant early to prevent check, there is great risk in planting out dahlias too early. A very few degrees of frost will destroy their soft foliage in late spring. Generally it is not safe in this country to plant until the May frosts have passed, and they are usually at their worst from 12 May to 19 May, although in some districts in the Midlands they are known to come a little later. In southern districts, especially in the south-east, one is fairly safe after the 19th, but in districts where May frosts are known to prevail it is wise to withhold planting for another week or a few days longer. The locality must be considered and in most districts there are usually weather-wise people able to say when danger is likely to cease.

The dahlia is considered edible, but humans have not acquired a taste for it as a vegetable, as they have for the potato. This appears to apply to pests, too, because the dahlia is not attacked extensively. However, this matter will be dealt with later on in Chapter 32.

At one time the dahlia was said to be disease proof, but it is now sometimes troubled, in a few districts, with a disease known as a virus. This too, will be dealt with in Chapter 32, so I will refrain from dealing with it now.

One should remember that the duration of the flowering period of dahlias varies greatly according to seasonal vagaries. In a hot summer, if well prepared, unchecked plants are bedded out, and flowering begins in mid-July and sometimes earlier. The bedding types will flower at the end of June, but sometimes in a cold, wet season flowering of the taller types is delayed until early autumn. Dahlias are sometimes cut down in autumn by an unfortunately early frost, but are capable of flowering well until winter approaches, and I have seen brilliant displays of dahlias during the whole of October. On more than one occasion, because of mild autumns, they have been exhibited at chrysanthemum shows in November. It is our most brilliant decorative autumn flowering plant.

A good choice of varieties is important. Nowadays there are

many types and sections and a wealth of varieties ranging from giants, fourteen to sixteen inches across, to tiny pompons an inch or so in diameter. I could not, of course, give a list of varieties which would suit everybody and it would be equally impossible for everyone to try the innumerable varieties available today. To aid dahlia lovers, the National Dahlia Society has done good work in recent years in classifying types, sections and varieties, and those I now give are selected according to this classification. Perhaps there are some equally good varieties omitted, but those chosen are likely to fill a useful place in any garden.

Single Dahlias

Clematis	Chancellor
Caldicot Castle	Mia Karston
Crawley Beauty	

Star Dahlias

White Star	Bognor Star
Gatton Star	Epsom Star

Anemone-Flowered Dahlias

Southern Cross	Vera Higgins

Collerette Dahlias

Admiral	Balmoral
Bonfire	Canopus
Erika	Kangaroo
Julian Rose	Swallow
Tuskar	Trossachs
Mrs O. M. Courage	Kingsbrook Scarlet

Small Peony-Flowered Dahlias

Bishop of Llandaff	Sarah Peach
Norah Bell	Morning Glow
Lunar Beauty	Symphonia

Giant Decorative Dahlias

Dorothy Tattam	H.M. Queen Elizabeth
Liberator	Woodlands Wonder
Edith Morrell	Lily Vendyk
Clara Carder	F. Riley
D'Arcy Sainsbury	Dora Ramsey
Charlotte Collins	E. G. Ramsey

Large Decorative Dahlias

Anna Benedict	Elsie Sutton
Evelyn Ogg	Golden Dawn
Halifax	John Busbridge
Puritan	Frank Serpa
Elsie Wilding	Sanchican's Cameo
Mat Tandy	Earl Baldwin

Medium Decorative Dahlias

Audrey Leggatt	Autumn
Ballegos Glory	Blaze
D-Day	Deuil du Roi Albert
Florence Wilson	Jersey Beauty
Thos. Edison	Cherry
O. J. Prince	Fortune's Gift

Small Pompon

Burwood	Doria
Jill	Little Beeswing
Master Michael	Mrs J. Telfer

Giant Cactus Dahlias

Satan	Searchlight
Volkeart's Champion	Sampson
Miss Glory	Crimson Beauty

Large Cactus Dahlias

Betty Holmes	Doreen Blackman
Enkarts Prima	Hawaii
John Woolman	Beaute

Medium Cactus Dahlias

Dignity	Grandeur
New Vision	Sunlight
Vic	Kalorama
Future	Ecstasy
George Lawrence	Resplendent
Madame C. Jussiant	Torch

Small Cactus Dahlias

Andries Orange	Elsje
Ruby Glow	Belle
Dainty	Tip

Dwarf Bedders

Maureen Creighton	Rita
Constance Bolton	Park Beauty
Hockley Bedder	Little Marvel

Although it seems scarcely possible that a plant despised for a century should ever become popular, nevertheless the dahlia is now part of the landscape in all temperate and some semi-tropical lands, where it has come to stay. Few garden schemes would be complete without it.

· 19 ·

Coverings for Walls and Fences

IN the gardens surrounding many houses there are unsightly objects which could be beautified by climbing plants. I use the word 'climbing' in its popular sense, because few plants really climb by themselves, but have to be supported in some way. Perhaps the offending object is the back of a neighbour's shed, the blank wall of an adjoining house, a screen round a rubbish heap, or the chestnut paling dividing two gardens. Or perhaps a love of climbing plants makes you want to cover the walls of the house. This needs much consideration. Some types of houses could be mercifully hidden, if only to mask poor design, bad workmanship, or sheer ugliness, but there are houses built of good material and of dignified design, both old and new, that one should hesitate to hide. Such houses, perhaps with a classical exterior, rendered or whitewashed, have a satisfying dignity. This is partly because the clean lines contrast sharply with the living green drapery of the English garden, and to cover them with untidy festoons of creepers or to obliterate walls with one of the few self-climbing plants is only to cut out something beautiful.

On the other hand, houses built of cheap materials, of niggling design, or those houses haphazardly built in instalments throughout the centuries can often be greatly improved by a little green drapery judiciously employed.

On the subject of creepers, I have seen great numbers of letters whose writers all asked for self-clinging climbers. There are few. Apart from ivy, ampelopsis, and the clinging hydrangea there are not many satisfactory plants which cling. There are many varieties of ivy, and one should hesitate before using one of them, for the plant which is so pleasing in its early stages becomes a gnarled and twisted filcher of bricks and mortar in its old age. Stones of any size are nothing to it, for the slim creeping shoot which insinuates itself underneath a block of half a hundredweight succeeds, a generation later, when as thick as a man's arm, in dislodging it and sending it hurtling to earth. It will lift roofs, allow damp to get in, and provide rodents with easy access to a dwelling. The history of most ivy plants on dwellings is that the first generation is pleased with such a trouble-free plant, the second, seeing cracks in the fabric, feels doubtful, and the third generation has to strip it away to repair and save the building. If it is needed for one generation only, then ivy is the best self-clinging creeper.

But even ivy needs a good start. It is no use packing the roots of a plant into any sort of soil in any position. The ground should be prepared liberally. If it is around the dwelling, the soil must be suspect, for goodness knows what builders do to it or leave in its depths hidden for posterity. Ivy, and indeed most climbers, for the sake of successful transplanting are grown in pots by the nurseryman, and therefore can be planted at most times, although no one would choose the height of summer or attempt to plant on an ice-bound day in winter.

When knocked from the pot, roots are generally found intertwined closely in a mass at the bottom of the ball, and these should be gently disentangled and spread out in a hole wide enough for the purpose. The growth will be found tied to a stake from which, after planting, it should be detached; it should then be secured to the wall or fence. Curiously enough, ivy, the best self-clinging climber, is also the worst after transplanting, for it does not usually support itself by clinging until established for several seasons, and in the meantime has to be attached to wall or fence by means of wall nails and string or shreds of cloth.

Ivy is evergreen and loses its leaves during the spring and summer months, and these being very leathery constitute a great nuisance. To obviate this they should be trimmed off closely in March with a sharp reaphook, a tool better than shears for the purpose. Ivy, however, in spite of its doubtful attention to a house, is splendid for covering lattice screens placed to hide unsightly objects from view. The best varieties are:–

Hedera hibernica. Medium-sized with green leaves.
Hedera atropurpurea. Leaves of deep bronzy purple.
Hedera caenwoodiana. The five-fingered Ivy. Leaves of medium size with white veins.
Hedera Cripsii. Small to medium sized leaves variegated silver.
Hedera Mrs Pollock. Leaves of bright gold.
Hedera dentata. Very large dark green leaf.

The second best self-clinging creeper of importance is undoubtedly Vitis inconstans Veitchii, a vine better known as

Ampelopsis Veitchii. Its foliage is beautiful in all stages and especially so in the autumn when few autumn-foliaged plants can touch its glorious shades of red. However, the truth must be told. This plant clings in the same way as ivy and it is an even worse destroyer of buildings. In speed of growth it far outstrips the ivy and its thick stems, looking like twisted and knotted ship's cables, soon obtain a strangle-hold on bricks and stone. Generally, it has to be cleared from a house in fewer years than ivy, but nevertheless as a short-term climber there is nothing more effective or beautiful. It is perfectly hardy, thrives in any situation, and like ivy does not cling very readily at first, but having once begun there is no stopping it. For covering unsightly sheds and walls where its destructive nature is of secondary importance it is ideal. As it is grown in pots it may be planted at any time of the year within reason.

Another vine, Vitis quinquefolia, better known as Ampelopsis hederacea, is the true Virginian creeper. Although self-clinging by means of pads on its tendrils it also festoons walls and buildings with hanging growths many feet in length. Its large green leaves become brilliant scarlet in autumn. Although not so destructive in its clinging habits even this vine needs restriction or the contraction of its twining growths may in time become a nuisance.

A third vine, Vitis Henryana, resembles Vitis inconstans Veitchii in all particulars except that its purplish green leaves are veined with silver and purple. These attractive leaves also turn to brilliant scarlet and crimson in the autumn.

There are many other ornamental vines, but one which should be given a place is Vitis Coignetiae, a rampant grower which needs the support of fence or trellis, to which it should be tied. Its very large shield-like leaves turn into many shades of purple, crimson, and scarlet in the autumn and persist until hard frost arrives.

From the few remaining worthwhile self-clingers only Hydrangea petiolaris deserves mention. It is fit for covering old tree trunks or for clothing large posts. Its dark rich green leaves are very beautiful and the large flat corymbs of white bloom striking in their unusual appearance. It is, however, a slow-growing plant, not to be compared with ivy and the vines already mentioned for quick coverage.

There are a number of plants which cannot cling but which support themselves on arches, pergolas, and trellis by twining and twisting. One of the most remarkable of these is Polygonum baldschuanicum, which, when established in congenial soil, sometimes makes as much as twenty feet of growth in a season. For covering sheds, summer houses, dead trees, or protective screens it is ideal, for in addition to lavish growth, milk-white feathery plumes of tiny flowers are borne in great profusion from July until the late autumn frost. There is a variety called Aubertii which flowers a few weeks earlier and sometimes a little more freely when in a young state. Both lose their leaves in winter.

Tecoma grandiflora (Bignonia grandiflora) is a handsome twining plant which provides quantities of orange-scarlet trumpet-like flowers, several inches long, in August and September. This plant, while being hardy, loves a warm situation and in such provides a beautiful display of blooms which look very exotic. A somewhat similar species, Tecoma radicans major, is slightly larger and a little brighter in colour.

Among the self-twiners is another remarkable plant, Aristolochia sipho, generally known as the Dutchman's pipe because its yellow and brown flowers are pitcher-shaped. Its ample foliage makes good coverage, while its flowers are interesting, especially as they come in June when there are few climbers in bloom. It is valuable too, because it thrives in a northern aspect.

Although it is not of such a closely twining habit and needs a little support, Solanum jasminoides cannot be overlooked, for it is one of our best and most beautiful flowering plants for wall covering. Its rapid growth and masses of pinkish white flowers form an unforgettable sight. In late summer and autumn it flowers so freely and is so intrinsically beautiful that it should be in every garden.

I cannot leave the twining plants without mentioning one of the best known, the Wistaria. This twining tree lives to a great age – centuries – and there are specimens in this country extending for several hundred feet with twisted trunks bigger than a man's body. Such ancient trees, when in bloom, are worth a pilgrimage, for the heavily scented racemes of bluish mauve in pendant tens of thousands create an impression not easily forgotten. Unfortunately, Wistaria is often disappointing, for in a congenial soil and a warm district it sometimes refuses to flower until it is old and growth ceases to be luxurious. Yet under such good conditions growth is often over twenty-five feet yearly and the long pliable thong-like shoots should be twined into the position finally required. The non-flowering habit of the early years may be partly overcome by pruning back some of the shoots to three or four eyes, while using others for extension. The species of which there are so many fine specimens is generally chinensis, but there is a much finer one called Wistaria multijuga which has racemes of lavender-blue approaching three feet in length. There is also a very good white form of multijuga known as multijuga alba. All wistarias flower in May and should be planted to face the south, south-west, or west.

There is a group of twining plants particularly suitable for British gardens – the honeysuckles. Although they luxuriate in rich soil they are quite happy in poorer ones and particularly happy over chalk. They love moisture but can endure drought, and while they are plants of the partially shaded forest are nevertheless comfortable in exposure. When established in good soil they become rampant growers and should not be planted where a flurry of foliage is not wanted. There are many varieties which flower over a long period and of which the following are some of the best. Most species and varieties are deliciously scented. Some are said to be evergreen, but the so-called evergreen ones all lose their leaves during or after severe frost.

LONICERA (Honeysuckle) japonica flexuosa. Purplish leaves with flowers of soft red outside and white within. Blooms freely from June until October.

Americana. Tubular yellow scented flowers creamy yellow within. Very profuse. Flowering in June and July.

Periclymenum serotina. The Red Dutch Honeysuckle. Beautiful reddish purple flowers with yellow interiors. Heavily scented. Masses of flowers from June until October.

Halleana. Rapid growing 'evergreen' variety with flowers of pale biscuit. Sweetly scented. This variety should be cut back each Spring. In flower from June until October.

Sempervirens (Scarlet Trumpet). A striking variety with long tubular flowers of rich orange scarlet and yellow within. Brilliant from June until October.

Tellmanniana. Produces large tubular yellow blooms in great clusters. Flowers in June.

On a warm sheltered wall facing south or south-west passion flowers should be found a place. They twine and cling but are better if they can be supported by a few wires. There are two which are hardy in all but very cold districts, Passiflora (passion flower) coerulea, a lovely shade of blue, and a white one, Constance Elliott, both of which later produce large fruits of egg size which are golden orange in colour. A wall covered with Passifloras in fruit is a very pleasing sight.

There are many shrubs and shrubby plants which although not able to cling or twine are used for the same purpose as real climbers by attaching them to wires, trellis, or some form of support, and perhaps the best of these is the rose; but as this will be fully dealt with in Chapter 21 I will not deal with it now.

There are several jasmines which are great favourites and perhaps the best of them is Jasminum nudiflorum, the well-known winter-flowering jasmine, beloved for its dainty yellow blooms in midwinter. In warm districts this sometimes starts to bloom in November and continues until spring, and as flowers are produced from wood made during the summer it should be cut back in spring after the flowering period. The fragrant white species, Jasminum officinale, should also be in every garden. It is very free growing, practically free from trouble, and possesses one of the old English perfumes which no one should do without. This jasmine flowers freely from June to August. There is also a beautiful pale pink form called Jasminum stephanense which grows very strongly and has the characteristic perfume which endears jasmines to most people. A yellow-flowered, nearly evergreen species which flowers late in summer, Jasminum revolutum, also has much to commend it, but needs plenty of room as it grows very strongly.

Clematis, on the whole, are unsuitable for wall covering–they are essentially plants for the specialist–but there is one delightful clematis which might well be in every garden, Clematis montana. This magnificent plant, capable of covering a large summerhouse by itself, has white anemone-like flowers in starry masses in May and is the ideal plant for such purposes; its rose-pink variety, Rubens, is a very fitting companion.

For making a temporary screen or for covering an old shed the merits of the common hop, Humulus lupulus, should not be overlooked. Few plants can make such a smother of foliage in such a short time or hide unsightly objects so effectively. It is a perennial which sends up fresh shoots from its base each spring.

Many people nowadays like to clothe their walls with fruit trees and thus combine utility and beauty, but as this is not a book on fruit I will content myself by saying that most of the tree fruits and all the bush fruits except black currants are suitable, and that raspberries, blackberries, and hybrid berries lend themselves admirably to this.

Many shrubs, some of them quite hardy, are used for the adornment of walls. Not all of them look well, however, when squashed against a wall in a narrow border where expansion is impossible. This usually results in an annual chopping back of such a drastic nature that still more unwanted growth is made each season, a sad state for which there is no remedy but uprooting.

The beautiful cydonias frequently suffer in this way. They are perfectly hardy, and therefore need no protection, but because of their hardiness are suitable for planting near exposed north and north-east walls where other plants survive with difficulty. It is unnecessary to torture them by a combination of hard pruning and tight pinning to walls; instead they should be planted at least three feet from a wall to permit their natural expansion. There are many good varieties, but in choosing due regard must be paid to background colour – orange scarlet and crimson do not harmonize well with bright red brick walls and some pale shades appear insipid against the yellowish drab of the brick used in London districts.

Good varieties are:

CYDONIA japonica Alpina (Maulei atrosanguinea)	Brilliant tomato red
japonica Simonii	Deep velvety crimson
Boule de Feu	Bright vermilion
cardinalis	Cardinal red
Falconet Charlot	Double salmon pink
Knaphill scarlet	This queerly-named variety has large flowers, salmon on the outside and terra cotta within

The cydonias, near relations to the apple, are exceptions to the rule of planting in good soil. Like the apple they produce most flowers when growth is partially starved; therefore, beyond preparing the soil for a good start, little is needed. Most of them produce regularly apple-like fruit of many shades of gold, highly fragrant and useful for jam making.

The red-berried cotoneasters which are splendid when grown as shrubs are also excellent for covering low walls on northern exposures. Some of the best for the purpose are as follows:

COTONEASTER Francheti	Grey green foliage on arched branches
horizontalis	A prostrate shrub very useful for covering low objects including the side walls of steps. Tiny leaves, densely borne
lactea	Oval olive green leaves on arched sprayed branches. Berries persist all the winter
rugosa	Attractive shiny leathery green leaves. Berries in clusters on arched sprays

All the above cotoneasters have scarlet berries.

The pyracanthas, often known as firethorns, are among our most beautiful shrubs. They can be planted in the most exposed site, and will withstand the rigours of the north. However, the building must be well chosen, for when laden with berries few of them appear at their best against a wall of bright red brick. They may be planted to grow freely at the base of a wall or trained to any desired pattern. The varieties below are striking:

PYRACANTHA coccinea Lalandii	Masses of white flowers in summer followed by orange-scarlet berries in autumn
Rogersiana fructu lutea	White flowers in summer and bright yellow berries in autumn

The beautiful ceanothus, with their flowers generally of soft shades of blue, in many districts need the protection of walls facing south or west. They are excellent wall shrubs. There are two sections, the so-called evergreen varieties which, however, sometimes lose their leaves after frost and which flower in late spring, and the summer flowering varieties which lose their leaves each winter.

Of the spring flowering sorts the following are recommended:

CEANOTHUS dentatus	Bright blue
florabundus	Pale blue
Veitchianus	Mid blue

These require little or no pruning.

The following are good summer flowering varieties:

CEANOTHUS Autumnal Blue	Large panicles of soft blue flowers
Burkwoodii	Bright indigo blue flowers from June until autumn

The summer flowering varieties should be cut back in spring.

The lists of shrubs could be continued indefinitely, but I have given enough for all to make a suitable selection. However, no one should attempt to cover every bare wall or building immediately. Only by living in a house and garden can one feel the intimate atmosphere or see their true possibilities.

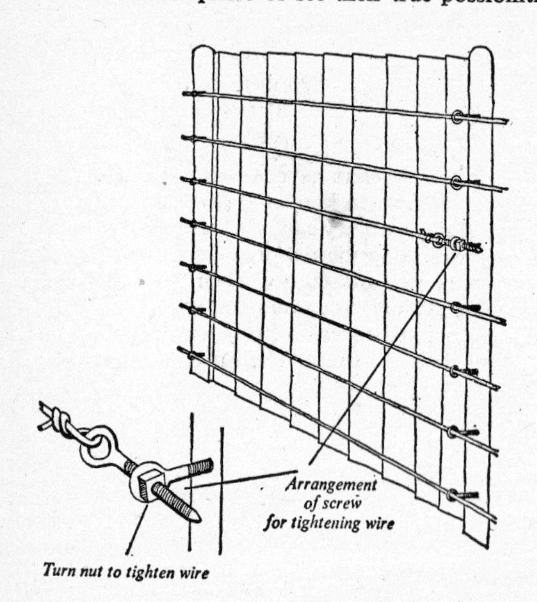

45. Method of wiring fences for attaching climbers.

Many people experience difficulty in fastening climbers to walls. Some use wall nails of the kind used for fruit trees and some use builder's nails and string. Both these methods are unsightly and not always efficient. By far the best method is to have the wall wired so that all shoots can be evenly spaced out or tied at any desired angle. This is done by stretching fourteen-gauge wire tightly between eyes driven into the wall at suitable intervals. One end of the wire is fastened to a stretcher which with a screw and nut maintains it in a state of tension. Wires should always be fixed two or three inches away from the wall for convenience in tying and to allow air to circulate between the tied branches and the wall. The wires should be placed about nine inches apart and can run horizontally or vertically according to the shape of wall or building or the general need. For many twining plants which are inclined to grow upright vertical fixing answers best.

Another workable plan is to make sections of light trellis by fastening builder's laths together in open squares of about four inches, fastening them to the wall with a two-inch space between walls and trellis, and thus providing a frame to which shoots can be tied. These frameworks of laths can be made to any desired shape and should be painted or stained a neutral moss green, thus being made as inconspicuous as possible.

Because there is a great wealth of plants available no one should attempt to crowd in too many or to convert house walls and buildings into a museum for climbing plants. Each should be chosen because of its suitability for the site with the idea of beautifying the general appearance – in much the same way as one would arrange a room.

Climbers, spaced and tied in as required, need little pruning except in those cases indicated. Nothing could be uglier than trees and shrubs hacked and slashed annually with the natural result that they produce thickets of brushwood always striving to restore a balance with the roots and becoming even denser in the process.

I have already said that climbers should be planted in good soil, a rule which should be strictly observed except where otherwise indicated, but climbers, unlike plants in the open, cannot always look after themselves – they need water. Because walls, buildings, and overhanging roofs prevent rain from reaching their roots and because of the porosity of much building material the roots of climbers are often dry when plants in the open are too wet – a state which should be remedied, at least in the early days before roots have had time to penetrate to moister areas.

The planting of all climbers should be done with deliberation and with suitable restraint, for climbers, like hedges and lawns, are mainly unproductive, and in time lead to much labour in upkeep. The cultivator should therefore ensure when planting that these unproductive items, taken together, do not saddle him with more responsibilities than he is able to undertake personally or by paid labour, or absorb time better used otherwise.

· 20 ·

Hedge Plants

NOBODY can deny that for sheer effectiveness the common quick beats all. It will thrive on any soil, endure much hacking after neglect, and yet submit to close clipping better than most. It is truly impenetrable, but not in the least interesting, so in this chapter I will mention other plants, some of which, though equally utilitarian, nevertheless have a good appearance and are not quite so dreary.

Hedges can be tyrants. Little is gained from the tyranny of hedge clipping, and this needs careful consideration before planting. Most garden jobs are productive. Directly or indirectly they give results in flowers, fruits, and vegetables, if only by building up valuable soil constituents or by improving texture and tilth, but in clipping, some hedges enforce an ever-recurring repetition of awkward movements with implements which lack the pleasant rhythm of the lawn mower, which does another unproductive job, but with more pleasing results. Such hedges are of quick, privet, and the like, which no amount of clipping effectively represses and which, if in good health, require much attention.

But there are other sides to the question. One that we cannot overlook is that the Briton loves to be enclosed. The American or the Colonial can have his open spaces if he likes, but the Briton, however friendly, likes to keep himself to himself. He enjoys privacy after business hours and so demands fences or hedges behind which he can work or play unseen, even though he can hear every word his neighbour says under similar conditions and knows that either can look over the fence or hedge occasionally. It is incontestable that failing a fence a good hedge is the best protection, so if privacy is really needed then a hedge it must be, with the attendant necessity of working often in summer, or, if it is neglected, in winter hard hacking at growth which could have been cut far more easily when in a soft state.

Hedges have other uses. They can be used to great effect for enclosing different parts of the garden. Thus the rose garden, the kitchen garden, and others immediately suggest themselves. Even the rubbish heap may need screening off and the dustbin by the back door – which cannot be concealed – may need obscuring by a friendly hedge or screen which might also temper the cutting draughts so ready to enter every back door. For this purpose, we are fortunate in this country. We not only have our well-known hedge plants, but a host of others far more interesting and beautiful and which give less trouble – but of these more later.

Let us first deal with the boundary hedge, which should be thick, impenetrable, of pleasing appearance, and, if possible, evergreen. Of all the true evergreens holly makes the most satisfactory hedge. Not the variegated or fancy-leaved varieties, but the common, English, prickly holly of the woodland. Although a native of the woods over chalk or flint where it is often partially shaded by large forest trees it is equally at home in any soil and aspect provided drainage is good.

For success, the soil for hedge plants should be as well prepared as that in the kitchen garden, and the holly is no exception; indeed good ground culture is a necessity for this plant. To grow as it should it needs much humus, which, in the woodland where it is so happy, it receives in abundance from the fallen leaves of the forest trees. Instead of taking the attitude 'It is only a hedge plant – it will grow anywhere' we should dig, delve, and manure just as we would for the onion or the delphinium – work I have fully described in Chapter 1. A strip of ground three feet wide should be treated generously both in labour and in farmyard manure, or compost, for this or any other hedge plant. A good start is important as it leads to the quick development of wood near the ground where growth is always greatly needed. As this soil treatment is applicable to any other hedge plant I shall mention, I need not refer to it again in this chapter.

Hedges with wide basal gaps between plants which have gaunt, scraggy bottoms are not uncommon and are directly traceable to two factors – scamped soil preparation and the use of plants which have become ungainly in the nursery bed, often the leavings of years. Such plants are usually purchased in the hope of obtaining a finished hedge quickly, for few people – even though they are young – are prepared to wait. This is no quick way to success. Tall, misshapen specimens rarely fit together into one homogeneous whole; they cannot, for they must be grown together. Neither are they time savers, except under very favourable conditions, for hardened ancient scraggs have a maddening habit of remaining semi-dormant, perhaps for several seasons, before they can be persuaded to grow again, while young unhardened plants generally grow away swiftly and uniformly each year. So choose small plants, as nearly alike as possible, and plant them firmly one foot apart in a single line. The double line is generally a mistake, for in time it forms a hedge too wide to manage, without having any corresponding gain in density or being less gappy at the base.

The newly-planted hedge must be looked after like any other valuable crop. Weeds must not encroach on it and a good mulching of manure is beneficial.

The early energies of the plants must be devoted not to becoming tall, but to thickening at the base, a state which, if not achieved in the early years of growth, is unlikely to be reached at all. For this reason a little judicious cutting back of leaders and other strong shoots should be practised until a foundation has been secured, and even then too much extension must not be expected annually.

The time of planting is important. Holly in expert hands can be planted successfully at any time between September and May, except, of course, in severe wintery weather, and at a pinch can be planted during the months of summer, but it is a fleshy leaved plant inclined to feel root severance and for that reason should be planted in a permanent position at a favourable time. In skilled hands the best time is at the end of April, just before the old leaves drop and as new growth begins. This entails swift handling to ensure that roots are not dried by cutting winds or by exposure to sunshine and the use of much water afterwards, because, if transplanted, hollies suffer from dryness in spring or early summer after a spring transplanting, they are likely to perish. For the amateur, therefore, able to work only at odd times with long intervals between, a cool period in September or October is best. In this case the work should be pushed on as quickly as possible so that the plants may regain a roothold before the rigours of winter.

Planting hedges is an art. It is not enough merely to take plants haphazardly and plant them in the proper stations – that is a rough and ready method which often takes time to give good results. The careful selection of plants and the dovetailing of branches will produce a faced-up hedge which looks as if it has been established for some time – a little more trouble, perhaps, but well worth while. A hedge is something to accept, much as wallpaper is accepted. Planting should therefore be carefully carried out, because if, through bad planting, the hedge is not a success, the result is a permanent eyesore instead of a pleasing background – perhaps a source of irritation for a generation. The boundary hedge becomes a frame enclosing the garden of which one should not be too conscious, but bad planting may lead to irregular growth and unhealthy plants showing various irritating degrees of debility. Because of this the temptation to pack the roots hurriedly into the ground because 'It's only a hedge' must be firmly resisted, holes should be large enough to accommodate the spread-out roots, and planting should be performed as carefully as with a fruit tree.

After planting, the soil should be trodden firm, the surface levelled with a fork, and the three-foot strip left about two inches lower than the surrounding soil to prevent water flowing away when watering during the first spring and early summer after planting. Above all, roots must not be exposed to the drying influence of wind and sun a moment longer than is necessary for the work of planting. Because of this, packages received from nurserymen should not be opened and their contents strewn around. If the work of planting can take place as soon as the consignment is received, well and good; in that case the plants may be taken from the package and laid out for sorting just before the job begins. Otherwise they should be taken from the package and 'heeled in' – i.e. planted in a temporary fashion to cover the roots – until planting proper can begin, a plan which has the advantage that when seen in this way individual plants may be easily selected according to shape and size. If, from the beginning, the plants shape up well and look happy, success is generally assured.

Late autumn planting usually ensures watering by natural means throughout the winter months, but, even so, should the spring months be dry a timely application of water may save much trouble and annoyance later on. Patching up hedges to replace random failures is not an easy job and is better avoided if possible.

Next on the list of evergreens comes yew, another native British plant which forms a splendid hedge. It is undoubtedly a fine hedge plant and one which should be treated similarly to the holly. Although comparatively slow growing it forms a very dense permanent hedge or screen provided it is planted closely when quite small. There also is a golden variety available for hedge planting, but it is expensive, and its shade of gold, though beautiful, does not always provide so good a background colour as the ordinary green variety. There are, of course, many other varieties, but none is better than the native type.

A third native, box, Buxus sempervirens, also makes a fine hedge, equally as good as the two evergreens already mentioned, but it is of woefully slow growth, and therefore cannot be recommended for general use. However, where a neat hedge of slow growth is required, the variety known as the Handsworth box is worth planting.

A fourth evergreen, the laurel, Prunus laurocerasus, forms a good hedge. It should always be used as a fine semi-natural screen where it can grow tall and expand. Although successful as an ordinary hedge it resents too much repression, and owing to the size of its spreading leaves is unsuitable for clipping with shears. It looks best in summer after being cut back by knife or secateurs in the spring just as new growth begins. Its appearance is good and sometimes impressive, but it has an annoying habit of casting its leaves during the summer months, and these, being very durable, if not gathered immediately, remain playthings of the wind for many months. Laurel should be sited eighteen inches apart and bushy plants about eighteen inches high are recommended. Latifolia is a good variety. The Portugal laurel, Laurocerasus lusitanica, also makes a very fine hedge, but like most laurels it is not altogether happy when repressed, and is better if allowed to grow freely as an informal screen when the long panicles of milky white bloom can be seen to advantage.

With the possible exception of box, the evergreens mentioned are suitable for tall screens and massive hedges as well as small containing hedges, but the one I now mention, Lonicera nitida, is fit only for hedges up to four feet high. It is a beautiful tiny-leaved evergreen which, with innumerable densely clothed shoots, forms an excellent hedge of pleasing appearance. Although extremely quick growing it is inclined to be flimsy; in its early days, therefore, it should be cut back hard for a year or two to induce a stout framework of foundation growth. The best hedges of this are formed by planting specimens a few inches high about nine inches apart in a single line. It is easy to clip and satisfactory if not allowed to extend too rapidly in height. A somewhat stiffer plant, Lonicera yunnanensis, forms a stouter hedge and is otherwise good and pleasing.

No chapter on hedge plants would be complete without some mention of privet, and I will deal with this gladly. Truly it is the king of hedge plants. It grows swiftly, is happy in all soils, is amenable to close and frequent clipping, and cheerfully endures being chopped down after neglect. Its general appearance is good, but, alas, nowadays drearily monotonous – one sees so much of it. Because of its many virtues and particularly its quick-growing qualities I have a feeling that most of my readers will use it in spite of anything I advise, and it is such a good plant that I cannot blame them. This plant, however, which grows so luxuriantly, needs much food, so that the initial treatment of the soil should be liberal. It is often misnamed. The best variety of privet, now in general use, is Ligustrum ovalfolium, not 'common Privet', which the oval-leaved variety displaced. The so-called common privet, once used extensively for hedges, has smaller paler leaves and a habit of flowering persistently if not clipped frequently. There is a golden-leaved variety of the oval-leaved privet as free growing as its parent.

Again, for complete success I make a plea for planting small specimens – year-old plants are best – and in a single line sited one foot apart. The oval-leaved privet is said to be evergreen, but this is not strictly true; nevertheless it retains most of its leaves until they are replaced in spring, unless very severe frost occurs, when it is liable to lose all of them suddenly. The common privet is not so evergreen, but is generally bare during the winter months.

I have already mentioned the effectiveness of quick or hawthorn, an accommodating plant which grows anywhere and suffers few disabilities. Most people look on it as a farm fence and regard it as normal to neglect it, perhaps for years, then to layer it angularly by partial severance and let it cover its wounds with fresh growth. At its best they associate it with an annual hacking down with the slashing hook. But treated well as a garden hedge there is little to beat it. It is cheap to buy and practically free from trouble. If planted closely in well-prepared soil when young – about nine inches apart from plant to plant in a single row – it will become a good hedge in a few years and sometimes outstrip privet. If clipped twice or three times when growth is soft no autumn hacking down is necessary. Although I do not recommend it as a garden hedge for general use, I do so enthusiastically in those cases where gardens are cut out of meadows and cattle must be excluded, for no British animal can pierce its prickly density when well established. However, it seems to be a good host plant, for seedling briars, brambles, honeysuckles, and a number of others quickly make use of its branches if not repressed, and for this reason planting in a single row, which offers greater scope for weeding, is laid down as a necessity.

The beech of the forest, Fagus silvaticus, which, when used as a hedge plant, retains its leaves all the winter, must not be overlooked. The leaves, of the well-known russet red, are very pleasing, and this plant is very valuable when used as a close wind-break rather than a hedge, although quite successful when clipped down. Small seedlings should be planted in a single row about fifteen inches apart and in the early growth stages treated liberally. There is a purple-leaved form of beech which, in addition to being a noble ornamental tree, is also good for its summer effect when used as a hedge or wind-break, but the winter colouring of the leaves is similar to those of the green-leaved beech.

Another forest tree, the hornbeam (Carpinus betulus), which is much like the beech in appearance but with smaller leaves, is, in the opinion of many, superior for the purpose. Be this as it may, it is an exceedingly good hedge plant or wind screen, which, though carrying dead leaves throughout the winter, gives the impression of vigorous life.

Another deciduous tree which, when 'hedged', makes an impenetrable fence, is Prunus myrobalum, the cherry plum. This, in the fruit-growing districts, is often planted thickly and unpruned to form a thick windscreen and one which sometimes bears heavy crops of fruit. As a closely-cut hedge it is equally happy and withstands neglect and hacking down almost as well as quick. It should be planted in a single row about a foot apart. In the prunus family, too, there are many ornamental plants useful for hedges, but one which deserves special mention is Prunus Pissardii, whose plum-like leaves are the same colour as the purple beech. Treated in the same way as the cherry plum it forms a hedge of character which does not grow out of hand too easily. Like quick, it is specially good for excluding cattle.

Most of us have seen evergreen coniferous trees used as hedge plants, generally sadly ill-treated and looking very unhappy. Nevertheless, if treated intelligently, several conifers form good screens and tall hedges. One of the best is Chamycyparis (Cupressus) Lawsoniana. When planting this and other conifers for screens most people make the mistake of using specimens which are much too large. The natural early habit of this and some other conifers is to be pointedly elliptical, or something like a long lemon stood on end; when planting well-grown specimens to form a hedge it is therefore found impossible to plant them closely enough together to prevent the formation of a large gap between each pair. Such a hedge or screen is gappy from the first, and as some lower branches decay in time the tendency is for it to become even more so as time goes on. My readers will readily see, therefore, that if conifers are to be used successfully they must be planted when small, and placed close together so that they develop an unbroken face from a few inches above the ground upwards. Conifers are very unhappy if clipped and few kinds and varieties will last very long if systematically treated in this way; instead they should be controlled by the judicious use of secateurs, which cannot give the surface the flat appearance beloved of enthusiastic hedge trimmers, but gives a pleasing matt effect, restful to the eye and one which does not look out of place in any garden.

For those who like blue and glaucous effects, Chamycyparis (Cupressus) Lawsoniana Allumii is excellent for forming a hedge or screen of distinction. This variety has foliage of a dark green shade underlying a blue grey which is very pleasing. Another fine variety, whose foliage colour is more grey than blue, is Chamycyparis (Cupressus) Lawsoniana Fraseri, which should be treated similarly to the other. The above Chamycyparis should be sited eighteen inches apart when planting or slightly closer if the provision of very small plants renders it possible.

A very dainty hedge can be made if Chamycyparis (Cupressus) Lawsoniana Fletcheri is used. It is a small-growing conifer which can easily be kept in bounds and whose columnar shape permits close planting. It is said that this variety will withstand close clipping, but even if this is true it seems foolish to take away all its character by the repeated use of shears. Its colour is a lovely bluish grey which shows well on unclipped feathery foliage. These slim conifers should be planted fifteen inches apart.

Some mention must be made of Cupressus macrocarpa, the most rapidly growing conifer and one much used for hedging. I cannot recommend this as it is hardy only in very mild districts and is unhappy except in maritime parts. For a time it will survive close clipping, but after a few seasons of this will often die suddenly, sometimes as a complete hedge and in other cases here and there. It is also liable to die after great drought and severe cold. As a hedge plant it is a failure, but as a specimen tree, grown untrammelled, a magnificent success, and in the opinion of many superior to the cedar. For this, however, it must be planted in the mild districts of south and south-west and near the sea; inland it is generally a miserable failure.

Before leaving conifers I must mention another, Thuya plicata, which somewhat resembles the Chamycyparis. It is a splendid hedge plant provided it is planted when quite small. Its bright green foliage is attractive and the branches intermingle so freely that a matt-faced hedge of distinctive character is formed. It should be planted fifteen to eighteen inches apart.

For hedges of less severe character there are many shrubs which beautify and enrich the garden, and one of the best of these is Cotoneaster Simonsii. It is stiff enough to form a hedge while giving a good show of bloom followed by scarlet berries which persist all the winter. Any pruning necessary should be done in the spring after the berries have fallen. Plant one foot apart.

There are several varieties of Berberis suitable for hedges. Among them are Berberis Darwinii, which gives masses of orange yellow flowers in summer, followed by purple blue berries which carry a rich bloom; Berberis stenophylla, which gives cascades of yellowish orange flowers and small dark foliage; and Verruculosa, with yellow pendant flowers in sharp contrast to the dark glossy leaves silvered underneath. These Berberis should be planted fifteen inches apart and pruned in early spring after the berries have fallen.

A dwarf but impenetrable hedge can be formed with Genista hispanica, which in May or June is densely clothed in bright yellow flowers. This will grow in soils impossible to many species. It is most attractive and durable. Any pruning necessary should be done in early spring.

In mild districts of the south and south-west the Escallonia flourishes, and if an informal and beautiful hedge is desired this should not be overlooked. Probably the best for the purpose is Escallonia Ingrami, a variety with rosy red tubular flowers which is hardier than most. Escallonias look best when unpruned, but need room as they have a spread of eight feet or more when fully grown. They can be pruned in spring if desired. Eighteen inches from plant to plant is a good planting distance. Escallonias should be planted in May.

In very mild districts hardy fuchsias make delightful hedges, and even in parts where they are liable to be cut back by frost the root bases are not usually destroyed, so that by hard pruning each spring new growth and a good show of bloom can be expected. Fuchsia Riccartoni, which has crimson and purple flowers, and Fucshia Thompsoni, with bright red and purple blooms, are both excellent. These, too, should be planted in May at fifteen inches apart.

This chapter would be incomplete without mentioning upkeep, for closely-planted hedges are less likely to look after themselves than other plants which have room to expand above and below. Often when a hedge shows signs of sickness after being satisfactory for some years the trouble can be traced to starvation. The reason is not hard to find. In a garden a hedge is generally competing with crops, often has its roots chopped off closely when trenching for other crops, and seldom, if ever, is allowed to retain over its roots leaves and debris blown there by the wind; it is therefore robbed of an annual supply of humus. Hedges in a farm, although neglected, have a much better time; often they are top dressed with accumulated inches of decaying leaves and the tops of weeds. Other crops seldom invade their root run and they have the benefit of much deposited manure, especially on grassland.

A garden hedge, robbed of natural food, with its roots closely packed into a few cubic feet of soil, faces gradual starvation and if, at any time, plants in a hedge make little growth, and look pallid or generally unhealthy, and if no symptoms of disease can be seen, starvation usually accounts for the trouble. In such cases a layer of good farmyard manure, several inches thick, applied in the autumn to a generous width on each side of the hedge centre generally works wonders, and if this is followed up annually there is little fear of the trouble recurring. Failing farmyard manure, garden compost, peat, leafsoil, or accumulated grass mowings will form excellent substitutes – even old potting soil would do good. As nitrogen starvation is generally more acute than that of other elements it is an additional aid to sprinkle the surface of the soil, before the mulch is applied, with six ounces coarsely ground hoof and horn meal per superficial square yard to ensure that supplies of nitrogen are always available throughout the growing season.

On thin dry soil no plant in the garden appreciates a copious drink more than the hedge plants, so, at a time when perhaps so many other plants need water, if a little can be found to care for the hedge, the results will be well worth while. And if the ground is prepared and manured for a hedge just as for some special crop, it will have a much better chance in life even though subsequently neglected.

And now about clipping. It is always easier to clip deciduous hedges in the summer when the wood is comparatively soft and green and, in the case of the free-growing privet, it is beneficial to do so on several occasions. Holly and yew are best clipped in early August so that enough growth will form during the autumn months to hide the stubble left by clipping but not enough to become unsightly and straggling. The laurels are best cut in early April as young growth begins. For convenience, beech and hornbeam may be clipped twice, once in early summer and again in August. Conifers generally should be cut in August, but they may be cut at any time in spring or summer, if necessary – never in the winter. Prunus of all sorts should be treated like privet, but if preferred can be cut back annually with secateurs while dormant in early winter.

Of the shrubs, Berberis should have little cutting, but any done should be in winter. Escallonias and Fuchsias I have already mentioned.

It is wise to obtain the best shears possible and have them sharpened and set from time to time. Good mechanical hedge clippers are now available driven by power taken through a long flex from a power plug or from a portable motor, of which many sizes and makes are procurable. Where there are many hedges these are a great boon and with them free-growing hedges can be clipped frequently and well. As they are almost as easily handled as domestic cleaning machines, I need not give instructions for their use, as most people would feel happy with them after a few minutes.

· 21 ·

Roses

No garden old or new would be complete without roses, which, as befits our national emblem, fit so happily into the English garden. Fortunately there are few gardens where roses will not thrive and wherever one goes in the British Isles there roses are to be found, excepting, of course, in a few bleak exposed northerly districts where few flowering plants could thrive.

Not many years ago it was considered necessary for good rose culture to have a garden of clay too intractible to grow other plants, and while this was partly true as regards a few varieties of hybrid perpetuals, generally grown for show purposes, it certainly was never true of the rank and file varieties, even in the days of this doctrine. It is not strange that the general culture of roses spread extensively when it became known that good roses could be grown on almost any type of soil without special preparation, excepting a few small areas on Bagshot sand, where they thrive with some difficulty. However, even in this poor sand, with a little extra soil preparation, fine roses are grown, and now there are nurseries producing splendid plants within this soil-hungry belt, an achievement which rose growers of past generations would have thought impossible.

Concurrently with this enlightenment came the introduction of the hybrid tea roses, composed mainly of roses of light build which bloom during most of the summer and autumn. Most of these are quite happy on soils of average quality, and some, indeed, thrive on land known to be much below average.

In general, the roses now grown in English gardens are hybrids and are known as hybrid tea roses, although there are some known as Pernetiana roses and a few older varieties known as hybrid perpetual roses – which, in the perpetual sense, they never were – still grown and loved by ardent rose growers.

The introduction of hybrid teas gave colours hitherto undreamed of and in most parts a continuous flowering season from June to late autumn, extending to Christmas in many mild districts. These roses, like many others before them, have an ancestry going back through the ages almost to the dawn of civilization, from which time roses have been revered, but few of the earliest raisers could have foreseen even the possibility of so much beauty, such an indescribable wealth of colour or such an infinite range of varieties. Some of the modern colour combinations of many varieties are strikingly beautiful in their rich refinement, and although a few varieties are not overblessed with petals, and, therefore, their flowers are not very plump, they can be forgiven for this because their myriad blooms, produced in a seemingly never-ending succession, compensate fully for any deficiency.

But how do we grow them? As with so many crops, success lies in thorough soil preparation. Although it can be said that no rose needs a plastic clay, yet heavy soils of good depth give the best results, provided they are well drained. In planting roses it should be remembered that for some years at least they will be permanent occupants of a bed or border and preparations should accordingly be on a long-term plan. For this the procedure advised in Chapter 1 is strongly recommended and good farmyard manure should be worked into the soil to a good depth. This should not, however, be placed near the top spit where it would come into contact with the roots of roses when planting. It is always a bad plan to place manure in the soil in sandwich formation, and quite wrong, when cultivating for roses, as, unlike the yearly soil preparation possible for many other plants, there will for several seasons be no chance to mix again into the soil by digging any additions or ingredients. All farmyard manure, or compost, therefore, must be mixed with the soil as thoroughly as possible, in the first instance.

Those with heavy fat soils may content themselves with supplies of well-decayed horse manure or even compost, and some fortunate ones need not bother about manure, as any good rose nurseryman can say that roses will grow well on some good soils with no additions before planting. However, those with sandy or gravelly soils can hardly be too thorough. For these poor soils results will be much better if some good farmyard manure is incorporated, and if compost can be added so much the better. On such soils, too, the addition of some good well-rotted turf from an old meadow, or top spit arable soil from a well-worked field on heavy sub-soil, will work wonders and greatly help to prolong the life of the roses. If the soil is deficient in lime, hydrated lime should be applied at the rate of 28 lb. per square pole and lightly forked into the surface before planting.

Some plants should be procured from a good nurseryman. It is obviously foolish to spend much labour, and perhaps expense, in preparing a piece of ground, then spoil all prospects of success by procuring cheap-jack plants budded on nondescript stocks and perhaps weakly and ill-formed through being badly grown. Thirds and throw-outs sometimes find themselves in the market-places of provincial towns where, on market days, they are sold by auction at prices far beyond their meagre value. Often the purchaser imagines he has obtained a great bargain, which, however, he usually regrets in the barren years which follow. Tied tightly into bundles, such roses appear good, but when separated they are generally found to be single-stemmed specimens which have made poor growth, those with faulty unions, and miscellaneous discards of every description. There is no guarantee that such roses are true to name, for unscrupulous dealers, who have no interest in horticulture, have been known to obtain a batch of labels of modern varieties and to tie them to any rubbish which came along and thus make the deception greater. So obtain the best from a reliable source – there are plenty of good nurserymen – and do not be afraid to ask your supplier for advice; his knowledge will enable him to tell you what succeeds in the neighbourhood.

Few roses are grown on their own roots; instead, they are budded or grafted – generally budded – upon an approved wild rose stock. At different periods in rose history first one stock and then another has been widely advocated by experts, but nowadays most authorities agree that for general purposes the wild dog rose of the countryside, Rosa canina, is the most suitable, and upon approved strains of this stock most roses are budded today. If you are situated on light land and you hear, however, that the roses you propose to buy are budded on Rosa rugosa do not despise them – this stock does well on very light land and on land a little on the poor side where Rosa canina is not at its best. It has one very annoying fault, that of throwing up from the base suckers which, of course, must be removed or the scion will be greatly weakened. However, even Rosa canina is not free from this habit – of which more anon.

The best time for preparing soil for roses is the autumn and the most suitable period for planting is undoubtedly early November, but there is no reason why roses should not be planted at any time from October to mid-March, provided soil and weather conditions permit. Indeed, in expert hands they may often be planted successfully in April, but the risk of loss then is greater. However, one should not spoil well-prepared land by attempting to plant when it is overburdened with moisture, but wait until there is a good friable tilth.

Dwarf roses, usually known as bush roses, should be so planted that the union of scion and stock is just below the surface when the newly-planted rose is firmly in position. To achieve this, a hole should be taken out with spade and fork sufficient to contain the roots with comfort, generally about fifteen inches square and about ten inches deep. Into this hole the roots, after having any jagged ends removed with a sharp

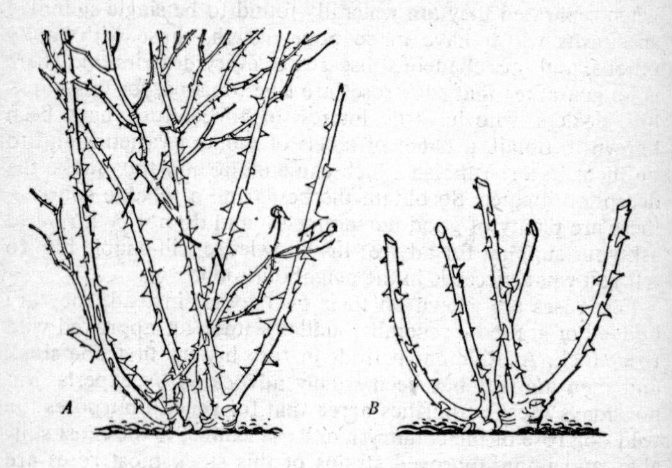

46. Bush rose: (A) Before and (B) after pruning.

knife, are spread out comfortably without crossing or bunching. The hole may have to be a little shallower or a little deeper according to the needs of individual plants, and the planter must proceed accordingly. A little soil is then placed on the roots and trodden firmly; the hole is then filled in with soil, which should be made firm in a similar manner. Finally, enough soil is placed on the surface surrounding the stem to restore the soil to the old level. On average soil roses should be sited about fifteen inches apart, but in good heavy soils the distance can be increased to eighteen inches with advantage. Some growers finish off by adding a dressing of 8 oz. of bonemeal per square yard to the surface soil and pricking it in with a fork to make a good finish and to add to the manurial value – a very good plan when the soil is poor. Rather less bonemeal can be used in cases where the soil, although not good, is not excessively poor. When sheer necessity compels planting in soil much too wet some experienced growers use a few handfuls of dry or slightly moistened peat to sprinkle on the soil over the roots to prevent it from becoming unduly compacted during the process. Generally,

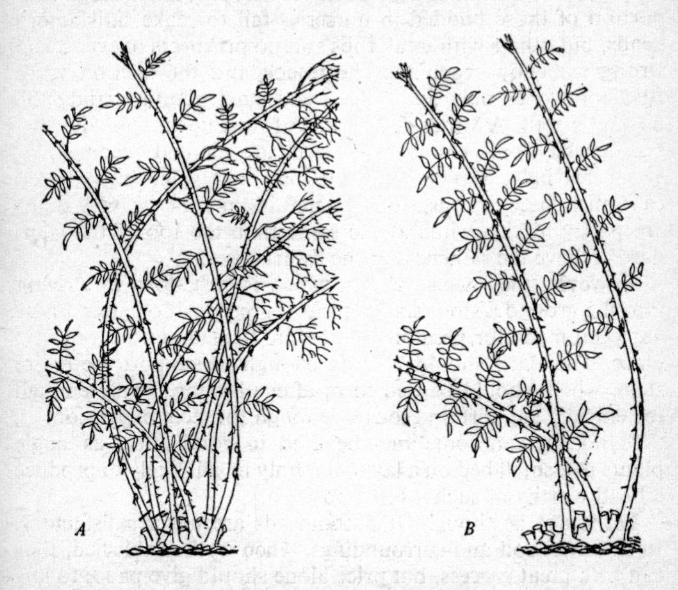

47. Climbing rose: (A) Before pruning; (B) After pruning, with the old flowering wood cut out.

however, unless the lateness of the season impels the grower to to something desperate, it is wiser to keep off.

All I have written so far applies to dwarf or bush roses, and now I will deal with standards.

In a way these are similar to bush roses, but they are budded on tall stems, three to four feet high, instead of at ground level. These stems are generally of Rosa canina or Rosa rugosa, although sometimes other stocks are used. Standards have a rare fascination for some people, who procure and plant them regardless of circumstances. Rarely do they appear happy when planted thus. It should be a general rule not to plant standards unless the soil is really good so that vigorous growth can be expected annually. Short stunted growth on a dwarf plant close to the ground is one thing, but unsatisfactory growth displayed on a tall stem right in the line of sight is quite another, and ill-developed standards can be positively ugly. Quite a large proportion of those budded in nurseries fail to make satisfactory heads, but others with weak tops and no prospects of ever being strong somehow reach the cheap-jack and the auction yard. Buy good ones only and before you start planting study the positions well. A windswept site is always unsuitable and any site in which only rows of standards are planted becomes unspeakably ugly. Standards are at their best when interspersed cautiously between bush roses so that in time their gawky stems are partly hidden while at the same time the top of the standards relieve the sameness of the dwarf roses.

However, they need staking, which is best done by driving into the ground a stout stake at the desired position after a hole has been made for planting and before the standard is put into place. The stake should be long enough to support the entire stem, which should be tied to it, after planting, firmly enough for efficient support and loosely enough for stem expansion.

Standards can sometimes be used to good effect as single plants in a small bed on a lawn, but only in soil likely to produce a head worthy of such a good position.

Let it not be thought that standards are never satisfactory. In the right soil and surroundings, when well established, they can be a great success, but price alone should give pause to any impulsive planting of standards in unsuitable soil and positions.

There is a great wealth of good varieties and from these I have selected fifty suitable for growing as dwarfs or as standards.

Fifty Good Roses suitable for Dwarfs or Standards

ANGÈLE PERNET (PERN.)	Orange yellow, shaded apricot
ANGELS MATEU (H.T.)	Flame, shaded gold
APRICOT QUEEN (H.T.)	Salmon, shaded old gold
AUTUMN (H.T.)	Orange, shaded pink
BARBARA RICHARDS (H.T.)	Maize yellow, flushed pale rose
BRASIER (H.T.)	Carmine shaded gold and scarlet
CAROLINE TESTOUT (H.T.)	Bright warm pink

COMTESSE VANDAL (H.T.)	Reddish copper, edged pale pink
CONDESA DE SASTAGO (PERN.)	Orange flame, reverse of petals gold
CRIMSON GLORY (H.T.)	Deep velvety crimson
DIRECTEUR GUERIN (H.T.)	Creamy yellow, centre golden orange
EMMA WRIGHT (H.T.)	Pure orange
ETOILE DE HOLLANDE	Bright dark red
FREDERICO CASAS (PERN.)	Bright orange, shaded copper
GENERAL MCARTHUR (H.T.)	Bright scarlet crimson
GLORY OF ROME (H.T.)	Colour variable between red and pink
GOLDEN DAWN (H.T.)	Pale lemon yellow
J. C. THORNTON (H.T.)	Bright scarlet crimson
JULIEN POTIN (PERN.)	Clear golden yellow
LADY FORTEVIOT (H.T.)	Golden yellow, shaded apricot
LAL (H.T.)	Salmon pink, shaded white
MAJOR SHELLEY (H.T.)	Intense scarlet
MARGARET MCGREDY (H.T.)	Geranium lake
MARY WHEATCROFT (H.T.)	Copper flame, dark bronze foliage
MCGREDY'S IVORY (H.T.)	Creamy white, shaded gold at base
MCGREDY'S ORANGE (H.T.)	Yellow, shaded orange
MCGREDY'S PINK (H.T.)	Pale rose pink, shaded gold
MCGREDY'S TRIUMPH (H.T.)	Fiery scarlet
MCGREDY'S WONDER (H.T.)	Coppery orange
MCGREDY'S YELLOW (H.T.)	Pale yellow
MME. BUTTERFLY (H.T.)	Pink, shaded apricot
MME. HENRI GUILLOT (H.T.)	Salmon pink, shaded orange
MME. JOSEPH PERRAUD (H.T.)	Bright orange, slightly shaded pink
MRS BARRACLOUGH (H.T.)	Carmine pink, shaded yellow at base
MRS EDWARD LAXTON	Old rose, shaded salmon
MRS SAM MCGREDY (H.T.)	Coppery orange, flushed scarlet
NINON VALLIN (H.T.)	Outside petals clear yellow, inside apricot
OPHELIA (H.T.)	Salmon flesh
PHYLLIS GOLD (H.T.)	Golden yellow
PICTURE (H.T.)	Clear rose pink
PILAR LANDECHO (H.T.)	Coppery orange, shaded pink
PINK DAWN (H.T.)	Salmon pink, shaded gold

PORTADOWN BEDDER (H.T.)	Orange yellow, flushed cerise
PORTADOWN FRAGRANCE (H.T.)	Orange, salmon pink and scarlet, all combined
PRESIDENT BOONE (H.T.)	Intense scarlet, shaded black
PRESIDENT CHARLES HAIN (H.T.)	Pale yellow, shaded cream
PRESIDENT HOOVER (H.T.)	Glowing orange yellow, shaded pink
SAM MCGREDY (H.T.)	Buff shaded cream
SIMONE GUERIN (PERN.)	Golden buff, shaded pink
THE DOCTOR (H.T.)	Bright silvery rose

Next we have roses for covering pillars, pergolas, old tree stumps, walls, and the like. There are roses specially adapted for this and undoubtedly there is no wall covering which has so many advantages as the rose, especially now that we have varieties which flower continuously for long periods.

For walls the climbing forms of hybrid tea roses, tea roses, and hybrid noisette roses are the most suitable, although the Wichuraiana ramblers, which are generally more suitable for pillars and pergolas, can be used if desired. The general procedure for planting is the same as that for other roses, except that being near walls the soil is sometimes too dry – a condition which demands that a copious drenching of water be given after planting.

In this section there are some old favourites which should not be overlooked. In sheltered districts in the south and south-west everyone should try the fragrant golden yellow Maréchal Niel. It is grown in pots by the nurseryman and is best planted in the spring so that it can have a season in which to become established before winter arrives. A sheltered southern or south-western exposure is best. It is far hardier than is generally supposed, but it is useless to attempt its culture out of doors in the Midlands or north. Undoubtedly, although old, and lacking form, it is one of our most beautiful flowers.

Gloire de Dijon, another old-fashioned rose, is hardy and its buff-yellow blooms are only slightly less beautiful than those of Maréchal Niel.

Another rose for covering the house is climbing Lady Hillingdon, which, although not so old, is delightful, for its orange-yellow blooms of good form are borne more or less continuously throughout summer and early autumn. It should be sited on a southern or south-western exposure.

Also, below I give a list of varieties suitable for this purpose, including a few Wichuraiana ramblers. They are as follows:

Roses for Walls with North and East Exposures

ALBÉRIC BARBIER
ALLEN CHANDLER
DR VAN FLEET
GLOIRE DE DIJON
CLIMBING CAROLINE TESTOUT
LADY WATERLOW
MARY WALLACE
MME ALFRED CARRIERE
PAUL'S SCARLET CLIMBER
THELMA

Roses for Walls with South, South-west or West Exposures

CHAPLIN'S PINK CLIMBER
CLIMBING LADY HILLINGDON
MARÉCHAL NIEL
MISS HELYETT
CLIMBING MME ABEL CHATENAY
CLIMBING MME. BUTTERFLY
CLIMBING OPHELIA
PAX
PHYLLIS BIDE
RÉNÉ ANDRÉ
ZÉPHIRINE DROUHIN

Then there are ramblers peculiarly adapted to clothe dead tree trunks, pillars, whether composite or single, or any object which stands alone. Generally these are climbing forms of hybrid tea and other roses, and most of them flower continuously during the summer, have long stiff stems useful for cutting, and point upright or nearly so. As these pillar roses, as they are called, can be seen from almost any angle it is important that they should make good growth; preparations to receive them must, therefore, be on generous lines. I give below a list of these:

Roses suitable for Pillars

ALLEN CHANDLER
LADY WATERLOW
CLIMBING MME ABEL CHATENAY
MME ALFRED CARRIÈRE
CLIMBING MME BUTTERFLY
CLIMBING CAROLINE TESTOUT
MME. GREGOIRE STAECHELIN
CLIMBING OPHELIA
ZÉPHIRINE DROUHIN

Other roses known as Wichuraiana ramblers, popularly called 'ramblers', are eminently fitted for covering arches and pergolas. Generally they flower in clusters of many double or semi-double blooms, and as these are borne on long laterals they usually hang in pendant masses, last in bloom for a long period, and are very effective. All of them can, of course, be used on pillars and walls, but I feel that in such situations erect flowering roses are more in keeping with the surroundings and pendulous ones more effective on arches and pergolas, although I readily admit that a well-grown pendulous Wichuraiana which completely clothes a pillar with bloom is a fine sight. However, many of the Wichuraiana ramblers flower fleetingly, which is another reason why they should not be used for draping pillars. The following constitute a good selection:

Roses for covering Arches and Pergolas

ALBERTINE	HIAWATHA
BLUSHING LUCY	LADY GODIVA
CHAPLIN'S PINK CLIMBER	LÉONTINE GERVAIS
CRIMSON CONQUEST	MARJORIE FOSTER
DOROTHY PERKINS	MARY WALLACE
EASLEA'S GOLDEN RAMBLER	MINNEHAHA
EVANGELINE	PAUL'S SCARLET CLIMBER
FRANCOIS JURANVILLE	SANDERS' WHITE
GARDENIA	THE NEW DAWN

Occasionally Wichuraiana ramblers are budded on the top of very tall standards, sometimes up to eight feet in height. Unsupported, excepting the tall stems, both growth, and the laterals on which the bloom is borne, become pendulous, and well-grown weeping standards, as they are termed, are a glorious sight. However, as can be well imagined, several feet of unsupported growth, heavy with masses of pendulous bloom, becomes a plaything of the wind, and the staking of the main stem must therefore be very efficient. When these heads are in bloom and wet with rain their weight is tremendous; wooden stakes small enough not to offend the eye are almost useless, so that a stake made of circular iron rod three quarters of an inch in diameter should be used. Scraggy weeping roses are an abomination. It follows that only good well-grown weeping standards should be planted; they should never be placed in a draughty site and they should not be planted at all except on good soil where they have an opportunity to become well clothed and vigorous. For these, preparation cannot be too thorough. Six satisfactory varieties are given below:

Roses suitable for Weeping Standards

ALBÉRIC BARBIER	HIAWATHA
DOROTHY PERKINS	LÉONTINE GERVAIS
FRANCOIS JURANVILLE	MINNEHAHA

For bedding purposes, very interesting dwarf roses exist which are brilliant. They are known as polyantha roses and rarely exceed eighteen inches in height. The blooms are small, borne in dense upright clusters, in some cases continuously all the summer. They do not mix well with other types, and therefore should be accommodated in beds or borders of one variety. A few are inclined to bleach in strong sunshine, but as this generally occurs only in the summer of exceptional heat the risk is worth taking. The following are good varieties:

Some good Polyantha Roses

CAMEO	KATHARINE ZEIMET
CORAL CLUSTER	PAUL CRAMPEL
GOLDEN SALMON IMPROVED	WILLY DEN OUDEN

The polyantha rose crossed with those of other species has given us an important group known as hybrid polyantha roses. Generally both plants and flowers are much larger than the polyanthas, although with a similar bunch-flowered formation. As a rule they flower continuously during the summer and in time develop into imposing bushes. In good soil they make excellent hedges which, in summer, are as beautiful as they are utilitarian. In gardens where little labour can be given they are ideal for massing in beds and leaving to grow as they please, except for the removal of old flowering tips. I give below a list of twelve good varieties, any of which should make a good show.

Twelve Hybrid Polyantha Roses

BETTY PRIOR	KAREN POULSEN
CHEERIO	ORANGE TRIUMPH
DAINTY MAID	PERLE D'OR
DONALD PRIOR	POULSEN'S YELLOW
ELSE POULSEN	SCARLET QUEEN
FRENSHAM	YVONNE RABIER

Roses are not too happy when mixed with perennial or annual plants in the border; it is always more satisfactory to place them in a bed by themselves. Sometimes it is possible at one end of the garden or in a convenient corner to make a separate rose garden where all types of roses can be grouped. A circular garden with beds roughly representing the spaces left between the spokes of a wheel answers well. The hub of the wheel could form a central bed, and the segments, which together form the circular bed, could be linked with arches on the outer perimeter. A pergola might lead to such a garden and pillar roses might surround the beds. If it is thought desirable hedges of roses might enclose the whole very pleasantly.

For hedges, some of the hybrid musk varieties, Zephirine Drouhin, the thornless rose, the old favourite hybrid perpetual, Hugh Dickson, and some of the hybrid polyanthas mentioned above, are very good. All varieties of Rosa rugosa, known as Japanese roses, are also suitable. From the following a comprehensive choice may be made:

Roses suitable for an Informal Hedge

DAINTY MAID
DANAE
DONALD PRIOR
ELSE POULSEN
FELICIA
FRENSHAM
HUGH DICKSON
MOONLIGHT
PAX
RUGOSA ROSES AND THEIR HYBRIDS
SCOTCH ROSES
ZÉPHIRINE DROUHIN

Where a shrubbery acts as background for a rose garden, some roses can be planted to grow as shrubs, untrammelled and unrestricted. Many of the modern hybrid tea varieties are well fitted for this and need little attention beyond a judicious thinning and tip pruning. In addition to these I append a list which includes hybrid musk varieties, some species, and a few others.

Roses suitable for growing as Shrubs

DANAE
MERMAID
MOONLIGHT
MOYESII
PENELOPE
AUSTRIAN COPPER
AUSTRIAN YELLOW
HARRISONII
HIGHDOWNENSIS
HUGONIS
ROSA ECAE

Roses are delightful when out of season and those with a cool greenhouse or conservatory might do well to plant a few climbers to train on wires fixed about fifteen inches below the roof glass. There are many which might be used, but the four I give below are especially happy under these conditions:

CLIMBING LADY HILLINGDON
MADAME ABEL CHATENAY
MARÉCHAL NIEL
NIPHETOS

In a cold house or conservatory also roses can be grown in pots with a modicum of trouble. Maidens, as received from the nurseryman, should have their roots shortened sufficiently to allow them to be placed in a pot seven to eight inches in diameter. Compost consisting of equal parts of loam – in a rough state – and well-decayed farmyard manure, to which has been added a five-inch potful of coarse bonemeal to every barrow load, should be used. This compost should be consolidated well with a rammer when potting. The point of union of each plant should be just below the soil level, as is the case when planting outside. The pots should be plunged to their rims in soil or ashes until January, when they should be housed in any greenhouse with a low night temperature – 45° F. is quite sufficient in the early stages of growth.

Now I must deal with pruning. In the minds of many, pruning is an annual chopping back – a ritual which must be performed, or else there would be no roses. This is far from the truth, because pruning is not necessary for bloom production. It is true that in the days of the hybrid perpetuals – grown mainly to be big and fat and doomed to adorn a metal tube in a flat board at the flower show – pruning became an obsession, leading the grower to think that unless he pruned almost to ground level he would get no roses. This pruning was, of course, primarily intended to produce oversized roses for show purposes, but the principles have persisted and thousands of roses not intended for show are needlessly slaughtered annually.

Roses are pruned for several reasons – to improve the size of bloom, to correct the shape of the plant, and to remove weak, unripened, and dead wood.

When hybrid tea and Pernetianas are grown for garden decoration they will make a good show if dead and unripened wood is removed and the stronger growths are slightly shortened. This leads to the production of a large number of medium-sized roses of good quality. If larger roses are required the strong shoots are shortened to four or five buds, and if it is intended to exhibit then the shoots are cut back to two or three buds. In each case the cut is made about a quarter of an inch above a bud, generally pointing outwards to keep the centre of the plant open to the sun. Some varieties, however, straggle outwards, and to control these they are pruned to a bud pointing inwards. Unwanted crossing shoots should be removed altogether.

A rose-grower of experience gets to know his varieties so well that he prunes each one according to its requirements, but this is a refinement which comes only with practice and need not bother the new grower. If a general rule of pruning the strong varieties lightly and the weak ones more heavily is observed all will be well, and if, through stress of circumstances, pruning is omitted for one season little harm will result; indeed, some of the varieties which automatically restrict themselves by dying back after frost delight in such neglect.

In the south, most hybrid teas can be pruned at the end of March, but in the midlands and north it is wise to wait a little longer. Growth starts rapidly after pruning and is liable to be cut back by May frost if too forward.

The climbing forms of tea roses should have all old flowering wood removed in early autumn, and in spring laterals on the new wood should be shortened to about three buds. No more is required.

Wichuraiana ramblers and polyantha ramblers need only have old flowering and overcrowded wood removed in autumn, and although the varieties of one section are said to be improved by the cutting back of laterals in the spring, all do well if thinned only, and this I advise.

Weeping standards need little attention beyond the removal of old flowering wood and perhaps a little judicious thinning of growth which is overcrowded. Sometimes, for the sake of appearance, some old wood must be left to fill up a gap and sometimes long shoots which trail on the ground need shortening.

Dwarf polyantha roses are pruned to within two or three eyes from the base if needed to make a show for bedding, but if in informal surroundings little pruning beyond the removal of dead wood and the removal of old flowering tips is needed.

Hybrid polyantha roses need little pruning except the removal of weak tips and dead wood, a procedure which also applies to this when it is used for hedges.

Nearly all roses used for hedges need little more than to be left in peace. Sometimes, however, a long straggling shoot needs taking out or reducing and weak tips and old flowering heads need removing.

Roses grown as shrubs should generally be left alone, but sometimes old flowering heads and dead tips need removal. If a variety or species is becoming leggy a shoot or two from the base must be cut back yearly to provide shoots to cover the legginess.

Climbing roses in a greenhouse should be pruned, generally by the removal of old flowering growths, after which young growth should be trained to cover the vacant spaces. Some varieties, however, and notably Niphetos, flower almost continuously, so the old flowering wood of these should be removed at any time when an opportunity occurs. Growth must be efficiently thinned; it is a mistake to let it become a jungle suspended underneath the roof.

Roses in pots are pruned in December or early January. If a few very good blooms are desired the shoots should be cut back to within an inch or two of the union of stock and scion, but if a heavier crop of slightly smaller roses is preferred three or four eyes should be left to give more shoots.

The pruning of standard roses offers little difficulty, for varieties and kinds should be treated in the same way as the same kinds and varieties not on standards.

There is a system of growing roses known as 'pegging down' whereby strong shoots of dwarf roses, three to four feet long, are arched over and fastened by means of a peg holding their tips down to the ground instead of their being reduced in the ordinary way of pruning. Only strong varieties are useful for this system, which should not be attempted on poor soil. Pruning consists of removing the pegged-down shoots which have flowered and pegging down others to replace them.

Roses are economical in general annual upkeep and there is little to do after pruning but gather up the prunings, apply a dressing of 8 oz. bonemeal per square yard and lightly fork in. On poor soil it is a good plan to mulch with a three-inch layer of farmyard manure in the autumn, but this is not advisable on heavy soil which is generally very wet in winter. Spring mulchings should be avoided; they are a nuisance and greatly impede the hoeing which is so necessary for roses. Weeds are hosts for pests and disease; it is not enough to let them grow and then pull them up by hand: they should be precluded by frequent hoeing, weekly or bi-weekly.

Some roses are prone to sucker production from their stocks, and if these are left unmolested they quickly form a formidable bush, while the budded variety (scion) dies out. Suckers should be removed immediately they are seen, and while doing this it is wise to search for and remove the piece of root from which each sucker springs or many more will follow.

Now I must deal with pests and diseases. Books on roses deal with an astonishing number of pests and diseases, and if, unfortunately, the beginner starts with literature of this kind he naturally fears the worst. He can be forgiven if he thinks 'If I have to fight all these enemies it is not worth while growing roses.' Often he gives up the idea and contents himself with something else. It is true that all these fearsome pests and diseases can attack roses and it is also true that rarely indeed does every one of them attack the roses in any garden. Some of them are unknown even to growers of life-long experience. The new gardener can take heart. If he studies good cultivation and plants his roses on a suitable site possibly he will never see more than a very few of these enemies, but there are some marauders which attack roses in most gardens and these I will deal with next.

In pests, Aphides (the familiar green-fly) are the chief offenders. They usually appear in May and if not checked are capable of doing much damage. The remedy is to spray with a fine-nozzled sprayer immediately the insects are seen or better still before they become evident. It is wise, therefore, to start about the end of April and spray regularly once a fortnight throughout the early part of the season. Sundriesmen sell good nicotine and phosphatic insecticides for the purpose. These are very reliable if the directions given are carried out faithfully. Caterpillars sometimes appear, but if spraying against Aphides is carried out systematically these are automatically destroyed. It must be understood that attacks of many other insect pests will be prevented by this treatment; they may therefore never be seen by the grower.

There are many diseases of roses, most of which are very unlikely to appear, but there are two which sometimes prove troublesome, Mildew and Black Spot. Mildew first appears as small round whitish spots which spread, join up, and eventually cover the leaves in a felt-like grey covering which later turns brown and destroys the foliage. If the soil is too wet and cold, or the roses are planted in a draughty garden corridor or on a site troubled by cross currents, attacks may occur. A good remedy is to spray with a colloidal sulphur preparation used according to directions. In a district liable to mildew it is a good plan to begin to spray as soon as the leaves appear and continue at fortnightly intervals throughout the season. A few varieties, of most sections, which have very smooth glossy leaves are almost immune, and in a bad district it would be wise before purchasing to consult a local nurseryman for advice about varieties which prove mildew-resistant in the district. Some growers spray with Bordeaux Mixture while the plants are still dormant in spring, but this, although helpful, cannot be claimed to give complete immunity.

The second dangerous disease which appears almost everywhere, Black Spot, and is usually worse during wet summers and on wet ground, comes in the form of brownish black spots on the leaves which spread until the leaves turn colour and drop, leaving the plant entirely leafless. It should be combated early and frequently with a good colloidal copper spray fluid applied every ten days. The disease nearly always appears about mid-June, but is later in some districts.

Good hygiene demands that all prunings and fallen leaves should be collected carefully and burned and, as I have already mentioned, rose sites – and indeed all others – must be kept weed free, so that no host plants exist to infect or reinfect the roses. If this and good culture is practised trouble from pests and diseases need not be feared. In gardens, the ancient proverb 'A stitch in time saves nine' truly applies, as any new gardener will soon appreciate.

· 22 ·

The Cool Greenhouse

So many people think that a greenhouse is only useful to grow plants which need great heat. This is very misleading and only partially true, for most greenhouse occupants do not need tropical conditions. Although a well-heated greenhouse is a great convenience, much can be done in a cool greenhouse. By a cool greenhouse I mean one which has sufficient artificial heat to exclude frost in all but the occasional winter of great severity, when few greenhouses – including those which are well heated – are capable of excluding it. Even if not heated, a greenhouse is a great help, and if it is heated only enough to keep out frost, many floral seedlings can be brought on earlier, to say nothing of tomatoes, lettuces, etc., whose culture is outside the scope of this book.

Greenhouses can be heated in many different ways. The simplest method is to build a lean-to glasshouse against a southern or western wall. This not only gives protection from wind but also provides a little comfort, for the walls of an occupied house radiate a pleasant warmth. If the greenhouse can be placed against a wall with a flue built in from boiler or kitchen, so much the better. Builders often take advantage of a flued wall, which is nearly always warm, to heat garages, and if the chimney or flue is built projecting outwards, such a chimney will certainly keep a small greenhouse comfortably warm. After all, heating by flue is only a return to the original means of greenhouse heating, for our forefathers used to build a furnace – much like an old bread oven – and arranged for its heat and smoke to pass through a brick flue running all round the greenhouse, generally under the stages, before being allowed to escape up a chimney.

Many houses, however, owing to peculiarities of shape, are not adapted for accommodating a lean-to, so the next best thing is to build a span-roofed greenhouse in a sheltered but sunny spot not far from the house. The end of the garden will probably prove the worst possible place, and will lead to many unnecessary journeys to give it attention. In bad weather, a greenhouse in such a site may lead to neglect, for the fireside is difficult to leave when there are several inches of snow and slush outside and the greenhouse is fifty yards away. So near the house it must be. A greenhouse standing independently is always a few degrees colder than a lean-to; it must therefore be put on the snuggest side of the house where it will obtain some protection from biting winds. It should be remembered that a glasshouse is constructed to admit all possible light and to trap every sun ray – properties which make it very vulnerable to cold. One can scarcely imagine an appliance better fitted to lose heat quickly on a cold night than a greenhouse.

Probably the most satisfactory means of heating – not always the cheapest or easiest to handle – is a small boiler fitted in one of the end walls supporting the greenhouse. To these are fitted two four-inch hot-water pipes, a flow and return, which run the length of the house. Such boilers are fired with coke, anthracite, or low-grade bitumenous coal. As an alternative, two-inch flow and return pipes can sometimes be taken from the house boiler. This is a very handy arrangement in the case of a lean-to, but in an independent span-roofed greenhouse would necessitate efficient lagging of the connecting pipes to prevent losses between dwelling house and greenhouse.

In most districts, however, electrical heating, which is generally a little dearer than heating with solid fuel, is most convenient, for the heat can be thermostatically controlled and all stoking is abolished. However, in very frosty weather electrical heat cannot be increased so that to guard against risk from frost a double installation of heaters is necessary, the second lot to be switched on when severe frost occurs. Both lots are controlled afterwards by the thermostat.

There are oil heaters said to be reliable if properly cared for, and I do not doubt the truth of this. Whether with wicks or without their efficiency depends on scrupulous cleanliness, entailing daily attention. If neglected, or allowed to become foul in the burners, oil lamps emit smoke and fumes which are deadly to plant life, so that the work of nearly a year may be wasted in a very few minutes and in the case of orchids and other perennial occupants of the greenhouse the built-up stock of years may be wiped out.

When any system fails emergency heating must be resorted to. Three candles on a wide saucer covered with an eight- or nine-inch pot constitute a very efficient heater and as many as are needed can be placed in the house. A battery of hot water bottles can also be utilized. Foot warmers, which hold several gallons of hot water, still in use on out-of-the-way branch lines of the railways, are sometimes available as they are discarded – they are most efficient in giving out heat.

Now let us see what can be grown. In spite of the wishes of the owner there is a limit to the number of species and varieties which can be grown, because there are many plants which, requiring similar temperatures, need different treatment. Nevertheless there exists a wide range of plants which can settle down happily together.

Most people, nowadays, are fond of tomatoes, which frequently fill the greenhouse during the summer. After the tomatoes have finished ripening the greenhouse frequently becomes a museum for a heterogeneous collection of plants which need protection, or an extra cloakroom where gum boots, mackintoshes, and old coats, plus garden tools and sundries, can be dumped. This is a pity, for not only is it unhygienic but it is a great waste of space which might be devoted to winter and spring flowering plants. Within the pages of one chapter I could not possibly deal with this, but I can deal with several interesting subjects which will keep the greenhouse gay during the dull months.

Let us now think of greenhouse primulas, of which there are several sections, and which, although they enjoy slightly different temperatures, nevertheless will grow comfortably in one another's company. Of these, perhaps Primula Malacoides is the most accommodating and nowadays has a wealth of beautiful varieties. Like most primulas, these are at their best if allowed to flower in February or March when the worst of the dull days are left behind, but by sowing at the right time they can be controlled and induced to flower at Christmas. This is an easy arrangement for the average man because chrysanthemums, which follow tomatoes, pass out of flower at this time.

For Christmas flowering, seed should be sown during February in pots, pans, or small boxes filled with John Innes Compost No. 1. The seed should be sown thinly. A temperature of 55° F. is suitable, but if owing to cold weather there is some difficulty in maintaining a night temperature within 5° F. of this it would be wise to wait until the warmer days of March before sowing. When the seedlings are big enough to handle and before they become drawn and weakened they should be pricked out singly into three-inch pots and grown on in the greenhouse in a similar temperature. Seedlings are given a slight check when pricked out, however carefully handled, because no one can prevent a few tiny roots from being broken. If room is available it is therefore a good plan to sow seeds in groups of three or four in the centre of three-inch pots filled with John Innes Compost No. 1 and remove all seedlings but one by thinning. If a mixture of varieties is being grown it is important not to pull out the weak seedlings in favour of strong ones, for the best plants and colours often come from the small seedlings, which, although appearing weak in the early stages, generally develop into good plants later on. This plan obviates much check and at flowering time provides larger plants than those which have been pricked off and checked.

If the seedlings are in good health potting on quickly becomes necessary and is imperative when white roots can be seen emerging from the ball. It is always unwise to wait until the roots are matted and coiled in a tangled cushion at the bottom of the pot, for by that time the plant is already starving and sometimes badly checked. Successful plant growing depends greatly upon avoidance of check.

When the May frosts have passed, generally about 19 May, the seedlings can be placed in a cold frame irrespective of their size and state, and here they will grow comfortably until the moist nights of September make it imperative that they should be taken to the greenhouse, where the atmosphere is not so heavily charged with moisture and where they can obtain more air. In some moist districts there is a great tendency to damping off as soon as autumn arrives: hence the necessity for a dry and more buoyant atmosphere. When housed in autumn Primula Malacoides need only enough artificial heat to exclude frost on cold nights. In mild weather 40° – 50° F. is an adequate temperature.

To see this charming primula at its best it should be sown in mid-July and germinated in a cold frame – being brought into the greenhouse in September. Though late, some plants flower in March and April, and as a rule have one massive central spike and a large number of smaller ones symmetrically arranged around. The flowers on all varieties of Primula Malacoides become larger and have more depth to the colour as the spring advances. This primula, which can be grown by almost everyone with a greenhouse, now has some splendid varieties, and from these the following is a good selection:

Primula Malacoides

DELIGHTFUL	Clear rose pink
FEARLESS	Rosy crimson
MAUVE QUEEN	Rich mauve
LILAC QUEEN (Double)	Soft lilac
ENCHANTMENT	Purple mauve

Next we have Primula Sinensis with its wonderful range of types and varieties. This, introduced from China many generations ago, cannot now be found as a type plant growing wild. For many years, its symmetrical flowers were dull and lifeless, although they ranged from pure white to rose pink and magenta crimson. The arrival of a beautiful orange-scarlet mutation called 'Dazzler' introduced through its progeny a completely new range of colours from the softest salmon pink to the most fierce scarlet crimson.

It is sown and handled similarly to Primula Malacoides, but gives the best results when sown in June, although if needed for mid-winter it can be sown in February.

There are two main sections, the old type called Primula Sinensis and a lighter looser type called Primula Sinensis Stellata. The former is a dwarf neat plant not more than six inches high, while the latter sometimes attains the height of two feet and has myriad starry flowers. Both of these types have 'Giant' forms, i.e. varieties with an increased number of chromosomes, which have the effect of giving them more size and substance. The word 'Giant' is therefore fully justified. As these primulas enjoy a slightly higher temperature than Primula Malacoides they are generally more successful from a regular June sowing, and when housed should be placed in the warmer end of the greenhouse. If accommodated alone they should be given a night temperature of from 50° to 55° F. The following are good varieties:

Primula Sinensis

SCARLET KING	Vivid scarlet overlaid crimson
DAZZLER	Orange-scarlet
ROYAL WHITE	Ivory white
READING BLUE	Clear light blue

Primula Sinensis Stellata

FIRE KING	Rich scarlet crimson
GUARDSMAN	Star form of Dazzler
ENCHANTRESS	Rich salmon pink
BEACON	Orange scarlet and salmon
GIANT METEOR	Orange scarlet and salmon

There is a third indoor primula which has also made great strides recently, Primula obconica, the most easily grown of all the indoor primulas. If it is thought desirable, seeds of this can be sown at any time of the year, for under glass the plant seems to have no definite season. However, it gives the best results from an early autumn sowing in a temperature of 50° – 55° F. in a cold frame where there is much atmospheric moisture; it generally germinates badly in a high temperature.

The cycle of pricking out and potting is much the same as that for the two types of primulas previously mentioned, but in the winter months Primula obconica loves a lower temperature and is quite happy in a damp atmosphere and a night temperature of 40° – 45° F. This primula starts to flower at a very early age, but the flowers are small and should be pinched out regularly until the plants are established in six-inch pots, when they should be allowed to flower at will. Generally indoor primulas do not need additional feeding in pots if a good potting compost like the John Innes is used, but Primula obconica is a vigorous hungry plant which, when well established, needs extra food, and for this a good compound fertilizer made for indoor plants should be applied at weekly intervals. This can be obtained from any seedsman, nurseryman, or sundriesman and should be used strictly in accordance with the maker's directions. Good varieties are:

Primula Obconica

SALMON KING	GIANT CRIMSON
FIRE KING	GIANT WHITE
GIANT PINK	GIANT BLUE

All the greenhouse primulas named in this chapter are shade lovers and the frame or greenhouse in which they are grown should be shaded during the summer months. A dense shade is not desirable and it is sufficient to shade with openwork rush mats, scrim, hessian canvas, or even old sacks if nothing else is handy. Such shade, however, should not be applied before 9 a.m. and should be removed about 5 p.m. in mid summer with a correspondingly shorter period on each side of the longest day according to season. For those who have to be away from home daily a compromise can be made by painting the glass with a thin green preparation sold by sundriesmen for the purpose or a very thin mixture of whiting and water which is equally effective. The latter, however, is easily washed off by heavy rain, and therefore needs renewing accordingly.

Cinerarias too, are splendid plants for the cool greenhouse because they are quite happy in a low winter temperature, and, indeed, make poor plants if subjected to much artificial heat. Seeds can be sown at any time from February to September and plants resulting from an early sowing will not only be very much larger but will come into flower earlier. For the average person with a greenhouse a May or June sowing generally proves best, as if allowed to grow steadily, without recourse to high temperatures, plants resulting from these sowings generally flower just as the primulas are going out of bloom.

The seed, which is quite tiny, should be sown in groups of three or four in the centre of a three-inch pot filled with John Innes Compost No. 1, but only lightly covered with soil. In every case, as with primulas, discard the bigger seedling in favour of the smaller when reducing them to one to each pot, though not, of course, selecting weakly or unhealthy seedlings. It is very important that cinerarias should have ample room for lateral expansion, as, owing to the flattened habit of early growth, by which the leaves extend laterally as they grow, they need more room than most seedlings of the same age. For this reason the pots, each containing a single seedling after thinning, should be spaced about three inches apart; the spaces will be fully occupied by the time the seedlings are ready to pot on.

In April the seed should be germinated in a cool greenhouse, but in May a cold frame with the lights and the glass shaded answers better. In any case the seedlings should be placed in a cold frame to develop and should be shifted into larger pots before their balls of soil become matted with roots. Eight-inch pots and John Innes Compost No. 2 is needed for the potting, but plants resulting from later sowings may well be placed in six-inch pots – they will not need larger ones. In most districts cinerarias may remain in cold frames until October, and, although they will often survive a few degrees of frost, such exposure does not help them. They must be taken to a frost-proof greenhouse in which only enough artificial heat to exclude frost on cold nights is used and not enough to raise the temperature above 45° F. on mild nights or as low as the outside temperature when it is mild. No attempt should be made to force into flower during the many weeks of poor light in winter or the plants may become pallid and the flower stems lengthen, eventually to become too weak to support the flowers, which, consequently, bend over sharply and spoil their natural beauty by showing the underside of the petals.

Cinerarias have an old-fashioned charm not possessed by any other greenhouse plant. This applies especially to the large flowered varieties which have blooms three to four inches across, regularly circular with long slightly reflexing overlapping petals. Their old-world colourings and the many combinations of colour, especially the blue and purple shades, are not equalled by any other garden plant. The large-flowered varieties are dwarf, and symmetrical in foliage habit as well as in flowers, and this, combined with the old china appearance of the flowers, makes up a plant of great beauty. Some good varieties of the large flowered section are:

LARGE FLOWERED SINGLE HYBRID MIXED
ROYAL BLUE
PINK PEARL
WHITE

There are taller lighter forms which grow several feet in height and which produce thousands of starry blooms on a single plant, known as the stellata or star varieties. They are excellent when cut and last a long time in water. The colours embrace practically every shade known in cinerarias and the blues are especially good. The following is a good selection:

DWARF MIXED STAR
GENTIAN BLUE STAR
LIGHT BLUE STAR
PINK SHADES STAR

There is another beautiful race of stellata flowered cinerarias known as the Feltham beauty star. These are about twenty-one inches high when fully grown, larger in the flower than the true stellata type, and the blooms of each variety all have a creamy-yellow centre which imparts much lightness and grace. Good varieties are:

THE KING	Bright rosy carmine
THE PRINCESS	Sky blue
THE DUCHESS	Royal blue
FELTHAM BEAUTY	Mixed

Between these and the star varieties comes another race known as intermediate. These are truly intermediate both in foliage and leaf size as well as in height. The best varieties are:

SPECIAL HYBRIDS
BLUE SHADES
FORGET-ME-NOT BLUE

All the above are varieties of charming colouring and habit.

Next to flower is the schizanthus, often called the poor man's orchid. Seeds of this should be sown during mid August to produce plants for flowering in mid May or a little before. They can be sown in pots, pans, or shallow boxes filled with John Innes Compost No. 1, or a few seeds in the centre of a three-inch pot, also filled with John Innes Compost. The latter is by far the best method as, after the seedlings are thinned down to one, their fight for light and air ceases; they may therefore thicken in the stem and develop growth laterally to their hearts' content.

Like cinerarias they must have a low temperature for success in the winter; they should not be brought into the greenhouse until frost compels it, and then only a very cool house is needed. If for some weeks during the dead of winter the night temperature is only a degree or two above freezing, so much the better, for at no time do they enjoy heat and later on in spring, when solar heat forces up the greenhouse temperature, the ventilators must be used freely and a little shading sprayed on the glass.

They are great feeders with tremendous root action, and when ready should be potted successively into six-inch pots and again later in nine- or ten-inch pots, using John Innes Compost No. 2 for both pottings and reinforcing the compost for the last potting with a five-inch potful of coarsely-ground hoof and horn meal to each barrow load. This extra food would be insufficient to carry them through; the surface soil in each pot should therefore be top dressed at weekly intervals with a good compound plant fertilizer from the time they are well rooted into the final compost.

Almost from the beginning schizanthus need support, first with a thin bamboo or twig sufficient to hold the central stem upright, and later, when in the final pot, with a stout bamboo about three feet long. This should be plunged deeply into the soil in the pot, the central stem tied firmly but without compressing, and the many lateral shoots looped to it lightly when support is needed.

Stopping should not be practised at any time or the pyramidal habit will be lost and the plants develop an ugly flat head with many of the blooms hidden. Well-grown plants will continue to flower for many weeks and from good strains an enormous range of colourings is available including some found only in schizanthus. Good strains are Giant Hybrid and Pansy Flowered, the latter being all self colours and the petal formation of the flower resembling that of a pansy.

In the summer months my readers may choose between annuals in pots or tomatoes, but it must be emphasized that both cannot be grown in the same house together. If tomatoes are grown, provision must have been made beforehand to raise plants, and if annuals, seed should be sown in April and May in receptacles placed in a cold frame, where they should remain until all, or any, of the plants already named have passed out of flower.

For summer greenhouse culture, annuals are grown very simply. Pots ranging from six inches in diameter for the small growing annual to ten inches for the strong growing ones should be filled with John Innes Compost No. 2. In each pot a few seeds are sown in three equidistant stations and the resulting seedlings reduced to one to each station when of a size large enough to handle.

Almost any kind and variety is good for this method, but as room is limited, a selection according to colour should be made from those selected for the border in Chapter 6.

As annuals intended to flower under glass develop extensive growth and root systems, and the latter, being confined in pots, require much extra plant food, several inches of good decayed cow manure or farmyard manure should be placed over the crocks forming the drainage system, to be found by the roots when they most need it. For a similar reason, a weekly application of a good compound plant manure should be given from the time the plants are well established. Much water will be needed. The smaller kinds and varieties will also need adequate supplies of plant food but need not have quite so much manure placed on the crocks.

Under glass, there is always a tendency for annuals to become too large or luxuriant in foliage at the expense of flowers; this tendency can be checked by allowing their great masses of roots to be a little pot-bound in the early stages of growth, thus checking growth exhuberance. This slight check must be deliberate and not prolonged, and as soon as buds are visible feeding with a good compound manure must be practised weekly.

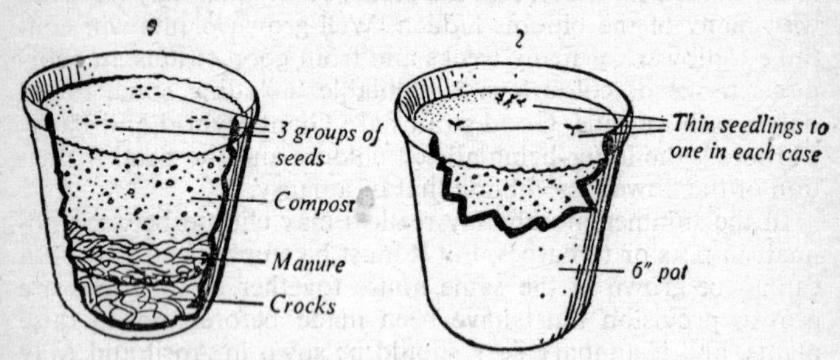

48. Growing annuals in pots from seed.

Annuals grown in pots in which they are to remain during the flowering period grow rather taller than those grown out of doors. They therefore require support, which, owing to the somewhat soft growth made under glass, must be given quite early in the life of the seedlings. The smaller ones can be held in place adequately by the use of short twiggy brushwood taken from the tops of pea stakes. These should be plunged into the soil in the pots between the seedlings immediately after thinning. At first they look a little ugly but the rapidly advancing growth will soon lean against the twigs and cover them with greenery. Some of the taller flowers require staking individually, and for this purpose nothing is better than willow stakes with the bark left on. Medium-sized plants and those which approach the tall stage can be supported by being tied with green twist or green dyed raffia to four willows at the edge of the pots; the main stem is thus confined inside while all laterals are left free to grow and hide the stakes.

If only one greenhouse is available it is always unwise to fill it completely with one plant or set of plants, because some space is always needed to bring on other flowering plants to succeed them. Annuals under glass flower profusely for six or seven weeks and occasionally longer, but in the heat of summer sometimes collapse quickly.

Tuberous begonias, started into growth by being placed in boxes of peat maintained in a moist state, can be potted into six-inch pots to occupy the greenhouse after the annuals. John Innes Compost No. 2 is excellent for this. When potting, the soil should be no more than moderately firm; ramming need not be practised. A hundred or so begonias, which in their starting boxes occupy little space, may later require all the bench area in the greenhouse. They should be grown in a moist condition, as they are great moisture lovers, but should never be over watered. They are able to withstand a modicum of sun, but are much happier if shaded lightly as advised for primulas.

Almost from the first, buds appear, and these should be nipped out, with the finger and thumb, regularly until the plants are well established. The single varieties need no attention in the way of disbudding, but the doubles produce both double and single blooms. The latter, the female flowers, should be pinched out, leaving the double ones, the male flowers, to develop.

Before the flowering period arrives tuberous begonias appreciate atmospheric moisture. All stages, floors, etc. should be thoroughly damped down with water from a rosed can at least once a day, but when they are in flower the atmosphere should be kept drier.

Some people prefer to grow only one crop and for this the modern perpetual flowering carnation is supreme. It is propagated yearly from cuttings, i.e. young growth without buds taken from the centre of a flowering plant. These cuttings, about four inches long, should be inserted into beds of sand in a box or a small propagating case in which a temperature of 50° – 55° F. can be maintained. Cuttings root quickly and are then potted into thumb pots in John Innes Compost No. 1, and later, when established, into three and a half inch pots filled with John Innes Compost No. 2. In a very few weeks the well-rooted plants will require a greater root run, so, when rootlets are seen emerging through the ball of soil, pot them into seven- or eight-inch pots. For this final potting, soil consisting of good turfy loam and well-decayed manure in equal parts should be used, and if to this enough sharp sand is added to ensure free drainage, so much the better for drainage. A little lime is sometimes needed, so about 8 oz. to a barrowload of soil should be added and thoroughly mixed in to ensure alkalinity. Carnations do not grow well in an acid soil.

When established in the final pots, perpetual flowering carnations need some support; this is best afforded by thrusting a stake about three feet long into the soil in the pot and attaching to this a circular wire, which also clips on the stake, to contain all the shoots within.

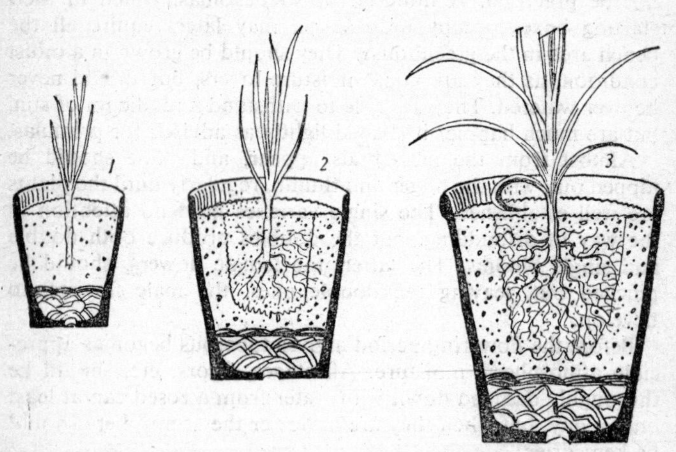

49. Potting on carnation cutting.

High temperatures are injurious to these carnations; at night the temperature should not be higher than 45° – 50° F. in the winter months and as low as possible in the summer or at any time when the temperature is higher out of doors.

In the following season the flowering plants can be potted on into eleven- or twelve-inch pots and encouraged to grow and flower for another season. Sometimes these potted on flowering specimens develop into very fine plants and produce some excellent blooms. A little shade is essential, but only in the summer months; for this a very thin mixture of whiting and water sprayed on the glass suffices well. In genial weather, all ventilators must be thrown open and even in winter the ventilators should never be entirely closed, except, perhaps, in frost of unusual severity. This type of carnation approaches hardiness and if on a very bad night a degree or two of frost is registered in the greenhouse, no harm results.

The begonias are past their best at the approach of October and chrysanthemums may well take their place. At night these need the lowest possible temperature consistent with the exclusion of frost from the greenhouse. When they are first taken inside some damping down of floors is necessary to reproduce the humidity of the outside atmosphere, but as the plants become used to their surroundings damping down should decrease until a dry buoyant atmosphere is assured which discourages damping off in the blooms. Watering should be cautious and no more water used than is necessary.

Bulbs potted in September and October will complete the full greenhouse cycle. They flower from December to late spring, but as they are dealt with separately in Chapter 27 I will not add any details now.

Where only an unheated greenhouse is available it might be put to a very good use to house border carnations in districts in the north in which they are not quite hardy.

The cool greenhouse, of course, has other pleasant uses. It is invaluable for raising bedding plants such as antirrhinums and the like which need a little nursing under glass in their early stages. This aspect is fully treated in Chapter 25, so I will not say any more about it in this chapter.

Chrysanthemums and dahlias can also be propagated to flower in summer and autumn; indeed, with a greenhouse it is always necessary to plan ahead. The possessor of a houseful of glorious flowering plants should always remember that other plants to flower in succession should always be in the process of propagation, or one day he will find himself with a good greenhouse completely devoid of bloom. This must be avoided, but not by collecting anything and everything which needs a little protection to form a hotch potch of nothing in particular. Bedding plants, of course, have their place in the greenhouse in the winter, but the homely geranium must be suspect, for it is one of the worst carriers of disease even though it shows no trace of it, and one disease in particular, which is bad if it gets into a greenhouse, is carried over from year to year by this plant. Similarly, old plants of this and that, long since starved and useless and which, although sickly, refuse to die and because of their nature cannot be cleaned properly, harbour not only disease but many insect pests which can be eradicated only by the destruction of these old host plants. On the other hand, carefully placed shelves, which by their position cannot spill their surplus water into plants beneath, are ideal places for keeping stocks of heliotrope, verbena, and the like. General cleanliness and good plant hygiene are most important. Wherever there is a dry spot underneath stages near hot water pipes or electric heater there insects gather, and it is almost useless to attempt to destroy pests on the plants themselves if plague spots and extensive colonies of insects are allowed to survive.

Once a year at least, the greenhouse must be thoroughly cleaned. For this, if a convenient time can be found in late summer when there are few plants inside, or just as a spent crop of flowering plants is turned out, all the occupants remaining should be placed outside while the inside is cleaned. To eradicate pests in cracks or crannies in the woodwork every part of the inside should be sprayed forcibly, through a powerful jet with insecticide, and afterwards glass, woodwork, and walls scrubbed thoroughly with soapy water mixed with an adequate insecticide. Inert soil, ashes, or gravel underneath the stages, which might contain disease germs and insect pests, should be removed and the site flooded with insecticide and fungicide. After this a fresh layer of clean gravel or ashes should be spread over all areas under the stages. Openwork lattice stages are rarely worth while in a greenhouse, so if the stages are faced with a layer of gravel, sand, or ashes, as they should be, this too must be removed, and the site sterilized and again faced with a two-inch layer of fresh moisture-holding material. Every avenue of re-infestation and reinfection must be sought out and cleansed.

Plants suffering from disease or infested by insects should be dipped in a combined insecticide and fungicide, such as nicotine and colloidal copper, to ensure that no disease or pest is re-introduced by foul plants. When the plants are taken inside all weakly ones or those of little value should be destroyed and a resolution made to grow the best only.

There are many other plants besides those mentioned which can be grown in a cool house, but one house can never hold everything. It is far better to make a definite plan to grow some of the things I have mentioned in regular sequence and later on thoroughly enjoy the beauty of the many varieties of each subject available. Instead of trying to grow every good variety it is better to make a cropping plan for several years ahead and in this way enjoy something fresh each year.

With good hygiene there should be little trouble with pests and diseases, especially if the plants are strong and healthy. Insect pests, as well as disease, are always more prone to attack weakly plants than those in good health. There is no excuse for allowing pests to multiply under glass, for a weekly fumigation with a good nicotine fumigant will effectively combat them, and if, because the atmosphere has become too dry, minute pests like Red Spider and Thrips obtain a foothold, abobenzine smoke bombs or disinsectation by the acrocide method – tiny particles of insecticide discharged by a gun into the air – will quickly destroy them or keep them in check.

Many more useful plants could be mentioned, but within the confines of this chapter I have no more space, and on diseases and pests, of which so much could be said, my readers will find more information in Chapter 32. The good grower, however, will seldom have recourse to that chapter, for if he treats his plants well he has little to fear.

· 23 ·

Potting Composts and Seed Sowing in Pots, Pans, and Boxes

IN the long chain of plant cultivation under glass the weak link is often found in the soil or compost used. It is useless to erect a good greenhouse, build robust cold frames, buy the best sundries and manures, and then use poor soil. Great consideration must be given to this. The roots of a plant growing in the open have several square feet in which to ramble for food, which, in most soils, is there in abundance. Such a plant, bedded out, would cease to grow only when autumnal weather conditions were unsuitable. By this time it would probably be a heavily clothed plant, possibly more than a foot high, but a similar plant grown in a greenhouse might be larger, although growing in a pot only five to six inches in diameter – a matter only possible with suitable compost. This is because, concentrated in the narrow confines of a pot, there are mineral constituents and humus in a small quantity of compost as great as those found in several cubic feet of well manured and cultivated soil.

It might be argued, reasonably, in the case of pot-grown plants, that the soil used is only a vehicle to carry plant food and that it would be easy to add enough of this and that to supply the plant's needs. This appears sound in theory, but proves unsound in practice, not only because plant roots have an antipathy to highly concentrated manures if these are used in excess, but also because the physical state of such soil is often faulty and not to be compared with well-worked garden soil, abounding in all that is necessary for the growth of plants, although not always in the right proportion.

Because of this, loam used for potting generally consists of deeply-cut turf from a meadow in which cattle have been fed for generations or from fine downland where there are deep layers of flint and loam on the chalk. Very poor fibrous turf taken from the sand of the Bagshot district or from the black sand of the Midlands is seldom of use and some is poor enough to be worthless. Some of the best loam comes from the Kettering district and from many districts in Surrey and Sussex where the plough has never operated.

Owing to the compression necessary when they are placed in pots, the physical condition of some soils, although quite good for garden use, is unsuitable for pot culture, and as only a small portion can be pressed into a pot, ingredients must be added, not only to improve it physically but also to reinforce minerals and humus. It follows, therefore, that the better the loam used as a base the fewer parts of other constituents will be needed to balance the mixture chemically and physically.

Good loam has other virtues. When cut and stacked, grass side downwards, the grass and its roots decay and in doing so provide a rich store of nitrogen. For this reason, new turf

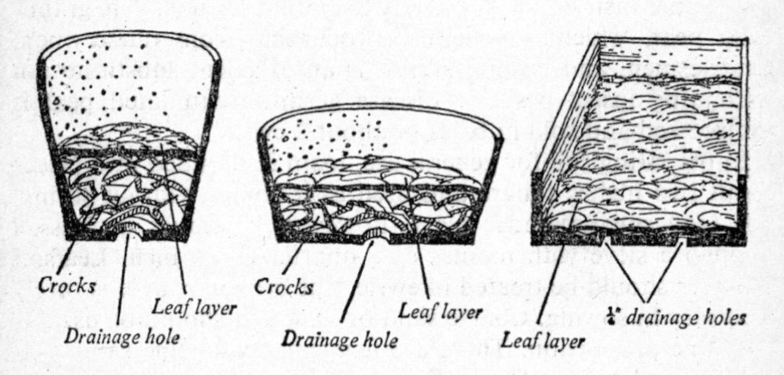

50. Sectional diagrams showing arrangement in crocks for seed sowing.

should not be used, as, with grass and roots both undecayed, the soil, unless reinforced with other nitrogen, would become poor, for the soil bacteria would be fully engaged in breaking down the new substance instead of enriching the whole.

Substances employed in potting composts to improve the physical properties are peat, leafsoil, mushroom manure, sand or grit, brick or mortar rubble, and sometimes burnt clay and charcoal. This is usually called 'making the soil lighter', a descriptive statement which is not wholly true, as in reality the inclusion of these substances permits the soil to be handled freely without clinging, improves its capacity to lose surplus water, and allows a moderate degree of compression in the pot without pastiness.

A good potting compost for general use for soft-wooded greenhouse plants is three parts loam in a rough state one part leafsoil or peat, half a part coarse sand or river grit and 8 oz. superphosphate per barrow-load of compost. If the loam used is very heavy and sticky, half a part of crushed brick or mortar rubble will materially improve the texture. As loam has so many variations in condition and quality no hard and fast rule can be laid down, but loam of a very tenacious nature may need considerably more of what is called opening material to prevent clogging when potting, and, in bad cases, leafsoil or peat can be increased up to fifty per cent – likewise the sand or rubble. Spent mushroom manure and well-decayed farmyard manure are both substitutes for leafsoil and peat.

In some districts it is difficult to obtain leafsoil, but granulated peat, which is generally procurable from nurserymen, sundriesmen, and general stores, is an excellent substitute not containing insect pests or disease germs. Granulated peat is compressed and sold in bales of about 2 cwt.

In preparing soil for general use, loam is chopped into pieces about two inches square and used as it comes without sifting. For seed sowing under glass, however, it should be passed through a sieve with meshes of a quarter of an inch. Leafsoil and peat should be treated likewise, but broken rubble is rarely necessary in sowing. Coarse sand or river grit should be used in the same proportion. There are few samples of fine sand suitable for soil composts and the inclusion of some types, similar to those used by the builders, would convert potting soil to concrete when dry and an impenetrable plaster when wet. If the loam is poor the inclusion of 8 oz. hoof and horn meal one eighth of an inch grist will correct matters, and if nitrogen is needed in the early growth stages 4 oz. dried blood is excellent.

Composts made deliberately or haphazardly on the Christmas pudding principle, i.e. a little of this and a little of that, are rarely successful. Often they are fermenting chemical mixtures in which plants cannot grow until harmful reaction ceases and do little more than give the mixer the satisfaction of having done something for the seedlings.

Pots, pans, or boxes should be thoroughly cleaned before being used for seed sowing and should be perfectly dry or the soil will stick to the receptacles, making knocking out impossible. Good drainage is necessary, and this is ensured by placing one big crock on the drainage hole, and for seed sowing by half filling the pot or pan with pieces of broken pots (crocks). Boxes should have drainage holes, or their equivalent, made by leaving the two pieces of wood which form the bottom about a quarter of an inch apart. Crocks will not be necessary for boxes, but these should have a handful of fresh leaves or litter placed on the bottom to prevent choked drainage, and a similar layer should be placed on crocks in pots to prevent the soil being washed through into the drainage and so choking it.

The fine soil should be put into the pots and pans, firmly, and levelled off smoothly, about half an inch below the rim. Making the soil firm is an art. If it is made too firm water cannot easily pass through and not enough air is admitted, and if too loose it is liable to be washed out when watering and will allow

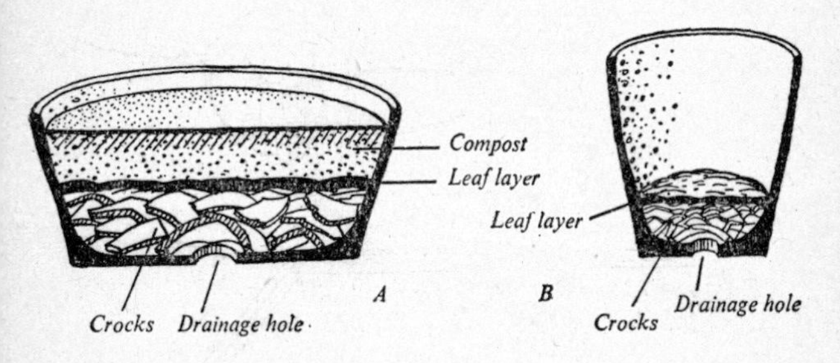

51. (A) Seed pan prepared for sowing; (B) Crocks for plant growing.

too much air to enter. Generally, if the soil is pushed in tightly with the fingers and made level, first with the fingers and afterwards with the bottom of a small pot, it will prove firm enough for germination. Successful germination depends on a little moisture, a little warmth, and some air, but not too much of any of these.

Most greenhouse soft-wooded plants have small seeds and in the cases of begonias and streptocarpus very fine seeds – almost as fine as flour. So fine are they that seeds numbering a thousand or so are almost invisible in an ordinary seed packet and to prevent their being told repeatedly that seeds are omitted from the packet seedsmen place the fine seed in transparent inner packets in which it can be seen. Having seen these seeds the grower will readily see the necessity for making the soil smooth, for even then these tiny seeds will drop into crannies many times deeper than themselves. In view of this, seed covering is hardly necessary, but if a very tiny layer of fine soil is spread over them, by means of a small sieve of perforated zinc, the grower can feel certain they will be consistently moist. This degree of moisture, however, is hardly enough for germination, so after seed sowing the soil must be thoroughly moistened either by the use of a water can with a very fine rose or by immersing the seed receptacles in a vessel of water. The

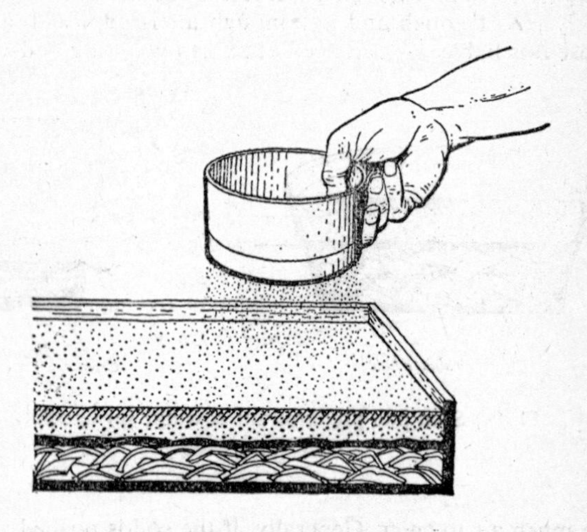

52. Sieving soil over seeds, or sowing fine seeds.

latter is the most satisfactory if care is taken that when immersing the soil level is always a little above water level; otherwise the fine seed will float away. When the surplus water has drained away the receptacles should either be covered with glass to prevent rapid evaporation or tied down with brown paper, jam-jar fashion. No water should be given until germination has taken place, when the covering can be removed. Seeds which germinate somewhat slowly and decidedly erratically like primula are often killed with kindness, for the anxious grower, feeling he must do something, generally seizes the water can and sprinkles water over the germinating seed; often he does this daily, nearly always causing the seed to rot.

Fine seed, in the process of germination, is frequently lost by malting. If precautions are not taken there is sometimes sufficient moisture in the soil to start germination but not enough to permit normal growth and the emerging cotyledon perishes. It is not unusual in these cases for the grower to imagine the seed is at fault, and people have been known to write irate letters of complaint to their seedsman; but if they had known that germination *had* occurred and that for want of water the embryo perished these letters would never have been written. Consistent daily soil moisture is necessary through the whole intricate process of germination; hence the necessity to water the soil and provide protective covering to prevent evaporation.

For those who find it difficult to mix their own soil compost the John Innes Compost, which is prepared according to a formula, answers admirably. It can be bought prepared for use in varying stages of growth, No. 1 being for seed sowing and the other numbers rising up the scale for plants as they need re-potting. Although mixed to a formula it cannot be just the same everywhere because loam varies so much in consistency and quality.

Because of this in some districts the standard mixtures need additions or modifications very similar to those I have already suggested. Putty-like soil requires something to lighten it, such as an extra quantity of leafsoil and peat, and perhaps some additional sharp grit to allow water to pass out freely. Very fine soil might need nitrogen additions like those I have already mentioned, even though the compost is based on a John Innes formula. But prepared John Innes Compost should not be mixed indiscriminately with any sort of soil just to make it go further, for by doing so it might be completely unbalanced. John Innes Compost is generally partially sterilized so that all weed seeds are killed – an added reason for not mixing it with other soil.

Before I leave this subject of loam I must mention how it can be improved in those districts where only poor stuff is available. If possible, it should be cut in early summer when bountifully covered with grass and herbage. After cutting, it should be stacked, grass side downwards, in regular layers and between each two layers a generous layer of farmyard manure should be placed as the work proceeds. Failing farmyard manure, garden compost or good leaves could also be used lavishly to produce a similar result. This stacked loam should be left undisturbed for a full year and cut down from top to bottom when supplies are taken from it. Such soil seldom needs any additional items, for it is already well reinforced.

When sowing three or four seeds in a three-inch pot the procedure is much the same as when sowing in larger receptacles, the only difference being that the few seeds are placed in the centre. For sowing in this way, however, the soil need not be sifted so finely and John Innes Compost No. 1 suffices. However, it is not easy to cover a whole batch of small pots with glass and still less easy to cover each one jam-jar fashion; it is therefore wise to cover the batch of pots densely with several sheets of coarse brown paper which should be tucked in well at the sides. Large seeds such as those of cyclamen, which are easy to handle separately, should be dibbled in singly into the soil-filled three-inch pots, in this case from a quarter to half an inch deep, or treated similarly in pans or boxes dibbled in about two inches apart in each direction. It is particularly necessary to observe the rule about watering immediately after seed sowing, because cyclamen need six weeks or more to germinate. Sometimes, indeed, in spite of precautions the soil becomes dry. In such cases water should be applied copiously – it is the daily flick-over with the rosed can which does so much damage.

The drainage of pots is important. When sowing seed, drainage crocks should occupy the bottom half of the pot because little soil is needed for germination and water should be given no excuse to remain in the soil too long. This would be wrong, however, for plant growing, because over-draining is as bad in its way as under-draining. Without drainage the closely impacted soil would drain out too slowly and probably the drainage hole would become choked, so only sufficient drainage to enable surplus water to pass out freely should be used. One big crock which almost covers the drainage hole is the keystone of pot drainage, and if half an inch of finely-broken crocks are placed on this, good drainage should be assured, provided a layer of leaves or the fibre of turf after sifting is placed on it to prevent the soil from falling, or being washed, into the drainage. This principle answers well for pots of all sizes, except the very large ones used for growing hungry plants such as chrysanthemums and tomatoes, which, if crocked in this way, would be overdrained. Such large pots for special plants are efficiently drained with one large crock to cover the middle hole or none if the large pot has three holes at the sides, as the three outlets in themselves form an effective drainage system. It is a good plan to place a three-inch layer of well-decayed farmyard manure in the bottom of these large pots to support their hungry inmates. When this soil is linked with such large pots there is no necessity to sift or chop the soil finely – instead pieces of turf loam three to four inches square may be used with advantage.

The physical side of turf loam is important. I fully realize that many of my readers may experience difficulty in obtaining fresh turf for stacking. If it is procured through a reputable source it is a little costly, mainly because charges for handling, re-handling, and transport are heavy. Nevertheless fibrous soil is a great advantage. As we have already seen when plants are grown in pots, much plant food has to be concentrated in a small space, and this, if packed in loosely, would lead to extravagantly soft growth which would prejudice success. To overcome this much compression is necessary, for even though great quantities of plant food are available they cannot be utilized suddenly if the root tips are unable to penetrate quickly; hence the use of a rammer to compress and consolidate and favour steady growth. Soil sifted or reduced in any way to fine particles, however, becomes an impermeable plaster which water passes through with much difficulty and, therefore, air can scarcely enter. In such soil plants progress with difficulty and because of the faulty physical conditions often starve in the midst of plenty; fine soil must therefore be placed more loosely in the pot or a delay in growth must be faced. Sometimes growers overcome this difficulty by including more lime rubble, broken bricks, or sand than is otherwise necessary in order to prevent soil packing and the exclusion of air, but this is scarcely a good way of restoring a good balance.

However, when fibrous turf is used in a partially decayed state only, the necessary soil consolidation may take place without the soil particles clinging too closely together.

Sometimes turf can be obtained from a building site for the cost of transport, if one can be on the spot in time, for builders find that heaps of turf prevent them from dumping building materials nearby.

By far the best source of nitrogen and humus is leafsoil from natural decay in the woods. Most leaves are valuable when decayed, but the leaves of the beech and oak are better than others. As a rule, in woodland districts permission is readily granted – sometimes for a small fee – to collect leafsoil. By the natural fall of the leaf, except when it is blown by the wind into depressions and deeper hollows, leaves are found in well-defined yearly layers, those at the top being less decayed. New leaves are difficult to handle, but leaves two years old are just at the right stage of decay to break down to add nitrogen to potting compost and to improve its physical condition. Leaves which are less decayed are invaluable for covering drainage crocks to prevent soil choking, and at the same time, by gradual decay, to afford additional plant food.

The part played by lime in potting compost cannot be overlooked. Some people, believing that lime is needed, are enthusiastic in its use and unwittingly convert their compost into a fermenting mass from which most of its nitrogen escapes in ammonia fumes. This is worse than allowing soil to be a little acid. If the truth must be told, most soft-wooded greenhouse plants give their best when the soil is slightly acid or about neutral. Growers should give this point consideration. Simple soil-testing apparatus can now be obtained very cheaply from most chemists and this should be used to determine the Ph value. Soil which has a Ph value of seven or slightly under is quite suitable for soft-wooded greenhouse plants without any additions. Chrysanthemums are happier in soil a little above this point and tomatoes also need more. Generally about 6 oz. hydrated lime per barrow-load mixed into the grit or sand and afterwards into the whole is sufficient. Lime is not a plant food and many plants said to be lime lovers are merely tolerant of lime; too much lime in the soil releases plant food far too rapidly, and therefore such soil quickly becomes poor, especially in nitrogen. On the other hand the use of just enough lime to turn the scale releases much plant food otherwise locked up in the soil. Many authorities, from time to time, have advised the use of mortar rubble, thinking that they were advising the use of lime. Generally this is not so, for in mortar the lime is so locked up that in reality the grower has done nothing more than improve the physical properties of his soil. This accounts for many improvements attributed to the use of lime.

For the benefit of many who are able to mix their own potting compost I give below the details of the John Innes Compost, but I cannot emphasize too strongly that the use of this formula cannot in itself make good potting soil or turn bad soil into good. The basis of all good potting compost is good loam.

John Innes Compost

No. 1. SEED COMPOST: Two parts medium loam, one part good peat, one part coarse sand (by loose bulk). To each bushel of this mixture are added 1½ oz. superphosphate (16 per cent. P.205), ¾ oz. ground limestone or chalk.

No. 2. POTTING COMPOST: – Seven parts medium loam, three parts good peat, two parts coarse sand (by loose bulk). To each bushel of this mixture are added 1½ oz. superphosphate (16 per cent. P.205), ¾ oz. ground limestone or chalk.

For those who cannot obtain good leafsoil, peat is an excellent substitute. The peat used for potting is decayed sphagnum moss taken from a partially decayed level, granulated to small particles, and forced under pressure into bales. Like leafsoil it is a source of nitrogen and humus. Unlike leafsoil it is sterile of plant diseases and pests and may be used in a raw state to mix with sterilized soil without fear of disease contamination and insect infestation. It is slower in decay than leafsoil; its nitrogen is therefore yielded up more slowly. It will absorb five to six times its weight in water, but when totally dry is difficult to re-charge with moisture. On this account soil containing peat used for potting must never be allowed to become dry, because sometimes, in a pot, patches and pockets of soil remain dry because the water used finds an easy way to escape through one channel only, leaving the remainder of the soil in the pot excessively dry. If an unaccountable debility in the plant leads the grower, in the absence of other evidence, to suspect this, the plant or plants concerned should be immersed in tank or bucket until all bubbling ceases, when the grower will know that complete saturation has taken place.

Sterilized soil is a great boon. Not only does it release nitrogen, but by killing weed seeds saves much unproductive work. A small quantity can be sterilized in a colander or sieve placed over a vessel of boiling water and small portable electric apparatus can be procured from nurserymen and sundriesmen. However, because mixed compost when sterilized sometimes has harmful interactions, all ingredients should be sterilized separately. Peat, already sufficiently sterile, need not be processed, neither should artificial manure, sand or lime, but bulky farmyard stall manure, garden compost, sand, grit, and leafsoil should all be treated.

Pricking Out

I HAVE referred already to 'pricking out' and in this chapter I shall endeavour to explain it. The term is seldom used to describe the process of handling seedlings out of doors, but in the greenhouse and frame it implies an early transplanting to give crowded seedlings more room for individual development. Most people sow too thickly, partly because some seeds are very small and hardly show when sown, and partly because of the age-old custom of sowing thickly to ensure enough seedlings. Country people, and old farmers in particular, sow thickly for another reason: they believe that when young seedlings are crowded in the drill or in a receptacle they shelter one another, and therefore make more rapid growth. The custom of thick sowing has been handed down through the centuries when adulteration was an integral part of the seed trade.

Most, if not all, of the seed sown in the early days of the greenhouse was heavily weighted down by cheap killed seed consisting of one or many worthless varieties in which the germ was deliberately killed by heating, the proportion of the new seed of the right variety being very small. Killed seed was bought and sold in the trade for this purpose. Because of this, thick sowing was a necessity. Through generations of nurserymen and gardeners this principle has been handed down. It is a most difficult habit to alter and even now, when adulterated killed seed is no longer used, operators who should know better often sprinkle on seed pan or pot a little more seed for luck, for to anyone handling fine seed it seems so little.

As I have already said, seed should be sown very thinly, for nowadays when it is tested repeatedly for germination before it is distributed to the public there is little to fear, and if germination is bad the cause must be sought elsewhere; rarely has it anything to do with the germinating qualities of the seed.

Pricking out is not a necessity for plant growing; it is only an expedient, which, when practised deliberately, permits the handling of many more seedlings than would be possible if the seed was sown in a way that rendered pricking out unnecessary. However well done, it is a form of check, for it is almost impossible, even for highly skilled operators, to prick out or re-plant seedlings under glass without breaking vital tiny rootlets, But facts have to be faced. Although it is well known that seedlings sown in their stations and allowed to grow without check are sturdier than those pricked out, nevertheless some pricking out is necessary, for the average greenhouse is not large enough to contain a large number of small pots in the early spring and to display plants in flower. So, to make enough room, seeds are broadcast in small pots, pans, or boxes; hence the necessity for

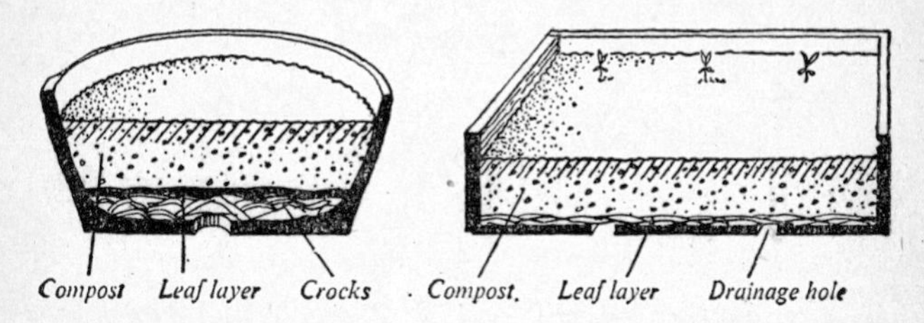

53. Boxes prepared for pricking out.

pricking out. Pricking out cannot be avoided after seed is sown in this way, which is a sound additional reason for filling seed pots half way up with crocks, leaving only the top half for soil, as these seed pots can be held upside down and by carefully knocking them on bench or barrow the ball can be split open so that the seedlings can be handled with little loss of root – a much better plan than digging them out of the seed pot with a label or dibber.

Now that we know that some pricking out is unavoidable, let us see what is necessary. Good well-balanced sifted compost is a necessity, and John Innes Compost No. 1 answers admirably. Pans or boxes which are to be used should be filled to within half an inch of the rim with this compost, which should be made moderately firm. After seedlings have been gently disentangled from the ball of soil, a dibber is needed about three quarters of an inch diameter at one end with the other carefully pointed conically. With this dibber a hole is made deep enough to receive the roots of the seedling fully extended without crushing or cramping them, and the seedling is dropped in and held in the finger and thumb of the left hand, while the other hand is using the dibber to anchor the seedling firmly by pressing it into the soil about an inch away from the original hole. This is repeated until the box or pan is filled. Most seedlings are sited about two inches apart in each direction, but some minute seedlings like begonias and streptocarpus do not need so much room, while seedlings with spreading flat leaves like nicotiana should be allowed more. If possible, seedlings should be pricked off singly into three-inch pots, from which they can be bedded

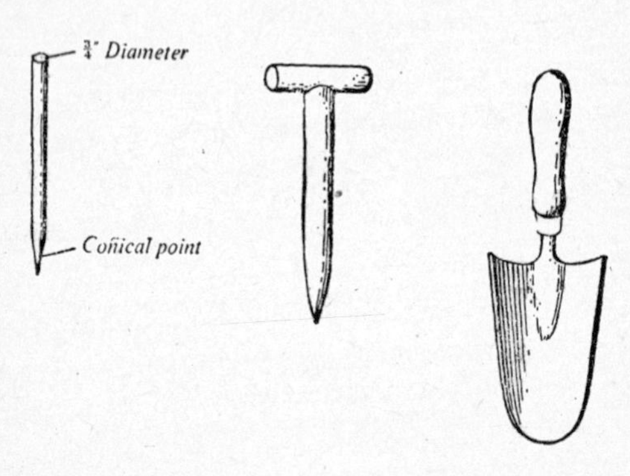

54. Dibbers, etc., needed for pricking out.

out without root disturbance or potted on as the case may be – a method which prevents more root tearing, for it is by no means easy to dig seedlings out of boxes, even though they are not overcrowded.

Generally seedlings are ready for pricking out just as they emerge from the cotyledon stage, i.e. when the first real leaf appears. Seedlings should never be allowed to suffer in the seedling pots, for even if sown thinly they cut out one another's light and steal one another's air and to escape can only grow upward, and, as they all try to do the same, they quickly become attenuated and badly checked, only to be checked again when pricked out. For seedlings at this stage, good drainage is essential, but over-drainage, by the use of too many crocks, leaving little room for soil, is very bad. To overcome the shortage of soil, which in itself leads to dryness, much extra water is needed and frequent watering leaches away much valuable nitrogen at a time when it is badly needed. All sorts of bedding plants can be treated in this way, and also plants for growing in the greenhouse, but true greenhouse subjects should, if possible, be pricked off into pots to save the wasteful method of growing roots merely to destroy them.

Sometimes it is necessary to prick out plants outside, such as polyanthus, Canterbury bells and the like, and in this case also they should be lifted from the seedling quarters with as little root damage as possible and dibbled in in a suitable spot four inches apart in each direction. Seedlings pricked out in summer on very well manured soil are apt to send down their roots deeply, which makes it very difficult to avoid breaking roots at lifting time. Because of this it is an excellent plan to place about four inches prepared seedling soil on a bottom too hard for roots to enter. It is then possible to cut the soil in squares and lift the plants with much less root disturbance.

55. Holding dibber and anchoring seedling.

For outdoor use a much larger dibber is used for plants which generally have more roots than those intended to grow outside.

Many half-hardy annuals which cannot withstand cold nights will need pricking off in frames, and here the principle of pricking off in rich soil placed on top of a hard bottom should be adopted. In this and all other pricking off, seedlings should be handled gently, for it is not uncommon for seedlings to die, apparently of some disease, but in reality through being pinched or bruised by the workers' fingers. When handling tender seedlings the nails should always be short.

The term 'pricking out' is usually reserved for seedlings under glass or for small seedlings out of doors, but there is another term which means much the same thing – 'transplanting'. This generally means the planting of larger seedlings, such as asters, stocks, and many other plants which are bedded out, or the planting of anything in the garden which is accomplished by the use of a trowel. Many seedling plants, especially perennials, come under this category.

Generally seedlings of any size are best handled by the planting out process rather than by pricking out, for the pointed dibber is a poor tool for making holes for a densely-rooted plant; indeed, many good gardeners have gone so far as to say that even brassicas, which will stand much ill-treatment, are much better if a trowel is used for their planting. With the trowel it is possible to make a wide hole easily and to ensure that roots can spread instead of being crushed while still tender into a conical hole. Most seedling perennials, such as delphiniums, lupins, and the like, are best treated in this way.

The soil for pricking out or transplanting out of doors should be friable and rich in humus and nitrogen. For friability the use of a little sharp sand or grit is an advantage, and good leafsoil or granulated peat well forked in will supply humus and some nitrogen. It should be remembered, however, that this is not a permanent planting, so the bed need not be deep. Means of watering should be close at hand. One should aim to produce seedlings with a spreading network of roots ready to make themselves at home in their permanent quarters when finally transplanted.

At the other end of the scale we have tiny seedlings scarcely visible with the naked eye, such as those resulting from the sowing of seeds of fine-seeded greenhouse plants such as begonias, gloxinias, streptocarpus and the like. These seedlings, germinated in high temperatures, sometimes are attacked by damping off disease while they are quite tiny, especially if they have been inadvertently sown too thickly. In such cases tiny seedlings must be pricked off to save them from a quick death, and this means picking them up by the point of a finely-pointed dibber or by forceps, very carefully to prevent bruising. 'Pricking out' in these cases is a misnomer, for the word implies the replanting of roots, great or small. These seedlings, however, have little or no root, and therefore none to plant, so the seedlings are carefully placed in a tiny depression made in a specially prepared sandy surface where they are well drained but always moist. Such seedlings are truly dependent on moisture in the atmosphere until they are able to make a little root penetration between the moist sand grains, and it follows, therefore, that when seedlings of this kind are being grown the atmosphere must be fully charged with moisture and the temperature must not drop below 65° F. Roof shading is essential and sometimes the seedlings are happier if paper is spread over them during the sunniest part of the day. In any case, whether damping off or not, seedlings resulting from the sowing of fine seed must be pricked off in the early days after germination, and, incredible though it seems, grow rapidly into healthy plants, after an apparent standstill of several weeks, provided a warm moist atmosphere is provided.

Half-hardy Annuals including Antirrhinums

It is fortunate indeed that in Britain we are able to grow such a wealth of flowers and to assemble them from many distant parts to grow here cheerfully – although sometimes with the seasons reversed.

We have already seen how hardy annuals can be grown by simple means, but unfortunately there are other annuals equally hardy, when planted out in summer, but which require a longer season of growth to bring them to perfection. These are usually termed half-hardy annuals, because they have to be sown at a time when conditions are much too bad out of doors, and therefore must be carefully tended under glass. There are many of these, and among them plants which have been cherished for centuries, although many of them are not native.

The most outstanding example is the antirrhinum, which is descended from the purple bi-colour snapdragon which we knew years ago. It grows on old walls or in crannies and in its new brilliance gives us a galaxy of colours and shades.

At one time it was necessary to grow antirrhinums from cuttings because they would not breed true to seed, but nowadays good strains will give a large percentage of plants exactly alike, and the rogue of the wrong colour and type is now almost a rarity.

Although half-hardy annuals require protection and some need to be sown several weeks before it is possible to sow hardy annuals out of doors, they do not need great heat and can be spoilt by coddling. Of this group the nearly hardy antirrhinum is a typical example.

Seeds of antirrhinums should be sown at the end of January or early February, very thinly in pots, pans, or boxes filled with John Innes Compost No. 1. To grow them exceptionally well a few seeds can be sown in the middle of a three-inch pot, but generally this is out of the question on account of lack of room. The seed is very small, so that care is necessary to sow thinly as it is scarcely visible to the naked eye. The precautions which should be practised generally about the conservation of moisture during germination apply very forcibly to antirrhinums. It is a mistake to put antirrhinum seed in a high temperature to germinate – one of 55° F. is admirable for its germination.

The seedlings are extremely soft and because of this they contract the damping-off disease (Pithyum de Barryanum) rather more quickly than some seedlings. It is imperative, therefore, that the glass covering the pot, or the paper with which the pots were tied down, should be removed immediately after germination.

As this stage it is a good plan to take the seedlings to a slightly cooler place, if possible, so that they may grow sturdily. When they are large enough they should be carefully pricked out, two inches apart in each direction in boxes three to four inches in depth filled with John Innes Compost No. 2. If very large plants are needed, and provided room is available, they should be pricked off singly into three-inch pots. Although these seedlings are very small and do not grow rapidly in the early days, high temperatures are harmful and a free circulation of air should be allowed at all times, whenever possible.

As the seedlings progress they should be ventilated still more freely, until, at the end of March or early in April, the receptacles in which they are growing can be placed in a cold frame, in which they can be hardened off preparatory to being planted in the open about the end of April.

Most people are inclined to look upon them as ordinary bedding plants which should be bedded out at the end of May or early in June just as many others are, but the antirrhinum is very near the edge of real hardiness and only needs a little protection in the early stages of babyhood. When it is well hardened there is no reason why it should not be planted out at the end of April because a few degrees of frost rarely harm it at this stage.

There are now many types. We have those known as giants which will grow five to six feet high. Then we have the Triumph strain which gives giant flowers on plants of medium height. There are, of course, the older intermediates which are certainly good for bedding and in which there are some wonderful colours, but most of these colours can be produced in the Triumph strains and with flowers several times larger. For general purposes the Triumph strain is better than most others. Antirrhinums known as bedding antirrhinums are available. They do not grow very tall but make great clumps of foliage which seem to sit down happily on the soil for some time but finally throw up spikes in great profusion.

At the lower end of the scale we have dwarf varieties sometimes known as Tom Thumb. Now that we have better bedding varieties these are not so much sought after, but they are still very valuable for edging. They may be had in several colours. Good varieties are as follows:

ANTIRRHINUM TRIUMPH
- Scarlet
- Bright Orange
- Rich Apricot
- Bright Yellow
- Buff Pink
- Primrose

BEDDING ANTIRRHINUM
- Scarlet
- Pale Apricot
- Bright Pink
- Deep Crimson

Then we have species of a much softer nature which appreciate a little more heat than antirrhinums, and which really need congenial conditions or they are unhappy. Among these we have balsams, celosias, and cockscombs.

The balsam is an old-world plant rarely seen now and is not much of an ornament unless grown very well. The seeds should be sown about the second week in February in the usual way in receptacles filled with John Innes Compost No. 1, and pricking out should take place immediately the plants are large enough to handle.

Unlike the antirrhinum this plant prefers genial warmth, and a temperature of 55° – 60° F. without cutting draughts and with little ventilation is much to its liking.

Soft-wooded plants, however, like balsam should never be allowed to be checked. As soon as the plants are big enough, therefore, they should be potted into three-inch pots, and returned to the same genial temperature. It is, of course, a great convenience and help to the plants if they are pricked out direct into three-inch pots instead of having an intermediate pricking out. In this same temperature they should be grown on steadily until May approaches, when they should be carefully hardened off for planting out in sheltered positions at the end of May.

Celosias and cockcombs require much the same treatment. Years ago they were treasured bedding plants and most people who grew them cherished their own strains of seeds. Specimens many feet in height were grown with imposing cypress-shaped bloom in the case of the celosia, and large combs in the case of the cockscomb. To do this check should be avoided at every point. Like the balsam they are tender in the early stages and require much the same treatment, which means that they should be grown steadily without check, and that they should never be allowed to be dry. Neither should they be permitted to become root-bound before potting on, and if it is necessary to pot into five-inch pots before they are planted out this should be done, otherwise stems become hardened and rarely have the capacity afterwards to produce impressive plants.

Almost in the same category come the lobelias. For some unknown reason this plant has always been associated with edgings and is rarely given its rightful place in a bed. That it makes good edging is indisputable, but it is far better massed in a bed, fully six inches from plant to plant. To grow to perfection the seeds should be sown as early in January as possible, and, as the seed is very fine indeed, nearly as fine as that of the begonia, great care should be taken when sowing. It is unwise to give more than a scattering of sand to the surface after the seed is sown on a prepared surface in pot, pan, or box.

As a rule lobelia seeds germinate well and regularly but need very early pricking out. It is a somewhat tedious but interesting job, as they should be pricked out when they can hardly be handled with the finger and thumb. A temperature of 55° – 60° F. is admirable for sowing, and they should be kept going in a similar temperature until they become a little more advanced. Then the temperature should be reduced and the seedlings hardened off preparatory to being placed in a cold frame, where they should be allowed to grow until bedding-out time, at the end of May, arrives. The bedding lobelia is a tender plant unable to stand more than a degree or two of frost.

Few people know the possibilities of lobelias of this type. From a July or August sowing they can be forwarded and grown under glass in cool conditions during the winter, although, as I have already said, they will not stand frost. Such single plants will develop until they are great clumps six or seven inches across with thousands of flowers per plant, and can hardly be recognized as the same species as that used for edgings when sown late in spring.

There are many shades of blue and white, and some pink and mauve varieties available; there are also varieties suitable for baskets and tall varieties for planting in gaps in the perennial border. A bed of really well grown lobelia massed closely is an almost unforgettable sight, but the same lobelia sown late in the season and used as a coloured ribbon in a border is not at all impressive. I give below a list of good types and varieties:

LOBELIA
- Cambridge Blue
- Bright Blue
- Basket (for hanging baskets)
- Ramosa (Tenuior, for greenhouse culture)

Dwarf ageratum may be treated in much the same way, but height difference spoils some modern strains, and they have not the regularity of colour or the interesting appearance of lobelia.

They can be propagated from cuttings from old plants lifted from the previous season, but this is a messy job and not always reliable. The general treatment when they are raised from seed is the same as that for the lobelia. They need thin sowing, careful pricking out, several months of growth in a congenial atmosphere, and finally hardening off in a cold frame for planting out at the end of May or early in June. It is a very easy plant to grow.

The beautiful salpiglossis may also be grown in much the same manner. When sown late in spring it attempts to flower early and is quite an insignificant plant. This also happens to some extent when seed is sown direct on the flowering site, as is possible if a sowing is delayed. From an early sowing, under glass, it can be magnificent. It embraces practically all the old-fashioned colours of great radiance and varied effect and the combination in some varieties is amazing. Perhaps its only fault is that when well grown it becomes tall, and therefore needs staking and much careful handling. It does, however, resent root disturbance, and is, therefore, not very happy after being pricked off, especially if the seedlings have been allowed to become too large beforehand. It is essential, therefore, that the seedlings should be handled with the utmost speed in the early days, and for good culture they should be pricked out direct into three-inch pots, or better still sown in three-inch pots and thinned to one seedling.

Salpiglossis generally have amazing root systems. When they have little top growth they nevertheless have masses of roots, and when quite small are ready to be potted on. It is important that they should be potted on whatever the size of the top, but with due regard to the root action; otherwise a check may occur which will prevent growth from starting again until it is too late for the plant to be well and truly formed.

For sowing John Innes Compost No. 1 is excellent and John Innes Compost No. 2 for potting on.

The varieties known as Chelsea hybrids are excellent and may be had in separate colours which breed true to type and colour. There is also another strain known as Triumph hybrids which are equally good but less lanky, and dwarf miniature strains which have all the colours of other varieties without being so tall. It must be said, however, that these dwarf varieties have blooms much smaller than the others.

Another beautiful half-hardy annual is the cosmea, which at different times has assumed several names. It is admirably fitted for growth in the English climate during the summer, but unfortunately that summer is very short and sometimes ceases before the cosmeas have started to flower. It is therefore necessary to start them under glass.

The end of January or the first week in February is not too soon, and after being sown in the ordinary way they should be pricked off when large enough to handle into three- or four-inch pots and placed in a temperature which is about 55° F. at night. As soon as they are well established, and before they need potting on, the temperature should be reduced to 50° F. at night; otherwise the plants will become leggy and almost useless for any purposes. If necessary, these should be potted on into five-inch pots, so that when large plants are placed out of doors early in June they are on the point of showing bud and will flower and continue to do so throughout the whole of the summer and early autumn months.

The modern large flowered zinnias are beautiful and interesting. Zinnias revel in heat when approaching the flowering stage, but if given too much in the early stages become thin, turn yellow, and die. For this reason they should be sown rather later than most of the half-hardy annuals – April is soon enough on account of their quick habit of growth.

They need very careful handling during pricking out, and if possible this should be done into a three-inch pot rather than into boxes so as to save another root disturbance.

They enjoy rich soil and although they are heat lovers they

also love moisture more than a number of other annuals. In the hot summer of 1949 zinnias made magnificent shows during August and September, and in October until caught by the frost. It is not uncommon for zinnia seedlings to turn yellow in the early stages and afterwards to acquire some disease and go off quickly. This is generally due to check, possibly through allowing the temperature of the greenhouse to drop too much on a cold night. To prevent anything of this kind it is wise to sow later than usual with half-hardy annuals and to keep the plants growing without check throughout.

Not so many years ago zinnias were not true to colour or name, but nowadays some very fine double strains are available which throw only a very small percentage of rogues, and therefore for all practical purposes may be described as true. I give below a list of good varieties:

ZINNIA GIANT DOUBLE WHITE
YELLOW
ROSE
ORANGE
SALMON ROSE
SCARLET

From South Africa we have had many tender annuals, nearly all of them brilliant in colour – generally in orange and buff shades. One of the best of these is Venidium fastuosum, a magnificent plant which has silky grey felted foliage from which long-stemmed brilliant orange flowers are developed. Generally, these have black centres and maroon markings on the ray petals, and sometimes these blotches are so well defined that they appear as a purple-black zone on the base of the petal. Occasionally seeds of this plant germinate badly. This cannot be avoided, so it is wise to make provision for it when ordering seeds. It is one of the most remarkable plants we are able to grow and one which begins to flower in June and continues until the frost.

In addition to the species fastuosum, there are now some exceedingly beautiful art shades. These have growths very similar to fastuosum, but the shades of grey are dissimilar and the colours are remarkable, as they vary from pure white to orange, with almost every ivory, cream, lemon, and yellow shade included in the same batch. Generally they have glistening black centres.

Another species, Venidium calendulaceum, has green foliage with brilliant orange flowers, most of which have a pale zone surrounding the central dark disc. The flowers are not so large as Venidium fastuosum, but are borne in very great profusion, making it a plant which should be included in every half-hardy annual border.

Another very fine plant from South Africa is Ursinia anethoides, an early April sowing of which will give a magnificent display during the whole of the summer and autumn. It is not quite so fastidious as Venidium fastuosum, neither is it so tall, but it does provide a wealth of glistening orange flowers which surpass in brilliance those of any other species grown in the garden.

In addition there is a smaller type known as golden bedder. The flowers are of a pale shade of orange with a deeper coloured zone in the centre making a very attractive combination. Like Ursinia anethoides it is extremely free flowering, but it does not grow much more than a foot in height. This Ursinia has great lasting power.

A smaller form of Ursinia known as Ursinia pulchra grows only to a height of six to seven inches, and the tiny flowers are a mass of brilliant orange. All these should be sown about the first week in April and grown on without check for planting out in the open as soon as the bad weather in May has passed.

Another fine plant from South Africa, the nemesia, which came to us as a brilliant orange, now possesses all the shades of the rainbow. It is a somewhat soft but very free flowering plant which succeeds best in the moister parts of England, in the extreme north or in Scotland. It is a great lover of atmospheric moisture and will sometimes flower within six weeks of the time of sowing. For most districts in the south, seeds should be sown early in April and care should be taken to prick out the seedlings immediately they are large enough to handle, for if they are allowed to become drawn they rarely recover.

There are two types, the hybrid type in which there are some brilliant colours but small flowers, and the large flowering section which has giant flowers much larger than the original species and which may be had in almost any shade including blue. This plant, although a sun lover, will grow in semi-shade.

It likes rich soil, resents check, and is unhappy in an open windswept garden.

The nicotianas are very beautiful and capable of tremendous development. If sown early and handled well many will grow to a height of five or six feet. At first seedlings require little room, but afterwards their leaves begin to spread so much laterally that a good deal of room is required in order for them to grow unmolested. A mid-February sowing in the usual way suffices for this plant, which should be potted on, if necessary, in order to prevent starvation. Planting out should generally take place at the end of May or early in June in soil as rich as it can be made within reason. With such a free growing plant it is almost needless to say that it appreciates quantities of well-decayed farmyard manure or compost.

These flowering varieties should not be confused with the several tobacco species used for making tobacco. At one time only the white one was available, but there are now hybrids which give almost every shade from pure white to deep crimson. There is a scarlet crimson which produces blooms true to colour and is known as Crimson King which gives very rich flowers, and there are some others. As most people know, these nicotianas are heavily perfumed and it is always wise to plant such scented flowers around the house where the perfume can be appreciated at evening. The flowers open widely at early sunset but do not close completely in sunshine, so that the nicotiana makes an exceptionally good bedding plant.

In addition to the best large-flowered varieties there is also a very neat miniature variety which sends up innumerable spikes of tiny flowers from dark green clean-looking foliage. Generally it should be treated in the same way as its larger brethren.

Of late years petunias have returned to favour as bedding plants. Although tender in the early stages they are easily cultivated and flower continuously from the end of June until the frost. They should be sown, pricked out, and potted on, and handled in the same way as others I have already described, but with soft plants of this description check must be carefully avoided. It is true that checked plants eventually recover after losing a month to six weeks of good growth, but as these plants are annuals they have no chance whatever to regain the lost time. They are essentially sun lovers but will make quite a good show in partial shade.

There are many beautiful colours including double striped varieties, and those known as bedding varieties, of which I give a list below:

PETUNIA BLUE BEDDER
PINK BEDDER
VIOLET BEDDER
CRIMSON BEDDER
WHITE BEDDER
STRIPED BEDDER

There are also large-flowered single varieties with a heavier habit of growth although quite good for bedding purposes. Petunias are very valuable for filling stone vases, baskets to beautify odd spots, and window boxes. They are much hardier than is generally supposed and will stand several degrees of

56. Petunia

frost in the autumn with impunity, but, of course, succumb when severe frost sets in.

The bedding verbenas, although unlike petunias in appearance, need somewhat similar treatment, and as they grow a little more slowly than petunias seeds should be sown at the end of February or in March. They are unhappy if they have much root disturbance, and, because of this, if they can be sown or pricked off direct into small pots much damaging check is avoided.

Many years ago the verbenas ranked among the best of our bedding plants, and they still are very valuable, especially now that they have new colours and forms.

Verbenas appreciate well-worked heavily-manured soil in which they sometimes grow rampantly. This disadvantage can easily be overcome by pegging down growth with wire pegs to cover the whole of the soil in the bed and eventually to clothe it with brilliant bloom.

There are many first-class varieties, of which I give a selection below:

VERBENA GIANT WHITE
PINK
BRILLIANCE
FIREFLY
BLUE
ROYAL BLUE

There are also two splendid varieties which have to be propagated by cutting: Laurence Johnston, scarlet, and Loveliness, mauve, which should be in every garden.

Another plant which can be grown out of doors and which probably makes a more brilliant bed than any of our half-hardy bedding plants is Dianthus Heddewigii. There are both single and double varieties, but for sheer brilliance the single varieties are by far the best.

In the early stages they are comparatively slow growing, and for this reason should be sown at the end of January or early in February, pricked off into boxes as soon as they are ready, and potted on separately when big enough to handle. Like most plants of this description they appreciate good treatment and are happy in good rich soil, but they are essentially sun lovers and are, therefore, unhappy in shaded positions. No stopping or pinching out of any kind is necessary.

Some people prefer the mixed strains to the separate varieties. This is a matter of taste, but I must say that the modern separate varieties, especially salmon and scarlet shades, are certainly very good. Below I give a selection of varieties:

DIANTHUS HEDDEWIGII
SALMON QUEEN
SCARLET QUEEN
DOUBLE PINK
DOUBLE CRIMSON

Phlox Drummondii is a plant which succeeds well in districts where there is good soil and much atmospheric moisture but with a heavy rainfall. It is a dwarf, almost creeping plant which does not closely resemble the perennial phlox of the border, although the build of the flower is much the same. These wiry trailing plants are magnificent in the south-west and the west of England. They should not be grown by anyone who has poor sandy or gravelly soil unless such soil can be treated as advised in Chapter 1, and water can be given in abundance daily.

Phlox dislike check; seeds should, therefore, be sown in three-inch pots and thinned to one seedling if possible, or the seedlings should be pricked out while they are still quite tiny into three- or four-inch pots. It is unwise to sow too early as the plants become too big and starved far in advance of the planting season. An early April sowing usually suffices.

There are large-flowered types which grow rather tall and smaller bedding varieties which are excellent if allowed to grow in their own way. The shoots of the large-flowered ones may, if necessary, be pinned down with wire pegs in the same way as verbena. There are also some very small compact varieties which need planting about nine inches apart in each direction to ensure a good show.

The following is a selection of the best varieties:

PHLOX DRUMMONDII
DELICATE PINK
VIVID SCARLET
PINK BEAUTY
SALMON BEAUTY
CRIMSON BEAUTY
BLUE BEAUTY

Those who are short of greenhouse room can raise most of the kinds and varieties I have mentioned very successfully in a frame over a hot bed and sometimes in a cold frame, delaying the date of sowing a fortnight or three weeks and thus taking advantage of the increasing spring sunshine. If in doing this the hot bed is looked upon in the same way as a greenhouse, and if a cold frame is available, seedlings can be handled in just the same way as if they were placed in the greenhouse to germinate. But there are two half-hardy annuals especially associated with village gardens – asters and stocks – which, if sown about mid-March, in a greenhouse with a temperature of 50° – 55° F. at night, will produce good seedlings for pricking out about a month later. These can easily be pricked out into boxes or pans in the same way as other half-hardy annuals, but they do much better if pricked out in lines on about four inches of soil placed in a cold frame and with a hard base. They should be sited about three inches apart in each direction and the lights used to protect them for the first few days. Afterwards, as soon as they become well established, the lights should be removed daily and allowed to remain off at night as soon as the danger of frost has passed. Although seedlings require a certain amount of nursing in both greenhouse and cold frame they should not be kept too hot or ventilated badly; indeed, it is necessary to ventilate freely on every possible occasion to prevent the plants becoming too forward or drawn and sometimes useless.

Stocks in particular require very rich soil; indeed, it is almost impossible for the ordinary person to make his soil too rich with farmyard manure or compost, and as this plant is much hardier than most half-hardy annuals a certain amount of risk can be taken in planting out early in May on any day except when danger of May frost threatenes.

There are a great number of types and varieties, but the ten-week stock usually proves better for garden purposes than most others. Of this type there is a fine strain known as Perfection in which there are many colours. Of these I have made a selection:

STOCK PERFECTION WHITE
YELLOW
DELICATE PINK
CHAMOIS
CRIMSON
MAUVE

There is also a dwarf form which is known as bedding stock. The type known as intermediate is also very valuable, and should be sown early in February; there are winter flowering varieties which, if sown early in July, can bloom in profusion in the early spring months. I have made a suitable selection of all these below:

STOCK INTERMEDIATE EAST LOTHIAN WHITE
PINK
SCARLET
MAUVE
PURPLE

Annual asters (Callistephus) form a very large family useful for garden decoration in August and September. At one time the plants were short and squat, and the flowers stiff and formal and of little use for cutting purposes, but now there are very tall-growing varieties, long-stemmed and with very fine flowers which are admirable for house decoration.

It would scarcely be possible for any one grower to include varieties of the many sections in one garden. Instead it is better to grow one type each season and have something fresh and interesting. Probably the best of the bedding types is one known as ostrich plume, of which there are many colours and shades ranging from white through many shades of rose pink to scarlet, blue and deep blue, all orange shades being absent.

A section of tall varieties called mammoth will give plants three feet or more in height with stems eighteen inches or more in length, very valuable for cutting in August, September, and sometimes October. Some people take advantage of this by sowing rather late, and lifting their plants in September so that they can flower for several months more in the greenhouse.

In addition to the two main sections I have already mentioned there are incurving varieties known as giant French in which there are several good colours, and good strains of dwarf bedding varieties which rarely exceed one foot in height.

Well-grown asters are worth a place in almost any garden, but have to be sited very carefully as their colours disagree with the orange, buff, or crimson shades of other plants. Their colours mix very well together but as a rule do not blend or mix with other colours in the border. It is therefore necessary to grow them in a patch by themselves where they can be enjoyed at leisure.

I cannot leave the asters without mention of the section of single varieties known as Southcote beauty. In a way they are similar to the single sinensis, but differ in that there is a smaller disc and larger ray petals, making up a most interesting flower. These single asters flower more freely than those of any other type, stand bad weather much better than those of the shaggy type, and can be grown in soil which is infinitely poorer.

On the whole, asters revel in rich soil and generally if checked just before the time of planting are not successful. Mid March is the best time to sow.

There are many other types and varieties of asters which space will not allow me to deal with now, but I have given sufficient varieties to last for several years, even in a large garden.

As the object of sowing half-hardy annuals under glass is to lengthen the season of growth, let it be noted that it can be lengthened still more if an autumn sowing is practised. Some kinds and varieties come through the winter badly and are tall and lanky, but if an early summer display is required thin sowing in September or October provides very fine plants. For this purpose the following are excellent when grown in this way:

AGERATUM
PETUNIA
VERBENA
LOBELIA
NICOTIANA
STOCKS
SALPIGLOSSIS

Asters are not quite so successful but can be treated in this way if sown about mid October.

Half-hardy annuals are very interesting and perhaps more useful than some plants in other sections, and, with the exception of some non-blending types and varieties, form a useful addition to the herbaceous border, particularly for filling gaps.

Taking Cuttings and Layerings

AFTER centuries of culture in this and other countries many of our cherished flowers are hybrids, of which a large number will not breed true to seed. To reproduce them they must be propagated vegetatively, which, in effect, means that every plant propagated thus, even to tens of thousands, is a part of the parent plant. Among the several methods practised the most simple and common is propagation by cuttings, generally called 'taking cuttings'. Cuttings can be taken of soft-wooded plants, which sometimes root in a few days, or of hard-wooded plants, in autumn, which take months or more to root. In this chapter we are most interested in soft-wooded plants.

The geranium – in reality a pelargonum – is perhaps the easiest example. Geraniums can be propagated the whole year round, but for convenience are propagated in late summer in a cool greenhouse or in early spring in a greenhouse with a temperature of 55° – 60° F. for preference, although rooting can be successfully accomplished in a lower temperature. In August and September well-ripened shoots – i.e. those grown in full sunshine, and not those from the shaded depths of the plant – should be cut away carefully. Usually these will be four to six inches long, possess several pairs of leaves, and approach half an inch in stem diameter. At a suitable point immediately below a joint (node) the stem is cut squarely at right angles, and all lower leaves – generally two pairs – which would inconvenience insertion, are carefully and cleanly cut away, leaving a bare stem below the foliage of about three inches. The cutting is now prepared.

Such cuttings should be inserted in pots or boxes filled with a clean compost of two parts loam, one part well-decayed leaf-soil or peat, and half a part of sharp sand. No manure, artificial or otherwise, should be added to any soil compost for propagating. Boxes are perhaps a little more convenient when large numbers are propagated, but pots are easier to handle and generally give the best results.

The general principle of taking cuttings is that they should be firmly anchored in the soil and that the stem cut to a right angle should rest on a sandy bottom. To achieve this the soil, either in pots or boxes, must be firm – a condition difficult to achieve when boxes are used but comparatively easy in the case of pots. When filling pots it will be found that if the pot is filled with soil and then made firm, although it is compacted enough

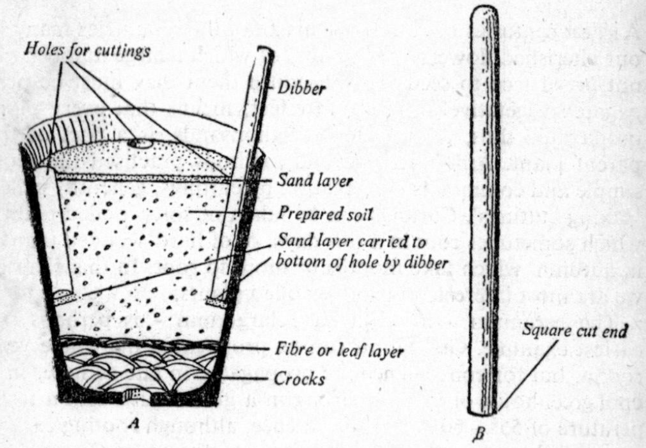

57. (A) Sectional diagram of pot prepared for cuttings; (B) Dibber.

at the top, it is far too loose for security at the bottom where the cutting will rest. To overcome this, the soil should be placed in the pot a little at a time and made firm with a downward thrusting movement of the fingers, the top not being smoothed over until all the soil is firm. In pots, whose earthenware sides prevent lateral movement, this is simple, but in boxes, where there is side play, although the soil can be successfully made firm, the job takes a little longer. In both cases a good level surface is necessary on which should rest a layer, a quarter of an inch thick, of coarse sharp sand.

A dibber should be made slightly larger than the greatest diameter of the stoutest cutting. This should be cut square at right angles and thrust down two to three inches at the side of the pot following its slightly tapering line. When withdrawn it should leave a clean hole with a layer of sand carried down. On this layer of sand at the bottom of the hole the cutting should rest evenly and should be made rigidly firm by thrusting in the dibber at the side of the pot an inch or so away from the inserted cutting and obliquely, so that the soil displaced thus by the dibber comes to rest gently but forcibly against the cutting and anchors it firmly. For this purpose, pots three to four inches in diameter are best, and not more than four cuttings should be inserted in each. The same method of making the cutting firm should be adopted with the boxes, though the job is not so easy. However, whether easy or no, a firm anchorage for cuttings is essential for good propagation. In time, after a little practice, an operator should be able to lift the cutting, pot and all, by one of the leaves without loosening or displacing it, and, in general, the mechanics of 'taking cuttings' should follow these lines. It is true that shoots of some soft-wooded plants root merely by

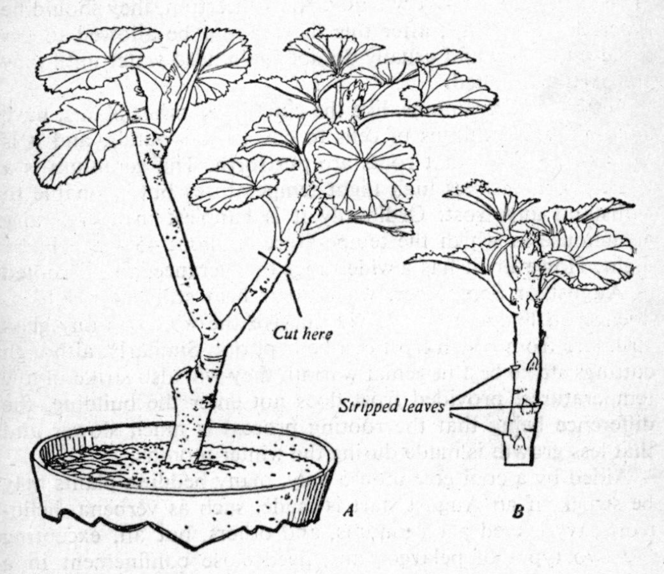

58. Geranium cutting: (A) Before taking; (B) Prepared.

having cuttings inserted loosely and without preparation in propagating houses where there is much heat and atmospheric moisture; but these are the exception. The rule is that most cuttings must be anchored safely, and then a good take, approaching a hundred per cent, can be expected.

Cuttings of fleshy-leaved plants like geraniums when deprived of moisture-carrying roots transpire badly, and until new roots have formed have no means of providing the tops with moisture. Shoots of many other plants flag too; hence the reason for placing cuttings in a very close atmosphere where, by cutting away the air supply, transpiration is greatly checked. Geraniums appear limp and lifeless after propagation and usually look far worse than they are. With these, as with other plants, transpiration can be almost prevented by placing them in a small propagating case – a small frame with light or a box covered with glass – not much bigger than the boxes or pots of cuttings, but if there are other plants needing attention, the geraniums can be placed on the greenhouse benches and allowed to flag – as they do – very badly. After insertion, they should be watered thoroughly; after this they should be allowed to become rather dry and usually do not again need water until they are partially rooted.

Cuttings of geraniums, like the cuttings of other plants, have first to form a callous of cells to cover the wounds, and it is from this callous that roots are put forth. The geranium is a plant which dislikes high night temperatures but is unable to withstand any frost. Ordinarily it is happiest in a cool airy greenhouse in which the temperature is about 45°– 50° F. by night. However, it has a wide range of tolerance, and if rooted in August or September, when solar heat still has much influence on temperature, it will survive the winter in any glass structure from which frost can be kept out. Similarly, although cuttings strike best in genial warmth they will also strike in low temperatures, provided frost does not enter the building, the difference being that the rooting process is much slower and that less growth is made during the winter months.

Aided by a cool greenhouse only, many bedding plants may be struck, if an August start is made, such as verbena, heliotrope, ivy-leaved pelargonums, and others, but all, excepting the two types of pelargonums, need close confinement in a small propagating case, which need be nothing more than a glass-covered box in the greenhouse.

I have used the geranium as an example because it is large and easily handled. All other soft-wooded cuttings are taken in a similar fashion, which seldom leads to the removal of more than two pairs of leaves and sometimes only one. Care should be taken when selecting soft-wooded cuttings of plants, which, if the climate permitted, would grow into hard-wooded shrubs, such as heliotrope, fuchsias and lemon-scented verbena, that the shoots selected are really soft, otherwise there may be much delay. Sometimes, indeed, these semi-hard-wooded cuttings refuse to root at all.

Now let us deal with the carnation. As everyone knows these are available at the florists all the year round, although they are more plentiful in the spring and early summer months. They are the so-called tree or perpetual flowering carnations, and no doubt the word 'Tree', which now is seldom used, was given to this class of carnation because it will continue to grow for several years as a small sub shrub. If allowed to do this, however, it quickly becomes unmanageable, as two or three feet of growth develop each year. Because of this it is usual to propagate yearly.

It is important when selecting cuttings to cut them from the part of the plant likely to produce healthy plants of strong growth. In the case of the perpetual carnation, cuttings taken from the top of the plant run to bud quickly, and rarely make a good plant. Cuttings from the bottom are usually too hard and lead to a plant which is good in appearance but too slow in growth to be of much use. Those taken from the middle usually prove best because they develop enough growth to build up a good foundation on which flowers are freely borne. Shoots should be selected about three inches long, and owing to the grass-like formation of the leaves the general rule about stripping cuttings does not apply. Carnations, which have so many more leaves than most plants, produce shoots which are sometimes puzzling as their dense growth of leaves is sufficient to hide their stems. Enough of these should be stripped away to leave a clean stem of about one and a half inches, which, if inserted to the full length of the cleaned portion, should give excellent results.

Carnations can be rooted in soil similar to that advised for geraniums, or, much quicker, in a sand bed, into which they should be dibbled firmly about two inches apart in each direction. Cuttings cannot be made very firm when inserted in sand, owing to its shifting nature; neither is it necessary that they should be, for the technique suitable for manipulation in soil is quite different to that needed when sand is used. The sand bed should be made up in the propagating frame in the greenhouse, in small boxes and even in pots, depending upon the number to be dealt with. Carnation cuttings will strike in a comparatively low temperature if required, but are then much slower and a night temperature of 55° F. will be found more satisfactory. January has proved to be the best time for propagating.

If sand is used growers should pot up the rooted cuttings, as soon as they have roots half an inch long, into compost made of finely-sifted loam and decayed farmyard manure in equal parts, with half a part of sharp sand to ensure that water passes out freely. Sharp sand or river grit is needed for propagating

59. Inserting carnation cutting in pot.

beds, but fine builder's sand with all its impurities is useless for the purpose.

All carnations can be rooted in this way, but in the case of the border carnations and the pinks a method known as 'layering' is used. This entails stripping the growth stems until no leaves are left but a tuft on the top which looks like an unsevered cutting. On this stem, at the first point where it would be severed, were it a cutting, a long tongue extending to half the stem diameter should be cut on the underside, and the stem bent at the point, and pressed into the soil with a wire peg which effectively secures it and keeps the growth upright. Over the slit and layered stem a couple of good handfuls of fine sandy soil is placed and well moistened with water. In a few weeks roots will have formed from the tongue into the new soil, the stem can be severed close to the tongue, and the new plant, complete with roots, placed in a three-inch pot preparatory to growing in a cold frame all the winter. If intended for culture out of doors, instead of in the greenhouse, the severed layers can be planted out direct into permanent quarters. Malmaison carnations are also propagated by layering.

Chrysanthemums are prepared in the same way as the geranium, but before preparation great care is needed in selecting cuttings. Large strong shoots which spring up from the base in the autumn and which already have roots rarely make a good plant. January is the accepted time for these and short fresh cuttings from the base are the best. Woody cuttings, with or without buds, are unsatisfactory and not worth the trouble they entail. Cuttings can be inserted three in a three-inch pot or in trays in a mixture of half loam and half sand, or they can be dibbled into a bed with compost of a similar character. To save the miserable dejection these cuttings exhibit when flagging, chrysanthemums can be placed in a propagating frame, but this is not really necessary as the flagging soon ceases and the rooting cuttings pick up quickly. Chrysanthemum cuttings should be potted immediately they are rooted, for the rooting medium possesses little plant food. A temperature of about 50° F. suits chrysanthemums. January and February are the best months.

Dahlia clumps placed in the greenhouse soon develop shoots large enough for cutting. These are trimmed in the same way, and inserted in pots or boxes in finely sifted half loam and half sand or in a bed placed in a propagating frame. In a temperature of 55° F. they root readily and should be potted on quickly before starvation occurs.

The examples I have mentioned of soft-wooded cuttings will serve for many other plants, but there are others not quite hardy which need the protection of a cold frame during the winter months. Two of the flowers which need this treatment – violas and pentstemons – are valuable in any garden.

Viola cuttings should be taken late in September or early in October. Good growing shoots are chosen and prepared like other cuttings and are dibbled into sandy soil in a cold frame in which they will spend the winter. When first inserted the frame should be kept closed for a few weeks to check transpiration, but after becoming rooted they should be ventilated freely and in good weather the lights removed as they are for the winter culture of sweet peas. In frosty weather the protection of litter, straw, sacking, or even soil on the frame is needed to protect them, but all coverings must be removed quickly when thaw occurs.

Hybrid pentstemons, which are brilliant bedding plants of a sub-shrubby nature, should be treated similarly, but hardened cuttings are of little use. Soft cuttings must be found for successful propagation.

Then we have many families of perennial plants best propagated from cuttings although they can be increased in a rough and ready way by division. A family which lends itself to propagation by cuttings is the perennial aster (Michaelmas daisy) which puts forth many shoots in spring. Strong shoots should be selected for cuttings and inserted four in a pot in a mixture of fine soil as for geraniums. As perennial asters root readily in a few weeks without artificial heat only a cold frame is necessary, and if after being well watered the pots are plunged up to the rim in moist peat the soil in the pots will be maintained in an equable condition of moisture. A glass-covered box will suffice for a small quantity. Cuttings of all sections can be treated thus, but all varieties of Aster amellus do not root as quickly as the varieties of other sections. Most of the cultivated species can be increased in this way.

Phlox decussata is another plant which throws up good cuttings early and if treated like asters does not require more than a cold frame or a small box. Cuttings of phlox do not root so quickly as asters and if put in during April generally require three weeks longer.

The delphinium is another example of a plant which gives quantities of cuttings in early spring and sometimes does so over a long period. Generally the best cuttings are those taken early, and delphiniums differ from all other plants I have mentioned in this chapter because their stems are tubular and the walls of the tube very thin. Because of this when selecting shoots the soil should be scraped away from the crown so that each cutting can be removed with a woody heel, for if cut short at right angles across the tube, callousing and subsequent rooting is done tardily, if at all. In the case of delphiniums the woody-ended cuttings should be inserted singly in the centre of each pot, the directions for soil and insertion being similar to those already given for asters, etc. It is essential that delphinium cuttings should be made firm and that the soil be always moist. After the initial watering the cuttings should be placed in a close propagating frame in a cold greenhouse or frame. Some people say that heat is necessary, but as delphiniums will strike well in a cold frame or cold greenhouse, although much more slowly than in heat, there is no reason to crush them into some corner of the greenhouse where, in the spring, every inch of room is required for plants which need warmth. In a cold house or

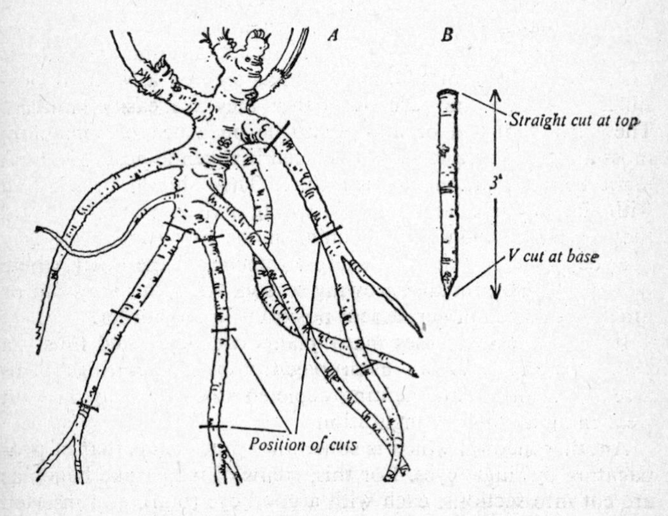

60. Diagram of root cuttings of lupin.

frame, delphiniums need from six weeks to two months in which to strike.

Mention must be made of numerous plants which, although they can be propagated by cuttings and divisions, nevertheless grow into fine plants if grown from root cuttings. In some cases they are stoutly-rooted plants like the lupin, in others fine-rooted ones like the phlox.

In the case of the lupin a section of thong – as the roots are termed – is cut away from the cat o' nine tails root system and cut into lengths almost three inches long. For identification, the end of the cutting farthest from the crown is cut into a wedge shape and the end nearer the crown cut square at right angles to the length. Then they should be inserted in threes in three-inch pots for which the compost advised for asters and other plants should suffice. The thong should be placed upright, resting firmly anchored against the side of the pot. Its square-cut portion should be just covered with soil after completion and must be very firm. These too, will root in a cold frame or box, but certainly will give better results if given the advantage of a little heat, 50° F. at night sufficing.

Phlox decussata can be struck from cuttings, as I have pointed out, but makes much finer plants when propagated from root cuttings. For this, plants are lifted in late autumn, their roots washed quite free of soil, and rootlets secured as long as possible. Although they are quite thin they are easily handled. These roots should be allowed to lie on a bed of sphagnum moss and sand in a receptacle placed in a gentle heat, 50° F. at night being a suitable temperature. They should be covered with similar material and when spring arrives it will be found that buds or shoots are forming on the tiny roots, and they may be scattered thinly in shallow trenches in the open, where they can remain for one growing season. After this they can be lifted and placed in permanent positions in the border.

If the necessity arises many plants can be treated thus – a valuable thing to know – as propagation by root cuttings forms a ready means of augmenting depleted stocks rapidly without weakening a plant's constitution.

Another method which is sometimes practised is that of propagating by single eyes. For this, stems of plants like begonias are cut into sections, each with a good eye (bud), and inserted upright in small pots, the base of the eye resting on the soil after completion. This method, which gives a high percentage of failures, is sometimes resorted to when it is imperative to increase stock rapidly. A moist atmosphere and a temperature of 65° F. is necessary for this. Hard-wooded plants can also be treated in this way if it is thought desirable.

Allied to this is propagation by leaf cuttings, a method widely practised for begonias, especially the winter flowering varieties in the days before begonias (tuberous) and gloxinias bred true to type and variety as they do to-day. Winter-flowering varieties do not produce seed except occasionally by a lucky accident, and there are many people who exhibit monstrous plants at chrysanthemum shows each autumn who believe that large vigorous plants cannot be produced in any other vegetative manner. For this, boxes of sandy soil are needed with the surface covered by a quarter of an inch of sharp sand. On this bed leaves are pinned down flat with small wire pegs, after the principal ribs have been nicked with a knife. Close contact between leaves and sand is needed, for without this decay is likely to set in. This method of rooting is rather slow, as over two months is generally needed before a callous is formed, and, finally, leaves and roots are emitted at the cut ribs. For this, a temperature of not less than 65° F. is desirable. Propagation by this method should begin under glass during February, and is essentially the method for the expert.

Other methods of vegetative propagation are for plants outside the scope of this book, so I refrain from dealing with them, especially as I have already given enough food for thought for a long time.

Flowering Bulbs

A FLOWERING bulb is, like an onion, built up of many successive fleshy layers. These layers, when the bulb is well grown and old enough, shelter an inflorescence complete in every detail and ready to emerge when they are cultivated and the season permits. The term bulb covers a wide range of plants and is also used to describe other bulbous-looking plants which do not develop sheaths but whose reproductive reserve is a solid mass. These are corms in the case of begonias, gloxinias, and the like, tubers in the case of dahlias and potatoes – to use a homely example – and bulbs only when sheath-like growth builds up the reserve. When the average man thinks of bulbs, he thinks of hyacinths, narcissus, and tulips, and it is these that this chapter will refer to.

Bulbs prepared for sale, whether in Holland or Great Britain, are several years old. They are grown on yearly until they become of a size and age to give their flowering maximum. They are received from the bulb growers in late summer and often suffer through being kept out of the ground too long – a point worthy of more attention than it gets. As most people know we receive a large proportion of our bulbs from Holland, a country with centuries of experience in growing bulbs and bringing them to perfection. In addition, quantities are grown in our own Eastern Counties – sometimes under Dutch supervision – of a standard as high as that of bulbs from Holland.

While general improvement has taken place in all families of flowering bulbs, the greatest advance has been made with the narcissus or daffodil, which all belong to the same great family in which such outstanding advances have been made. The beauty of some of these modern aristocrats is appreciated throughout the whole of the horticultural world, but as each novelty begins as only one seedling, which has to be slowly increased by bulb multiplication yearly, advance is necessarily slow. Of modern novelties – those of the last two generations – there are plenty of remarkable beauty from which to choose.

Narcissi, or daffodils, as they are generally called, having been thoroughly developed by the bulb grower, need only moist soil to bring to them to flower. It is true that they can be brought to perfection by the use of a jam jar of water and a few stones placed inside to give anchorage to the roots, but most of the plant's energies are utilized in developing the embryo flowers, and without soil the future of the bulb is compromised for several seasons while the plant is being nursed back to productiveness in the soil. But let us see what we need to make a display in the garden.

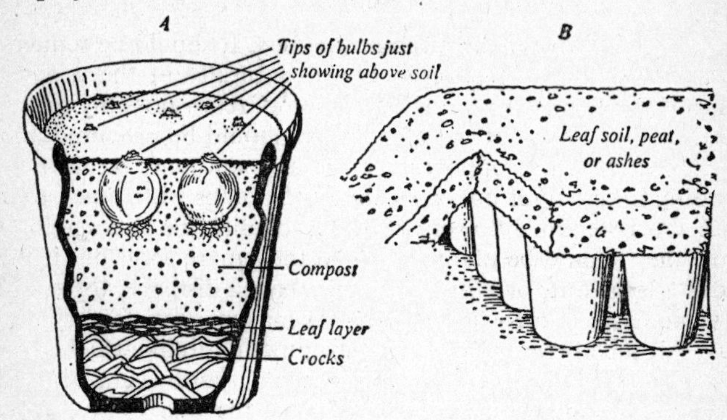

61. (A) Potting bulbs; (B) Block of potted bulbs covered with leaf soil, peat or ashes.

If we wish to have a bed of narcissi or daffodils we must remember that it cannot be permanent if we are to follow with summer bedding, for the narcissus bulbs have to be lifted before they have matured to make room for the summer occupants. When bedding out time arrives one must be prepared to sacrifice the bulbs in favour of the new occupants. For flowering purposes no special land cultivation is needed, for moist earth alone will allow good bulbs to develop. For displays in beds those known as trumpet daffodils make the best show and the following are recommended:

EMPEROR	Pale yellow and golden yellow
KING ALFRED	Deep golden yellow
GOLDEN HARVEST	Deep yellow, an outstanding variety
DAWSON CITY	Clear soft yellow

Those who like white trumpet daffodils should try:

IMPERATOR	White perianth with creamy-white trumpet
MRS E. H. KRELAGE	Ivory white

In addition to the above there are trumpet daffodils known as bicolours, of which those given below are good bedders:

BOSWIN	White perianth and pale yellow trumpet
QUEEN OF BICOLOURS	White perianth and canary yellow trumpet

All of the above make an imposing bed. It should be remembered, however, that narcissi grown naturally in the ground without lifting have only a short season of rest – possibly only a week or two, and that therefore bulbs should be procured and planted at the first opportunity in early autumn. A delay in planting until winter puts a strain on the bulbs which may produce short-stemmed flowers of poorer quality. To make a good show they should be planted four to the square foot, but if the bed is a large one, or if it is seen only from a distance, three and in some cases two to the square foot makes a satisfactory display. All the above are known as trumpet daffodils which have trumpets as long as, or longer than, the perianth segments.

A trowel should be used for planting the bulbs about four inches deep, and, apart from the usual firming of soil around the bulb, there is no special technique needed for planting.

Then there are those narcissi which are worth more intimate planting near the window or door or anywhere round the house. One section of these is known as large cupped narcissi. They have a cup or corona more than a third but less than equal to the perianth segment. Of these I give a list below:

CARBINEER	Rich yellow perianth with bright orange red cup
DAMSON	Cream perianth with cup of Fuchsia red
ELDORADO	Golden yellow perianth, cup edged bright scarlet
JOHN EVELYN	Creamy white perianth, apricot orange cup, heavily frilled
HAVELOCK	Bright yellow self
SCARLET ELEGANS	Deep orange red cup and bright yellow perianth

Much like the above, but with the cup less than a third of the perianth segments, are many exquisite narcissi which deserve to be planted in well-chosen spots:

BATH'S FLAME	Yellow perianth with orange red cup
FIRETAIL	Creamy white perianth with flattened crimson scarlet crown
LA RIANTE	Glistening snow white perianth with bright orange cup
PEGGY	White perianth and rich yellow cup

The double varieties should not be overlooked for nowadays there are some very fine varieties. I give a good selection below:

INGLESCOMBE	Bright sulphur yellow
HOLLAND GLORY	A fine soft yellow
INSULIND	Cream and deep orange
MARY COPLAND	White and orange red

Some people are very fond of the bunch-flowered varieties, of which those below are really good:

GERANIUM	Five or six flowers to a stem each with white perianth and orange cup
GLORIOUS	White perianth and orange cup
HALVOSE	Buff yellow perianth with orange red cup
PRIMROSE EXCELSIOR	Primrose yellow

There are, too, good poet's narcissi or poeticus narcissi:

ACTEA	Pure white with scarlet rimmed eye
RED RIM	White perianth with yellow cup edged red

For the intimates of the house border the fragrant jonquils should be included in the following varieties:

IMPROVED CAMPERNEL	Pure yellow
GOLDEN SCEPTRE	Rich golden yellow

All varieties above are given on the assumption that fresh bulbs will be procured annually, but many people wish to establish them in the garden. Narcissi love deep cool loam and are generally unhappy on a site which becomes hard baked and arid during the summer. Semi-shade is not objected to and leafsoil in abundance should be incorporated. Failing leafsoil, good garden compost or peat should be utilized. Narcissi look well if planted in clumps round a shrubbery, provided they are not crammed in. They are particularly happy in moist districts where the rainfall is heavy, provided they are left in peace. For establishing them in this way the bulbs should be planted a foot apart in each direction to give them room for natural bulb expansion and multiplication.

Among narcissi there are a few which are worth growing in pans in the cold greenhouse. These should remain undisturbed for several seasons or can be planted in suitable spots on the rock garden. Of these, cyclameneus, with reflexed perianth and tube-like yellow trumpet with a maximum height of six inches; minimus, a golden yellow flower which grows only three inches high, the yellow hoop petticoat of about six inches; and caniculata, the miniature polyantha narcissi, are admirable for the purpose

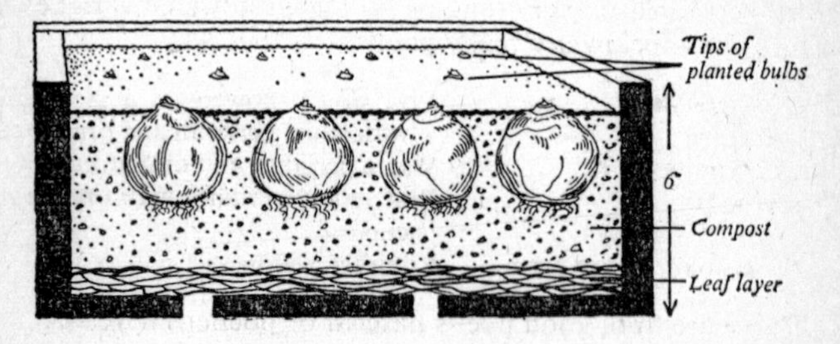

62. How to place bulbs in boxes.

Narcissi of all types are excellent when grown in pots for home decoration or in boxes for cutting. For this an early start should be made. A September potting or boxing of bulbs is excellent and the end of October should be looked upon as the last satisfactory date for potting. Elaborate soil mixtures are not required, and compost consisting of two parts loam, one part leafsoil or peat, and half a part of sand answers admirably. Pots six to eight inches in diameter are most suitable and in these are packed as many bulbs as will go in comfortably, with the bulb tips just showing through the soil after potting. They should be watered copiously, the pots stood together in a block and covered completely with a six-inch layer of leafsoil or peat, or, as an alternative, the pots can be buried in the ground so that they are covered with the same depth of soil. Here they should remain until growth is about an inch and a half above the pot and the ball of soil in the pot well permeated with roots, when they should be taken to a cold frame to be lightly covered with shading until the pallid tops have become green, when shading must be discontinued. The next step is to the cold greenhouse and after a few weeks of this to a warm greenhouse, if such exists, until finally they are given a temperature of 65° F. Treated in this manner, and if heating facilities permit, it is easy to have narcissi in flower from December until they can be cut out of doors. Some varieties force better than others, so I give a list below of suitable ones from all sections:

For November and December Flowering

PAPER WHITE
SOLID D'OR

Both of these are Polyanthus varieties.

For Gentle Forcing for Succession

KING ALFRED	CROESUS
GOLDEN HARVEST	FORTUNE
MAGNIFICENCE	HELIOS
REMBRANDT	BATH'S FLAME
JOHN FARQUHAR	MRS BARCLAY
SPRING GLORY	GERANIUM ORANGE CUP
CARLTON	

These should be potted early and by forcing a few each week a succession of them is easily maintained. All the above varieties are useful for growing in ornamental bowls in fibre. For this purpose prepared fibre should be procured and some coarse charcoal. A few sticks of this should be placed in the bottom of the bowl, followed by a layer of moistened fibre. The bulbs are then put into place as if they were being potted in soil and the fibre is packed tightly between the bulbs until all is quite firm. Bulbs growing in bowls should be kept uniformly moist and when water is required the fibre should be well watered by immersion. The bowls should then be put in a dark cool place until the shoots are an inch and a half long, when they should be taken out of darkness and the growing leaves gradually inured to light. Narcissi in bowls may be grown in a cool greenhouse or in a light living room, and both these and narcissi grown in pots should always be forced by easy stages. If narcissi are grown for cutting only, the bulbs can be packed into any boxes with a depth of six inches, brought on in easy stages and cut from the boxes.

Narcissi are delightful when naturalized in woodland and wild garden, where they should be planted as informally as possible. For this purpose offsets and single-nosed bulbs can be procured cheaply and all bulbs forced and used for cutting can afterwards be planted out in permanent positions. For this and all other purposes I have been able to give only a few of the many splendid varieties of narcissi, to which many novelties are being added yearly.

63. Bulbs in bowl.

Now to deal with hyacinths. The first of these to flower is the dainty fragrant Roman hyacinth, whose chaste white bells are always welcome. Cultivation is simple. To ensure Christmas flowering, bulbs should be potted during August, three bulbs being placed in a five-inch pot. The usual procedure of forcing by easy stages must be practised, and if the bulbs are slow great heat may be used in the last few weeks. It must be said, however, that the spikes are much finer if only gentle forcing is practised.

Miniature hyacinths known as cynthellas, which can be procured in several colours and whose delicate spikes are something like those of the Roman hyacinth, may also be had in flower at Christmas.

Named varieties of hyacinth are splendid for potting and for growing in bowls; the general directions given for growing narcissi in pots or bowls apply. Early potting is essential and it is important to remove them from beds of leafsoil and fibre before the buds, which are only partially protected by the foliage, become damaged. They form most effective beds for early spring display, but flower rather early, so that there is a big flowering gap, between these and bedding plants, put out at the end of May. For bedding they may be bought according to colour description a little more cheaply than the named varieties. Hyacinths are not good for naturalizing, and even in borders, where they sometimes exist for years, they do little more than produce a few weak spikes. However, I must admit a hankering for a few near the house, if only for fragrance, especially as they flower early. Even if the spikes are poor they have homeliness and an old-fashioned charm.

Below I give a selection of good varieties for potting and growing in bowls:

WHITE	L'Innocence
ROSY PINK	Princess Irene
SALMON PINK	Lady Derby
BRIGHT PINK	Queen of the Pinks
SCARLET	Jan Bos
	La Victoire
DARK BLUE	King of the Blues
	Marie
LIGHT BLUE	Blue Herald
	Dr Lieber
	Perle Brilliant
	Queen of the Blues
YELLOW	City of Haarlem
MAUVE	Lord Balfour

And now for tulips. These with their clear-cut elliptical outlines are always welcome. They have been cultivated for centuries, but like narcissi were greatly improved between the two World Wars, especially the late flowering sections. They are well adapted for forcing and can be grown and forced for house decoration in any drained receptacle, but are not at home in undrained bowls. They are, therefore, not usually grown in fibre like narcissi and hyacinths, although, in the hands of an expert, this is not impossible. They also lend themselves to culture in boxes for cutting, and for this purpose they can be packed in closely. There is an important early flowering section, the members of which are adapted for early forcing. They are equally at home in beds, although they are rather small, and, compared with the late flowering tulips, short on the stem. When forced they must be brought on by easy stages; this applies not only to this kind of tulip, but to all other tulips as well as the bulbs already dealt with. Potting follows the same general lines, and for indoor culture where room is precious, it is accepted that the bulbs may touch each other so that as many as possible can be accommodated in each pot.

The covering with fibre or some other substance is followed, as with all other bulbs for forcing, for it is important to build up a good root system before the top becomes too excited. With tulips, however, there is one important difference: they should never be allowed to become dry at any stage, or blindness will occur – i.e. the bud dies in the centre of the plant. Narcissi and hyacinths, which love moisture, and which will produce flowers when planted in water and stones, will withstand an occasional dry-out, but tulips usually suffer and sometimes go completely blind if allowed to become really dry only once. Below I give a selection of early flowering varieties:

BRILLIANT STAR	Scarlet
COULEUR DE CARDINAL	Crimson scarlet
DUCHESSE DE PARMA	Crimson and orange
IBIS	Deep pink with silvery edges
KEISERKROON	Bright red and golden yellow
PINK BEAUTY	Soft pink
PRINCE OF AUSTRIA	Orange scarlet
RISING SUN	Golden yellow
SUNBURNT	Chrome yellow
THOMAS MOORE	Rich orange
VERMILION BRILLIANT	Vermilion
YELLOW PRINCE	Golden yellow

In the same early flowering section there are double varieties splendidly adapted for bedding, as they withstand bad weather and last in flower for many weeks. I give a good selection below:

FIREBALL	Vivid orange scarlet
MARECHAL NEIL	Golden yellow shaded orange red
MURILLO	Creamy white and rose
YELLOW MURILLO	Pure yellow
PEACH BLOSSOM	Rosy pink
WILHELM CORDES	Beautiful orange

There is another section with varieties noted for their beauty known as May flowering or cottage tulips. Most of them are exceedingly good, and generally they may be mixed indiscriminately without colour clashing. A good selection follows:

ADRANE	Poppy red with bluish sheen
CARARA	Pure white
DIDO	Cherry red and orange salmon
DILLENBURG	Orange red with bronze edge
GOLDEN HARVEST	Golden yellow
INGLESCOMBE YELLOW	Primrose
LEMON QUEEN	Soft lemon yellow
LOUIS XIV	Rich purple, bronze and old gold
MRS JON SCHEEPERS	Clear yellow
MRS MOORE	Canary yellow
PRINCESS MARGARET ROSE	Rich yellow and orange red
MARJORIE BOWEN	Buff and salmon

The last section is that of the Darwin tulip, of which there are many good varieties. Generally these are tall, stiff, self-supporting, and good for cutting. Most of them force well and they are as excellent for growing in pots or boxes indoors as they are for bedding. All of them have the clean-cut statuesque beauty which makes them such a joy, and most of them have contrasting colours on the inside base which is attractive when the blooms open in sunshine. I have selected twelve of the best below:

AFTERGLOW	Soft apricot orange
ARISTOCRAT	Lilac rose
BLEU AIMABLE	Mauve and purple
CAMP FIRE	Blood red
CITY OF HAARLEM	Crimson scarlet
FARNCOMBE SANDERS	Rose red
GOLDEN AGE	Deep yellow
LA TULIPE NOIRE	Deep maroon
WILLIAM PITT	Deep scarlet
CLARA BUTT	Soft pink
YELLOW GIANT	Golden yellow
ZWANNENBURG	Pure white

In the last few years a new race has been bred which has the princely appearance of the Darwin tulip with the earliness of the early flowering varieties. At the moment of writing they are expensive – a state of affairs which cannot be altered until heavier stocks have been built up. The flowers of some varieties are very large, but without a trace of coarseness. Below I give a list of these:

AIRMAIL	Madder red with bluish sheen
AMBON	A superb yellow
BRIARCLIFF	Pillar box red
BRIDESMAID	Creamy yellow
DON JUAN	Brilliant scarlet
ELIZABETH ARDEN	Salmon and cherry
FIELD MARSHAL	Pale cream
FIERY CROSS	Cardinal red
GREY HUSSAR	Apricot
HAPPY DAYS	Rich pink on white
MENADO	Deep golden yellow
MODERN TIMES	Lavender
PACIFIC	Red overlaid with rose

All the above will force well and are excellent for pots. The descriptions given fail to do justice to the colours, which are unusually beautiful.

I could hardly leave this chapter without referring to tulip species which are excellent for a cold greenhouse. There are several worth growing in large pots or pans to introduce a little colour in early spring. While there are many which might be used in this way I give a short list below:

TULIPA CLUSIANA	White striped red
TULIPA ESCHLERI	Crimson scarlet shaded bronze
TULIPA KAUFMANNIANA	Carmine red on white ground

For those with a cold greenhouse who do not wish to use it as a forwarding place for other plants there are many dainty bulbous plants suitable for permanent pan culture. In winter and spring they might occupy the greenhouse, but in summer and autumn they could be placed out of doors. The following is a good list:

CHIONODOXA	In variety
ERYTHRONIUM	Mixed
MUSCARI	Heavenly blue
IXIAS	In variety
IRIS RETICULATA	In variety
SCILLA	In variety
TRITONIA	Prince of Orange
GALANTHUS (Snowdrop)	In variety
CROCUS	In variety
ANEMONE APENNINA	

Late Flowering Chrysanthemums

LATE flowering chrysanthemums belong to the same family as the early flowering chrysanthemums dealt with in Chapter 13, but, whereas good early varieties have slowly evolved to flower in late summer, the late ones have been bred to continue the flowering period from 1 October until January – and sometimes after. As we have already noted the chrysanthemum has been grown in this country for centuries and in the East for countless centuries, but we know little about its early culture and its origin. We do know, however, that after many vicissitudes it became popular some sixty years ago, a time which heralded the beginning of the new incurved and loose-headed varieties known then as Japanese – a name which most old growers will give up grudgingly, if at all.

Between the two World Wars many good varieties were distributed representing a number of types and sections, and some of these, and those which followed during the last few years, are found in most gardens where there is a greenhouse to shelter them. In almost every flower shop they are to be seen in a wonderful array of splendidly grown specimens, for a great market industry has grown up around them. The business man seeing these when going to and fro to the city envies them, and although he has a garden and greenhouse, generally sees that those in the shops are much better than his productions, and wonders how it is done. Really, it is quite simple if only a few simple rules are followed which automatically cut out starving and check.

Late flowering chrysanthemums, like their early flowering brethren, are propagated from cuttings. Suitable cuttings are of great importance. Some suppliers of chrysanthemums propagate only from selected stock – generally known as rested stock – secured by planting out rooted cuttings as soon as conditions permit in late spring, and by cutting back repeatedly; this effectively prevents the plants from flowering while refraining from any form of feeding. Few people are able to do this, but everyone can ensure that the cuttings selected are in a sound healthy condition. For this, all plants which have ceased to flower should be cut down to within six inches of the base to encourage the formation of fresh growth. The stools should not be neglected, but should be tended, and the greenhouse ventilated, just as if fresh young plants were there.

During the mid-winter period the greenhouse, or perhaps a heated frame, should be maintained at a night temperature of 45° F. It is an excellent plan, at this stage, to fumigate it with a good nicotine vaporizer every ten days or fortnight to keep down aphides.

Propagation should start early in January. Some persons find this very puzzling, for on the great majority of stools – as old plants are now called – there are several kinds of shoots. Some will be big and fleshy at the end of long stolons rooted already, and because of this and of their vigorous appearance many people are tempted to take them. Some shoots will be found growing from the stems and some will be neat fresh-looking shoots springing from the base. It is possible that a few plants will show all these, but generally the various types are found on individuals of these habits. The best type of cutting is the young fresh shoot about three inches long taken from the base. The fat vigorous fellows springing from a stolon are generally useless. These are called Irishman's cuttings. At first, with their rude growth, they are encouraging; later they refuse to grow, and become stunted and useless. On the other hand, stem cuttings sometimes persistently produce flower buds and make no real growth, while the unassuming basal cuttings usually develop with steady progress.

There are some varieties, however, which fail to give any basal cuttings, but instead produce a multitude on the lower stems. In such cases there is nothing to do but take the lowest of these and hope for the best. Whatever type of cutting is available must be free from pests, so look for trouble and if aphides or other pests lurk in the leaves, in spite of fumigation, then dip the cuttings bodily into a good nicotine insecticide before insertion.

As we have seen in Chapter 26 cuttings must be made firm after insertion – a pleasant task which is much easier to perform when good compost has been prepared. As this has been fully dealt with already I will not labour the point now. Suffice to say that the compost for the cuttings must be well drained, should not contain any artificial manure, and is of such consistency that good firming is possible.

For practical purposes a temperature of 50° F. is enough, as we have already noted, and though the provision of a propagating frame to check transpiration is of benefit in striking cuttings quickly it is not a necessity, as cuttings will strike in the ordinary atmosphere of the greenhouse, although a little more slowly. They will flag horribly, but only because they have no roots to counterbalance the moisture given off by the leaves – not because they are dry or need water. Do not, therefore, be kind to them – as you think – by sprinkling them with water daily while they have no roots, for this, if continued, leads to failure: the frequent application of water to unrooted cuttings brings basal decay and loss before the cuttings are able to form new roots to deal with the surfeit. It is, however, of benefit to spread newspaper over the cuttings to shade them from direct sunshine. The flagging period passes quickly and ten days after insertion you will notice flagging growing less; a few days later it ceases altogether and is followed by renewed growth shortly afterwards. At this stage most growers feel that the cuttings have hung about long enough and are anxious to make them grow quickly. Consequently they keep the greenhouse too close and perhaps give a little too much artificial heat. This is generally a mistake, for rarely, if ever, do chrysanthemums require a high temperature. Instead, every endeavour should be made to keep the rooted cuttings growing slowly and contentedly and developing stoutly as they grow.

From the propagating beds or boxes the rooted plants should be transferred to pots three inches in diameter, using John Innes Compost No. 2. When potting the soil should be finger tight firm – loose potting encourages soft foliage and shoots. The plants should never be encouraged to grow inches high; instead healthy lateral development commensurate with steady upright growth on a single stem should be looked for. For this reason, when giving the rooted cuttings their first pots do not crush them together rim to rim, but space the rims two or three inches apart, thus preventing plants from shading one another as their leaves grow longer and permitting air to circulate and light to enter.

While not in any way condoning the sin of over-watering, which is so harmful, it is important to observe that a chrysanthemum should never approach real dryness, for this not only leads to a loss of feeding roots, but if the practice of keeping plants on the dry side is systematically practised woody stems are encouraged, and woodiness is the last thing chrysanthemums require at this stage. It is true that later on wood on an early grown plant approaching the bud stage does require some hardening to perfect good blooms, but premature hardening restricts growth and automatically ensures toughened small growth which is incapable later on of producing fine clean blooms.

Unless spring is very late, after a few weeks' growth plants in three-inch pots will be all the better for being transferred to a cold frame, where, in a low temperature, atmospheric moisture is generally suitable. Cold nights may occur and for these the grower must be watchful. Ordinarily the solar heat trapped by day is sufficient to protect the plants, but if severe night frost threatens the frame will need some protection, usually most of all soon after dawn. As long as frost is just excluded the chrysanthemum will be quite happy and if not touched here and there by frost can be ventilated immediately the covers are removed. Should frost have entered the frame do not uncover it, but with a little ventilation allow the frost to pass away slowly. Quick thawing leads to dire results. Slow thawing and shading from direct sunshine will often save plants so tender that theoretically they should be destroyed.

Potting into six-inch pots should be timely. It is a job to do by degrees, not only because members of the same variety vary in rate of growth, but also because with so many varieties of differing growth habits it is impossible for them to be ready for potting at one time. This is fortunate, because few growers are able to deal with a large batch quickly, and if they all became ready together some would inevitably starve and become hard while waiting to be potted. At first the grower will have to verify his judgement by knocking out some of those which look most advanced and observing the condition of their roots. Chrysanthemums and most other plants need re-potting when the tips of white roots are piercing the ball all round. No one should wait until masses of fine white roots are wound inextricably round the ball, for by that time the plant has already experienced starvation, and, although it does not show signs of suffering, will hang fire for a long time after potting, while those potted on at the exact hour of need grow steadily onward. The grower, therefore, should select the most forward plants which, after a time, he will easily judge by growth appearance, irrespective of variety, and in this way he will be able to keep plants under control. John Innes Compost No. 3 with the turf loam broken up or chopped in rough pieces is good for potting. No one should allow that crippling pest, aphis, to infest chrysanthemums, because timely fumigation at intervals of a fortnight will eradicate it. Ventilate freely on every occasion and on good days remove the roof lights altogether.

At this stage in spring the grower realizes that space is valuable and that plants expanding as rapidly as the chrysanthemum take up much valuable room above and below. If any weeding out has to be done, the time of potting into six-inch pots is opportune, for it is foolish to pot more than can be comfortably handled and accommodated in frames and greenhouse.

Hardly will the last ones be potted into a six-inch pot than some of the first potted will need shifting into ten-inch pots. The soil for this potting should be John Innes Compost No. 3 with the turf loam in a very rough state. Before this final potting begins, some varieties which become top-heavy because of extensive growth will need a light stake, not for final support, but to keep them from bending and the stems from cracking until they are provided with stouter stakes later on. These should be long enough to support them, but short enough to be housed in the cold frame.

Final potting, in ten-inch pots, is a more lengthy proceeding than previous pottings. For this a rammer is needed – not to impact the soil into an impermeable mass through which water can pass with great difficulty and air barely enter, but to work the new soil firmly into the space between ball and pot and to make it firm enough to prevent rank growth while encouraging that of a thrifty nature. After potting the plants should be taken again to the cold frames, which, if necessary, should be raised by bricks at each corner to give enough head room to the rapidly growing plants.

There is always a little difficulty about this because well-grown plants are invariably ready to be potted before danger of frost has ceased, generally about 22 May; hence the necessity for raising frames on bricks or some other support to enable lights to be placed on in cold snaps. Some growers overcome this difficulty by deferring potting into the final ten-inch pots until all danger from frost has passed; this enables them to stand the big pots out of doors – a method with much risk of starvation which they obviate by feeding the plants, while they still remain in six-inch pots with a compound chrysanthemum

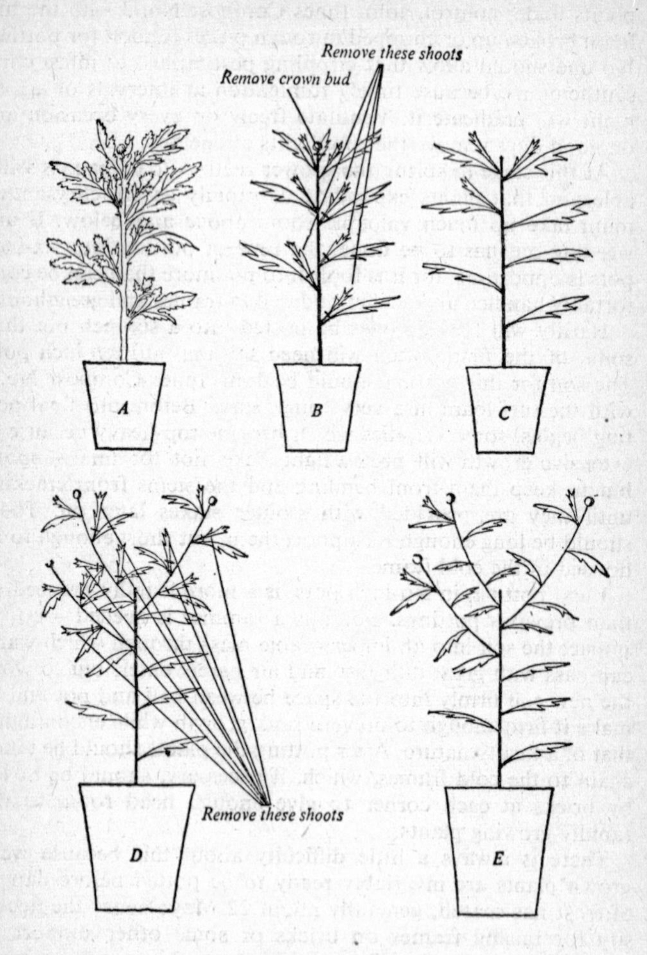

64. Stopping: (A) Chrysanthemum ready for first stopping and surplus shoot removal; (B) Diagram of the same plant before stopping and shoot removal; (C) After first stopping and shoot removal; (D) With first crown buds showing and ready for second stopping and surplus shoot removal; (E) After second stopping and surplus shoot removal.

manure. This works well in the hands of an expert. Those who attempt this, however, should remember that plant food given in this form is not instantly soluble, and, if it were, the plant could not utilize it instantaneously; applications of manure intended to prevent starvation should, therefore, be given several weeks before the risk appears to be present, so that when extra plant food is needed it is available in a partly assimilated form.

Ten-inch pots utilized for this potting have one drainage hole at the centre of the base and three at the side of the base. At this stage, and still more later, the chrysanthemum is a very thirsty plant and there is risk that if the usual drainage methods are adopted the plant will be overdrained. To overcome this and at the same time provide adequate surplus water disposal, place one large crock on the central hole and one large one over the side holes, and over these place some tufty loam, or if the compost is without much fibre a handful of leaves or strawy manure, all of which will prevent the drainage holes from becoming choked and provide a little plant food as gradual decay sets in. Again, for potting, the rammer will be needed. Potting must be firm, but no plant should be finished off with its surface soil puttied or plastered. This is the last potting, and now, having made the plants comfortable for the summer, we must look into the vexed question of stopping and disbudding.

In the minds of many stopping is looked upon as a prerequisite of flowering: no stopping, no flowering. This is far from the truth. Most chrysanthemums when left alone flower freely, but as there is no shoot restriction, blooms remain small and perhaps flower at the wrong time. The former can be remedied by shoot restriction and the latter by stopping the leader at a suitable time. Before we can go into this more deeply we must examine the general structure of the indoor chrysanthemum. When the plant is about eighteen inches high, and sometimes a little taller, it produces a bud at its tip. This bud has several shoots closely surrounding it, and below them, if the plant is healthy, a shoot springing from almost every leaf axil. At this stage all are about two inches long. The bud is known as the break bud. If the bud is removed and three of the topmost shoots are allowed to grow, all three will in time develop a bud in the centre. This is known as the first crown. The first crown bud also has shoots surrounding it and if all but one on each shoot are removed, and the three remaining shoots allowed to grow, these in time will produce buds. These are known as second crown buds. Shoots surrounding this bud also grow until finally they produce buds, but this time the shoot, instead of being surrounded by growth, is closely ringed by other buds, and these also appear down the stem from each leaf axil. This last bud is called the terminal bud because no more growth buds are produced.

Years ago a great number of large flowering chrysanthemums flowered on the second crown bud and a few on the terminal bud, but nowadays a large number of our best varieties flower on the first crown bud with no stopping or manipulation other than the restricting of the growths to three and the removing of all other lateral shoots below these three. It is possible to grow a large collection of large flowered (Japanese) to perfection without knowing anything about stopping by selecting varieties suitable for this treatment, and even if other varieties are used which need to be controlled by stopping this is by no means as intricate as it at first appears.

Some varieties which produce their first crown bud too early flower at the right time on the second crown, which means that one shoot is selected from each of the first three shoots after the removal of the first crown bud. Sometimes, however, the natural first crown is too early and the second crown too late, and to overcome this instead of waiting for the natural break the tip of the leader should be nipped out in mid April, thus forcing the three wanted shoots to appear some weeks earlier than they would naturally. Sometimes it is necessary to stop shoots resulting from the first stopping, because some varieties flower best on the second crown bud. A careful record should be kept of all stopping, including the removal of the break bud. This is very necessary because chrysanthemums vary in habit in different districts, and although nurserymen indicate the time of stopping of most varieties the dates they give can only be approximate. Notes taken during one season therefore become a material help during another.

Before the plants reach the stage when bud selecting is done they must be placed in their summer quarters. If possible the standing ground should be surfaced with ashes or gravel on which the plants should be stood in lines. As it is not desirable that they should root into ashes or gravel a slate or tile placed under each pot is a great help. Planks, of course, are ideal for this purpose. At each end of the rows posts should be erected, and between these wires should be strained to which the stakes supporting the chrysanthemums should be tied. Stout bamboo canes of a length suitable for adequate support should be thrust into each chrysanthemum pot and the main stem tied to them, loosely enough for stem expansion and tightly enough to prevent chafing or swaying with the wind. When long enough the shoots resulting from the removal of the break bud or a previous stopping should also be lightly looped, and this looping should be supplemented by other ties as the rate of growth demands. During this period, as extensive growth and large leaves make greater demands for moisture, much watering will be necessary, sometimes even in wet weather, because the extensive leaf cover effectively sheds water away from the pot below.

About mid-August the bud is 'taken'. This term, used whenever chrysanthemums are grown extensively, is misleading, for in reality the bud is selected, not taken. From this date buds should be selected to remain – all growths, irrespective of which crown they are being grown, and all side shoots or unwanted buds being pinched off or rubbed out with the finger and thumb. From this stage some extra food will be needed, and for this a peck of sheep or cow manure with a peck of soot placed in a 40-gallon tank, diluted by using two parts and one part liquid manure, is excellent. After a week or two of this an application weekly of a good compound manure made specially for chrysanthemums is very beneficial. Weeds sometimes appear in the pots and should be removed with great care, because now almost every square inch of soil in the pot is part of a complex root system and much damage can be done by carelessness.

So far we have dealt with the large flowered exhibition (Japanese) chrysanthemums. These are now sub-divided by the National Chrysanthemum Society into three sections – large flowered exhibition (Japanese), medium flowered exhibition (Japanese), and exhibition incurved varieties. These last have petals which curl inwards regularly, while those formerly called Japanese have petals incurving in tangled masses or reflexing regularly or irregularly. There are other sections equally important. The most important of these is the decorative section, which includes most of the very fine varieties one sees in florists' shops to-day. Some, but not all, of the large-flowered we have dealt with can be treated as decorative simply by leaving more shoots per plant, which to some extent determines the size of the blooms. Conversely, there are decorative varieties, which, if allowed to carry only three blooms, are as good as those generally used in this way, but there are some which are good only when grown as decoratives.

Decoratives are also loosely called bush chrysanthemums and in the early stages their culture is similar to that of the exhibition varieties. Up to the time of being placed in large pots there is nowadays nothing to choose between them, although formerly it was considered necessary to stop them when a few inches high and to do so repeatedly until mid-June. A moment's reflexion will expose the fallacy. Most people stop bush chrysanthemums to make them break, i.e. send out more shoots. In other chapters we have seen how the top of a plant intimately balances the root system. Because of this, it is obvious that the more a plant is sub-divided into innumerable shoots, increasing regularly with each stopping, the smaller must the stems and finally the blooms become. Because of this, no decorative or bush chrysanthemums, with one small exception, should be stopped or interfered with in any way until the natural break bud appears. By this time the single-stemmed plant has a stout stem sometimes nearly half an inch in diameter. From this thick stem laterals will emerge of great stoutness and, apart from other factors such as general health, treatment, feeding, etc., it follows that the size of the bloom is in direct proportion to the number of shoots allowed to remain. Thus growers may leave all or only half a dozen – it all depends on the size of bloom required – but by the no-stopping system twelve to eighteen and sometimes more good straight-stemmed blooms may confidently be expected.

All bush varieties should stand out in rows, staked like the exhibition varieties and watered, fed, and maintained in just the same way, but in August and September a well-grown decorative offers tremendous wind resistance, and therefore needs efficient support. When gales threaten a rough and ready method is to place a band of fillis string to enclose all shoots, thus making a kind of loose bundle; this, however, is unsatisfactory later on. A better plan is to loop each shoot separately to the central stake, tightly enough to keep the raffia or fillis string in tension and loosely enough to allow stem expansion. If you intend to allow all shoots to remain, it is a good plan to remove some of the lower shoots which grow immaturely, as blooms from these will be of little account. As decoratives carry a tremendous leaf area at the end of the summer they need abundant supplies of water. They should never be dry.

Business men away all day might, with advantage, stand each pot in a large saucer, and by watering the plant before leaving in the morning and filling the saucer with water ensure immunity from midday drought.

There are two other types which I have not specifically mentioned, the two forms of singles, large flowered and small flowered, and the anemone flowered. These do not make satisfactory bushes when unstopped and are treated differently. They should be struck in early January, stopped about the middle of February, and two shoots selected from the resulting break. These should be stopped again in mid-June and from the shoots then produced three are chosen. These types are interesting. The singles may have more than one row of ray florets and the disc florets form a glowing golden centre. The anemone flowered may have one or more rows of ray florets with shorter florets, generally of contrasting colours, forming a dense cushion in the centre.

When September arrives, with its cooling nights contrasting sharply with warm days, the plants must be housed. By this time chrysanthemums which have weathered the heat of summer have become used to low night temperatures and much cool atmospheric moisture. To house these in a greenhouse with a dry atmosphere and much heat would be folly, for there is no better way of predisposing to a bad attack of mildew. At first the grower should endeavour to reproduce, in the house, the conditions obtaining out of doors; the house should therefore be hosed down thoroughly and every portion of soil border and all unusable areas under stages and hot water pipes saturated. All doors and windows must be thrown wide open. Before the plants are brought in they should be sprayed thoroughly with a good colloidal sulphur spray to keep down mildew.

During the first few days in the greenhouse it is of service to damp down lightly with water, but this and all other sources of interior moisture should be discontinued gradually until the atmosphere of the house is as dry as it can be made. With days of decreasing light, damp is the great enemy, and to combat this not a drop of water should be spilled unnecessarily. Although no plant should suffer from want of water it is equally important that no plant should be watered before it is dry and that no water should be wasted in the process. Very large blooms will need nearly six weeks to develop fully and will sometimes keep in good condition for several weeks after. As chrysanthemums are not really happy in a very dry atmosphere a little atmospheric moisture must always be present, but this is provided almost automatically by the water which seeps away from the pots when watering. At the housing stage it is an excellent plan to fumigate with a good nicotine fumigant, even though no trace of aphides can be seen. Generally by the time aphides are noticed it is too late to prevent the dire results of an attack, for in autumn it is not the leaves which are attacked but the blooms, and these insects can remain hidden safely for many days until one day a dirty-looking bloom betrays their presence. Regular careful fumigation is a good insurance. Should severe frost occur – the first heavy November frosts always seem to synchronize with the chrysanthemum flowering – it is unwise to attempt to hold the temperature at a high level. Ordinarily for developing and flowering periods 45° – 50° F. with a little ventilation is ideal, but on very cold nights as long as frost can be kept out the grower should feel content. This is much better than causing an excessively dry atmosphere in an attempt to equalize the temperature by hard firing and overheated hot water pipes.

The chrysanthemum is not troubled greatly by pests, but sometimes earwigs attack the buds. These are easily kept at bay during the summer and early autumn by spraying regularly with D.D.T., and can be trapped by tying to the plants pieces of bean haulm or anything hollow. In these the pests hide by day and can easily be shaken out and destroyed.

The grower who begins with clean stock and who practises good culture has little to fear from other pests which do not readily attack the healthy. However, aphides, which at certain seasons will attack almost any plant, sometimes appear in considerable numbers about the end of May. They may be easily destroyed by a spraying with H.E.T.P., one of the substitutes for nicotine, which is more deadly and which seems to act as a tonic to the plants, for instead of looking a little dejected after spraying, as most plants do, they appear much fresher and more alert. To catch successive broods of these pests spray regularly at weekly intervals. Aphides rarely attack after mid July, but are likely to attack again when the chrysanthemums are housed. H.E.T.P. is highly concentrated; it is imperative therefore that measurements be accurate. A little added for luck when mixing might easily spell disaster.

The capsid bug sometimes appears during the summer. Its presence is easily betrayed by distortion of the upper growth and by yellowing irregular patches. Fortunately it is easily controlled by dusting the growing tips and upper leaves with D.D.T. powder occasionally.

During the last few years a pest from America has given a little trouble. It is called the chrysanthemum midge. It is a small brownish fly whose grubs devour plant tissues and whose presence can be detected by reddish brown galls. It breeds and

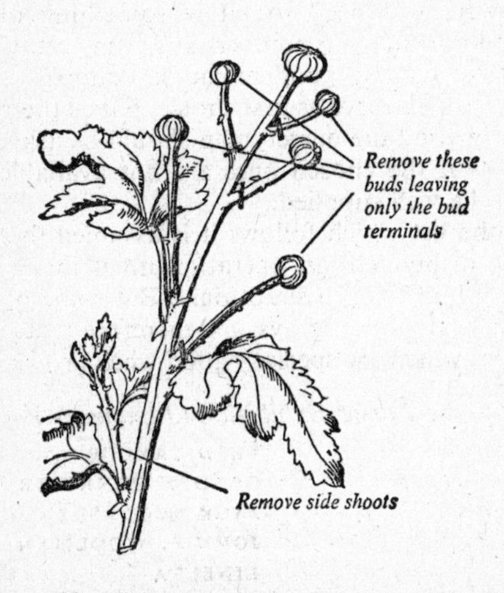

65. Disbudding a chrysanthemum.

destroys leaves at any season. It can be controlled by spraying twice weekly with H.E.T.P., but the only effective way of dealing with this pest is to destroy all infected stock by fire.

Of diseases I have already mentioned mildew, which can attack at any season but rarely does so. It can be controlled by spraying with a good colloidal sulphur spray which, in areas where mildew is prevalent. It rarely appears until the cooler nights of late summer, but, if neglected then and afterwards when the chrysanthemums are housed, much good foliage will be lost and the blooms will be poor in consequence. At the first sign of mildew in summer, spraying with the sulphur solution should begin and be repeated at weekly intervals.

My readers will remember that it is most important not to house infested plants. Years ago, when diseases were little understood and we heard much less of them, the fine old gardeners of the period controlled disease by the ruthless and immediate destruction of the first infected plant, and not, as the tendency is to-day, by making a museum piece of it. This old-fashioned plan had much to commend it and if carried out with common sense, combined with preventive spraying, is a means of retaining plant health.

Most growers will need to know something of varieties. These abound now in great numbers and many attractive sets of varieties almost equally good might be compiled. Of these I have selected lists to serve as first choice, but as there are others almost equally good the nurseryman should be asked to supply other varieties if the chosen ones are not available. In either case you will be well supplied.

In giving the list which follows it is assumed that most varieties will be disbudded, an operation involving the retention of one central bud to each shoot only. But some people prefer chrysanthemums in loose sprays, and therefore I have included a list of varieties which are specially good when grown in this way.

Twenty-four Large Exhibition (Japanese) Varieties

JESSIE HABGOOD
SHIRLEY CHAMPION
ALFRED SIMPSON
BERT WEBB
JAFFA
SHIRLEY CHESTNUT
SHIRLEY DESIRE
SHIRLEY TRIUMPH
BERTRAM JONES
D. M. POCOCK.
EDITH WOOLMAN
FRED BAKER
FRED TAYLOR
GOLDEN HENRY TRUEMAN
JACK MCGLASHEN
JOHN F. WOOLMAN
LINELLA
MAGNOLIA
MAJESTIC
POCKET'S MAROON
PRIMROSE CANDEUR
RED MAJESTIC
RISE OF DAY
SHIRLEY MASTERPIECE

Twelve Medium Exhibition (Japanese) Varieties

HYACINTH
LEONARD SHOESMITH
MISS SHIRLEY KEMBER
PATRIA
SHEILA PARKINSON
APRICOT ELEGANCE
HAROLD ALSTON
CRIMSON MONA DAVIS
ELEGANCE
MONA DAVIS
SALMON STRAUSS
WHITE MONA DAVIS

Twelve Exhibition Incurved Varieties

ANNIE CURRY	MILTON GRAY
PINK CURRY	MRS F. JUDSON
CAPTAIN KETTLE	ONDINE
CHAS. HOPKINSON	PROGRESS
GOLDEN CURRY	W. J. HILL
LILAC TIME	WOLVERINE

Twenty-four Decorative Varieties to be Disbudded

APRICOT LOVELINESS	SALMON CRENSA
BALCOMBE PERFECTION	SAY EDGAR
CONSTANCE BAKER	WHITE AVONDALE
CREAM LADY	YELLOW ACE
CRENSA	BALCOMBE GIANT
ENID GOFFE	GOLDEN GLOBE
HARRY MORRIS	GOLDILOCKS
LATE DELIGHT	MABEL CROW
LILAC LOVELINESS	MAY SHOESMITH
LOVELINESS	SALMON LOVELINESS
RED CRENSA	WHITE LOVELINESS
ROYAL CRENSA	WORTHING GOLD

Twelve Decorative Varieties to be grown in Sprays not Disbudded

PETER RAMSEY	MARKET RED
BRONZE MOLLY NICHOLSON	MAY WALLACE
CRIMSON VELVET	NORAH BEVES
EVENTIDE	OCTOBER RED
GOLDEN PATTISON	OLDLAND KING
GOLDEN PRIDE	FIRE GLOW

Twelve Single Varieties to be Disbudded

BETTY WOOLMAN	FANTASY
SATAN	LISA
BROADACRE	MARGARET LEMON
CAROLINE	PETER ROBINSON
CRIMSON CROWN	SHIRLEY SUNRISE
DESERT SONG	YELLOW CLEONE

Six Anemone Flowered Varieties

ANNIE BAXTER	CALEB COX
BEAUTIFUL LADY	CHARLOTTE
GRACELAND	NORMA

· 29 ·

Geraniums (Zonal Pelargonums)

THIS chapter is either forty years too late or a few years too early, but I have a feeling that it is not much too early, because the geranium must soon come into its own again. In Victorian times it was a bedding plant in almost every garden, large or small – in many cases sadly ill-treated. It was common to see flaming scarlet varieties placed against bright red brick walls or swamped in a garden clothed in green foliage in which they were utterly incongruous. It is not happy in any garden which is typically English, for our green mantle of foliage is too much for it; but in formal gardens of white stone, large or small, or on terraces of the Italian type, there is still no plant to beat it for beauty, effectiveness, or continuous flowering during our short season. It has other advantages which I will deal with later.

As we have noted from Chapter 26 the geranium is propagated from cuttings. It is a very obliging plant and can be propagated at any time of the year, but cuttings taken in August or September strike more readily and form a good foundation of roots before the winter season. It is usual to place these rooted cuttings into three-inch pots and afterwards, if there is room in the greenhouse, into pots five or six inches in diameter, in which they make good growth before being planted out at the end of May or early in June. The geranium will stand low temperature but cannot withstand frost. It will, however, endure the greatest heat with impunity and does not complain if it is denied water occasionally; indeed when it is not treated too well it usually flowers best. Rooted cuttings put into three-inch pots will go through the winter comfortably in any greenhouse from which frost can just be excluded, and such plants need little water.

Throughout this book I have stressed the necessity for adequate water supplies for pot plants, but the geranium is an exception. It is a fleshy-stemmed plant which has natural reserves of water, and therefore to give water when it is not needed is merely to invite decay and loss in the winter. The general rule should be that if the temperature is between 50° and 55° F. it should be watered very cautiously, but with temeratures below that, and those in cold weather which drop ometimes nearly to freezing point, little if any water is required or several months; in fact it does the plant good to become ry in the dark days of winter and in low temperatures.

In addition to raising young stock, many people are conerned with preserving the stock they already have, for old lants do well and make a useful addition to next year's bed. ll geraniums which have been used for bedding and are lifted hen the danger of frost arrives, or which have perhaps been lightly cut by frost, should be lifted, their main shoots cut ack half way down, and used as cuttings, if necessary, and the lants themslves potted into the pots of the smallest diameter nto which the roots can be forced. This kind of potting needs ttle soil as the grower is more concerned in saving the geranım until spring than in making a perfect plant. If room exists uch plants can be potted on into larger pots when they have nade sufficient new roots, but if no such room is available they an remain starved in the small pots and take little harm if, in pring, they can be given a little more generous treatment.

An adaptation of this plan is to push three or four old cutack plants into the smallest pot which accommodates the oots, and in spring pot them without division in a six-inch pot r separately into the smallest pot which contains the roots. Iowever, if room is very scarce numbers can be packed into oxes about five inches deep in enough soil to cover the roots nd these should be put in a greenhouse from which frost can ıst be excluded. The ideal night temperature for geraniums uring the winter months is 40° – 45° F. with a little ventilation nd a rise of 5° – 10° F. by day. In such temperatures little ater is needed.

I know that many people's greenhouses have to be kept at a emperature which suits some other occupants – perhaps primlas – and that the geranium will have to take pot luck. Fornately such treatment does not inconvenience it greatly. If ne house is too warm a little more growth is made and if it is oo cool it ceases to grow but remains healthy, and, in the verage greenhouse, it will probably have to go, packed in oxes or pots, on a shelf where it is not too much in evidence.

The saving of geraniums in a greenhouse, when one is availble, is not difficult, and providing the plants get through the orst of the winter months and begin to grow again, propagaion of shoots can go on merrily and quite a big stock be worked up. It is, however, much more difficult to house and protec geraniums during the winter when no slightly heated green house is available. The geranium is very tenacious of life an because of this can be kept a long time in bad conditions. Man people manage to keep them during the winter in cold frames

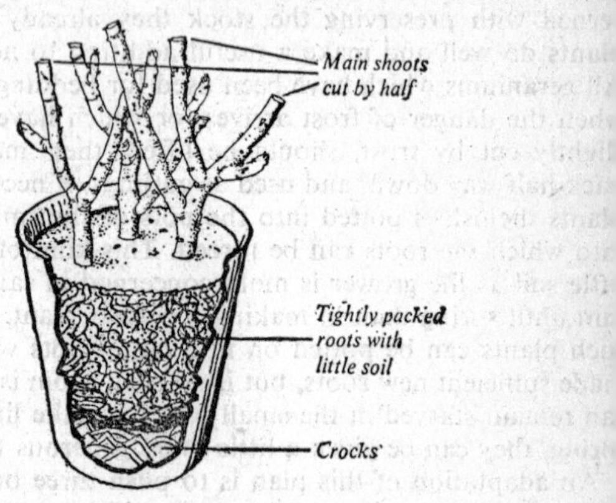

66. Old geraniums potted for the winter.

These are kept dry and protected from bad weather only i severe frost or very heavy rain. Ventilation is given wheneve possible and there is no coddling of any kind. With this methoc however, it is a good plan in frosty weather to close the roc lights of the frames early to trap, for the night, as much sola heat as possible. At night the frame should be protected wit litter, straw, mats, hessian, or any material handy, includin peat and soil on the top of the frame. The cold frame is not a ideal place as generally it has too much atmospheric moisture but people with spare upper rooms often manage to stan their geraniums on window sills and sometimes on floors wit saucers underneath the pot, and by withholding water, excep very occasionally, manage to keep them alive until bedding-ou time again arrives. Fortunately, as the geranium is a long suffering plant, the long semi-bleached shoots, a picture o misery when emerging from their winter quarters, soon cove themselves with fresh green leaves and make magnificent plant

I have know people without attic spare rooms who have su cessfully kept their geraniums from one season to the next tie in bundles in a cool cellar. This sounds impossible, but under certain conditions it is not. The geraniums before being taken in are put on the ground to wilt and to lose as many as possible of their leaves before being stored. They are then tied into small bundles and suspended from the roof with the roots uppermost. During the first few weeks after being stored in this way they lose most of their leaves and look a very sorry sight – the plant merely has a green tip showing above bleached stems. At the end of the season they come out looking washed-out and pallid with little sign of fresh growth, but by the use of a cold frame in April they quickly can be induced to start again and can then be made more shapely by cutting back. Some of the best shoots can be used for making cuttings, for almost any geranium shoot will root if handled properly and not given too much water.

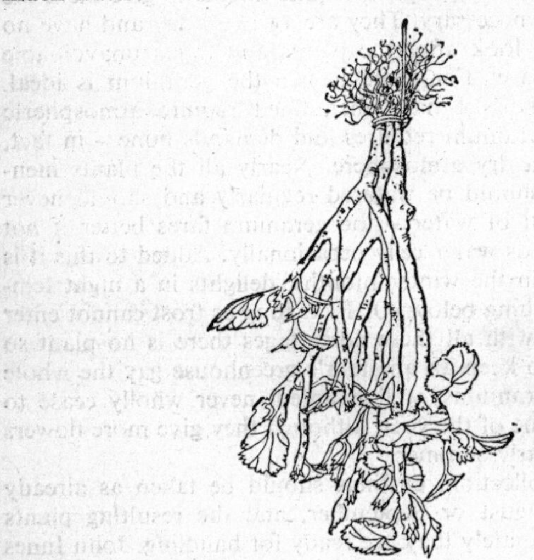

67. Old geraniums tied and hung for the winter.

Geraniums are known to live in cottage windows for generations and in the west of England one can see them tied to latticed frames proudly displayed in many windows. Unless it is given too much water, which, in the winter months, is slow death to them, the geranium will exist in nearly all conditions, short of being subjected to severe frosts – a point worth noting at any time.

In addition to the geraniums used for bedding there are many other varieties. A couple of generations ago there were many cherished varieties in an immense colour range, which did not include blue and yellow, although at one time there were a few dirty mauve sorts to be seen. In the height of the geranium craze there were several nurserymen who devoted their efforts entirely to the raising of new geraniums and their dispatch to customers, not for bedding, but for greenhouse decoration, and it is for this that the plant will return. Perhaps the time is not very far away.

Throughout this book I have mentioned many plants suitable for the cool greenhouse and given an account of their culture, but I know that many people are quite unable to give them the attention that is necessary. They are away all day and have no one at home to look after the plants and much unavoidable neglect takes place. For these people the geranium is ideal. Most of the plants I have mentioned require atmospheric moisture: the geranium requires and demands none – in fact, it flourishes in a dry atmosphere. Nearly all the plants mentioned already should be watered regularly and should never suffer from want of water – the geranium fares better if not watered and needs water only occasionally. Added to this it is a plant which, in the winter months, delights in a night temperature of anything below 40° F. as long as frost cannot enter the house, and with all these advantages there is no plant so well equipped to keep an amateur's greenhouse gay the whole year round. Geraniums, well handled, never wholly cease to flower at any time of the year, although they give more flowers in spring and early summer.

To raise a collection, cuttings should be taken as already described in August or September, and the resulting plants potted on immediately they are ready for handling. John Innes Compost No. 2 is excellent and they require a dry atmosphere. If the geranium is to have the whole house the plants should be grown on until they require shifting into six inch pots, again in John Innes Compost No. 2. Potting, in this case, must be firmer than for the majority of soft-wooded plants, as the intention is to build up vigorous hard growth capable of giving many flowers during the autumn, winter, and spring months.

As soon as weather permits, at the end of May, the geran-

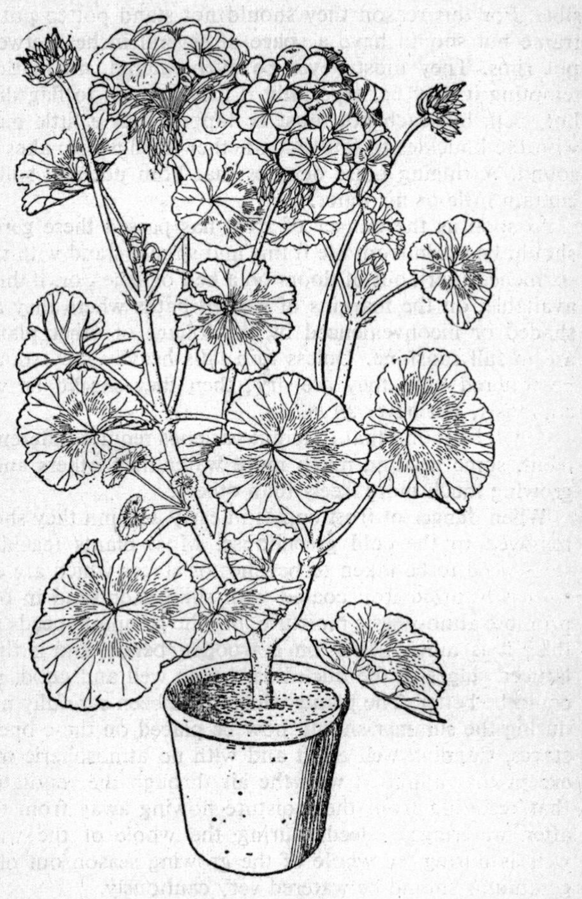

68. Geranium in pot.

iums, in their six-inch pots, should go out into cold frames. Before this stage they should have been stopped by pinching out the tip and now must be induced to grow as bushily as possible. For this reason they should not stand pot to pot in the frame but should have a space of several inches between the pot rims. They must never be over-watered, no matter how tempting it may be, especially if they happen to flag during a hot spell, but each pot must be tapped with a little mallet or with the knuckles to find out whether it rings or makes a dead sound. A ringing noise denotes that both pot and soil inside contain little or no water.

As soon as the danger of frost has passed these geraniums should be taken from the frame and should stand with the pots six inches apart, out of doors on a bed of ashes, or, if this is not available, on the margins of garden paths where they are not shaded or inconvenienced by the foliage of other plants and are in full sunshine. Unless rain falls heavily they should not be watered until they are dry; then they should be watered copiously, but never *en masse*.

It will be found that different varieties require different treatment, some needing much more water than others and some growing much more freely than others.

When danger of frost comes in early autumn they should be removed to the cold greenhouse. Most plants reaching this stage need to be taken to benches or stages which are covered with galvanized iron coated with shingle or sand in order to promote atmospheric moisture, but the geranium needs none of this; it is much better on a wooden bench, and if there are latticed stages of the duck-board type well and good, nothing could be better. The plants which have been carefully nurtured during the summer should now be placed on these open-work stages, standing well apart and with no atmospheric moisture except that admitted with the air through the ventilators and that resulting from the moisture flowing away from the pots after watering; indeed, during the whole of the winter as well as during the whole of the growing season out of doors, geraniums should be watered very cautiously.

In the spring and summer season geranium buds on plants intended for winter flowering should be picked off as they appear, but after the plants have been housed a fortnight or so all buds developing should be allowed to remain and in a month or six weeks every plant will be ablaze. With a little care in watering and with due regard to the possibilities of good ventilation, without cutting draughts, geraniums can be coaxed into bloom during the whole of the dead months and in spring they will spring into a riot of bloom which will continue most of the summer. When summer again returns these old plants can be potted up, if it is thought desirable, into pots eight or nine inches in diameter and stood out of doors during the summer to make strong specimens for flowering indoors in the winter.

There are few flowers for the amateur which give such good returns. It is true that geraniums are not very effective as cut flowers, except for very low vases on the dinner table or for special occasions, but they more than make up for this with the amount of bloom they give continuously for such a long period in the greenhouse itself.

Geraniums can be used for clothing greenhouse pillars, where they will grow twenty to thirty feet in height if required. They are very effective for clothing bare greenhouse walls, which, when well wired to receive them, can soon be covered in flaming colours. For filling fancy vases out of doors in the summer, or furnishing large pots or pans with masses of colour which can be taken to room or conservatory, they have no equal.

I do not know how long geraniums would live if left alone in good conditions. It is known, however, that in countries where frost is not sufficient to kill them geraniums form great bushes and grow for years. With development they become soft-wooded flowering shrubs, and although few people have a greenhouse to allow them to develop thus, some idea of their capabilities can be seen when they are planted against wall or pillar. I can truthfully say that I have never known a geranium die from old age.

The geranium has one fault – it is a well-known carrier of disease, even though it does not always show disease symptoms and is apparently not affected itself. It is one of the chief carriers of the spotted wilt of tomatoes which affects so many greenhouse plants, and because of this all discoloured or yellowing leaves should be removed immediately they are noticed and burnt.

Generally, and for the reasons I have already stated, the geranium is far happier with a house to itself than in a mixed house. A mixed house demands a good deal of attention, and for those who are unable to spend much time in the greenhouse I heartily recommend it, for it will give a rich reward in brilliant and beautiful blooms.

Below will be found a selection of good varieties which are worth trying:

Zonal Pelargonums (*Geraniums*)

ASTRACHAN	Dark crimson
DR OGIER	Fiery garnet
FRAICHEUR	White, edged rosy crimson
F. V. RASPAIL	Scarlet
KING OF DENMARK	Salmon
LADY ILCHESTER	Pale satiny rose
LAVE	Brilliant orange scarlet
MLLE. MEINDRE	Salmon pink
PINK F. V. RASPAIL	Soft pink
RYECROFT WHITE	
SCARLET KING OF DENMARK	Fine scarlet
THE SPEAKER	Rich fiery salmon

In addition to the geraniums we know, in reality zonal pelargonums, whose leaves are marked with a zone or band of a dark green or dark brown which contrasts sharply with the green of the foliage, there are other varieties used for bedding with silver or gold foliage or a combination of many colours, and some with three zones called tricolours. We are not so concerned with these now, as they are purely bedding varieties, but even with these it should be remembered that, as with the greenhouse varieties, any type of geranium is far better in a bed by itself than mixed with other occupants of the border or merged into some bedding scheme. Some of the ribbon borders in our forefathers' time, which had a row of geraniums, a row of marguerites, and a row of calceolarias, finished off with a thin streak of blue lobelia, would not appeal to us nowadays, but geraniums boldly bedded by themselves with no other plant surrounding them, provided there are no local incongruities, are still excellent bedding plants.

Varieties known as ivy leaved geraniums are also good bedding plants. Their foliage is recumbent and droops if given a chance. Their leaves are shaped like ivy leaves and their stems are somewhat brittle. They are excellent for furnishing large tubs, vases, or hanging baskets, and clothe beds effectively if pegged down to cover all the ground. There are two good varieties now in general use, Souvenir de Charles Turner, soft pink, and Galilee, bright cerise scarlet.

· 30 ·

Annuals in the Greenhouse

THIS chapter is almost an extra. It is occasioned by the thought that there are many people who, for various reasons, would be unable to utilize the greenhouse in many ways I have suggested, and to them annuals flowering in pots in the greenhouse are a great joy. It will not be a long chapter because cultural methods are so simple that there is little to say now that I have already written a chapter on annuals generally.

There are two main methods: sowing in the autumn, which usually involves some potting, or sowing, in the spring, direct into the flowering pots, which is probably the method most people will employ. For an autumn sowing the procedure is generally to sow a few seeds direct into three-inch pots in cold frames. The time varies with the plant, but with most late September or early October is the best time. Exceptions to this are salpiglossis, lobelias, and antirrhinums, all of which are better if sown in July. Clarkias and godetias give their best when sown in August, but all can be sown at one time if necessary and brought through the winter in a greenhouse from which frost can just be excluded.

The most magnificent annual grown under glass is the salpiglossis. The somewhat flimsy plant we know when it grows out of doors changes into a fine upstanding one of much strength and vigour. It seems almost a miracle. To achieve this three or four seeds should be sown in the centre of a three-inch pot filled with John Innes Compost No. 1, about mid-July. The seed pots should be placed in a cold frame shaded from direct sunshine. Germination is rapid, and as soon as the size of the seedlings permits, they should be thinned out so that one only remains in each pot. After germination the protecting lights should be removed and the seedlings encouraged to grow as sturdily as possible.

When sown in the open or under glass in the spring for bedding, salpiglossis seedlings always look very fragile, but in a cold frame, as autumn approaches, they look very different, for the stout sturdy foliage is almost a stiff rosette of green, so vigorously do they grow. They are deceptive in other ways too, for while they are quite tiny they develop a stout root system which makes potting on quickly imperative, or they will be checked and ruined even though they possess little top.

Salpiglossis hates root disturbance and for this reason intermediate potting must be forgotten; instead they should be shifted direct into pots eight inches in diameter in John Innes Compost No. 2. The cold frame which has accommodated them admirably since sowing will now be too cold, so a place under glass should be sought with a night temperature of 50°–55° F. After potting they should be well watered, but from this stage watering should be very cautiously performed – no plant being watered at any time unless its soil is really dry. Even though

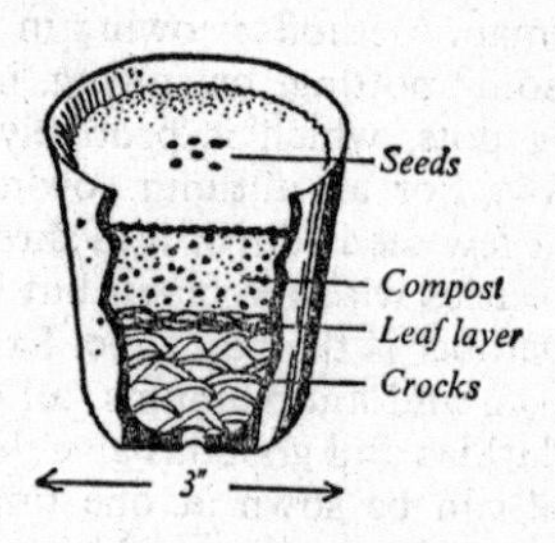

69. Seed sowing: Salpiglossis in pot for transplanting later. Seedlings to be thinned to one.

they do very well little top growth will be made, but the rosette of leaves will thicken, become stouter, and finally, in response to the urge of a vast root system, which until this stage has seemed disproportionately large compared with the top, begin to grow rapidly. Top growth will now be very rapid and staking will be necessary. Half measures are useless, for the plants are likely to be very tall. Stakes six to eight feet in height will be required, and nothing is better for this than good hazel stakes. Much head room will be needed and some of the tallest may have to stand on the floor. Do not imagine that this means a gawky unmanageable legginess – far from it, for from a stout central stem the plants will branch out laterally from the pot upwards.

In April some extra food will be needed; liquid manure

should be given and to supplement it – for salpiglossis is a great feeder – a weekly top dressing of a good approved compound manure is an advantage. Grown in this way blooms will be nearly as large as a gloxinia, with all their velvety richness, and borne in succession from April to August and perhaps later. It is well worth giving up one's greenhouse for the whole winter to have an array of colours such as these, which are rarely seen together in such a galaxy. Occasionally they need to be tied to stakes, and this reveals the plant's only handicap – it is sticky to handle. But after all this is a mild handicap set against so much beauty.

Another plant which often appears miserably bedraggled in the border is Leptosyne maritima. Under glass it is a revelation. Sow the seed in August in a cold frame in three-inch pots and keep it in the cold frame until frost threatens. Pot on as it becomes necessary and reinforce the soil liberally with a five-inch potful of hoof and horn meal ground coarsely. Finally pot each specimen into a twelve-inch pot and cultivate in the cool greenhouse throughout. You will be amazed. The straggly plant of the border becomes a column of handsome foliage six feet high, surmounted and smothered with large dahlia-like blooms on two-foot stems budding in endless profusion and in a richness of yellow colouring which is rarely seen. It will need much additional food and should be treated liberally both with liquid manure and with compound food, and to reward you these plants will continue to flower for months.

Then we have lobelia which gives blue shades superior to any in the garden. However, it is a mismanaged plant which often, in our borders, is merely a line of faint blue edging. Sown in July and kept growing in a cold frame a single plant will often make a specimen completely smothered in blue a foot across. Badly-grown plants in a thin long line are pathetically inadequate – lobelia needs splashing about in bold groups in both border and greenhouse. Single plants only should be pricked out in three-inch pots of John Innes Compost No. 1, potted into five-inch pots with John Innes Compost No. 2 when ready, and taken to the protection of the cool greenhouse only when severe frost makes it imperative.

There are many shades, the dark blue so often used for edging being the least impressive. Bright blue and Cambridge blue are two of the best varieties, and are both well adapted for greenhouse culture.

O

Plants like those I have mentioned will sometimes flower for many months if fed regularly.

Trailing lobelia is also a miserable wisp of growth flecked with blue if treated badly. Sow it also in July and grow on steadily in a cold frame, housing it only in times of danger from frost. When spring comes pot it on and place it on a shelf and let it hang. Fed well it will last for many months, flowering profusely.

And there are others – multitudes we have gathered together from all parts of the world and condemn to quick death in our short-summered land when we make them annuals flowering briefly out of doors. Given a long season of growth they are amazing. Clarkia elegans in all its many varieties is superb from an August sowing. Sow it in pots, and single to one when large enough. Grow steadily in a cold frame until frost comes, then accommodate it in a greenhouse from which frost can be excluded. Pot it on gradually, without stopping any growth, into a twelve-inch pot, and behold in April and for many weeks after a six-foot column of bloom. A tall stake will be needed for plants of this length and the shoots must be laced in enough to hold them upright.

Grown in the same way tall godetias also flourish. They grow even more vigorously than the clarkia. Their treatment is similar and they require even more food. They flower later than the clarkia and sometimes become much taller. They must have plenty of food and must never be dry. Good varieties are double shell pink and double cherry red.

South African plants which rarely are seen at their best are nemesias. Sown out of doors in spring they are quick growing and often come into flower before a sufficient framework of growth has been made. From a September sowing they are superb. Possibly this is because the cool winter conditions approximate to those of their mountain home in South Africa – cool, moist, and with a temperature which just keeps above frost level. Sow them in three-inch pots as you would the others I have mentioned. Thin out to one and pot on when necessary into six-inch pots. When frost threatens take them inside but keep the night temperature above 32° F. and below 40°F. if possible. Under this treatment they will become thick hefty plants which begin to flower in April and continue for many months. All varieties can be treated in this way, but the following is a good collection of striking varieties:

LARGE FLOWERED WHITE	LARGE FLOWERED BLUE
PALE YELLOW	HYBRID AURORA
RICH ORANGE	TWILIGHT
SCARLET	BLUE GEM
CRIMSON	FIRE KING
ROSE PINK	

All members of the tobacco family, Nicotiana, flower freely rom enormous branched plants when grown in this way. Seeds hould be sown in August and the resulting seedlings thinned to one in each three-inch pot. Pot on as required, using hoof and

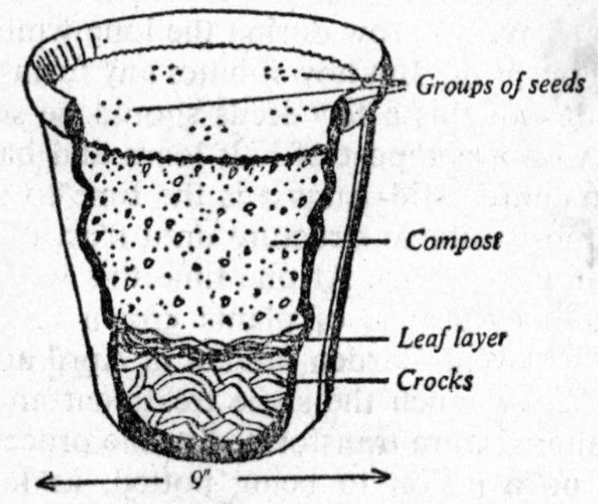

70. Sowing seeds in their permanent stations in pots. Each group of seedlings to be thinned to one.

orn meal in the final potting. They must be kept cool throughut until, when they are flowering in a ten-inch pot, their manyranched stems will be superbly fragrant. For their perfume, tand them in hall or porch when they are in flower and enjoy hem thoroughly.

Another plant which is almost transformed when grown in arge pots from an autumn sowing is the annual chrysanthemum. From an August sowing in a small pot placed in a cold ame seedlings result from which, if they are potted on regurly as they require it, until they finally reach ten-inch pots, lants of astounding size and beauty result. So large do they ecome that a few plants only suffice to fill a large corner of the eenhouse with bloom for a considerable time. Chrysanthemum carinatum Burridgeanum and carinatum atrococcinium ake a wonderful show when grown in this way.

Sweet scabious, if given the long season of growth which an

August sowing allows them, also grow to giant size and yiel
an enormous quantity of long-stemmed blooms. Grown in th
same way as the chrysanthemum they form dense bushes ofte
six feet or more in height. A few only are needed, but the fe
are well worth while.

The homely calendula in all its variety is another plan
which more growing-time transforms. A September sowing i
best for this and if grown on progressively without being al
lowed to suffer it becomes a veritable sub shrub. Nothing les
than a ten-inch pot suits this attractive plant.

Although it never attains large proportions, mignonette i
happier if allowed to grow during the long winter months tha
when sown in spring. But how it hates any form of root disturb
ance! Because of this a few seeds should be sown in six-inc
pots filled with a compost of half loam and half well-decaye
farmyard manure. Mid-August is the time to sow and a coo
frame the most suitable structure until frost threatens, when
cold greenhouse suffices. At one time this was a great mark
favourite and thousands of plants grown in this simple wa
were sent to Covent Garden market in April and May.

Stocks require much the same treatment and these, usuall
grown as annuals, are transformed in the process. However, a
they have no aversion to being potted, as long as they ar
handled with care, the seeds can be sown in small pots durin
August, the resulting seedlings reduced to one and potted o
successively until eight- or nine-inch pots are reached. Like th
mignonette, compost of loam and well-decayed manure in equ
parts suits them admirably. Under this treatment any membe
of the giant perfection annual section are liable to grow thre
to four feet high with beautifully perfumed and lengthy flow
spikes borne in great profusion in April and May. East Lothia
stocks, which have a bushier habit of growth and flower late
should be sown in July. They give spikes of great beauty in th
spring, but are not quite so spectacular as the Perfection famil
In addition to rich potting soil, stocks need much addition
plant food, and liquid manures should be given freely at eac
watering, and a top dressing of an approved compound fertiliz
weekly from the time a good root system has been formed.

A beautiful large flowered lobelia, Ramosa (tenuior), whic
often attains two feet and more in height but which is general
grown as a greenhouse annual under this system, gives bl
flowers of a quality undreamed of. The flowers are much larg

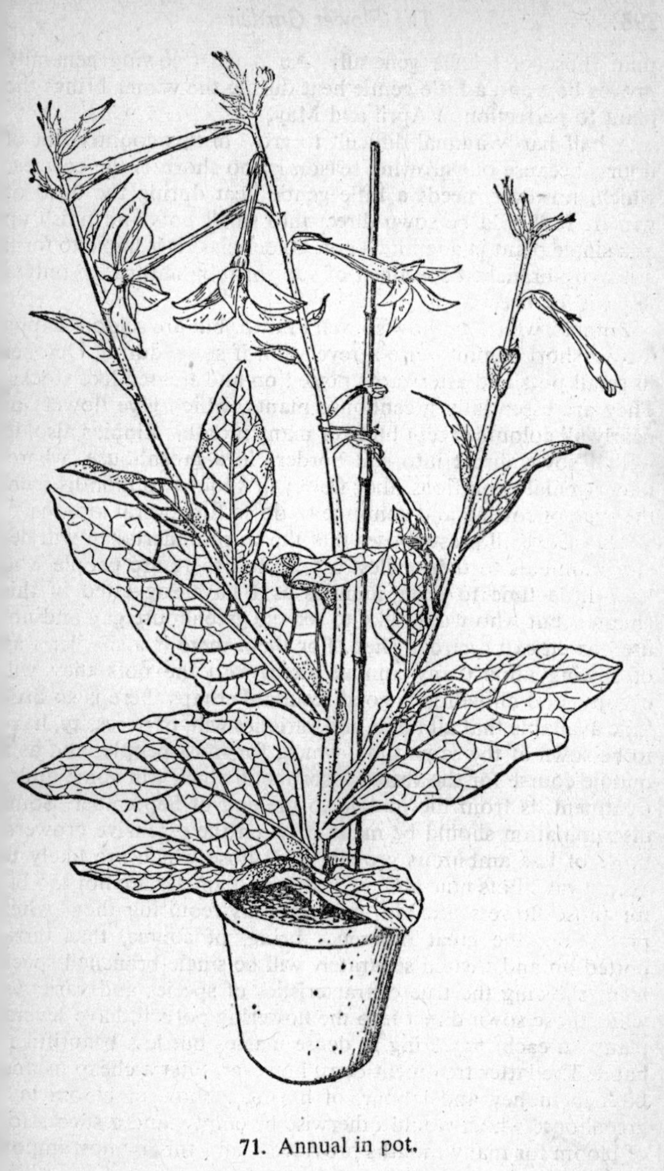

71. Annual in pot.

than those of lobelia generally. An August sowing generall
proves best and a little gentle heat during the winter brings th
plant to perfection in April and May.

A half-hardy annual difficult to grow in this country out o
doors, because our growing season is too short, is the cosmea
which, however, needs a little gentle heat during the dead o
winter. It should be sown direct into small pots and finish u
as a single plant in a ten-inch pot. Under glass it is liable to for
a heavily-branched specimen of sub-shrubby nature, so only
few will be needed.

Zinnias, which are now so well known, but are seldom happ
in our short summer, are a revelation if sown during Octobe
in small pots and afterwards potted on and treated like stocks
They are essentially greenhouse plants, which give flowers o
nearly all colours except blue for many months. Zinnias also d
well if sown direct into soil borders in a greenhouse, where
under genial conditions, they flower in about two months fro
the time of sowing and continue to do so for several months.

The above all presupposes that the work undertaken will de
velop annuals to their fullest extent, but there are people wh
have little time to grow annuals as I have suggested in thi
chapter, but who would like to see the greenhouse gay and no
used as an extra garden shed. For them there is a simpler wa
of sowing almost any annual direct into the pots they wil
occupy, and all will give good results. Perhaps there is so littl
time available that all kinds and varieties will, of necessity, hav
to be sown at the same time, which, for most people, and as
middle course for the varied assortment which will come unde
treatment, is from the middle to the end of September. Som
discrimination should be made between the extensive growers
those of less ambitious growth, and those which are likely t
keep dwarf. Pots nine and ten inches in diameter are not too bi
for those flowers already mentioned as requiring them whe
potted on, the great difference being, of course, that thos
potted on and treated separately will be single-branched speci
mens showing the true characteristics of species and varietie
while those sown direct into the flowering pot will have severa
plants in each, flowering in dense masses but less beautiful i
habit. The latter treatment does, however, offer a cheap mean
both in money and labour, of having a show of bloom in
greenhouse which would otherwise be empty, and a successio
of bloom for many months provided – and this is most impo

tant – that as soon as spring starts in earnest these very thirsty annuals never suffer for want of water. The full procedure is to fill the pots with John Innes Compost No. 2, then to sow several groups of seeds in several stations on the soil surface, water in and wait for germination. In September this will be rapid. As soon as the seedlings can be handled one seedling only should be retained at each station after a carefully manipulated thinning, thus leaving each pot, large or small, with several seedlings, spaced out at several stations and each with ample room to develop.

If possible, from this point, the pots containing the seedlings should not be crowded together, but should be spaced widely apart to give the developing seedlings elbow room and to counteract the tendency for them to be drawn upwards – a tendency which under glass always has to be fought. When the seedlings are about six inches high some support must be given – not tardily, because seedlings growing in the dead of winter are inclined to be a little fragile and liable to fall over. In supporting them it is wise to assume that under glass each will become twice its normal height, and that stakes will be needed accordingly high. Natural osier or hazel wands are best, and bearing in mind the plants' possible requirements the stakes should be left with a few inches to spare, for as soon as it is seen that growth in height is ceasing, unwanted stake tops can be easily nipped off with secateurs. The method is to insert four of these light osier or hazel wands deeply at the side of each pot, and tie round them bands of soft green twist or fillis string, always keeping the bands ahead of growth. Generally bands about five inches apart suffice, although this may vary with the plant.

As soon as the dark period of winter is over, with its many hours of bad light, and growth is actively renewed, stand each pot in a deep earthenware saucer to ensure that it always has a reserve of water. During the winter if frost can be excluded, well and good – there is no need to worry about high temperatures. Try to ventilate cautiously throughout the winter, and when spring arrives ventilate as freely as possible. When growth begins to alter in appearance and approach the bud stage, water with diluted liquid manure and apply a top dressing of a good compound fertilizer at weekly intervals. At this season there will be so many roots in each pot that over-watering should be impossible and all can be watered at once before you leave in the morning if it is desired.

But there is a still easier means of having a good show and that is by deferring sowing until February. This ensures a show nearly as great on plants not nearly so tall. The procedure is much the same, but thinning need not be nearly so severe, as with a shorter season of growth stems and foliage will not be so extensive. Most of the dwarf plants make a great show in large pans, particularly the South African annual dimorphothecas and ursinias with the dwarf godetias, Clarkia elegans and Clarkia pulchella – each a little flower-bed in itself. Almost any dwarf kind or variety treated in this way will flower well, while the blue annuals give a brilliance rarely seen out of doors. Phacelia campanularia, Nemophila insignis, and the large-flowered blue Nemsia are particularly beautiful.

Among the half-hardy annuals which lend themselves to such treatment, nicotianas, petunias and salpiglossis all do splendidly, without, of course, showing the complete glory of which they are capable when sown in the autumn and potted on.

The joy of seeing quickly-grown annuals at their best is dimmed only by the thought that being so quickly grown they cannot be expected to last long – the only penalty to pay for such brilliance. Looked on as an easy means of having a greenhouse full of blooms, annuals in the greenhouse are satisfactory.

Lawns

LAWNS generally suffer from neglect. Not that they are not regularly mown and rolled – far from it: usually they receive too much attention, particularly with the roller – but whereas the rest of the garden is dug and manured at least annually, the lawn, which cannot be dug, is flattened down by the roller until roots cannot breathe, and savagely repressed by the machine, which takes away the plant food – decayed grasses – which the grass would obtain in a state of nature. Few expect to feed a lawn, even those who believe in deep digging and good manuring. Instead they often grumble at its rusty appearance after drought, entirely forgetting that the maligned lawn is the only important thing in the garden which they have not fed.

But let us begin at the beginning and consider the question of upkeep later. The approach to the culture of lawns, like the approach to any other garden crop, should be thorough. The lawn, or the grass which forms it, should be looked upon as a crop, just like any other crop in the garden. There is this difference, however, that whereas most crops can have their soil exposed and aired, and food incorporated, at least once annually, the lawn has to go on indefinitely drawing on what is in the soil without additional plant food and without even the partial satisfaction gained from its own dead foliage. No leaves are allowed to decay on it, the grass box takes away all mowings, and generally the lawn repines yearly until in a dry summer it almost disappears – at least, the fine grasses of value, for only coarse-growing ones can stand continued repression and starvation. Few think of this, and most people are content, and some very anxious, to obtain any sort of turf to lay hurriedly, without soil preparation and with scant respect for levels.

Lawns should flow with the rest of the garden. Few gardens, except by a near miracle, are naturally dead level, and therefore, unless for some special reason, it is generally advisable not to alter it, for if this is done it so often looks wrong and the complications of banks and of conflicting lines and contours annoy.

Builders often turn out home and garden completely 'landscaped' with a lawn already made. Sometimes the lawn has been a good friend to the builder, for a sprinkling of soil and a skin of turf effectively hides debris which should have been taken away. It goes against the grain to rip away turf from the ground and to disinter the rubbish that only a builder knows how to leave, but often it pays to do so.

Haste is the enemy of a good lawn. If possible, one should start in the spring or early summer beforehand, to rid the soil of obstacles and rubbish of all kinds. If the soil is situated on limestone rock, gravel, or soil which contains a lot of flints no attempt to extract all the stones should be made. Many people have tried to do so by attempting to sort out with a sieve anything bigger than stones half an inch in diameter, only to find they have undertaken a colossal job and that soil so treated is generally unbalanced and spoilt. Large stones certainly get in the way and should be removed at the onset. Having got rid of bricks and boulders, there is the question of levels to consider. In contemplating these due regard must be paid to the relationship of the lawn to the rest of the garden. If the lawn is to be a tennis lawn then the nearer it is to being dead level the better, although few people would know if one end was lower by several inches, but if it is to be an integral part of the garden it should not only flow with it but should be indispensable. This being so, it should conform to the general slope and meet all paths and junctions at the right levels in order to avoid odd steps and steep banks, which should be avoided at all costs, since their upkeep is laborious and costly.

First of all it is necessary to find out what the lowest level should be, bearing in mind the possible height of unmade paths and borders, and, having driven in a builder's peg whose top represents the highest spot on the lowest level, to drive in pegs sited at the highest level. If the distance is small the levels between can be ascertained by stretching string tightly between the two pegs so that the running level made by the string coincides with the tops of the stakes. It is important to get the two sets of levels right, the top set and the lower set, and, having done this, to peg the site all over at intervals of ten feet, so that a straight edge is able to rest on pegs to give the correct running level as the work proceeds. Long lines of pegs between which tightened string would sag should be sighted over boning rods and pegged accordingly. Sometimes, owing to the general contour, it is necessary to have a running level in more than one direction – a matter which is easily adjusted with boning rods and pegs.

Having done this the ground must be prepared for the crop of grass, for that is what it amounts to. Some experts go as far as to say that the ground should be double dug or bastard trenched, and truthfully, if really well decayed farmyard manure and/or compost is used this is a good thing. Generally, however, if the ground is dug well all over one good spade in depth this suffices, provided good decomposed farmyard manure is used in quantity. This should be broken up finely and mixed into the soil thoroughly so that sinkage caused by ground consolidation and by the further decomposition of the manure should be as even as possible. Because of sinkage, lawns should never be made in a hurry. The consolidation problem is a real

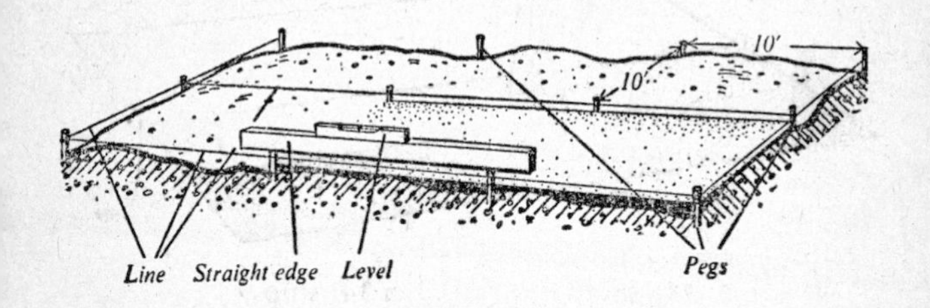

72. Levelling ground for lawn.

one, and time must be given for sinkage to occur and to abate, although a small gradual sinkage will inevitably take place for several years. In order that this shall be equal all over it is of great importance that all manures added should be well decomposed and thoroughly integrated. Consolidation of the bulk of soil should be proceeded with all the summer by treading on many occasions when the soil is not too dry or too wet but in good tilth. There is no better tool for packing the soil than two well-shod feet. A roller, which merely tightens the top inches, is almost useless at this stage. The old-fashioned ritual, still carried out in a few districts, of all hands turning out to tread the onion bed is one that could be followed with advantage.

If soil has to be moved to make levels see that it is put down in strata, not in patches, because later on if there are patches of clay, good top soil, indifferent subsoil, or poor sand in various parts of the lawn, their presence will be shown by a patchwork pattern of health and colour in the grass. As the process of building up and consolidating proceeds, all pernicious perennial weeds should be eliminated, leaving in the soil seeds of many annual weeds which will be a nuisance later on. As soon as the levels are right these various annuals are dealt with by allowing them to germinate and then cutting them off with the Dutch hoe – a process which if repeated often enough will in time destroy them, although seeds of the annual nettle and the annual grass, Poa annua – about the last thing needed in a lawn – sometimes remain in the soil in viable condition for years.

73. Sowing lawn seed in 3-ft strips.

Having achieved the right level and killed off as many weeds as possible, it is necessary to decide by which method the lawn shall be made. There are two – by seeding and by laying turf. The former is by far the most satisfactory method. Assuming that seed is to be used a reliable seed merchant should be consulted. He, by observing the grass of the district and the kind of soil, will know what kind of mixture to send. In dry districts and on some of the poor gravel soils, very fine grasses do not always succeed, but examination of the local wild grasses will quickly reveal this. It is far better to have a good lawn composed of somewhat poor grasses than a poor and patchy lawn of fine grasses which refuse to grow with vigour.

When the day of sowing arrives the soil should be raked down so that unwanted stones are removed and the surface is left as even as possible. Then, with a length of cord, the ground is marked off into strips a yard wide. Along this strip, grass seed is sown on the surface at the rate of not less than 2 oz. per square yard, which is the standard rate of sowing. In sparrow-ridden districts 3 oz. per square yard is a much better allowance, for birds will inevitably filch some of the seed, and, should the weather be dry, indulge in dust baths on the finely prepared surface. Patience and accuracy are needed to sow evenly and place the required amount into the allotted squares. When one strip has been completed take the second string to mark off another width and repeat the process by taking away the string from the side which has been sown to mark off the fresh strip, until all is completed. To cover as much as possible of the seed it is raked into the soil evenly and shallowly. Of course, some will still show on the surface, but sufficient should be covered to provide a 'good plant'. During the germination period scarecrows may be of some value. Sometimes they scare birds but often they but provide perching places for birds that tire of eating. Metal or glass reflectors which float in the air and glitter in the sun are far more effective.

After sowing some growers like to use a light roller to compress the soil and thus assist germination by ensuring good contact with the soil and making seed-finding more difficult for birds, but the disadvantages are many. Footprints are left, the roller itself leaves depressions, and, unless the land is dry, pulls up top soil in its passage, so that only in exceptionally good circumstances is it wise to use a roller.

Grass seed can be sown, if the need arises in many months of the year, but September and the early spring months are generally best. Mid-September is probably the best time of all, especially as this allows for thorough soil cleaning, as advocated already, during the summer months. Germination, too, is likely to be quicker in September, for the summer-heated earth is much better for germination than the barely-warmed soil of spring.

Assuming that a sowing is made in September, germination is rarely more prolonged than ten days and sometimes quicker – so much depends upon the atmospheric temperatures at the time. To see grass seed germinate and grow is a rare pleasure. When it is first noticeable there are only a few blades of green. Next day a thin green veiling shimmers in the wind. A day later the green veiling is shot with lurid green, and only a few hours afterwards the earth is completely mantled in a green that could only be that of young grass.

Now is the time for the roller, but both grass and soil must be dry. If not, the roller will skid at the turns and the soil cling to the steel, pulling up handfuls of tender grass in the process.

And the roller must be a very light one. Most rollers used on lawns are too heavy for the grass's health at any time, and at this tender stage too heavy an instrument will do harm. The object is threefold – to compress the soil, to push stones into the soil so that they do not obstruct the knives of the lawn mower, and to assist the young grasses to 'tiller out'. If September is warm, grass will grow quickly, and a day or two after rolling a light lawn mower should be passed over the grass. For the first cut the cutting blade and knife cylinder should be adjusted to cut the grass about an inch from the surface. Some prefer not to cut the young grass until it has grown unmolested for several weeks, but there is danger in this, for should the weather be warm and muggy, with little air circulation, the young grass growing densely together remains all day in a moist clammy condition almost inviting an attack of fungus disease – a subtle enemy which will sweep through a whole lawn in a couple of days if given the suitable conditions of humidity, which dense uncut young grass affords. Sometimes, indeed, the 'damping off' fungus will afflict young grass which has been mown and is not altogether dense, and if so all decaying foliage should be removed and the patch dressed with a powder containing copper in a colloidal form, which can be purchased at the usual seed stores.

For the first cutting it is important that the machine be in first-class condition. The knife cylinder and the bottom cutting plate against which the cylinder knives grind should have been ground. These knives should be adjusted so that when revolving they grind gently against the plate – an adjustment which can be tested by holding a piece of paper between knives and plate. If the paper is cut easily and cleanly the adjustment for young grass cutting can be considered good. Until cooler weather allows the grass to settle down to thicken mowing will be needed twice a week, and as November approaches once a week will suffice. Mowing is rarely needed in November, but should the weather keep mild and the grass grow, it is wise to cut it rather than face a tangled mat in the spring. For this late cutting, however, it is important that the grass should be dry before any attempt is made to cut it.

In spite of all efforts to dispose of weeds before sowing, some may appear. Perennials should be carefully gouged out and the larger annual weeds pulled out carefully by hand. The lawn mower, by continuously cutting off the top of small annual weeds, will easily account for these. A lawn of young grass on a well-prepared site which has been well cared for in the autumn should come through the winter well – even though it is a hard one.

Sowing in the spring should follow much the same lines. Anxiety to do something should not be allowed to overcome the cautionary practice of waiting until the soil is in good tilth. Although grass can be sown at almost any time it is always better to wait until the soil, of whatever character, works freely, and when the land is fit to sow onions or annuals, it is also fit to receive grass. In a mild spring, growth may be very rapid and if, owing to this, it is incumbent to cut the grass every other day, then do so, for the labour of cutting grass, at this time, before it is old enough to choke the machine, is little more than that of pushing a carpet sweeper. If only for this reason the young lawn should never be neglected. To cut grass with a lawn mower after neglect of several weeks is not only hard labour but bad for the operator and hard on the grass.

In sowing a lawn from seed, which can be very good or equally bad, it is worth while to take every step to ensure success. A lawn is something you must have, like a carpet in a room, a necessary part of your garden which you will see from your windows for who knows how long. It is your everyday landscape, and therefore it must be good and pleasing.

Excellent lawns can be made of turf – if possible that of the district. People who have seen the wonderful sea-washed turf of the Cumberland coast and other humid districts have been so impressed that at great expense they have brought it to their gardens in the south and have been bitterly disappointed. When laid it was perfect, but in spite of much care their lawns have become shabbier with each season. Not only this, but after a time indigenous grasses have usurped the place of the fine fescues, making the lawn a patchy eyesore. Because of the difference in annual rainfall and atmospheric humidity, it is rarely possible to bring turf from Cumberland with anything but transitory success. In many places on the north-western seaboard the annual rainfall is double and in some places treble that of the south-east, east and Midlands. In the districts of great rainfall not only is the soil – often only sand – always very wet but the atmosphere also is heavily charged with humidity. Except in a few districts in the west and extreme south-west nowhere in this island are these conditions reproduced, as many people have found to their cost.

Often in a person's own neighbourhood there is a good meadow turf. True, this is sometimes infested with ranunculus (buttercup) and other weeds. If when the turf is cut it is turned upside down on box or bench the worst perennial weeds can be pulled out with ease and the turf after mowing will be quite presentable. There are other districts near the Downs where excellent almost weed-free turf can be procured, and on the upper slopes of the Cotswold, Mendip, and Malvern Hills there is good turf of downland character. But while it is going through your hands weed it. It is infinitely easier to do this when it is upside down on box or bench than when it is in place, for weeding on hands and knees is unpleasant. Selective weed killer will certainly help afterwards, but if the turf is laid down clean it is a job done well. Clean turf is a joy to the eye and if you are able to remove the weeds from local turf you will have a green sward which will not change in character, because you will be laying down, in turf form, the grasses of the neighbourhood.

The initial preparation for turf laying is the same as for sowing seed, and, above all, a regular soil solidity in depth is essential. The system of pegging out is similar, except that due allowance should be made for the depth of the turf – generally about two inches. It matters little of what size the turf is cut, whether

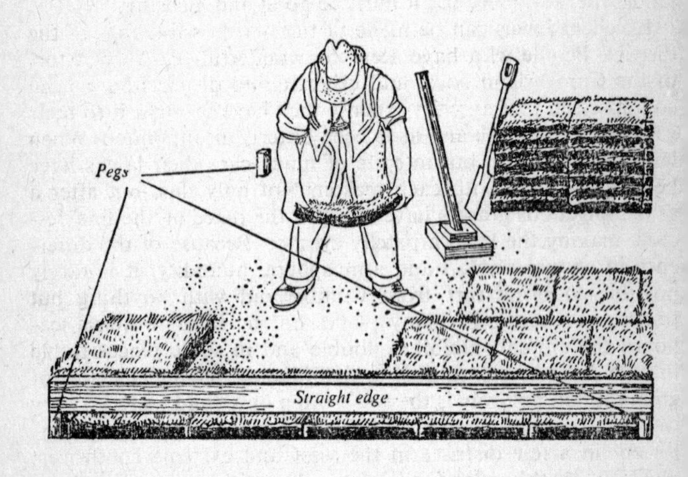

74. Laying turves.

three feet by one foot – in which case it is usually rolled for convenience; two feet by one foot – a most convenient size; or one foot by one foot; but it is a great help in turf laying to have turf which is cut all of the same thickness. Turf cannot be laid on the ground anyhow, and any inequalities brutally beaten out with a turf beater; instead the straight edge should be used from peg to peg to ensure that each turf conforms to its proper level. If a turf is too shallow, it must be packed up with fine soil. If it is a little too thick the level beneath it must be altered to correspond. Any weak or shallow spots in the turves occasioned by damage or faulty cutting must be packed up individually by using the hand underneath the turf. All joints should be butted together tightly, and when complete, to seal the joints, and to make up any minor depression, a thin layer of sandy soil which has been passed through a sieve with quarter-inch meshes should be spread on the surface and well brushed into the joint seams, holes, and inequalities with a birch broom. The turf beater should be used only to obtain some necessary consolidation, not to beat turf laid too high down to the surrounding level; sometimes, indeed, with turf cut from heavy soil, it is better not to use it at all. Similarly with the use of the heavy roller. Often one sees turf being laid carelessly with little regard to the finer levels, after which an excessively heavy roller is used to squash it into place.

The lawn is part of the general garden picture; you will see it often and a little extra work to ensure good detail at the time of sowing and/or laying is preferable to setting up a perpetual eyesore. As it is essential that turf should knit together quickly one should not be in too much hurry to use the lawn mower on newly-laid turf, but on the other hand, to leave it too long without trimming is to risk a mangled appearance which may persist for a long time. So when there is enough grass to warrant a comfortable cutting get out the roller mower and cut it, and do so thereafter every few days. With proper precautions turf can be laid at any season, except, of course, when frozen stiff, or when overwhelmed by heavy rain. Providing turf is moist enough to cut it can be laid in the heat of summer if water can be applied afterwards, but turf laid in the winter season, which afterwards has its share of heavy rain, is much more likely to be satisfactory than that laid under a handicap. Whether sown or turfed over the area treated should overlap the site by several inches all round, so that when established an edging iron and line can be used to form a clean-cut edge and give a neat and finished appearance.

For a few years a new lawn will have reserves of plant food on the soil from the initial preparations, but in time this will become exhausted. One of the best ways to feed a lawn is to spread on it in early November, or in October if growth ceases early, a dressing of three inches thick of well-decayed farmyard manure. The weather will disintegrate this during the winter and when spring arrives the residue can easily be brushed into the turf with a birch broom, leaving, as a rule, little debris to remove. If this dressing cannot be made, a mulch of about 7 lb. granulated peat per square yard in the autumn, followed by a dressing of 4 oz. hoof and horn meal, one eighth of an inch grist will provide humus and a supply of nitrogen throughout the growing season. If a more quickly acting nitrogenous fertilizer is needed, dried blood applied at the rate of 4 oz. per square yard is very good. Bonemeal should not be used on account of its phosphatic content, nor should any form of phosphatic fertilizer, as these have a tendency to encourage clovers to which most people object and which form treacherous slippery patches – which also wear badly – on playing lawns. For a similar reason, lime, which on some soils releases phosphate, should not be applied unless the soil reaction is very acid.

In addition to suffering from repression and starvation grass on lawns suffers greatly through the sealing down of the top soil caused by the heavy roller. On almost all soils, if a roller lawn mower is used the garden roller will not be required, except for a first rolling before the lawn mower is used at the beginning of the cutting season. Through the plastering down of the surface for years, grasses on many lawns suffer from lack of air; this can be remedied by the use of a fork to pierce holes an inch or two deep in the turf or a small light spiked roller which does the same job more quickly. In some cases, too, where repression has gone on for years, the grass is all the better for being allowed to grow towards the close of the season, coupled with a dressing of decayed farmyard manure, even though it may then be a little difficult to mow when spring arrives.

Even when carefully cared for some weeds will appear in the best of lawns, and for this the modern selective weed killers which destroy leafy weeds without harming the grass are a great boon. It must be remembered, however, that for a month or two after application the dead, dying, and distorted leaves are a great eyesore, and that therefore a time for application should be chosen when the lawn is not specially needed.

The frequent use of the birch broom has much to commend it, and cutting at least once a week, or better still twice a week, is a great saver of time and exertion. With a good lawn mower the exertion is slight when it is done frequently, and the lawn will never suffer in the way lawns do when long grass with decaying base is forcibly torn away. A good lawn mower is a great advantage. With it, drudgery can be turned into pleasant exercise, provided not more than five days elapse before cutting again. But it must not be too cumbersome. Many people think that if they have a wide machine they are able to cut the lawn more quickly, but rarely is this so. Such a machine is very tiring to use, and possible only when everything is favourable, whereas with a machine with twelve-inch cutters there is no loss of mobility, and it is far quicker and cheaper to use.

In dealing with a lawn one must never forget that one is growing a crop of grass under difficult conditions, and that, in time, it will need plant food. Recourse should always be had to farmyard manure, or organic manure such as hoof and horn meal and dried blood. There is no particular harm in an occasional dose of sulphate of ammonia, but the repeated use of any quick-acting nitrogenous fertilizer will in time spell ruin, whereas with natural manures one can continue feeding indefinitely, if need be, provided the drainage is good. Should it not be well drained, the use of nitrogenous manures will encourage moss, so in the few cases where drainage is suspect this must receive the attention advocated in Chapter 11 on Carnations.

So much depends on good preparation, which leads to permanent good health. With this many of the obscure diseases which threaten lawns rarely occur. In growing grass on a lawn one must first of all be health-minded, just as if any other important crop was being grown.

· 32 ·

Diseases and Pests

THIS is the last chapter; it will be brief, but not the least im portant. Throughout I have stressed that plants must be give good culture, that when this is done robust health follows an that, given this, pests and diseases seldom appear. During th last few decades scientists have given us startling remedies fo the eradication of disease as well as pests. Because of this som growers in difficulties neglect many things which are conduciv to good health and say to themselves; 'Never mind. If I do ge so and so, a spraying with so and so will soon put it right.' Thi comforting doctrine, though perhaps it leads to a check o disease or pests, is fundamentally wrong, for the grower's ulti mate aim is to grow good plants which are not readily attacked not poor plants which easily contract disease and suffer infes tation. The grower must become health-conscious, for wit good cultivation plants can be raised which do not invite attack

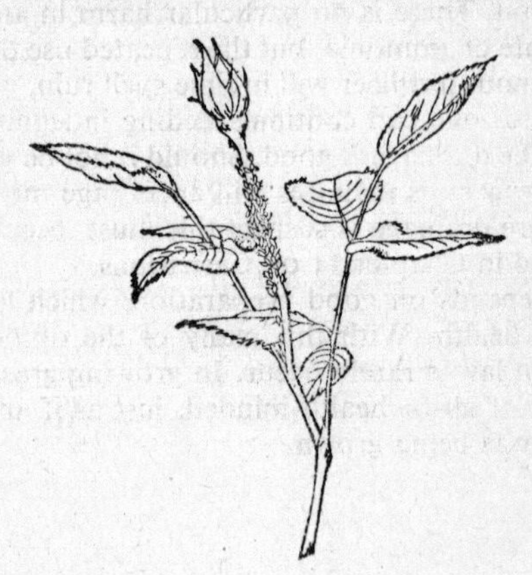

75. Bud attacked by aphis.

It is true that occasionally healthy plants are attacked by som virulent disease or pest, but this is the exception, not the rule It is equally true that infestation or infection may come fron a neighbour's neglected garden – often a matter beyond th grower's control – but that it is quite a different matter. The inefficient gardener is the insecticide maker's best friend.

Let it not be thought that I am opposed in any way to the march of science. Far from it. On more than one occasion I have

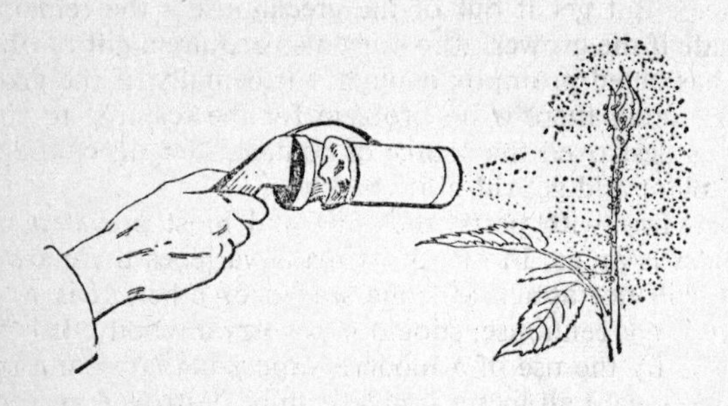

76. Dust blower.

had recourse in emergency to the latest discoveries of science and I acknowledge this with grateful thanks. But it has not caused me to look on these wonderful remedies as pillars of good culture, but only as something to be used when dire emergency demands it. The grand old gardeners who founded horticulture knew little of science, but through application to their work, which most of them loved, they had a very highly developed sense of observation which stood them in good stead. They produced plants of very high quality without the aids we have to-day, and knowing that disease spread rapidly, although they did not know how it spread, they had a very rigid rule – to destroy by fire, immediately, any sick plant. This is a rule any grower should make for himself.

Nowadays a sick plant is made into a pet. Often it is put in a special corner of the greenhouse while leaves of it are sent for microscopic examination to this and that authority. It is shown to everybody. Its leaves are turned up by finger and thumb to be examined, and healthy leaves are handled in the search for traces of disease by the same unsterilized finger and thumb, and so the disease is carried. Replies from reputable authorities come tardily and meanwhile aphides attack it. Carrying the disease with them in their rapid wanderings the aphides in taking their food infect other plants, and soon not one but all the plants are infected – perhaps with some minute virus disease for which science is still seeking a remedy. Destruction is far preferable to this. It is understandable that a good grower should want to know more about a disease which afflicts his plants, and in such a case it is far better to send the whole plant to some authority, or portions of it to several people who might help. But get it out of the greenhouse – the remainder will be safe if the grower, who must also acquire a gift of observation, has acted promptly enough. Incidentally, if the grower does this, often there is no problem for the scientist to solve, for he has destroyed the source of contact. Get rid of the first infected plant and get rid of it quickly.

To deal first with pests, the chief and most prevalent pest under glass is aphis. In one of its many varieties there are few plants it will not attack at some season or other. It is a pest which, in the greenhouse, should not worry anybody. It is easy to destroy. By the use of a modern vaporizing lamp and some nicotine fumigant all living aphides can be destroyed promptly,

77. Knapsack spray.

and if the vaporization is carried out automatically every ten days there will be no aphis problem, for successive broods will be caught as they hatch and the grower will see none of them. It is now known that aphides migrating from plant to plant are the chief means of spreading the worst diseases, so that by destroying them disease is prevented. How right our forefathers were, when, fearing something worse to come, they destroyed the first infested or infected plant? Regular vaporization is cheap insurance.

78. Using a stirrup pump sprayer.

Nowadays, when most people have only cool greenhouses, and tropical houses are rare, there are few other pests to worry about. Sometimes thrips, minute insects which can be detected by white markings and patches on the leaves, and red spiders, also minute insects which show reddish specklings on the leaves and which are generally found in each other's company, can be destroyed by an occasional fumigation with abobenzine smoke bombs. Their presence, however, shows that the atmosphere in the greenhouse has been too dry, either because of too much artificial heat, or because there has been a long dry period. Apart from fumigation the general remedy is to use less artificial heat, ventilate freely but carefully, and use the syringe or spray to moisten the foliage of plants daily, together with the systematic damping down of floors, walls, and stages daily.

Out of doors, aphides are the worst offenders. There is a

great variety of these and they attack many species, but all are vulnerable to regular sprayings of nicotine insecticide and H.E.T.P. – a modern phosphatic insecticide. Both should be used according to the maker's instructions, and it is particularly necessary to be accurate with H.E.T.P. as it is in a highly concentrated form and a few drops extra 'just for luck' may injure plants. It also acts as a great refresher to plants. Diseases out of doors are also carried by aphides. Particular watch should be kept on young sweet peas.

Aphides on chrysanthemums indoors can be kept down by fumigation, and out of doors by H.E.T.P., which also controls capsid bug and chrysanthemum midge. For all these spraying should be timely. It is an easy matter to spray the flower heads of lilies which aphides seem to enjoy greatly; H.E.T.P. is safe for this if used carefully. The tips of dahlias also can be sprayed with this if needed.

Violets in a dry season, if left unwatered, are sometimes attacked by red spider, which, however, is seldom in evidence if the violets are kept well watered. The remedy is to water them well and spray them with H.E.T.P.

Aphides are the chief pest of the rose, but there is little difficulty in controlling them with H.E.T.P.

As we have seen, aphides, which are the principal enemies of plants in the greenhouse, can be controlled quite simply by regular fumigation, which also, by destroying the chief carriers, precludes virus diseases.

With regard to diseases it cannot be said that plants in a well-managed garden are greatly troubled. Mildew on delphiniums and roses is probably the worst enemy. Luckily mildew, which sometimes looks forbidding, can be controlled by spraying with a good colloidal sulphur or colloidal copper fungicide, and if spraying is begun early in the season, it can generally be prevented from appearing. This also applies to the mildew of chrysanthemums and many other plants.

As I have already shown, virus diseases of sweet peas and dahlias, which are generally insect-borne, are controllable by the destruction of insects; therefore the good gardener who sprays or fumigates in good time against insects is unlikely to experience much disease. I must conclude on the note I began with: be health-minded, study and practise good plant hygiene, wage war on occasional insect attacks early, and you will see little of disease.

Index

Some other flower and gardening books are described on the remaining pages

BRITISH WILD FLOWERS

John Hutchinson

If a book like this had been published a hundred years or so ago, it would probably have been called a *Florula Britannica* (a Little Flora of Britain), though Latin titles are not now so much in vogue as they were in those days.

But this is just what it is, and it will enable anyone to find out the name and learn something about most of the lovely and interesting wild flowers with which our islands are still so richly endowed. It should enhance the pleasure of those who like to get more than a whiff of fresh air out of their rural rides and rambles.

In the two volumes each species is described and illustrated by a black and white drawing, with full details of floral structure, showing the more important features which in combination determine the species, genus, and family. (A330, 331)

GRASSES

C. E. Hubbard

Grasses are the most abundant, widely spread, and useful of all flowering plants, so much so that without them it is difficult to understand how man could survive. They provide the bulk of his cereal grains, green herbage and dried fodder for his domestic animals, and a variety of valuable by-products, such as fibres, paper, sugar, aromatic oils, adhesives, starch, and alcohol. Their special type of leaves withstands close and frequent cutting, providing the familiar green carpets of our parks and gardens.

In the British Isles there are about 152 different species of grasses, each of which is illustrated and described in this book. (A295)

SOFT FRUIT GROWING

Raymond Bush

The author tries to guide the amateur in the growing of soft fruits and the subject is dealt with methodically. The general questions of aspect, soil, nursery material, and planting procedure are reviewed first. Then follows a discussion of the specific cultural details associated with the various soft fruits. The vagaries of temperature and climate, the use of the compost heap, the need for and practice of spraying are all separately and exactly explained. (PH 1)

TREE FRUIT GROWING

Raymond Bush

'Experts will agree that it is hardly possible to speak too highly of Raymond Bush's two Penguins, *Tree Fruit Growing*. One is Apples and the other Pears, Quinces and Stone Fruits. To provide these two experience-packed, brightly written and painstakingly illustrated books is a great public service. Every branch of fruit growing is honestly dealt with.'– *Countryman*.

'There seems to be nothing left out in these books – varieties, pest troubles, pollination, spraying, pruning, good illustrations both diagrammatic and photographic. . . . The man who has on his shelves these books has no excuse if later on he does not also possess a most profitable and trouble-free fruit garden.' – *Fertiliser Journal*. (PH 2, 3)